Common Core Curriculum World History,
GRADES 3–5

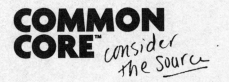

A Wiley Brand

Cover design by Chris Clary
Cover image: Graffiti on the Berlin Wall © Junophoto

Published by Jossey-Bass
A Wiley Brand
One Montgomery Street, Suite 1200, San Francisco, CA 94104-4594 www.josseybass.com

Detail of Hammurabi Receiving the Law from the Sun God, Shamash on the Stele of Hammurabi | © Gianni Dagli Orti/ Corbis

Jossey-Bass books and products are available through most bookstores. To contact Jossey-Bass directly call our Customer Care Department within the U.S. at 800-956-7739, outside the U.S. at 317-572-3986, or fax 317-572-4002.

The content in this book also can be found online. See "The Alexandria Plan" at commoncore.org.

Wiley publishes in a variety of print and electronic formats and by print-on-demand. Some material included with standard print versions of this book may not be included in e-books or in print-on-demand. If this book refers to media such as a CD or DVD that is not included in the version you purchased, you may download this material at http://booksupport.wiley.com. For more information about Wiley products, visit www.wiley.com.

Library of Congress Cataloging-in-Publication Data

Common Core Curriculum: world history, grades 3-5/Common Core, Inc. – First edition.
    pages   cm. – (Common Core U.S. and world history)
  Includes index.
  ISBN 978-1-118-83524-1 (pbk.); ISBN 978-1-118-84095-5 (pdf); ISBN 978-1-118-84085-6 (epub)
1. History–Study and teaching (Elementary)–United States. I. Common Core, Inc.
  D16.3.C679 2014
  372.89–dc23

                                              2013045501

Printed in the United States of America

FIRST EDITION

PB Printing 10 9 8 7 6 5 4 3 2 1

Contents

Era Summaries

Introduction: How to Use the Alexandria Plan

The Alexandria Plan is Common Core's curriculum tool for teaching United States and world history. It is a strategic framework for identifying and using high-quality informational texts and narrative nonfiction to meet the expectations of the Common Core State Standards (CCSS) for English language arts (ELA) while also sharing essential historical knowledge with students in elementary school (kindergarten through fifth grade). These resources can be used in either the social studies block or the ELA block during the elementary school day. The curriculum helps teachers pose questions about texts covering a wide range of topics: from the caves at Lascaux to King Tut's tomb, Chief Joseph to Kubla Khan, and the birth of democracy to the fall of the Berlin Wall. These books tell stories that thrill students. Accompanying text-dependent questions (TDQs) will elevate student learning to a level that will help them master the new CCSS for English language arts (CCSS-ELA).

We call these curriculum materials the "Alexandria Plan" because we enjoy thinking about the role that they—and the teachers who use them—play in passing along important knowledge to future generations. In ancient Egypt, the Library of Alexandria, along with a museum, was part of a grand complex that sought to collect and catalog "all the knowledge in the world." It became a center of learning, attracting scholars, philosophers, scientists, and physicians from all corners of the earth. Though it fell to fire, the spirit of Alexandria remains. Some twenty-three hundred years later, a new library stands near the site of its ancient ancestor, and the story of Alexandria and its great library inspires our efforts to help teachers illuminate the future by inculcating in their students an understanding of the past.

The Alexandria Plan is the second in a suite of curriculum materials Common Core is developing to help educators implement the CCSS. In 2010, Common Core released its Curriculum Maps in English Language Arts. The Maps are a coherent sequence of thematic units, roughly six per grade level, for students in kindergarten through twelfth grade. Now known as the Wheatley Portfolio, these resources connect the skills delineated in the CCSS with suggested works of literature and informational texts and provide sample activities that teachers can use in the classroom to reinforce the standards. The Wheatley Portfolio will soon grow, with resources to help educators enact the instructional shifts while cultivating in students a love of excellent books—all based on featured anchor informational and literary texts, poetry, and the arts. In summer 2013, we began rolling out a comprehensive, K–12, CCSS-based mathematics curriculum known as Eureka Math, with embedded professional development. Please watch our website, commoncore.org, for future releases.

HOW WILL THE ALEXANDRIA PLAN HELP ME, MY SCHOOL, MY DISTRICT, OR MY STATE IMPLEMENT THE CCSS-ELA?

The CCSS-ELA emphasize the importance of literacy across the curriculum. Indeed, CCSS architect David Coleman has said, "There is no such thing as doing the nuts and bolts of reading in kindergarten through fifth grade without coherently developing knowledge in science, and history, and the arts—period." Unfortunately, research has illustrated that history is one in a group of core subjects that have been squeezed out of many classrooms. The Alexandria Plan guides educators through the process of reprioritizing the teaching of history in the classroom and will assist teachers in addressing key CCSS-ELA while also meeting state social studies standards.

HOW ARE THESE RESOURCES STRUCTURED?

The print editions of the Alexandria Plan, each organized by subject and grade span, present essential content knowledge in United States and world history. United States history is separated into eighteen eras, and so is world history. To make this knowledge accessible to students in elementary school, we established two grade spans: lower elementary (kindergarten through second grade) and upper elementary (third grade through fifth grade). Each book contains one subject area (United States or world history) as well as the resources for teaching to one grade span (lower or upper elementary). Learning expectations articulate the key ideas, events, facts, and figures to be understood by students in a particular grade span. Suggested anchor texts; text studies (comprising TDQs and exemplar student responses, and accompanied by performance assessments based on one or more featured anchor texts); and more select resources flesh out the content for each era. The following is a detailed breakdown of what is contained in a given era of the Alexandria Plan as well as in the accompanying collection of era summaries that provide additional historical content for teachers.

Overview

Each overview captures the essence of the history presented in a given era. The paragraph concludes with a brief description of what students will learn and be able to do after completing the associated text study.

Learning Expectations

This section describes what our teachers have identified as being appropriate and necessary for students to know in each grade span. It is this knowledge that students need to master so that they will be prepared for later grades. Teachers can break down the content indicated into grade-specific expectations that fit their classroom.

Suggested Anchor Texts

For each era of U.S. and world history, we provide a well-vetted list of suggested anchor texts that can be used to impart essential knowledge found in the "Era Summaries" and "Learning Expectations." So that educators can select the book that is best suited to their classroom, we provide text recommendations covering an array of topics in the era. These carefully curated selections include exceptional works of narrative nonfiction, informational texts, and historical fiction. The texts are rich in historical content, well written, fair in their presentation of history, and often beautifully illustrated, allowing for the development of text-dependent questions that illuminate both the historical content and the authors' and illustrators' craft. These texts may also serve as mentor texts for students' own writing.

Featured Anchor Text

Teacher-writers selected one or two of the suggested anchor texts to illuminate in a text study aimed at the higher end of a particular grade span. Although all of the suggested anchor texts are worth exploring with students, each featured anchor text captures a particularly pertinent aspect of the era in which it is featured. Occasionally, the featured anchor text is paired with a supporting text to provide additional content to support student understanding.

Text Study

Each text study provides teachers with detailed guidance about how to lead students through a close, patient reading of a featured anchor text. Using a carefully crafted sequence of TDQs, teachers can effectively guide students through a detailed reading of a complex text. The questions lead students to use evidence directly from the text to explain and support their answers. Such close reading leads students to absorb key historical knowledge while honing essential CCSS-ELA skills. Answers are provided for each question. These TDQs are followed by at least one comprehensive performance assessment for each study. Both the TDQs and the performance assessments require students to support conclusions or opinions about the text with specific text evidence.

Performance Assessments

Each text study is followed by at least one performance assessment that allows students to demonstrate (typically, through a CCSS-based writing assignment) their understanding of the key ideas, historical events, and figures discussed in the featured anchor text. These performance assessments flow naturally from the progression of TDQs about the featured anchor text. Suggestions of activities that can be used to extend or expand instruction, labeled as extensions, are often included.

Connections to Common Core State Standards for English Language Arts

Each text study also includes CCSS-ELA citations for nearly every one of the TDQs, performance assessments, and extensions, along with explanations of how each of these items helps address the CCSS-ELA. Please note that our citations for the standards follow the established CCSS format: strand.grade.number.

More Resources

We include a list of related resources, including works of historical fiction, art, poetry, music, primary sources, and multimedia resources, that teachers can incorporate into lessons, use to extend or enrich instruction, or simply use to build their own content knowledge. Teachers often ask for quality primary sources that they can use in elementary grades, so Common Core sought out engaging, relevant, and accessible primary sources for teachers and their students. Sources of essential geographic knowledge are also incorporated where appropriate. Like our suggested anchor text selections, these resources have been carefully curated to save teachers countless hours of searching for resources to extend students' knowledge of history.

Era Summaries

Each of the eras in the Alexandria Plan also contains a concise and compelling summary of the history of that era—all collected together at the end of each print edition—highlighting the people, events, places, and ideas that constitute essential knowledge for teachers to share with students. The content of the summaries was guided by exemplary state social studies standards, written by a historian with expert knowledge of those standards. Nationally recognized historians vetted each summary and meticulously reviewed them for accuracy. These easy-to-read summaries contain what college- and career-ready high school graduates should know about each era. The summaries also make it convenient for teachers to review the history of the era in preparation for lesson planning and deeper research.

HOW WERE ANCHOR TEXTS SELECTED?

Teacher-writers with decades of classroom experience reviewed hundreds of historical fiction, narrative nonfiction, and informational texts, selecting the most engaging and content-rich among them. Each anchor text conveys an essential aspect of the history addressed in the "Learning Expectations" for each era. The list of texts is neither comprehensive nor exhaustive. In other words, a text has not been selected for every aspect of the history contained in the era summaries, nor do we imagine that we have identified all of the great texts available that are relevant to an era. The list represents a great start—a set that we look forward to building over time.

We were looking for rigorous, accurate, well-written, and wonderfully illustrated texts, considering the following criteria:

- *The text should enliven historical events in ways that nurture children's innate curiosity.*

  We sought texts that bring to life the historical setting, events, and story being told. Although our focus was on the selection of complex, content-rich texts, we also recognized that the texts needed to be age appropriate. Much consideration was given to readability, and whenever possible, we have placed texts in appropriate grade bands, based on their Lexile level. Where Lexile levels may pose ostensible challenges for teachers, we have explained how teachers might approach instruction (for example, reading the text aloud or scaffolding the amount of text students are expected to read).

  In addition, we have geared our questions and answers to the upper level of each grade band. Teachers will have to use questions that are appropriate for their students and look to the answers provided as guides for where to lead students, building understanding over time. Teachers who have piloted these materials have often reported being surprised at how successfully students mine and appreciate these texts, even when the texts were at first considered "too hard." They have told us—and we believe—that it is important not to underestimate what students can do when they are presented with compelling, high-quality texts.

- *The text should make teaching more fun, by engaging the teacher in compelling history.*

  One of the key instructional shifts called for in teaching to the CCSS-ELA is the significant increase in the amount of time and attention students are asked to devote to evidence-based analysis of what they are reading. Instead of focusing on metacognitive reading strategies at the expense of content, teachers can now focus on the content of the text, confident that it lends itself well to the kind of analysis demanded in the CCSS-ELA, but also giving students a chance to immerse themselves in the content, making learning more interesting for students and teachers alike.

- *The text should serve, in its quality and complexity, as an exemplar for teaching the literacy skills defined in the CCSS-ELA.*

  The third criterion for text inclusion was that the text should be significantly complex enough to support the rich text study, including the focus on important English language arts standards. If the texts weren't well written and compelling, they simply would not lend themselves to the kind of analysis that the CCSS-ELA demand—and that teachers and students enjoy. These texts, by celebrated authors including Peter Sis and Diane Stanley, exhibit the power of narrative history, the efficacy of great illustrations, the effect of figurative language, and the strength of arguments that are supported with clear evidence.

HAS THE ALEXANDRIA PLAN BEEN PILOTED?

Yes, extensively. We asked teachers from rural, urban, charter, and private schools across the country to pilot a selection of the materials and to share their experience. Nearly one hundred teachers participated, including new teachers, National Board Certified teachers, and veterans who have been recognized by their respective districts for excellent teaching. Their generous feedback helped us both improve these materials and explain more clearly how to use the features of the curriculum. Rather than speak for them, here are two testimonials from pilot users:

> The Map made it very easy for the teacher by giving information about the book as well as historical information. The direction of the lesson was centered around the character of Christopher Columbus and the vocabulary used to describe him—*brave, studious, curious, patient, dreamer.* The students described Columbus and were able to defend their answers. I never really thought about the character of Columbus and all that he went through to make his dreams come true. He was a true leader. Our school is a "Leader in Me" school, and this lesson illustrated several of the habits (character traits) we want our students to exhibit.
> –Trudy Phelps, kindergarten teacher, Dolby Elementary School, Louisiana

> The text was the core of the social studies lesson. I worked from the text out. In most social studies lessons you start from the outside and move in. Students related to the characters and seemed to feel they were there. They simply had a better understanding of the history behind the text. The text, with a well-balanced set of questions, made the experience easier as they developed an understanding of the history.
> –Jayne Brown, kindergarten teacher, Avery's Creek Elementary School, North Carolina

WHY ARE THERE SO MANY TEXT-DEPENDENT QUESTIONS?

It is important to note that we do not expect teachers to ask *all* of the questions we've provided. Our rather exhaustive sets of questions are intended to support teachers in the scaffolding that will be necessary to meet the needs of all learners. Further, careful study of these questions, including how they are constructed, will help teachers craft text-dependent questions for other high-quality texts on their own. Indeed, the curriculum can be used as a professional development tool and as a means of understanding what is expected of students according to the CCSS-ELA. Please contact Common Core through commoncore.org if you would like to learn about our professional development services.

DOES THE ALEXANDRIA PLAN REQUIRE ME TO ADOPT A PARTICULAR METHOD OF INSTRUCTION?

No. The way teachers choose to prepare students to approach the study of a text depends on their teaching style and the needs of students. A teacher may choose to have students read short sections of text with a few assigned questions, preparing students to participate fully in discussion. Or a teacher may choose to have students work in pairs or small groups to read and to discuss questions, preparing to pull their ideas together for a rich whole-class seminar discussion. Or a teacher may want students to grapple with the text independently at first. During their first reading of the text, students might circle passages where they are confused and/or underline points that they thought were interesting. Students might annotate the reading selection with questions and notes. As the teacher circulates during the independent reading time, he or she might note themes of questions that students generate as they read. The teacher could then use the TDQs, as needed, to clarify misunderstandings and to go deeper into the text than the students were able to go on their own. We offer these questions for teachers to use as they see fit.

HOW CAN I SCAFFOLD UP TO A TEXT?

If a teacher wishes to use one of the suggested anchor texts but feels it is too difficult for his or her students, using more accessible texts to build background knowledge might be considered. This strategy involves reading aloud less challenging texts to prepare students to tackle the more difficult text. Following is an example of how to build skills and rigor up to the featured anchor text for U.S. era 11, *Abraham Lincoln: Lawyer, Leader, Legend* by Justine and Ron Fontes, recommended for lower elementary students.

At a Lexile level of 790L, this text is certainly at the upper range for the age level, and we are not suggesting that K–2 students read this book independently. Instead, we suggest that they follow along (with their own copy or using a document camera) as the teacher reads it aloud. Even still, it might be best to first introduce some of the vocabulary and concepts through easier books on the same topic, such as the following:

- *Abe Lincoln's Hat* by Martha Brenner: 330L
- *Mr. Lincoln's Whiskers* by Karen B. Winnick: 420L
- *Looking at Lincoln* by Maira Kalman: AD480L
- *A. Lincoln and Me* by Louise Borden: AD650L
- *When Abraham Talked to the Trees* by Elizabeth Van Steenwyk: 670L

Each of the books tells interesting stories about Abraham Lincoln as a person and a leader, creating a whole reservoir of background knowledge. This mounting knowledge arouses curiosity in the children, prompting a desire for more information. By the time the teacher is ready to share the more challenging *Abraham Lincoln: Lawyer, Leader, Legend*, the students know that Lincoln stored important things in his hat, grew whiskers because a young girl thought it would make him more dignified, stood tall to make hard decisions, and practiced his speeches on stumps in the woods. This background knowledge will make the complex text easier to understand.

From First Fire to First Community: Humanity Evolves

(ca. 200,000 BCE to 3000 BCE)
GRADES: 3, 4, 5

OVERVIEW

Modern humans evolved from primates and, over many thousands of years, settled the farthest reaches of the globe, adapting to the exceedingly different environments they encountered. Archaeological finds of ancient structures, tools, burial remains, and even music instruments and cave paintings document their early societies and cultures and the rise of farming and trade. Over time, they developed more complicated social institutions: religions, economies, and hierarchies. Our ancient ancestors were vastly different from modern humanity but still had the same basic needs we have today. Lower elementary students will read *Discovery in the Caves* and explore what cave paintings reveal about how early humans lived. *Early Humans* prompts upper elementary students to use the evidence in the text to write about the methods archaeologists use to determine how our ancestors lived.

○ ○ ○

Interested in learning more about this time period? Read a more complete history in the "Era Summaries."

LEARNING EXPECTATIONS

Lower elementary: Our very distant ancestors—who lived well over one million years ago—made stone tools and fire and lived in social groups. Students should understand that much of what we take for granted—such as towns, farms, and metal tools—did not exist for the great majority of the human past and appeared only within the last ten thousand years. They should know that those changes completely altered the entire direction of human history in that they moved people toward complex communities and cultures.

Upper elementary: Most scientists think that humans arose in Africa and developed over millions of years. Students should know that we are still learning from new fossil finds about the patterns of human evolution. Modern humans appear to have moved gradually out of Africa and across the world; students should realize that artistic and musical expression, and rituals with spiritual significance, began among these early humans. Students should understand that in the last ten thousand years, humans transitioned from the enormously long Paleolithic, with its hunter-gatherer lifestyles, to settled, agricultural Neolithic communities—with increasingly sophisticated cultures, rituals, technologies, and trade. Students should realize that this transition was one of the most important in human history, because it laid the crucial groundwork for all later human civilizations.

SUGGESTED ANCHOR TEXTS

Early Humans by DK Publishing
Adventures in the Ice Age by Linda Bailey and Bill Slavin
Ice Mummy: The Discovery of a 5,000-Year-Old Man by Mark Dubowski and Cathy East Dubowski

FEATURED ANCHOR TEXT

EARLY HUMANS BY DK PUBLISHING

This book was selected because of the wide variety of topics covered and for the way it handles the content so that elementary students can grasp the most important information. Using clear, vivid photography of artifacts, students are treated to a museumlike experience. The distinct topics, addressed briefly but responsibly throughout the text, provide opportunities to examine the relationships among the ideas developed in each section. These questions focus on the first thirty-three pages of the text, but the combination of content-rich text, vivid illustrations, and photographs make this text worthy of further exploration—at various grade levels.

TEXT STUDY

These text-dependent questions address students' ability to use both text and illustrations to develop an understanding of a wide swath of history and archaeology. The questions ask students to compare information and make connections across eras discussed in the text. The performance assessment enables them to summarize and synthesize the information in an informative/ explanatory essay.

1. **Based on the information in "Human or ape?", where and when did the first humans appear?**

   • On pages 6 and 7, the author shows drawings and photographs of archaeological finds, such as the scene at Laetoli in East Africa and the upright "Lucy," excavated in Ethiopia in East Africa.

   • A map of Africa is included, showing the places in South and East Africa where early humans have been found.

   • According to page 6, "around six million years ago, the ape family had split into two distinct branches . . . one that led to humans."

   Note: Teachers can point out that the caption on the map of Africa suggests that it's still an open question whether early humans emerged in Africa or if they migrated there after emerging elsewhere.

   The caption on the map might lead to a discussion on the questioning that guides science.

2. **How does the author use comparison on page 7 to support the claim that early humans had distinct differences from apes?**

    - In the upper right illustration, the caption explains that the Australopithecines' brains were just a bit bigger than the gorillas' brains at the time, but still bigger than the gorillas' brains of today.

    - The caption associated with the picture of the oldest skull, featured in the center of the page, explains that early human muzzles and teeth were arranged differently than the apes', despite other similarities between the two.

    - In the bottom right set of diagrams, comparisons are made between human and gorilla neck, feet, and hips.

    - These comparisons make it clear that early humans were distinctly different from the apes.

3. **On page 8, how does this author define *hunter-gatherer*?**

    - The author defines *hunter-gatherer* as "living off the game that they hunted and the plants that they gathered."

4. **Describe the diet of the hunter-gatherer.**

    - Prehistoric people ate what they could hunt.
      ○ They hunted elk, stags, and seals, as pictured in the illustrations on page 9.

    - Prehistoric people ate what they could gather.
      ○ They ate nettles in soup and used the juice to make cheese.
      ○ They used dandelion leaves for salads, herbs to flavor foods, and spices, such as coriander, for digestion.
      ○ They ate and stored many grains, seeds, nuts, and berries or used them to flavor food.
      ○ They gathered eggs and fished for salmon with spears.

5. **According to page 10, why was man called *Homo habilis*? Explain what the human brain had to be able to do to make tools. Contrast this human toolmaking ability to an animal's limited tool-using ability.**

    - *Homo habilis* means "handy man." People were given this name because they were able to make tools.

    - The human brain had to be able to use memory, plan ahead, and work out "abstract problems" before it could make a tool.

    - According to the caption in the upper right quadrant of page 10, chimpanzees would use items from nature as tools. Humans were able to "use one set of tools to make other tools."

6. **According to archaeologists, how did the use of tools by *Homo erectus* improve on the way *Homo habilis* used them?**

    - According to page 14, *Homo erectus* developed a greater variety of tools. A hand axe from this era, for example, was "held in the fist, and the axe was used for cutting meat or digging up edible roots." (The hand axe is shown on page 15.)

    - *Homo erectus* was likely the first to create fire deliberately; they are believed to have used it to cook food and keep warm, but also as a tool for hunting animals, driving them into traps.

7. **On which continents have the bones of *Homo erectus* been found?**

    - According to the map on page 14, bones have been found in Africa, Europe, and Asia. (The caption specifically names the countries of China and Java.)

8. **According to the text, how did the coming of fire change the way people lived?**

   - On page 16, the author says that fire kept them warm in a very cold climate.
   - The text also says that fires kept the wild animals out of the living areas, providing safety for the people.
   - Fires enabled the people to roast meat and boil water for cooking.
   - Fire hardened the tips of wooden spears.
   - When people used fire to burn off a forest, they created fields for farming.

9. **Using the text and illustrations on pages 18 and 19, describe the scientist's view of the lifestyle of Neanderthals.**

   - Neanderthals lived in a cold climate and may have lived in a similar way to the Inuit people.
     - They made stone weapons and tools.
     - They made their own clothes out of deerskin.
     - They buried their dead, showing some evidence of religious beliefs.
     - Evidence suggests that they cared for disabled people who lived with them.

10. **How does the view of the Aboriginal people of Australia differ from the scientists' view of them?**

    - According to the text and caption on page 19, the Aboriginal people believe "they came from the land and have been in Australia forever."

    Note: *Students may be interested to look at the base word* original *within the word* aboriginal.

    - Scientists believe humans, in the form of *Homo sapiens*, may have boated to Australia from the islands of Southeast Asia.

11. **According to page 20, how have the scientists learned about Ice Age hunters?**

    - Because there are so few archaeological finds to tell about life in the Ice Age, scientists have studied the way the Inuit people live today.
      - Because they live along frozen coastlines and inland in Greenland and North America, the Inuits suggest how it was possible to survive in such extreme conditions.
      - Scientists have studied the way Inuits hunt, fish, make kayaks, and harpoon seals, walrus, and whales.

12. **Cite evidence from pages 22 and 23 to describe *Homo sapiens'* lifestyle of about ten thousand years ago.**

    - Modern man populated every continent, except Antarctica.
    - They used a wide variety of tools and stone blades.
    - Villages and tribes communicated with each other, and the settlements were larger.
    - People communicated "through the spoken word and through art, engravings, sculpture, and music."

13. **Why are the four skulls pictured on the bottom of page 23?**

    - The skulls represent "a classic view of the evolution of humanity from the apes," as described by Charles Darwin.

14. **After reading pages 24 and 25, describe the relationship between hunting ten thousand years ago and the earliest works of art.**

    - According to pages 24 and 25, the earliest art was found on the cave walls and roofs of Lascaux in France. The paintings illustrate animals the humans were going to hunt.
    - Carvings were done on animal bones, showing a human hunting a bison in one example.
    - People carved charms on antlers for good luck in hunting.

15. **According to pages 30 and 31, farming was "humanity's greatest-ever advancement." How does the author support that claim with evidence?**
    - People could control their own sources of food by growing plants and raising animals rather than depending on wild plants and animals.
    - It meant they could stay in one place and feed more people, growing the population.
    - Towns developed because groups of people would gather in one area.

16. **What is the purpose of the photograph of three sickles on page 30?**
    - The three sickles represent the stages of tool development during early times.
      ○ The photograph illustrates the flint-cutting edge of the Stone Age, the bronze-cutting edge of the Bronze Age, and the iron-cutting edge of the Iron Age.
      ○ It shows the progression of farm tools during the prehistoric ages.

17. **Compare the clothing of the Ice Age with the clothing of the Iron Age, as described on pages 32 and 33.**
    - The Ice Age people wore skins and furs of animals, cured and stretched to make clothing.
    - Eventually, wool was made from sheep in the late Stone Age.
    - In the Iron Age, fine fabrics were woven using sophisticated looms for the weaving.

PERFORMANCE ASSESSMENT

Using the completed questions related to this text, create a list of scientists' claims in one column and identify the archaeological evidence gathered to support that claim in another column. Use this work as a warm-up for the writing.

Give students the following task:

- Write an informative/explanatory essay describing at least two or three claims made by the author of this Eyewitness book, *Early Humans*. Introduce your topic, describe three to five examples of scientific claims made in the book, and explain how they are supported by the archaeological evidence presented in the text, illustrations, and captions.

Students should write a sentence that introduces their topic, use facts and definitions to develop points, and provide a concluding statement or section. At earlier levels, students may draw or dictate their informative/explanatory text and/or write a label, sentence, or series of related sentences. See standards for more details.

CONNECTIONS TO COMMON CORE STATE STANDARDS FOR ENGLISH LANGUAGE ARTS

- Question 1 asks students to use both illustrations and text to glean information about the central topic of this section (RI.3.1,2,3,7; RI.4.1,2,3,7; RI.5.1,2,3,7).
- Question 2 addresses the author's craft, asking students to note how the author compares two objects to make the differences between them clear (RI.3.1,2,3,8; RI.4.1,2,3,8; RI.5.1,2,3,8).
- Questions 3, 4, 6, 7, 8, and 11 require students to recall information presented in the text (RI. 3.1; RI.4.1; RI.5.1).

- Question 5 requires students to recall information from the text, but it also asks them to cite evidence from the text to explain that information (RI.3.1,2,3; RI.4.1,2,3; RI.5.1,2,3).
- Questions 6 and 17 give students a chance to cite and compare information presented in two different sections of the text (RI.3.1,2,3; RI.4.1,2,3; RI.5.1,2,3).
- Using illustrations and text, students must synthesize the information presented in both forms in order to answer question 9 (RI.3.1,2,3,7,8; RI.4.1,2,3,7,8; RI.5.1,2,3,7,8).
- To answer question 13, students must understand the information presented in the "evolution" paragraph, as well as the illustrations and their captions, but they must also synthesize that knowledge with information they have learned in previous sections (RI.3.1,2,3,7; RI.4.1,2,3,7; RI.5.1,2,3,7).
- Question 14 asks students to make connections between two related ideas presented in the text that are enhanced by accompanying illustrations (RI.3.1,2,3,7; RI.4.1,2,3,7; RI.5.1,2,3,7).
- Question 15 focuses on how authors support their claims with evidence. (RI.3.1,2,3,7,8; RI.4.1,2,3,7,8; RI.5.1,2,3,7,8).
- Question 16 asks about the author's purpose in including a particular photograph (RI.3.1,2,3,5,7,8; RI.4.1,2,3,5,7,8; RI.5.1,2,3,5,7,8).
- The performance assessment offers students a chance to revisit the wealth of information they have learned from this book, organize it, and present their understanding of it in an informative/explanatory essay (W.3.2; W.4.2; W.5.2).

MORE RESOURCES

PRIMARY SOURCES

Chauvet Cave paintings, ca. 30,000 BCE (Metropolitan Museum of Art)

Shard of decorated pottery bowl, ca. 6,000 BCE (British Museum)

Image of archaeologists uncovering Shanidar skeleton, 1953 (Smithsonian Institution)

35,000-year-old flute (Smithsonian Institution)

Oldest playable flute, Ancient China, 9,000 years old (Brookhaven National Laboratory)

   Includes links to listen to the flutes being played

USEFUL WEBSITES

Museum of the Stone Age

Stonehenge archaeological excavation article, 2008 (*Smithsonian* magazine)

Human Evolution Evidence (Smithsonian Museum of Natural History)

Photo gallery depicting the evolution of domestic dogs from wolves (*National Geographic*)

Civilizations Emerge: The Power of Words and of Bronze

(ca. 3500 BCE to ca. 1000 BCE)
GRADES: 3, 4, 5

OVERVIEW

As mankind improved its use of natural resources and farmed more efficiently, specialized crafts and professions could develop. The first distinct cities arose in major river valleys, and civilization began. From Mesopotamia to Egypt and India to China, cities began to pull people together into societies with varying rules, institutions, religions, and cultural identities. With the advent of bronze technology and the written word, the cities developed greater capacity to function, build, innovate, trade—and make war. The discovery of King Tut's tomb will fascinate younger students after they carefully read *Tut's Mummy: Lost . . . and Found*. Mesopotamia prompts older students to report on essential features of the ancient region that covered a major portion of what we now call the Middle East.

o o o

Interested in learning more about this time period? Read a more complete history in the "Era Summaries."

LEARNING EXPECTATIONS

Lower elementary: Students should understand that cities, arising in several world regions, marked the beginnings of what we consider civilization. They should also know that the development of writing and bronze technology for tools and weapons were crucial elements that enabled these complex new communities to function.

Upper elementary: Students should know the different regions in which cities first appeared. They should understand the importance of writing and of bronze tools and weapons in enabling these new urban civilizations to function and expand. They should understand that important Bronze Age cultures arose in Mesopotamia, the Indus Valley, China, the Aegean, and Anatolia—and that there were important ties between many of these cultures. They should know that civilization saw the rise of major buildings (temples and palaces with rich art and ornamentation), literature, and written laws.

SUGGESTED ANCHOR TEXTS

Mesopotamia by Don Nardo
Ancient Egyptian Culture by Katherine Gleason
Ancient Egyptians by Philip Steele
Ancient Mesopotamia by Allison Lassieur
Communication in the Ancient World by Paul Challen
The Egyptians by Richard Platt
Life in Ancient Africa by Hazel Richardson
The Gilgamesh Trilogy retold by Ludmila Zeman

FEATURED ANCHOR TEXT

MESOPOTAMIA BY DON NARDO

This book was selected because of the detailed information and beautiful illustrations depicting the cultures and archaeological artifacts of the ancient region of Mesopotamia. Don Nardo tells the story of the dawn of civilization through the art of the era. Charts, a time line, a detailed glossary, and an index round out this rich resource that is useful to the study of ancient history.

TEXT STUDY

These text-dependent questions offer students a chance to explore an informational text that treats several related concepts in depth. By examining and interpreting illustrations and the author's use of evidence along the way, students will be able to track and understand the rich amount (and kind) of information presented in this text. The performance assessment enables students to summarize and synthesize what they have learned in an informative/ explanatory essay.

1. **A *civilization* is "an advanced society with a high level of culture, science, industry, and government." Using evidence from pages 4 and 5, explain why the "dawn of civilization" came to the area of Mesopotamia.**

    - The word *Mesopotamia* comes from Greek and means "between the rivers." Because this region was between the Tigris and Euphrates Rivers, there were farmlands for the first farmers in history. Farms cause people to settle down because the land is fertile, and the produce feeds the people. The first major civilization was the Sumerian; Sumerians lived in the fertile valley.

2. **The word *mute* means "completely silent, unable to talk." What does the author mean by the ruins of ancient cities standing "as mute witnesses to the region's amazing past?"**

    Note: *Teachers may discuss that in contemporary English, this word is also used as a verb.*

    - There were four major cities in ancient times that left hints as to their beginnings of civilization—Sumerian, Babylonian, Assyrian, and Persian—and they changed the world forever. These ruins stand there as evidence, telling the world that they were advanced groups of society, even though they cannot speak aloud.

3. **According to page 7, why did life change from nomadic to settled farming?**

   - Historians believe that about twelve thousand to eleven thousand years ago, nomadic people who hunted for and gathered their food settled in the Fertile Crescent on the edge of the Mesopotamian region. This farmland made it possible to have a "permanent, secure food supply."

4. **These farming villages were small. How did these small village cultures spread into the Mesopotamian plains?**

   - Farmers need land. The numbers of people grew, so about six thousand years later, people moved into the very fertile land between the rivers. Because of the water source, they could irrigate their land and grow more crops. When they had more food, they were able to support more people and the population grew.

5. **According to pages 9 and 10, what were the "important elements of civilization" seen in the Sumerian culture?**

   - The towns became cities with thousands of people. Villages and farms with irrigation systems surrounded the cities, creating "city-states."
   - The city was walled for protection and ruled by a king.
   - The Sumerians traded food, crafts, cloth, and other goods with other city-states.
   - The Sumerians invented writing using wedge-shaped cuneiform pressed into clay tablets.

6. **According to page 14, there was a "relentless cycle of conquest, empire, and decline, followed by new conquest" in Mesopotamia. What examples does the author give of this cycle?**

   - Sargon of Akkad took over southern Mesopotamia, defeating the Sumerians.
   - Babylon's ruler Hammurabi later created a huge city in Mesopotamia.
   - Tukulti-Ninurta I of the Assyrians took over Babylon.
   - The "Sea Peoples" burned and "looted" the cities.
   - There was the Persian Empire, the Greeks, and the Parthians. Then the Sassanians, and finally the Arabs took over the land with the Muslim army in 651.

   Note: The succession of kingdoms and conquerors is so long and confusing that the author created a chart on page 15. You may choose to have the students simply interpret the chart of information, instead of wading through all of the meaty paragraphs to answer this question.

7. **Using the illustration on page 16, explain how archaeologists use art to learn about ancient societies.**

   - Slaves on a relief suggest that Mesopotamians owned slaves.

   Note: A relief is a type of art in which a sculpture projects from a plane; for example, a flat piece of clay that has been carved on one side.

8. **Using evidence on pages 17 through 20, describe the women and children in the societies of Mesopotamia.**

   - Families were "patriarchal"—ruled by the men. Possessions and property were passed down from father to son, if there were one.
   - Although women were under men in the home, either the father or the husband, they were allowed to have a job in the community. Some women were scribes, artists, and doctors. They helped in the fields and made cloth.

- Women were "expected to marry and have children." Males in the family usually arranged the marriages.
- Children played with toys such as "jump ropes, balls, and hoops." There is evidence that boys played with toy chariots and slingshots and girls had dolls.
- Adoption was common.

9. **How do historians know there were schools in ancient Mesopotamia? What have they learned about these schools?**

- According to page 21, they found vocabulary lists from 3000 BCE. They have found ruins of schools in Mesopotamian cities.
- They have learned that students sat on benches and wrote on wax-covered wooden writing boards. They wrote with a stick on the wax. They could reuse the board by smoothing the wax.

10. **According to pages 22 and 23, why is it that we know so little about the artists in ancient Mesopotamia? Describe the art of the Mesopotamian people as described on pages 23 through 27. What were the purposes of Mesopotamian art?**

- Writers told of the nobility and wealthy in society; artists were thought to be "lower class," so not much information was recorded about them.
- The Assyrians sculpted "kings, gods, animals, and mythical beings." They made a creature called a "bull man." These guarded the entrances of palaces.
- War scenes were etched in "bas-reliefs." Their purpose was decorative, but they were also meant to impress their people and foreign visitors to the city.
- The Persians carved reliefs into the sides of rocks and cliffs. They sculpted scenes that told of a king's reign, with images of conquered enemies.
- Murals made with etched plaster and paint decorated the homes of wealthy people.
- Cylinder seals were made to create an imprint that "identified a person, family, or social institution."
- Mosaics were created for decoration, but they also depicted military scenes of the victors from battle.

11. **What are ziggurats? Why did they not last long?**

- According to page 28, a ziggurat is a "gigantic pyramid-like structure with stepped platforms used for religious purposes."
- The ziggurats of Mesopotamia did not last long because they were made of clay and reed bricks. "The region had very few forests to supply wood and very little native stone." Because they were not strong, "rain, wind, and sun caused the bricks to crumble very quickly."

12. **The text says that the ancient Mesopotamians were "devoutly religious." According to pages 31 through 33, what did the gods require of the people?**

- The gods required the people to follow basic social rules.
  - They had to tell the truth.
  - They had to behave in a civilized manner.
  - They had to seek justice.
  - They "expected the kings to make constructive laws and their subjects to obey them."
- The people had to perform "rituals of worship."
  - They had to pray and make offerings to the gods.
  - They held religious festivals.

13. **What can you conclude from the table showing the "Major Sumerian Gods" on page 34?**

   - The people believed in many gods—not just one.

   - If these Gods are called "major," there were probably more Gods who were "minor."

   - Their gods came from nature and the universe—the water, the heavens, the sun, the moon, the underworld. They also exhibited fine qualities, such as love and wisdom.

   - The Sumerian gods and the Babylonian gods were similar.

14. **According to pages 40 and 41, what is the country now occupying the area once called ancient Mesopotamia? How is the present-day country similar to the ancient region?**

   - Iraq now occupies the area known as ancient Mesopotamia.

   - Modern Iraqi street markets are very similar to the ancient markets.

   - Until recently, people still lived in small mud-brick houses. People who lived near the marshes lived in reed huts.

   - People still made reed boats and played similar games.

PERFORMANCE ASSESSMENT

Review the definition of *civilization*. Give students the following task:

- Write a three- to five-paragraph informative/explanatory essay explaining two or three features of a civilization that developed in the ancient region of Mesopotamia. Be sure to name the features, describe them, and describe how historians know about them.

Students should write a sentence that introduces their topic, use facts and definitions to develop points, and provide a concluding statement or section. At earlier levels, students may draw or dictate their informative/explanatory text and/or write a label, sentence, or series of related sentences. See standards for more details.

EXTENSION

Read one or more stories from the *Gilgamesh Trilogy* by Ludmila Zeman to students. Have the students write an informative/explanatory essay in which they explain how the events and people in the story reflect the religion and culture of the people of Mesopotamia.

Students should write a sentence that introduces their topic, use facts and definitions to develop points, and provide a concluding statement or section. At earlier levels, students may draw or dictate their informative/explanatory text and/or write a label, sentence, or series of related sentences. See standards for more details.

CONNECTIONS TO COMMON CORE STATE STANDARDS FOR ENGLISH LANGUAGE ARTS

- Questions 1 and 2 focus students' attention on key vocabulary words and ask them to use evidence from the text to explain the use of phrases containing these words (RI.3.1,2,4; RI.4.1,2,4; RI.5.1,2,4).

- Questions 3, 4, 5, 9, 11, 12, and 13 ask students to identify key details from the text (RI.3.1,2; RI.4.1,2; RI.5.1,2).
  - Question 13 also asks students to make a specific inference.
- Question 6 requires students to identify the evidence that the author provides for an important assertion. Students may use the timeline, giving them practice in interpreting this structural feature of an informational text (RI.3.1,2,3,5,8; RI.4.1,2,3,5,8; RI.5.1,2,3,5,8).
- Question 7 addresses the interpretation of illustrations as well as a key vocabulary word (RI.3.4,5; RI.4.4,5; RI.5.4,5).
- Students must cite the author's evidence and detail key information from the text when answering questions 8 and 9 (RI.3.1,2,8; RI.4.1,2,8; RI.5.1,2,8).
- Question 10 is multifaceted. It asks students to recall key details, convey their understanding of the author's description of a key concept (Mesopotamian art), and describe the author's explanation concerning the purpose of that concept (RI.3.1,2,3,8; RI.4.1,2,3,8; RI.5.1,2,3,8).
- Question 14 requires students to recall a simple detail from the text and also to compare and contrast two related concepts from the text (RI.3.1,2,3,8; RI.4.1,2,3,8; RI.5.1,2,3,8).
- The performance assessment gives students an opportunity to reread closely to gather evidence for a well-organized informative/explanatory essay that conveys their understanding of key concepts in this informational text (RI.3.1,2,3,5,7,9; RI.4.1,2,3,5,7,9; RI.5.1,2,3,5,7,9; W.3.2,9; W.4.2,9; W.5.2,9).

MORE RESOURCES

HISTORICAL FICTION

The Egyptian Cinderella by Shirley Climo and Ruth Heller

Seeker of Knowledge: The Man Who Deciphered Egyptian Hieroglyphics by James Rumford

The 5000-Year-Old Puzzle: Solving a Mystery of Ancient Egypt by Claudie Logan and Melissa Sweet

How the Sphinx Got to the Museum by Jesse Hartland

Ickstory: Unraveling the History of Mummies around the World by Sylvia Branzei and Jack Keely

Secrets of the Mummies by Harriet Griffey

Pyramid by David Macauley

The Best Book of Mummies by Philip Steele

Bill and Pete Go down the Nile by Tomie dePaola

Egyptian Gods and Goddesses by Henry Barker

Skippyjon Jones in Mummy Trouble by Judy Schachner

Temple Cat by Andrew Clements and Kate Kiessler

Mummies in the Morning by Mary Pope Osborne

PRIMARY SOURCES

Sumerian cuneiform tablet, ca. 16th to 15th century BCE (Metropolitan Museum of Art)

Code of Hammurabi stele, ca. 1792 to 1750 BCE (Louvre)

Ancient Egyptian board game of Twenty Squares, ca. 1500 to 1200 BCE (Louvre)

Oldest known text in Hurrian language called *Urkish Lion*, ca. 21st century BCE (Louvre)

Chinese Zhou ritual vessel with inscription, 11th century BCE (British Museum)

Page from the *Book of the Dead* of Hunefer from Thebes, Egypt, ca. 1900 BCE (British Museum)

POETRY AND MUSIC

"The Tale of Sinuhe," Egyptian, 1850 BCE (British Museum)

ART AND ARCHITECTURE

Two panels with striding lions, ca. 604 to 562 BCE (Metropolitan Museum of Art)

Bas-relief of Prince Khaemwaset, ca. 1550 to 1069 BCE (Louvre)

Orthostate relief: seated figure holding a lotus flower, ca. 9th century BCE (Metropolitan Museum of Art)

USEFUL WEBSITES

Ancient Mesopotamia teaching resources (University of Chicago, Oriental Institute)

Online tour of Egyptian antiquities (Louvre)

From Iron to Ideas: Religion and Freedom Take Shape

(ca. 1700 BCE to 400 BCE)

GRADES: 3, 4, 5

OVERVIEW

Many Bronze Age cultures and cities were in decline about the time the technology to make iron tools and weapons emerged. During this time of migration and chaos, two peoples rose to prominence: the Israelites and Greeks. The ancient Israelites' belief in a single deity would have an enduring impact on ensuing centuries. The city-states of ancient Greece twice defeated the Persian Empire as they laid the groundwork for democracy. *Ancient Greece and the Olympics* gives K–2 students knowledge insights into the guiding principles of this ancient civilization and how they still influence present-day America. Older students deepen their understanding of cultural interactions by reading *Ancient Israelites and Their Neighbors* and writing about the impact of surrounding communities on ancient Israel.

o o o

Interested in learning more about this time period? Read a more complete history in the "Era Summaries."

LEARNING EXPECTATIONS

Lower elementary: Students should understand that more and more people began to develop important civilizations as the great Bronze Age cultures fell. They should know that the ancient Israelites were the first to worship a single god, which powerfully affected later history, and that Greece laid the roots of much of Western culture. A major contribution by Greece was the idea of democracy, or government ruled *by the people*.

Upper elementary: Students should know that iron replaced bronze in the first millennium BCE, enabling the advent of more advanced technology (and harder-fought wars). They should know, also, that the Iron Age witnessed the birth of many cultures that still have powerful influences today. These include the ancient Israelites, the ancestors of modern Jews and creators of the religious tradition that would also spawn Christianity and Islam, and the ancient Greeks, whose art, architecture, philosophy, and democratic ideas powerfully affect the world to this day–even though the high point of classical Greece was brief.

SUGGESTED ANCHOR TEXTS

Ancient Israelites and Their Neighbors: An Activity Guide by Marian Broida
Greek Myths: Stories of Sun, Stone and Sea by Sally Pomme Clayton and Jane Ray
The Greeks by Richard Platt
Life in Ancient Greece by Lynn Peppas
One City, Two Brothers by Chris Smith and Aurelia Fronty
Tools of the Ancient Greeks by Kris Bordessa

FEATURED ANCHOR TEXT

ANCIENT ISRAELITES AND THEIR NEIGHBORS: AN ACTIVITY GUIDE BY MARIAN BROIDA

This book was selected because of the strong focus on ancient Israel's religious legacy. Although this book teaches about the Israelites, Philistines, and Phoenicians, this set of questions will focus on the people of Israel. The combination of archaeology, sacred writings, and other writings provide students with experience working with primary sources in the study of history. Rarely seen in historical texts, the activities are well designed to give students opportunities to follow directions in the context of learning more of the daily life of ancient people. The text also includes a detailed table of contents, a foreword, a timeline, a carefully constructed introduction, maps, a glossary, links to additional resources, a bibliography, an index, and other structural features of informational text that make it a great resource for students to learn how to navigate a rich informational text, especially one that addresses several related but different topics.

TEXT STUDY

These text-dependent questions require students to read closely. They mine this rich informational text for questions about its structure, its use of irony, and its strategic use of insets and illustrations. Many of the questions ask students to compare and contrast information from various sections of the text and make inferences about the significance of events described.

1. **According to the information found in the section "What Is This Book About?" on page xiii, create one informational sentence about each of the people groups featured in this text.**

    Note: Answers can vary.

    - The Philistines wrote in an ancient alphabet on scrolls and played music on a stringed instrument called a lyre.

    - The Israelites farmed hillsides of grain and fruit trees.

    - The Phoenicians sent sailors in ships boldly to "far-off lands."

2. **According to this author's introduction on pages xiii and xiv, how are time periods organized in ancient history?**

    - Time periods are organized in two different ways in ancient history.
      - Ancient history is organized by numbers such as 1200 BCE and 538 BCE. According to this text, BCE stands for "Before the Common Era," or how many more years until the year 1. Because you are counting backward from the year 1, the greater number denotes the

older time period. Some people refer to the dates as BC, meaning "Before Christ" and refer to the time after the number 1 as AD, meaning "Anno Domini," which means "the year of our Lord" in Latin.

- Ancient history is also organized into ages based on the materials used to make their tools, in this order: Stone Age, Copper Age, Bronze Age, and the Iron Age.

3. **According to pages xvii through xix, how have historians gathered information about the ancient Israelites, Philistines, and Phoenicians?**

- The historians gather information from the Bible, other ancient writings, and archaeology.
  - The Bible is mainly a religious book, and it tells sacred stories, and about history, the law, and also daily life.
  - The other writings from the Greeks, Romans, and Egyptians tell about these people and events on carvings.
  - Archaeology uncovers ruins that may have been a house, a temple, or a workshop.

  Note: *Throughout this text, the use of the three sources is evident and usually they are used to question or confirm interpretations of findings.*

4. **According to pages 3 through 5, who were the Israelites and what was their legacy as described in this text? Why was that legacy so important to history?**

- The Israelites are described as an obscure people with poor settlements and crude tools who settled in Canaan's central hills. The stories of their origin are told in the Hebrew Bible, listing seven people: Abraham, Isaac, Jacob, Sarah, Rebecca, Rachel, and Leah.

- They left a religious legacy, a belief in one God.

- The religion of the ancient Israelites began three of the great religions of history: Judaism, Christianity, and Islam.

  Note: *The inset on page 5 goes on to explain the similarities and differences among the three religions.*

5. **According to the inset on page 5, what do Jews and Muslims have in common? How are these two religious groups different?**

- Both Jews and Muslims believe they descended from Abraham. They also name Moses as their prophet. Both Jews and Muslims believe there is one God.

- These two religious groups also have differences.
  - Jews claim Isaac, a son of Abraham, as their father and the Muslims claim Ishmael, another son of Abraham, as their father.
  - Jews claim the Hebrew Bible as their holy text. Muslims claim the Quran as their holy text.

6. **How does the inset entitled "Did King David Really Live?" prove that historians use a variety of primary sources to look for information about a historical event or person?**

- According to page 7, the Hebrew Bible says that King David really lived, but there were no other writings that confirmed it.

- Then in 1993, archaeologists discovered an inscription on a broken piece of stone with "a king of Israel" and "the House of David" on it. This find confirmed that David was really a king in ancient Israel.

- All three sources—the Bible, ancient writings, and archaeology—were used as primary sources to study history.

7. **According to page 13, how did the Israelites arrange their "pillared houses" to provide protection for families? How did cities provide protection?**

   - The houses of the Israelites were sometimes connected with their back walls forming a ring, leaving a gap to allow people out to farm fields. If the towns grew large enough, they built a wall.

   - Cities had huge walls with gates that were opened in the morning and closed in the evenings.

8. **What is ironic about the source of information about the ways Israelites dressed?**

   - According to page 16, the enemies of the Israelites were the ones who left the archaeological evidence about the Israelite's style of dress. There were carvings in rock by the Assyrians, showing the capture of the Israelites and displaying the way they dressed.

     Note: *The irony lies in the fact that the history of their dress would have been lost had they not been captured and the information had not been recorded by the enemy.*

9. **Using evidence from the text, explain how the Babylonian exile changed the way the Israelites wrote their language.**

   - According to page 25, the Israelites had been using the Phoenician alphabet until they were taken to Babylonia. While they were there, they learned a new alphabet called the Aramaic alphabet. All of their future Hebrew writing was recorded with this new alphabet.

10. **Explain how the Israelites wrote and what kinds of materials they used, citing evidence from the text.**

    - The Israelites mainly wrote on three different materials: parchment, papyrus, or potsherds. Parchment was "tanned animal skins," papyrus was an Egyptian imported material made from papyrus stems mashed into a kind of paper, and potsherds were broken pieces of pottery.

    - Seals pressed into clay were used to sign someone's letter or to impress clay pottery. They also "sealed" a private letter written on papyrus. If a message arrived with a broken seal, the recipient would know the letter had been read.

11. **On page 31, the author wrote, "Terrace farming meant turning a hillside into something like a staircase for giants." Explain what was meant by that simile, what terrace farming is, and why terrace farming was necessary for the Israelites' way of life.**

    - From the diagram on page 31, one can see how a terraced hillside looks like giant steps going up an inclined piece of land.

    - A terraced farm was created when Israelites "first built a long, stone wall around the hillside, then heaped rubble behind the wall until the ground there was flat. Finally, they covered the rubble with soil." They would continue doing this up the hill, creating long, narrow fields up the whole side of the hill.

    - This type of terracing was necessary for the Israelites because they lived in a hilly land but needed to grow many crops for their own provisions of food. They would grow olives on trees and wheat on the same terrace. On other terraces, they would grow grains, fruits, or legumes.

12. **How does the way in which the ancient Israelites prepare their food reflect their religious culture? Cite evidence from the text to support your answers.**

    - According to page 36, the Israelites did not eat pork because the Bible had forbidden it. According to page 38, honoring the Sabbath meant that no work could be done. This meant the hard work of baking bread would not happen seven days a week, because on the Sabbath there was no bread making.

13. **According to page 42, why was "you shall have no other gods before me" such a new idea in the culture of ancient Israel?**

   • The idea of worshipping a single god was a rare one. Most cultures at that time worshipped multiple gods. Each god was prayed to for a specific purpose. They would pray to a specific god for protection and to another god for healing or a good harvest.

   • The text proposes that even the Israelites didn't actually abandon belief in multiple gods at first. It took centuries for them to believe that there was only one God.

   Note: Page 44 goes on to say how archaeological indications and the recordings in the Bible give evidence of worshipping multiple gods, even though their religion taught otherwise.

14. **Cite evidence from the text to explain how the destruction of the temple in Jerusalem affected the religious practices of the Israelites.**

   • According to page 45, the temple in Jerusalem, built during the reign of King Solomon, had become the center of worship and sacrifice of animals for the Israelites. The smaller centers of worship located in other places had been destroyed, but when the temple in Jerusalem was destroyed, many people were sent to Babylonia. When they returned, they began to focus more on prayer, the Sabbath, and holy texts. They no longer centered their worship on animal sacrifices in the temple.

PERFORMANCE ASSESSMENT

Give students the following task:

• Using the evidence in the text, write an informative/explanatory essay telling how events involving other cultures affected the Israelite culture. For example, the alphabet of the Israelites was affected by the Babylonian captivity when the alphabet changed from Phoenician to Aramaic. The Babylonian captivity also changed the way Israelites worshipped, as the loss of the temple in Jerusalem led to a cessation of animal sacrifice.

Students should write a sentence that introduces their topic, use facts and definitions to develop points, and provide a concluding statement or section. At earlier levels, students may draw or dictate their informative/explanatory text and/or write a label, sentence, or series of related sentences. See standards for more details.

EXTENSIONS

1. Have students work in pairs to choose one of the Israelite activities. Instruct students to gather the materials they will need and follow the directions to create the piece of clothing, writing stamp, pillared home, and so on. After all of the projects are completed, have students set up an ancient Israelite museum with summary cards telling about the project. Give the students the following task:

• Explain how you created your ancient Israelite project. Be sure to include the materials you needed and the steps you followed to complete the project. Explain how this project represents an important image of the daily life of the ancient Israelite culture.

Students should write a sentence that introduces their topic, use facts and definitions to develop points, and provide a concluding statement or section. At earlier levels, students may draw or dictate their informative/explanatory text and/or write a label, sentence, or series of related sentences. See standards for more details.

2. Continue the studies of the Phoenicians and Philistines of the Iron Age, using the other two-thirds of the text. Have students create an informative/explanatory essay comparing the

three cultures living in close proximity to each other. Have students consider how the Iron Age not only helped the farmer with stronger tools but also increased the damage in war with stronger, more durable weapons.

3. Have students read books on the Greek culture during the Iron Age. In an informative/ explanatory essay, have students compare and contrast the legacy of Greek myth and art to the Israelite legacy. Ask students to look closely at how different these two cultures were, although they existed during the same era.

CONNECTIONS TO COMMON CORE STATE STANDARDS FOR ENGLISH LANGUAGE ARTS

- Question 1 asks students to summarize and—potentially—synthesize information learned from the introduction. They must convey their understanding in complete sentences (RI.3.1,2,3; RI.4.1,2,3; RI.5.1,2,3; W.3.2; W.4.2; W.5.2).

- Questions 2, 3, 4, 5, 7, 9, 12, and 13 ask students to recall important information from the text and cite evidence to support their assertions (RI.3.1,2,3; RI.4.1,2,3; RI.5.1,2,3).
  - Question 4 also requires that students infer and explain the significance of the information provided (RI.3.6; RI.4.6; RI.5.6).
  - Question 5 also requires students to compare information read in one section to that in another. They must also use a structural feature of informational text (an inset) to glean key information (RI.3.5,9; RI.4.5,9; RI.5.5,9).

- To answer question 6, students must again extract information from an inset about the use of primary sources (RI.3.1,2,3,5; RI.4.1,2,3,5; RI.5.1,2,3,5).

- Question 8 helps students consider and understand the concept of irony, which is used not only in literary texts but also in informational texts (RI.3.1,2,3; RI.4.1,2,3; RI.5.1,2,3).

- Question 10 prompts students to recount information—some procedures—described in the text (RI.3.1,2; RI.4.1,2; RI.5.1,2).

- Question 11 addresses a number of Common Core State Standards (CCSS) skills: students must first recall and explain information that they have read (using text and illustrations), interpret a simile that the author used to describe the information, and then explain the significance of the information (RI.3.1,2,3,4,7; RI.4.1,2,3,4,7; RI.5.1,2,3,4,7).

- The performance assessment task enables students to summarize and explain cause-and-effect relationships among the peoples and events discussed in this informational text (RI.3.1,2,3,5; RI.4.1,2,3,5; RI.5.1,2,3,5; W.3.2,9; W.4.2,9; W.5.2,9).

- The performance assessment involves a number of related CCSS skills: students must follow directions to complete a project, summarize the significance of their work, then write an informative/explanatory essay that explains what they have done, how, and why their project is reflective of important concepts in the text (RI.3.1,2,3; RI.4.1,2,3; RI.5.1,2,3; W.3.2,9; W.4.2,9; W.5.2,9).

- The first extension gives students a chance to explore other cultures related to the ones discussed in this text and convey their understanding of the similarities and differences among the cultures in an informative/explanatory essay (RI.3.1,2,3,9; RI.4.1,2,3,9; RI.5.1,2,3,9; W.3.2,9; W.4.2,9; W.5.2,9).

- Similar to the first extension, the second extension directs students to research a topic related to material in the anchor text, then convey their research in an informative/explanatory essay that compares and contrasts the new information with what they learned from the anchor text (RI.3.1,2,3,9; RI.4.1,2,3,9; RI.5.1,2,3,9; W.3.2,7,8,9; W.4.2,7,8,9; W.5.2,7,8,9).

MORE RESOURCES

PRIMARY SOURCES

Zhou dynasty bronze sword, ca. 5th to 4th century BCE (British Museum)

Phoenician sculpture, head of a woman, ca. 5th century BCE (Louvre)

Phoenician coin showing Heracles and Zeus, ca. 330 to 327 BCE (British Museum)

Kushite statuette of Taharqa and the Falcon God, ca. 690 to 664 BCE (Louvre)

The Mesha stele, ca. 800 BCE (Louvre)

Ancient Hebrew letter on pottery, ca. 6th century BCE (The Israel Museum)

Marble stele of an athlete from archaic Greek period, ca. 550 BCE (National Archaeological Museum of Athens)

ART AND ARCHITECTURE

The Siren vase depicting Odysseus passing the Sirens, ca. 480 to 470 BCE (British Museum)

USEFUL WEBSITE

Ancient Greek Sites and Ancient Greek Ruins (Historvius)

The Classical Era: Hellenistic Greece and Rome Flourish

(400 BCE to 476 CE)
GRADES: 3, 4, 5

OVERVIEW

The ancient Greek and Roman cultures comprise what is called classical civilization because of their great contributions to philosophy, statecraft, architecture, art, and literature. These two cultures laid the foundation for the governance form we know as democracy. Each had vast impact on world civilization as well as the arts of government and of war. Christianity emerged during the early Roman Empire. Lower elementary students will unearth details of what life was like prior to the famous volcanic eruption in the Roman Empire through a close read of *Pompeii . . . Buried Alive*. After reading *Roman Diary*, upper elementary students will produce dictionaries of words that derive from ancient Rome and recognize how aspects of Roman culture persist to the present day.

o o o

Interested in learning more about this time period? Read a more complete history in the "Era Summaries."

LEARNING EXPECTATIONS

Lower elementary: Students should understand that the Greeks and the Greek-influenced Romans (who were further influenced by the rise of Christianity) profoundly and permanently affected Europe and much of Asia: they left political, literary, artistic, and religious legacies throughout the world.

Upper elementary: Students should know that the conquests of Alexander the Great helped bring Europe and Asia into greater contact, blending the two cultures with important long-term consequences. They should know that the Greek world gave way to Rome. The Roman republic helped create crucial political ideas and provided a model that strongly influences governments to this day. Rome's empire, which ultimately replaced its republic, spread Greco-Roman classical culture and the expanding religion of Christianity over an enormous area. Although the Roman Empire decayed and collapsed, its influences were permanent and profound.

SUGGESTED ANCHOR TEXTS

Roman Diary: The Journal of Iliona of Mytilini, Who Was Captured and Sold as a Slave in Rome,
  AD 107 by Richard Platt and David Parkins
Alexander the Great by Demi
Ancient Rome by Robert Snedden
Ancient Rome: A Mighty Empire by Muriel L. Dubois
Brave Cloelia by Jane Louise Curry
Roman Numerals I to MM by Arthur Geisert
Tools of the Ancient Romans: A Kid's Guide to the History and Science of Life in Ancient Rome
  by Rachel Dickinson

FEATURED ANCHOR TEXT

ROMAN DIARY: THE JOURNAL OF ILIONA OF MYTILINI, WHO WAS CAPTURED AND SOLD AS A SLAVE IN ROME, AD 107 BY RICHARD PLATT AND DAVID PARKINS

This book was selected because it is written as an engaging first-person, fictionalized diary from the unique viewpoint of a young slave in the ancient Roman culture. The wealth of information in the informational section at the back of the book enhances the enticing diary with basic information about the Roman Empire's technology, society, sports, and religion. The glossary of terms and the timeline of historical events make this a complete text for an elementary walk-through about life in ancient Rome. The illustrations will grab the students' interest and are large enough to use as a shared text.

TEXT STUDY

These text-dependent questions focus students' attention on a wealth of important historical information about life in ancient Rome. Many questions focus on understanding academic vocabulary, summarizing and synthesizing information, and comparing the fictionalized account to the supplemental informational text, designed to give students more background and other information about ancient Roman culture and accomplishments.

1. **According to the text and the illustrations on the cover of this book, what was true in the featured era of Roman history?**

   - According to the subtitle, people were captured and sold as slaves during this Roman era.

   - Rulers were crowned with wreaths of leaves.

   - This was the era of men fighting each other with swords in great arenas.

   - Men and women wore white robes.

   - Writing was done on scrolls.

     Note: *These are only sample responses based only on what is visible on the cover. Students might have prior knowledge to know that there is evidence of a mosaic style of art, columned architecture, togas, gladiators, laurel wreath, and so on.*

2. **According to page 5, what was Iliona's life like in Greece? Why were they leaving to go to Alexandria, Egypt?**

   - Iliona had a wonderful life in Greece.
     - She lived on an island called Mytilini, in a "fine, big house."
     - Her father was a businessman.

   - Iliona's family was traveling to Alexandria, Egypt, to live for at least two years. Her father's warehouse had burned down and they would need to be there while it was being rebuilt.

3. **According to page 5, how would Iliona be doing her writing?**

   - She would use goose quills, sharpened with a knife and dipped in ink.

   - She would write on fine, smooth papyrus, rolled in a scroll, as seen on the cover.

4. **According to page 6, what did the pirates mean by "self-loading cargo"? Why was Iliona allowed to keep her writing tools?**

   - As the ship was traveling toward Egypt, it was overtaken by pirates who captured people whom they were later to sell as slaves in Rome. They were not interested in taking anything they would need to carry, such as the cargo hold full of wine. They wanted to take those human beings who were healthy and would be able to walk onto the pirate ship on their own.

   - According to Iliona, the pirates allowed her to keep her ink, pens, and papyrus "because they think I will fetch a higher price if it is obvious that I know my letters."

5. **Summarize Iliona's experience from her arrival in Rome until she arrived at the home of the senator, Gaius Martius.**

   - According to pages 8 through 11, Iliona and her brother were sold together as one unit at three different auctions within a few days of arriving in Rome. They were dirty, with creatures crawling in their hair, before they were cleaned up to be sold to a senator of Rome, Gaius Martius. Iliona's value came from her ability to teach the Greek she knew. She and her brother were separated by the overseer and taken to another place to work. Iliona stayed with the mistress named Lydia.

6. **How was Iliona's life as a slave better than the life of poor Romans?**

   - According to page 12, she had clothing, food, and rest. The poor Romans did not have those basic needs met.

   - "The poorest Roman citizens," she says, "are worse off than slaves."

7. **In this text, it says that Cestius was the "boys' *pedagogus*." (See pages 12 and 13.) How does the context (surrounding text) help to explain the meaning of the word *pedagogus*?**

   - The context says the students were going to school with Cestius. The picture caption says that Cestius was "an old slave: part tutor, part guardian."

     Note: Teachers might ask students if they know what a tutor or guardian is—and how they are like teachers. Teachers might also explain that the contemporary English word pedagogy refers to the work of a teacher. Students could confirm their understanding of this word by looking up pedagogy in the dictionary, where they can trace its etymology and make the connection to the Roman word.

8. **Cite evidence from the text to explain how the school in Greece differed from the schools in Rome. How were they similar? Does the text imply that Iliona would have received an education in Greece?**

   - The schooling in Greece took place in a "grand building" with a hundred other boys. School in Rome was more of a small tutoring session with a teacher and a few students, and the place was unimportant. Some Roman boys sat in the street for studies and some in small rooms.

- According to page 13, there were some similarities: for example, they wrote on the same type of tablet coated in wax, using a stylus to write.

- It seems that in Greece, Iliona would have received an education, but she would have studied at home because she was a girl. In Rome, she was allowed to go along with the boys to school.

9. **According to page 14, why did the Romans say, "What could be worse than Nero, or better than his baths?" Describe Nero's baths.**

   - The Romans are contrasting the cruelty of Nero, a former Roman ruler whom they hated, with his wonderful invention of the bathhouses.

   - The baths were luxurious and valued in the culture of the Roman people.
     - The baths were housed in great buildings that were similar to palaces.
     - The baths were very inexpensive and allowed people to "soak all afternoon."
     - The water came from aqueducts, described in the book as "a river on legs."
     - According to the illustration and captions on page 14, there were three different temperatures of the water baths: frigidarium (very cold), tepidarium (warm), and caldarium (very hot).
     - According to the illustration and caption on pages 16 and 17, the baths were very noisy and held many people.

10. **According to pages 15 through 19, what is the likelihood that Iliona will be free someday?**

    - Although her master suggested the idea of manumission as hope for freedom, her fellow slave explained to her the value of money in Rome. The money required to buy her freedom would be "three lifetimes of work." This collection of money makes the likelihood of her ability to buy her freedom close to impossible.

11. **According to pages 20 to 25, what happened following a Roman victory?**

    - According to the account on these pages, the Roman soldiers returned home to celebrate the victory. There was a parade of soldiers in triumphant stances on floats. There was the emperor on a cart in the parade, being reminded of his humanity, throughout the journey. There were chained prisoners who were walking to their public death.

12. **From the information on page 26, who were the Senators of Rome and what did the Senators do in Rome?**

    - The Senators were the richest and greatest men of Rome. They met together and wore "purple-edged togas and special red shoes."

    - The Senators made Rome's laws. They also discussed the future of Rome. They were an essential part of the government system of Rome.

13. **How does the "Technology" section on page 60 help to inform the fictionalized diary on pages 28 through 31?**

    - Pages 28 and 29 are about the water supply to Rome. A wealthy man is angry about the cutoff of water supplied to his home while the public fountains are still flowing. Iliona also mentions the smell of the sewer in the July heat.
      - The "Technology" page explains how the water of Rome came to the city from the countryside by way of water channels called aqueducts. The source of the water would be springs up to fifty miles away.
      - The "Technology" page also explains how the people of Rome had a sewer system underground to drain toilets and sinks.

- Pages 30 and 31 tell about the trip taken by Iliona via the very hard road on her journey to the country.
  - The "Technology" page describes the process used to create a layered construction of roads. The cross-section shows how large stones were at the bottom with tightly packed gravel above, covered by cemented small stones, and finally stone slabs on the surface. There were ditches along the road to deal with the drainage of rain water.

14. **What are the clues on page 33 that Apollo is not treated as kindly as his sister? How are those clues verified on page 35?**

- According to page 33, Apollo was thinner, had bruises and scars, his eyes "darted back and forth," and he had an expression "that I once saw on the face of a stag as it fled from the hunt." Apollo was afraid to speak when asked a question, and when he answered, it was about how well he was treated, how the work was not hard, and how he had enough to eat. Iliona noted in her diary how he was a terrible actor, implying she did not believe his account.

- According to page 35, there had been a cruel overseer who had treated the boys as prisoners. They had to work in chains and were always hungry. When the Senator found out about the abuse, he fired the overseer and hired a former slave to be in charge of the boys.

15. **According to pages 38 and 39, how does Cestius describe what the Roman Empire is to Iliona? Refer to page 56 for more information about geographical location and area of Ancient Rome.**

- On page 38, Cestius explained to Iliona about the wide area ruled by Rome. Cestius made the point by showing her that the area ruled by Rome was in red, and how most of the map was red. He also proved his point by showing how much in the marketplace, or the Forum, was from all over the world.
  - The grain was from Egypt.
  - The oil was from Spain.
  - The salt pork was from Gaul.
  - There were hides and fabrics from Egypt, Africa, Britannia, and Asia Minor.
  - There was even marble from Greece.
  - "So you see," he concludes, "almost everything we have in Rome comes from distant regions that our great city rules."

- On page 56, there is a map showing how far ancient Rome had spread through conquest of all of the areas near the Mediterranean Sea, the Black Sea, and the European countries near the Atlantic Coast.

16. **Why was the "gladiator" fight called a "deadly game"?**

- According to Iliona's diary description on pages 40 and 41, the crowds of people entered the arena of ancient Rome, not to watch a game, as one would today. The games were "real battles between two slaves, called gladiators, who fight with razor-sharp weapons." Although the "games" were put on for sport and for the enjoyment of the crowd, often the game ended in the death of one of the gladiators.

- According to the informational text on page 59, the Romans called the gladiator games *munera*, meaning "battles to the death," fought in the Coliseum of Rome. These battles would escalate to being animals versus people or actual naval battles in a stadium flooded with water.

17. **What was surprising to Iliona concerning the structure of the walls of the new bathhouse? How does the information on page 60 support this type of building?**

- She was surprised to see the walls were not solid marble, but were filled with a mixture of lime, water, and dust poured between molds.

- One of the technologies invented by the Romans was concrete. It was made with a mixture of lime, water, and sand from a Roman town called Pozzuoli. After it was poured and set, it was "hard as rock."

18. **According to page 53, how was Iliona finally freed?**

    - After her master died, she found that he had given her freedom in his will. Because of her bravery in saving his daughter from the burning building, she was able to leave the life of slavery with her brother.

19. **According to the informational text on page 59, how did the religious views of the Roman people change over the years?**

    - At first Romans worshipped "spirits of the natural world and of their dead ancestors."
    - After becoming acquainted with the Greek's belief in gods and goddesses, the Romans "merged their own gods with the Greeks."
    - As the Romans included more people in their kingdom, more religious beliefs such as cults were accepted.
    - Eventually the Roman Empire was influenced by the spread of Christianity. Christianity became the official religion of Rome in the fourth century.

20. **According to the information on pages 60 and 61, what evidence of the Roman Empire is still present in today's culture?**

    - The Romans influenced our laws and our system of government with the Senate and two houses of government.
    - Our months are determined by the phases of the moon.
    - Much of our vocabulary is derived from Latin, the language of the Romans.
    - Our alphabet is based on the Roman alphabet.
    - Arches and domes find their beginnings in the architecture of the Romans.
    - Somewhere in the history of the Roman culture, writing changed from being housed in scrolls to being in books with pages.

PERFORMANCE ASSESSMENT

Give students the following task:

- Scour this text for words that come from the Roman language. Using at least ten words, create a carefully illustrated dictionary showing the meaning of these words through a definition and a short paragraph displaying the proper use and context of the word.

Students should write a sentence that introduces their topic, use facts and definitions to develop points, and provide a concluding statement or section. At earlier levels, students may draw or dictate their informative/explanatory text and/or write a label, sentence, or series of related sentences. See standards for more details.

EXTENSION

Using the index of this book, create a class alphabet book based on the contributions of the Roman Empire. Have students choose one important word from the A's such as *aqueduct* and create a page for the word. Have students show a then-and-now comparison of how the aqueduct looked during Roman times and how that idea has evolved today.

CONNECTIONS TO COMMON CORE STATE STANDARDS FOR ENGLISH LANGUAGE ARTS

- Question 1 requires students to note information from the cover and title of the book (RI.3.1,2,5,7; RI.4.1,2,5,7; RI.5.1,2,5,7).

- Questions 2, 3, 4, 6, 8, 9, 10, 11, 12, 15, 18, and 20 ask students to recall important details from the text (RI.3.1; RI.4.1; RI.5.1).
  - Question 4 also requires students to consider a context clue (definition) as they focus on a key phrase (L.3.4; L.4.4; L.5.4).
  - Question 8 also asks the students to make an inference from information presented (RI.3.5; RI.4.5; RI.5.5).
  - Questions 10 and 11 also require that students integrate information that is presented over several pages of text (RI.3.3; RI.4.3; RI.5.3).
  - To answer question 15, students might refer to the supplemental section (page 56) mentioned in the question (RI.3.6; RI.4.6; RI.5.6).

- Question 5 asks students to summarize a series of events in the text (RI.3.1,2; RI.4.1,2; RI.5.1,2).

- Question 7 addresses the author's use of context clues and helps students infer and then confirm their understanding of an important academic vocabulary word (RI.3.1,2,4; RI.4.1,2,4; RI.5.1,2,4; L.3.4; L.4.4; L.5.4).
  - Question 7 also presents a new vocabulary word and asks students to consider the surrounding illustrations as well (RI.3.7; RI.4.7; RI.5.7; L.3.4; L.4.4; L.5.4).

- Question 13 gives students a chance to make connections between what they have learned in the narrative and the factual information in the supplemental sections that enhance the narrative (RI.3.3,6; RI.4.3,6; RI.5.3,6).

- To answer question 14, students must track and compare information presented over several pages of text, taking some things at face value and making inferences in other cases (RI.3.1,2,3; RI.4.1,2,3; RI.5.1,2,3).

- Questions 19 and 20 ask students about information in the supplemental section, requiring them to track the development of key concepts (RI.3.1,2,3,6; RI.4.1,2,3,6; RI.5.1,2,3,6).

- The performance assessment gives students a chance to convey their understanding of key academic vocabulary through informative/explanatory writing (RI.3.4; RI.4.4; RI.5.4; L.3.5; L.4.5; L.5.5; W.3.2,9; W.4.2,9; W.5.2,9).

MORE RESOURCES

PRIMARY SOURCES

Gold coin depicting Alexander the Great, ca. 196 to 217 CE (British Museum)

Pair of gold bracelets from the Persian Empire, Achaemenid period, ca. 350 BCE (Louvre)

Head of Alexander the Great sculpture, ca. 2nd century BCE (Istanbul Archaeology Museums)

Greek student's writing tablet with Sumerian, Babylonian, and Greek writing exercises, ca. 3rd to 1st century BCE (British Museum)

Roman bronze medallion depicting Rome's founding mythology, ca. 50 to 150 CE (British Museum)

ART AND ARCHITECTURE

Othryades the Spartan dying, sculpture, ca. 1779 (Louvre)

Aphrodite, known as the *Venus de Milo*, ca. 100 BCE (Louvre)

USEFUL WEBSITES

"Treasures of the Sunken City," resources on the Pharos lighthouse (PBS: NOVA)

Ancient Rome (The History Channel)

Resource on ancient Roman Britain (BBC)

Religion and War: Driving Change in Asian Empires

(1750 BCE to ca. 1650 CE)

GRADES: 3, 4, 5

OVERVIEW

Since ancient times, Asia has been a crossroad of conquest, culture, and trade. India, China, and the civilizations of Japan, Korea, and Indochina went through a process of growth, turmoil, and change similar to that of Greece, Rome, Egypt, and other Euro-Mediterranean-based civilizations. New religions were formed: Buddhism, Hinduism, Daoism, and the ethical code of Confucius arose. The migration and the integration of various peoples created complexities of interaction and culture among India, China, Japan, and Korea. Lower elementary students will explore how one Chinese ruler was motivated to accomplish great things by the proximity of his enemies through a close reading of *Hidden Army: Clay Soldiers of Ancient China*. Upper elementary students will identify and explain how leadership effected change in Asia after a close reading of *Kubla Khan*.

o o o

Interested in learning more about this time period? Read a more complete history in the "Era Summaries."

LEARNING EXPECTATIONS

Lower elementary: Students should know that India's many states and China's long-standing empires produced great cultures with tremendous artistic, literary, philosophical, and scientific achievements that heavily influenced Asia and the West. They should also know that both countries, especially India, were influenced in turn by the West.

Upper elementary: Students should know that India saw a succession of native states and foreign invaders that fused to produce a rich and enormously influential culture, exporting Buddhism and Hinduism throughout Asia. They should know that China developed a long series of powerful empires, unifying vast territories and producing a culture that dominated Asia. They should understand that Japan, Korea, and Southeast Asia, though heavily influenced by China, developed important cultures of their own.

SUGGESTED ANCHOR TEXTS

Kubla Khan: The Emperor of Everything by Kathleen Krull
Ancient China by Natalie M. Rosinsky
Ancient China by Robert Snedden
"Hairy Barbarians on the Silk Road," *Muse*, May/June 2002
Life in Ancient China by Paul Challen
Marco Polo by Clint Twist

FEATURED ANCHOR TEXT

KUBLA KHAN: THE EMPEROR OF EVERYTHING BY KATHLEEN KRULL

This book was selected because of the well-illustrated and detail-filled account of the life and rule of Kubla Khan. The cultural differences in Asia between the nomadic lifestyle of the Mongols and the refined civilization of the Chinese are explored as the great Mongol leader unifies the cultures for one brief period of history. The European travels of Marco Polo are relayed and the eventual exploration of the New World is foretold. This text pulls together the East and the West during a very transformative time in history. While conveying a rich narrative history, this text also exhibits a rather colloquial style, which is interesting to consider, especially its effect on the reader; elementary school students will surely appreciate it. The text also contains structural features of informational text that students should be learning to use effectively (for example, maps, a "Who Was Kubla Khan?" introductory note, an author's note, an illustrator's note, and list of additional sources).

TEXT STUDY

The text-dependent questions ask students to read closely in order to understand and explain how illustrations work with text to convey meaning and how authors support their assertions with evidence. Students also have an opportunity to analyze key academic vocabulary words. The performance assessments give students a chance to discuss key concepts and details before writing either an opinion or an informative/explanatory essay that conveys their understanding of the text and of its main character.

Note: You may want to judiciously read page 11 of the text. It may not be wise to have to explain the one hundred children of multiple wives and concubines to your students.

1. **Study the map on the inside cover of the book. What lands made up the "World of Kubla Khan and the Mongol Empire"? What other places are shown within Kubla Khan's kingdom? Who are the people shown on the map?**

    - The world of Kubla Khan included China, Tibet, Russia, Persia, Mongolia, and Korea.

    - One can see the Great Wall of China, the Grand Canal, Xanadu, and the city of Beijing.

    - It shows Marco Polo meeting the Great Khan.

      Note: *You may need to cue the students to notice the color key showing the Mongol Empire; the colors are subtle.*

2. **According to page 2, what makes Kubla Khan noteworthy in history?**

   - Kubla Khan was a great conqueror. During his lifetime, he enlarged his kingdom to be the greatest empire in all of history up to that time. He was able to keep his kingdom united for thirty-four years.

3. **How does the author describe the land of Mongolia on page 3?**

   - The author described the country as "unique, beautiful and cruel."
     - The summers were very hot, the winters "fearfully cold."
     - There were high mountains and expansive, dry plains.

4. **Using the illustration and the text on pages 3 and 4, describe Kubla Khan's training as a young child.**

   - He learned to ride a horse when he was only three years old. This was typical for children born in Mongolia.

   - As a young child, he hunted with a bow and arrow while riding his horse.

   Note: *You may want to highlight that Kubla Khan's grandfather, Genghis Khan, mentioned on page 2, was a former warlord of the Mongol Empire.*

5. **According to page 5, what skills did the warriors of Mongolia learn?**

   - The training for a warrior was completed by the age of fourteen.
     - They learned how to shoot with bows and "long-distance arrows."
     - They learned how to shoot with "perfect accuracy in any direction while at full gallop."

6. **According to pages 5 and 6, how would you characterize the Mongol attacks? Support your characterization with details from the text and the illustration.**

   - The Mongol attacks on villages and towns were sudden, vicious, and ruthless.
     - The warriors would swoop loudly into a town with a "hit-and-run raid" and then "vanish like smoke."
     - The warriors would kill and destroy everything in their path.
     - In the illustration, it appears that they left a town burning to the ground.

   Note: *Student answers will vary, but they should characterize the attacks in a similar way.*

7. **Explain Mongolia's transition from multiple "khans" to "Khan of all Khans."**

   - According to page 5, the "khan" was the leader among a group of nobles in a Mongol tribe. There were many tribes and many leaders of those tribes.

   - The change came when Genghis Khan became the khan of his tribe, and then managed to unite all of the tribes into one united Mongolia. In 1206, he was named the "great Khan of all Khans."

8. **What evidence does the author provide that the lifestyle of Mongolian nomads contributed to their reputation for being "tough" people?**

   - The nomadic lifestyle meant that people were never comfortably settled down; they searched for food year-round.
     - They were also in constant search for water and grass to feed their animals.
     - According to page 3, they lived in all kinds of weather: from "blistering hot" summers to "fearfully cold" winters.
     - They lived in felt-covered tents, not in warm permanent structures.
     - Food was sometimes scarce, so they would drink the blood of horses if there was no water.

9. **On pages 9 and 10, how does the author describe what Kubla Khan's mother was like? What was her goal for her sons and how did she achieve that goal?**

   - His mother is described "as a woman nobody messed with."

     Note: *You might ask students why they think that the author uses this figurative language (for example, to catch the reader's attention).*

   - His mother's goal was to "mold all four of her sons into great leaders."
     ○ She educated them well and allowed their curiosity to guide their learning.
     ○ She taught them to value the people they would rule and to protect them.
     ○ She taught them tolerance of other people's beliefs.
     ○ She watched for opportunities to show off her sons', especially Kubla's, leadership abilities.

10. **What evidence does the author provide that Kubla Khan demonstrated excellent leadership skills?**

    - He tolerated the practice of many different religions, which was unusual during the time.
    - He had ambitious goals to expand the Mongol kingdom, especially to conquer "all of China."
    - He was a "brilliant military leader," sometimes taking "up to a year to prepare for a battle, considering every angle of his strategy."
    - He offered people the choice to submit to his rule before killing them.
    - After he conquered a town, he ruled well. The author says, "As a ruler, he was considered unusually fair. True, he captured towns by force, but once in control, he wanted to govern wisely (not just make himself richer)."

11. **How does the practice of having advisors from all over his empire offer advice (in sealed envelopes) support the assertion that Kubla Khan was a thoughtful, tolerant ruler?**

    - The religious leaders of all kinds of faiths would give him advice in sealed envelopes. He would reward the advice that was appropriate for his decision making, but he would *not* punish the people whose ideas he chose not to use.
    - He accepted the advice from people of all kinds of faiths, from more than forty advisors from all over his empire: Confucian scholars, Buddhists, Muslims, Turks, and Tibetan lamas.

12. **According to the dictionary, *civilized* means "having an advanced culture." What details does the author provide to support the assertion that China's culture was advanced and so appealing to Kubla Khan? What kept him *out* of China?**

    - Kubla Khan, coming from a tough, nomadic culture, admired how China was more refined.
      ○ The fabrics they wore were soft, made of "fine silk brocade."
      ○ They made beautiful ceramics and textiles.
      ○ They "were renowned for exquisite scroll paintings and poetry."
      ○ They practiced an ancient form of medicine called acupuncture.
      ○ They "invented the most advanced printing methods in the world."
    - The walls around China, the Great Wall, kept enemies like Khan out.

13. **How did Kubla Khan overtake China? Why did he move to China?**

    - According to pages 15 and 16, he took down the walls protecting China by force using "boulders and flaming torches hurled from catapults."
    - Kubla Khan moved to China because the Chinese people greatly outnumbered the Mongol people. To be in control, he would have to rule from China, in a way that the Chinese people would understand.

14. **How does the description of Kubla Khan's Imperial City support the suggestion that he loved the finer things of China? How does the text suggest that he savored what he loved of Mongolia?**

   - The text describes how the Imperial City was filled with luxurious places and extravagant objects and activity.
     - Twenty-eight thousand workers constructed the lavish city.
     - The streets "were so wide that nine men on horseback could ride abreast."
     - "There were splendid houses (with bathrooms inside), shops, hotels . . . all surrounded by lakes, gardens, bridges, and trees."
     - The palace had four hundred rooms decorated with the silk, jade, and ermine he loved.
     - The illustration on page 18 shows the beautiful paintings on textiles and the ornate decorations.
   - He spent the summers in Xanadu, where it was cooler and he could hunt. While there, he lived in a "lavish Mongolian tent." The text said he could "relax in khanlike style" and drink "mares' fermented milk."

15. **According to pages 23 through 26, how did Khan support the advancement of the Chinese civilization?**

   - He loved the arts.
     - Production of the blue-and-white porcelain, famous in China, began during his rule.
     - He supported weaving artisans, bringing together different ideas of craft.
     - Theater was expanded to include more courtroom plays and comedies.
   - He advanced literacy by making books more available through government printing of books.
   - Muslim medical experts advanced the work of medicine and opened the Imperial Academy of Medicine.
   - Mapmakers created more accurate maps of the world.
   - Astronomers created a more accurate calendar.

16. **How does the author describe how Khan helped make the lives of the people better?**

   - Better ways of farming and irrigating were created through his "Office for the Stimulation of Agriculture."
   - People who were hungry were fed.
   - Education was available to more of the boys in the kingdom than ever before.
   - Postal services were improved.
   - Paper money was invented.

17. **How does the illustration, on pages 27 and 28, support the text's description of the advancement of agriculture?**

   - The illustration shows the way the fields were irrigated with water from a nearby river. From the illustration, it appears these may be rice fields.

18. **What were Khan's two great projects, encouraging trade within his kingdom and between his and other kingdoms?**

   - He created the Grand Canal, the "longest manmade waterway in the world," and managed to provide transportation from the Yangtze River to Beijing, the capital city of the kingdom. The goods from within his kingdom could travel to Beijing for trade.
   - He helped to improve the safety and quality of the Silk Road, encouraging trade from outside his kingdom.

19. **What most impressed Marco Polo in the kingdom of the great Khan?**

   - He was impressed by the paper money because to him it represented creating money "out of nothing."

20. **How was the Asian world after Kubla Khan's death similar to the world before he reigned?**

   - Eventually China closed itself off again to the Europeans and any foreigners.
   - The Mongols returned to the arid, vast areas in the mountains to live as nomadic people.
   - The European traders stayed away.

21. **In what way did Kubla Khan's rule influence Christopher Columbus's eventual discovery voyages?**

   - When Marco Polo visited Kubla Khan's world, he was impressed and wrote about the lavish supply of Asian goods.
   - He later wrote about his experiences in "Cathay" (China) in a book entitled *The Travels of Marco Polo.*
   - The book was finally printed for all to read in 1477. Christopher Columbus read and studied the book, carrying it with him as he traveled across the Atlantic to the Americas.
   - In this text the author wrote, "In his own over-the-top way, Kubla Khan introduced the East and West to each other."

PERFORMANCE ASSESSMENTS

1. This book examines the leadership of a famous khan, Kubla Khan. Work together as a class to construct a list of his leadership qualities. Discuss the way his leadership qualities led to his outstanding accomplishments.

Give students the following writing task:

- Choose one leadership quality Kubla Khan exhibited as the "Khan of all Khans." Using evidence from the text as your support, write an informative/explanatory essay showing how that leadership quality had positive effects during his rule.

Students should write a sentence that introduces their topic, use facts and definitions to develop points, and provide a concluding statement or section. At earlier levels, students may draw or dictate their informative/explanatory text and/or write a label, sentence, or series of related sentences. See standards for more details.

2. Give students the following writing task:

- After discussing Kubla Khan's leadership style, write an opinion essay explaining whether you think his leadership had more positive or more negative effects. Be sure to use evidence from the text to support your opinion.

Students should write a sentence that introduces their topic, use facts and definitions to develop points, and provide a concluding statement or section. At earlier levels, students may draw or dictate their informative/explanatory text and/or write a label, sentence, or series of related sentences. See standards for more details.

CONNECTIONS TO COMMON CORE STATE STANDARDS FOR ENGLISH LANGUAGE ARTS

- Question 1 focuses students' attention on the important historical information they can gather from examining the map on the inside cover (RI.3.1,5; RI.4.1,5; RI.5.1,5).
- Questions 2, 3, 5, 13, 15, and 19 ask students to cite evidence from the text when recalling key details (RI.3.1; RI.4.1; RI.5.1).
- Students must synthesize information from illustrations and text to answer questions 4 and 17 (RI.3.1,2,7; RI.4.1,2,7; RI.5.1,2,7).
- To answer question 6, students must summarize information and support their own interpretation of events with evidence from the text (RI.3.1,2,6,7; RI.4.1,2,6,7; RI.5.1,2,6,7).
- Questions 7, 18, 20, and 21 ask students to recount the import of a series of historical events (RI.3.1,2,3; RI.4.1,2,3; RI.5.1,2,3).
- Questions 8, 9, 10, 11, 12, 14, and 16 require students to determine the details that an author provides to support key concepts or assertions (RI.3.1,2,8; RI.4.1,2,8; RI.5.1,2,8).
  - Question 12 also enables students to wrestle with word meanings, parts of speech, and shades of meanings among related words (RI.3.4; RI.4.4; RI.5.4; L.3.1,4,5; L.4.1,4,5; L.5.1,4,5).
- The performance assessments enable students to discuss and analyze as a group an important aspect of the Kubla Khan text and then write an informative/explanatory or an opinion essay that addresses a specific question about the text and coalesces learning done during the class discussion about leadership (W.3.2; W.4.2; W.5.2).

MORE RESOURCES

PRIMARY SOURCES

Statue of river goddess Ganga, Gupta era, ca. 5th century BCE (National Museum, New Delhi)

North Indian goddess with weapons in her hair, ca. 2nd to 1st century BCE (Metropolitan Museum of Art)

Sandstone statue of Buddha, from East India, ca. 11th century CE (British Museum)

Chinese chariot fitting in shape of animal head, Zhou kingdom, ca. 5th century BCE (British Museum)

Han Dynasty artifacts, ca. 206 BCE to 220 CE (Metropolitan Museum of Art)

Silver coin from Mongol culture, minted on authority of Genghis Khan, ca. 1206 to 1227 CE (British Museum)

Japanese Jomon culture artifacts, ca. 10,500 to 300 BCE (Metropolitan Museum of Art)

Zao Gongen statue, Heian period of Japan, ca. 11th to 12th century CE (Metropolitan Museum of Art)

Korean statue of Buddha, ca. 8th century CE (Metropolitan Museum of Art)

POETRY AND MUSIC

Audio recordings of Bhagavad Gita in Sanskrit

> *Provided as reference because it showcases the native period language and the native period music, just as a background for teachers*

ART AND ARCHITECTURE

Daoism and Daoist Art (Metropolitan Museum of Art)

Life of the Buddha artifacts (Metropolitan Museum of Art)

USEFUL WEBSITE

Silk Road Virtual Lab (Stanford Program on International and Cross-Cultural Education–SPICE)

The Rise of Islam: Religion Travels on a Road of Silk

(ca. 610 CE to 1500s)

GRADES: 3, 4, 5

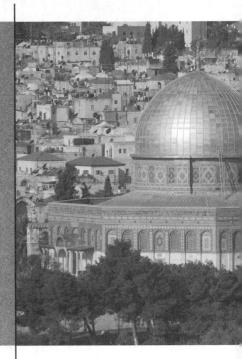

OVERVIEW

Islam was the last of the three major monotheistic world religions to develop. Arising in the seventh century CE, it quickly expanded through military conquest and conversion of conquered peoples. Like earlier civilizations, the Islamic empires were marked with the combination of internal political strife and great cultural achievement. However, one of Islam's greatest contributions to world history was the unique cultural bridge it created among China, India, and Europe. *We're Riding on a Caravan* gives younger students details about the famous Silk Road trade route that they then present as a class. Older students will use *Traveling Man* to analyze the writings of the famous Moroccan and give historical context to the beautiful quotes from the famous traveler.

o o o

Interested in learning more about this time period? Read a more complete history in the "Era Summaries."

LEARNING EXPECTATIONS

Lower elementary: Students should understand that Islam was the last major world religion to arise and that it quickly expanded to control a large territory in and beyond the Middle East. They should also know that Islam was responsible for notable cultural achievements and that its conquests brought it into conflict with the Christian West.

Upper elementary: Students should know that Islam was the last major world religion to appear and that it shares roots with Judaism and Christianity. They should also understand that it expanded very quickly because of military conquest and persuasion of conquered peoples. They should know that the shifting empires of Islam's complex history produced highly significant cultural achievements and created a cultural bridge among China, India, and Europe. Students should also realize that Islam's determined expansion and its possession of the Holy Land caused conflict with the Christian West when the European Crusades sought to reconquer the Holy Land and when the later Ottoman Empire pressed deeper into Europe.

SUGGESTED ANCHOR TEXTS

Traveling Man: The Journey of Ibn Battuta, 1325–1354 by James Rumford
1001 Inventions and Awesome Facts from Muslim Civilization by National Geographic
Muhammad: Prophet of Islam by Jessica Cohn
Tales Told in Tents: Stories from Central Asia by Sally Pomme Clayton
The Wise Fool: Fables from the Islamic World by Shahrukh Husain

FEATURED ANCHOR TEXT

TRAVELING MAN: THE JOURNEY OF IBN BATTUTA, 1325–1354 BY JAMES RUMFORD

This book was selected because of its exquisite, multilayered retelling of a fourteenth-century, seventy-five-thousand-mile, almost thirty-year journey into the East. In the retelling of Ibn Battuta's story, the students will experience an Islamic pilgrimage to Mecca, multiple modes of travel, and a peek into the cultures of the known world during this period of history. The author's creative use of Arabic writing, path-shaped sentences, ancient maps, and the color gold makes this a perfectly engaging book from which to teach.

TEXT STUDY

The text-dependent questions offer students a variety of opportunities to explore the inextricable and clever relationship between the illustrations and the text. They address author's craft, academic vocabulary, and the purpose and effectiveness of structural features of this informational text. The performance assessment and extensions enable students to convey their understanding of key historical information in this and other related texts in the form of informative/explanatory essays, posters, or presentations.

1. **What makes the description of place interesting in the first page of this text? What does this description tell the reader about how people viewed the world then? How does the description draw the reader into the story?**

    - The description of the setting is mysterious.
      - The time is described as "in the days when the earth was flat and Jerusalem was the center of the world."
      - The text says that Ibn Battuta lived "on the very edge of the earth, near the shores of the Ocean of Darkness."
      - It says that "nothing but night lay to the west, but to the east lay the golden world" and that Ibn Battuta had "dreamed of traveling across it."

    - The description of place shows us how much they did *not* know about geography at this time.

    - The mysterious description makes you want to know more about Battuta's possible pilgrimage and what he might find beyond his own city.

2. **What does paragraph 3 on page 1 tell the reader about Battuta's character? How does the illustration on the cover and on page 2 help to enhance understanding of that paragraph? Why was this combination of illustration and text about maps important at the beginning of this book?**

   - "On maps, he would trace his finger along scarlet roads to reach the vermilion stars that marked the great cities of the world. On hot afternoons, in an imaginary boat, he would cross cool, peacock-colored seas to the eastern edge of the earth and sail fearlessly into the Ocean of Ignorance."

   - The boy was fascinated by maps and would spend hours tracing the red ("scarlet") lines representing the roads on the maps, showing words that led to cities in the "golden world," also marked in a shade of red ("vermilion"). Then he would spend his afternoons imagining he was on a boat sailing to those places beyond the blue-green ("peacock-colored") water into unknown areas of the Ocean of Darkness.

   - The cover illustration shows Battuta traveling on the "scarlet" roads with the cities identified and starred in "vermilion." The illustration on page 2 shows his parents sitting with him as he studied the map of roads and cities.

   - The focus of this book is Traveling Man. It was important for the author to show the reader how maps captured Ibn Battuta's imagination from when he was very young. It was also important to show how his parents supported his curiosity.

3. **According to page 1, what did the author want the reader to know about Ibn Battuta as an adult? How does the glossary define the key words in the description of his adulthood? What does each of the definitions have in common with the others?**

   - As an adult, he wore the turban of a scholar, could recite the Koran, and headed to Mecca as a pilgrim.

   - According to the glossary, the *Koran* is "the holy book of the Muslims." *Mecca* is a "holy city in Saudi Arabia for Muslims." A *pilgrim* as used in this story is a "Muslim who goes to Mecca."

   - Each of the defined words has *Muslim* in the definition. The terms indicate he believed in the religion of Islam.

4. **What is the effect of the text's design on pages 3 and 4?**

   - The text is written on a "road" on the ancient map used by Ibn Battuta as a child.

     Note: *Notice the scarlet road and the vermilion stars denoting cities.*

   - The text of his good-byes to his parents and his joining with merchants is written from "west to east," in the direction that he traveled.

   - The words flow across the page as if on a journey themselves.

5. **How does the storytelling method change on page 3?**

   - On page 3 begins Battuta's own account of his adventures, told in the first person (in his own voice), first "along the road" on pages 3 and 4 and then in boxes with subtitles, such as the first one, "The Lonely Road," on page 5.

6. **How does Battuta describe the downside of travel during this time of history (page 5)? Give examples from the text that exhibit how Battuta dealt with the difficulties.**

   - Battuta says, "Bandits roamed the countryside like wolves." He uses a strong simile to explain that there were many bandits—thieves—who looked for people traveling alone or behind their group. This made it absolutely necessary to keep up with the group of merchants with whom Battuta traveled.

- Battuta fell ill, but one had to keep on going. In this example, Battuta had to tie himself to the camel with his unwound turban.
- Travel was lonely, because you were going to places where you knew no one. Battuta was welcomed into a stranger's home and found a new friend. He said about travel, "It makes you lonely, then gives you a friend." It seems like he tried to keep up a positive attitude.

7. **How did Battuta explain that the Egyptians were generous?**

- On pages 7 and 8, he likened the people to the Nile River, which had been generous by giving the Egyptians "gold, incense, and abundant food."
- He then said that the Egyptian people gave to him "alms." The alms were "food, money, and a place to sleep."

8. **According to the text on page 9 and the glossary, what was significant about traveling to "Mecca" and kissing "the Black Stone of the Kaaba"?**

- Traveling to Mecca was the goal of a Muslim pilgrim, as noted on page 1. In the glossary definition of *pilgrim*, it adds that all pilgrims were expected to make a journey to Mecca at least once in their lives.
- According to the glossary, the Black Stone was a sacred, or holy, stone built into the wall of Kaaba.

9. **According to page 11, how did traveling turn Battuta into a storyteller?**

- He tells of the amazing beauty of traveling by boat down the coast of Africa. He talks about "ivory and ebony, of gold dust, and leopard skins." He says it was so beautiful it left him speechless.
- Then he says that the "sultans" would ask him about his travels and he would begin to find the words to describe his travels, becoming a storyteller.
- "Traveling—it leaves you speechless, then turns you into a storyteller."

10. **Gather evidence from page 16 for the meaning of *sultan*. After finding all of the context clues, suggest a definition. Look up the word in the glossary and in a dictionary to see how close you came to the meaning.**

- These are the clues from the text.
  - The sultan's palace in Delhi was described as huge.
  - Catapults flung gold coins to the people in the Great Hall of the Palace.
  - The sultan would give money to those who pleased him and would kill those who did not.
  - The sultan had international relations because he offered to send Ibn Battuta to China as his ambassador.
- According to this text, a sultan was a wealthy man who held great power over the people in the city and maintained relationships with other countries.
- The glossary defines the sultan as "a ruler or king."

  Note: *The dictionary defines a* sultan *as "the sovereign of an Islamic country" or "an absolute ruler."*

11. **How were the events described on page 17 foreshadowed earlier in the book?**

- On page 8, the holy man in Alexandria had told him that when he got to India, "my brother Dilshad will save your life."

12. **According to page 21, how does the author use contrast to tell about Battuta's life goals?**

- The author tells of how a "vizier" gave him position as a judge and wealth in a chest of jewels. Riches did not satisfy Battuta.
- When Battuta saw a small family on an island, owning nothing but a small house, he knew that a family and a home was what he wanted.

13. **What seemed to impress Battuta about China?**

- He mentions the word *silk* four times in the second paragraph. "Everywhere there was silk: the black silk of merchants, the flowered silk of girls, the heaven-colored silk of priests." And then he uses words that could be used to describe silk as he described the life in China as "alive, moving and fluttering."

14. **According to page 27, what had happened in Battuta's home area?**

- A plague had brought "death as black as night" and the cities were "peopleless."
- His father had died of it and his mother died just before he arrived home.

  Note: *Students may want to study the effects of the Black Death (bubonic plague) on the culture of that day.*

15. **According to page 30, what was Ibn Battuta's contribution to the fourteenth-century world?**

- He shared his memories through writing, telling stories of his travels.
- He opened listeners' eyes to the world—"took friends across peacock-colored seas and showed them new horizons."

16. **Why is the glossary an important feature of this book?**

- The book is filled with Arabic words and words from different times and places. Although many of the word meanings can be understood by using context clues, the glossary gives a succinct meaning to the word.

  Note: *Teachers may also wish to discuss the usefulness and effect of other text features, such as the "Map of the World 1325," the present-day map of the world, and the blue drawings at the beginning and end of the book.*

PERFORMANCE ASSESSMENT

Have students answer the following question, using evidence gathered from the text:

- What does Ibn Battuta learn about travel?

Direct the students to start by rereading the text, looking for all of Battuta's quotations about travel. Ask each student to choose one of the following quotations to use as the basis of writing an informative/explanatory essay on travel through the eyes of Ibn Battuta. Explain the historical and geographical context for the quotation and what he meant by it.

"It offers you a hundred roads to adventure, and gives your heart wings."
"It leaves you speechless, then turns you into a storyteller."
"It offers you a hundred roads. How does a holy man know the one you'll take?"
"It captured my heart, and now my heart was calling me home."
"It gives you a home in a thousand strange places, then leaves you a stranger in your own land."
"All you do is take the first step."

Students should write a sentence that introduces their topic, use facts and definitions to develop points, and provide a concluding statement or section. At earlier levels, students may draw or dictate their informative/explanatory text and/or write a label, sentence, or series of related sentences. See standards for more details.

EXTENSIONS

1. Lead a study on "Life in the Cities of the Fourteenth Century." Allow students (individual, partners, or small groups) to choose one of the cities mentioned in Ibn Battuta's travels, such as Tanjier, Jerusalem, Mecca, Beijing, Timbuktu, Istanbul, Delhi, or Calicut. Students will need to keep secret the name of the assigned city.

Have the class generate a list of things to learn about each city (location, language spoken, religion[s], history, distinguishing features, architecture and art, famous residents, and so on). Have students create informative/explanatory posters (or a multimedia presentation) describing key information about each city but lacking the name of the city. Have students in the class try to match the name of the city to the poster by rereading *Traveling Man*, studying the maps in the book, and looking for more information.

Teachers may wish to observe in discussion with students how many of the cities had already been affected by the spread of Islam.

2. Study Marco Polo's journey of a century prior, using an informational book such as *Marco Polo: History's Great Adventurer* by Clint Twist. Have students write an informative/explanatory essay in which they compare and contrast the journey of Marco Polo with the journey of Ibn Battuta. Lead a Socratic seminar asking text-dependent questions such as, "How did the travels of Marco Polo open the world to more travelers?" "How were each of the travelers motivated to keep going?" "How does travel change the traveler?" "How does the traveler affect the people he meets?"

CONNECTIONS TO COMMON CORE STATE STANDARDS FOR ENGLISH LANGUAGE ARTS

- Question 1 asks students to consider the aspects that make the author's opening engaging (RI.3.1,2,8; RI.4.1,2,8; RI.5.1,2,8).

- Question 2 is multifaceted: it asks about the characterization of the main character, it focuses attention on the vivid description of setting, and it helps students make connections between the illustrations and the text to enhance their understanding of characters, setting, and the central ideas of this text (RL.3.1,2,3; RL.4.1,2,3; RL.5.1,2,3; RI.3.1,2,3,7; RI.4.1,2,3,7; RI.5.1,2,3,7).

- Question 3 is also multifaceted: it asks students first to identify key details from the text, then leads them to use the glossary to enhance understanding of essential academic vocabulary, and finally they must synthesize information from the text and the glossary definitions (RI.3.1,2,4,5; RI.4.1,2,4,5; RI.5.1,2,4,5).

- Question 4 reiterates the close connection between the text itself and the way the text is designed and illustrated; both are integral to the telling of Buttata's story (RI.3.1,2,3,5,7; RI.4.1,2,3,5,7; RI.5.1,2,3,5,7).

- Question 5 requires students to note a shift in the way the author chooses to tell the story, switching the point of view (RL.3.6; RL.4.6; RL.5.6; RI.3.5,6; RI.4.5,6; RI.5.5,6).

- Question 6 asks students to identify how the author supplies key details to support a central idea (RI.3.1,2,8; RI.4.1,2,8; RI.5.1,2,8).

- Questions 7, 9, 13, 14, and 15 prompt students to cite key details and summarize information (RI.3.1,2; RI.4.1,2; RI.5.1,2).

- Question 8 requires students to cite evidence about key details when describing the significance of an event in the text (RI.3.1,2; RI.4.1,2; RI.5.1,2).

- Question 10 focuses students' attention on an academic vocabulary word, asking students to use context clues to guess the definition, then asking them to confirm their understanding of the word by using the glossary and the dictionary (RI.3.4; RI.4.4; RI.5.4; L.3.4; L.4.4; L.5.4).

- Question 11 asks students to identify foreshadowing events to make connections between events in two different sections of the text (RI.3.3; RI.4.3; RI.5.3).

- Question 12 addresses the author's craft and the structure of this historical narrative, focusing on a point of comparison and contrast (RI.3.1,2,5,8; RI.4.1,2,5,8; RI.5.1,2,5,8).

- Question 16 concerns the usefulness of a structural feature of informational text (RI.3.5; RI.4.5; RI.5.5).

- The performance assessment offers students a creative way to reread the text closely and write an informative/explanatory essay that summarizes the essential ideas about the text (RI.3.1,2,3; RI.4.1,2,3; RI.5.1,2,3; W.3.2,9; W.4.2,9; W.5.2,9).

- The first extension gives students a chance to learn more about important places mentioned on the text and to render their findings in informative/explanatory posters or multimedia presentations (RI.3.1,2,3; RI.4.1,2,3; RI.5.1,2,3; W.3.2,9; W.4.2,9; W.5.2,9).

- The second extension gives students a chance to compare this text with a similar one and to participate in a Socratic-style seminar that addresses a related question or questions (RI.3.1,2,3,6,9; RI.4.1,2,3,6,9; RI.5.1,2,3,6,9; W.3.2,9; W.4.2,9; W.5.2,9; SL.3.1,2,4; SL.4.1,2,4; SL.5.1,2,4).

MORE RESOURCES

PRIMARY SOURCES

Muhammad's call to prophecy and the First Revelation, Islamic manuscript page, ca. 1425 (Metropolitan Museum of Art)

Fragment of woven tapestry, Umayyad period, ca. 8th century CE (Metropolitan Museum of Art)

Astrolabe, Rasulid period, ca. 1291 (Metropolitan Museum of Art)

Islamic amulet from Egypt, ca. 11th century (Metropolitan Museum of Art)

Building inscription commemorating the rebuilding of the walls of Jerusalem, Ottoman period, ca. 1535 to 1538 (The Israel Museum)

Bronze figurine of a Moorish cavalryman, Roman, ca. 2nd century CE (British Museum)

Folio from the Blue Qur'an, Tunisia, ca. 9th century (Metropolitan Museum of Art)

ART AND ARCHITECTURE
Queen of Sheba drawing, Safavid dynasty, Iran, ca. 1590 to 1600 (British Museum)

USEFUL WEBSITES
Silk Road Virtual Lab (Stanford Program on International and Cross-Cultural Education—SPICE)
History of Hagia Sophia (Hagia Sophia Museum)

Europe after Rome Fell: The Middle Ages Descend

(400s to 1350)

GRADES: 3, 4, 5

OVERVIEW

After the fall of the Roman Empire, regional kingdoms of Europe became more distinct in language and customs, and feudalism sharpened divisions in societal class. Although Christianity was the dominant religion in Europe, doctrinal disputes ultimately split the church in two: the Catholic Church in Rome and the Orthodox Church in Constantinople. Despite this break, the Christian kingdoms of Western Europe united in crusades to "reclaim" the Holy Land from Islam, but a deadlier opponent emerged: bubonic plague. Reading *A Medieval Feast* enables younger students to study the lives of the rich and the poor in Medieval Europe. *Good Masters! Sweet Ladies!* provides the necessary details for older students to justify an opinion on whether life in a manor or a town during this era was easier.

Interested in learning more about this time period? Read a more complete history in the "Era Summaries."

LEARNING EXPECTATIONS

Lower elementary: Students should understand that Europeans gradually rebuilt their world after the fall of the Roman Empire. New peoples moved across Europe and adopted Christianity, one of the most powerful legacies of the fallen Roman Empire. The centuries that followed the empire's demise were not entirely a dark age. Rather, this was a complicated world of rising and falling states, opportunity and inequality, and rising achievements in arts, culture, and religious learning.

Upper elementary: Students should know that Germanic peoples settled across former Roman territory, gradually converting to Christianity and building new states and empires. They should understand the oppressive nature of feudalism and its eventual decline as people began to escape through new avenues of opportunity. They should also be aware that there was a consolidation of royal power throughout much of Europe, although it was challenged by powerful nobles and frequent warfare and by the continuing power of the Catholic Church. The Crusades—the Christian effort to reclaim the Holy Land from the Muslims—are one of the best-known features of the period. They helped inspire its embrace of knighthood and chivalry, but also had a darker side of persecution and death. Students should understand that the Middle Ages produced great cultural and artistic achievements and should also be aware of the Black Death's shattering impacts.

SUGGESTED ANCHOR TEXTS

Good Masters! Sweet Ladies! Voices from a Medieval Village by Laura Amy Schlitz
Barbarians by Steven Kroll
Castle by David Macaulay
Days of the Knights: A Tale of Castles and Battles by Christopher Maynard
Run Far, Run Fast by Timothy Decker
The Ink Garden of Brother Theophane by C. M. Millen
The Middle Ages by Jane Shuter
The Sword in the Tree by Clyde Robert Bulla

FEATURED ANCHOR TEXT

GOOD MASTERS! SWEET LADIES! VOICES FROM A MEDIEVAL VILLAGE BY LAURA AMY SCHLITZ

This Newbery Award–winning book was selected because of the creative, interwoven monologues from people of various social classes during the Middle Ages. The literary part of the text, written for performance, shows the different points of view during the same period of history. The informational part of the text ties directly to the recently read monologue. The illustrations are minimal but integral to the understanding of life on the manor and in the town.

TEXT STUDY

The text-dependent questions help students track carefully the many different kinds of people and their roles in medieval society by asking students to identify and explain key details and concepts gleaned from the text.

Note: *The author begins this book's foreword with the words, "This is a part of the book that most people skip." You will not want to skip this foreword. It tells "why the book exists and why the reader might want to read it." The author also explains the theme of the book, aspects of the medieval era, and the author's fascination with history itself. She calls it a "story of survival."*

1. **Look closely at the illustration on pages x and 1. What can you learn about the setting of the story?**

   - The geographical setting is a medieval manor in England in 1255.

   - The illustration shows the predominance of farming and gardening in the community.

   - A bridge to a castle links the western part of the community to another castle in the east.

   - The manor is built near water, with either natural or manufactured irrigation streams.

   - Barriers, such as fences, waterways, or rows of trees, surround each section of the manor.

- Everyone seems to be working, including the horses.
- There is a water wheel, perhaps running a mill.

  Note: *There are countless observations to be made in this illustration. You may want to continue to refer back to it as the book is read.*

2. **The structure of medieval society determined the classes of the people, their jobs, and their places in the community. What do the monologues of Hugo, Taggot, and Will teach the reader about the society living on the medieval manor?**

   - From Hugo's monologue, the reader sees the role of the hunter, nephew of the "lord" in medieval society.
     - He was encouraged to be a bold hunter. His response to the killing of the boar shows how the ability to hunt was highly valued in his family, a sign of becoming a man.
     - He went to school to learn Latin and grammar.
   - From Taggot's monologue, the reader learns about the role of women in the medieval society.
     - Women had limited access to working in a guild to learn a trade, but they could be trained by husbands and fathers to do work such as blacksmithing.
     - Marrying and having children were the usual adult activities of women.
     - All people in the manor admired and respected the lord of the manor and the nephew of that lord, also a knight.
   - From Will's monologue, the reader sees the life of the poor farmer on the medieval manor.
     - The farmer worked long days in the fields of wheat and barley.
     - Farmers used a system to rest their land, even though they were poor and needed the extra yield.
     - Farmers had limited rights and were not allowed to kill a rabbit without risking death.
     - All of the animals on the land, even those running wild, belonged to the lord.

     Note: *You could also discuss the cultural significance of celebrations noted here: the Feast of All Souls and the later celebration of May Day. According to page 62 of this text, the Middle Ages were marked by feast days instead of by a monthly calendar.*

3. **According to page 13, what were the reasons for the "three-field system" in the Middle Ages? What does this section teach you about the role of peasants?**

   - The landowners wanted the best harvest possible. They knew that fields could not be planted with the same crops year after year and still yield a rich harvest, so they rotated the crops through three fields, allowing one field to be "fallow."
   - Peasants were at the mercy of the lord.
     - The lord chose the placement of their farmland.
     - Peasants had to work all of the daylight hours to farm successfully.
     - Peasants worked together on their farms so they would always have a harvest to eat.

4. **What do you learn about the medieval practice of medicine from Thomas's monologue?**

   - The profession of physician was handed down from one generation to the next.
   - They used egg whites, eel skins, and bloodletting as remedies for injury and disease.
   - They believed good health depended on the balance of earth, air, fire and water as seen in the "four humors."
   - Doctors believed in astrology, the study of the stars.
   - Doctors learned to protect themselves by telling the patient they had waited too long to call the doctor.

5. **Why was Constance, the Pilgrim, headed to the well of Saint Winifred?**

   • Constance was deformed, hunchbacked, and crippled. During this time, deformities were thought to be signs of "God's displeasure." She was going to the well to be healed.

6. **On page 23 of this text, the author contrasts the medieval view of medicine with the religious prayer for healing. Cite the author's explanation for these opposing views and explain it in your own words.**

   • "Medieval people did not share our need to understand the world scientifically. They were convinced that water from a shrine or relics from a saint could cure disease—and it may well be that these 'faith cures' were as reliable as the hodgepodge of astrology and folk medicine practiced by medieval doctors."

   • The medicine of the day was not scientific like the medicine of today. It was based on looking at the stars and finding "cures" that were grounded in traditional beliefs, not in science. The pilgrimage to the tomb of a saint, and the prayer that came from it, were seemingly as dependable as the medicine of the day. The author adds that the pilgrimage to salt springs may have actually cured skin disease, even though the people were not seeking a medicinal cure but a faith cure.

7. **According to Mogg's monologue and footnote, how was a "villein" different from a peasant in social order? Why did Mogg trick the lord with the cow?**

   • A "villein" was a peasant who wasn't free. He could be bought and sold like a slave.

   • After Mogg's father died, it was the right of the lord to take the villein's finest livestock in exchange for the death of his slave. Mogg's family temporarily traded their fine cow, a family investment, for an old bony one when the lord came to take the livestock. The lord chose the best pig instead of the old cow. This left the family with their strong and healthy cow, named Paradise.

8. **What was the role of the miller in the medieval society? Why was he hated?**

   • According to pages 27 through 29, the miller was the one who ground the wheat of the peasant and villein. The miller didn't really fit in the society because he was placed above the peasants, but much lower than the lord.

   • Millers had a reputation of stealing from the peasants who brought their grain to be ground into flour. They would steal the ground flour and replace it with chalk.

   Note: *This monologue could easily move to a discussion on corruption in society, especially in a manor such as this where everyone needed bread to live.*

   Note the uneasy positions of the miller's son and Jack (pages 30 through 32) in this society. In a feudal society with well-defined classes, there were always people who didn't fit within those lines.

9. **According to Simon's monologue, what duties and qualities were included in the soul of chivalry for the knight? Why would Simon need to become a monk?**

   • The knight would "fight for the widows and orphans, Christ and His church." He would be "valiant, open-handed, frank, and pure of heart, and courteous."

   • Being a knight was expensive. The family had to sell land to pay for weapons, armor, and a horse. Simon's family had no money. His only choice was to be a monk because it was the only profession equal in rank in society.

10. **According to pages 36 and 37, why were the common people in the Middle Ages so willing to join the Crusades?**
    - The people in medieval society had no hope for good changes in their futures and had a desire to please the Pope, God's head of the church.
      - The Pope had told these Christian people they had a religious duty to kill the Muslims.
      - The people's lives were tedious, and they had no real hope for change. The Crusades offered them a chance to see the world.
      - The people living as slaves could leave their manor and freely fight for the Pope.
      - The Pope promised forgiveness of sins and a special place in heaven if they even started on the pilgrimage and died on the journey.

11. **According to pages 40 and 41, why was a trained falcon so valuable in the Middle Ages?**
    - The falcon was a hunting bird that helped to supply food for the lord's table.
    - Training falcons was very expensive because it took much time and patience to train a bird.
    - The gear made for the hawk was also very expensive.
    - The falcon was a status symbol, or an outward symbol of its owner's high place in society.

12. **Why does Isobel believe her father was made the "lord" of the manor?**
    - She believes it was because God chose her "father to rule" in the "same way he chose them to serve." She believed God determined each person's place in society.

13. **According to pages 50 and 59, how was medieval society poised to antagonize the Jewish people?**
    - According to the dialogue, Jewish people had to identify themselves as Jewish by sewing "a yellow badge" to their clothes.
    - According to the dialogue and informational text, Jewish people were blamed for things they had no part of doing. They would be fined and then still be "driven out of town."
    - The Jewish people were not allowed to own land, and money came from farming.
    - If people wanted to seal anything legally during this time, they had to say their oath in Jesus's name. The Jews didn't believe Jesus was God, so they could not seal legal documents.
    - The only way Jewish people could earn money was to lend their money with interest. Because the courts did not side with the Jewish people, they often lost court cases when the borrowers refused to pay back the money.

14. **According to pages 62 through 65, how did town life offer hope to the people in the Middle Ages?**
    - Living in a town gave people choices. An example given in the text referred to the monopoly of the miller in the country, but there was a choice of more than one miller in the town. This discouraged millers' dishonesty in trade.
    - Villeins from the country could live in a town for a year and a day, earning their freedom while hoping to find someone to train them in a skill.

15. **What must happen for Piers to inherit the glassblowing business?**
    - According to page 69, Piers must marry one of the glassblower's daughters to inherit the business. Being a talented glassblower is not enough.

16. **How did Giles and his father use the people's religious beliefs to make a living during the Middle Ages?**

   - Giles pretended to be a beggar on a crutch, with a crushed foot, as he entered a town exhausted from travel. He begs for money.

   - His father later enters the town, peddling religious "relics" thought to hold special healing powers.

   - The father and son perform a routine that looks to the people like a real healing. People give money to his father for drops of the healing water, obviously blessed by God himself.

PERFORMANCE ASSESSMENT

Give students the following task:

- If you grew up in the Middle Ages, would you want to be raised on the manor or in the town? Be sure to support your opinion with evidence from this text.

Students should write a sentence that introduces their topic, use facts and definitions to develop points, and provide a concluding statement or section. At earlier levels, students may draw or dictate their informative/explanatory text and/or write a label, sentence, or series of related sentences. See standards for more details.

CONNECTIONS TO COMMON CORE STATE STANDARDS FOR ENGLISH LANGUAGE ARTS

- Question 1 asks students to infer information from an illustration (RI.3.7; RI.4.7; RI.5.7).

- Questions 2 and 4 require students to identify and explain key details and concepts from this informational text by analyzing the accounts of several different characters (RI.3.1,2,3; RI.4.1,2,3; RI.5.1,2,3).

- Question 3 asks that students identify reasons for an important phenomenon explained in the text (evidence) and explain what this evidence teaches about the role of certain characters in this text (RI.3.1,2,3; RI.4.1,2,3; RI.5.1,2,3).

- Questions 5, 7, 8, 9, 10, 11, 12, 13, 14, 15, and 16 all ask students to identify and explain key details and concepts from the text, citing textual evidence (RI.3.1,2; RI.4.1,2; RI.5.1,2).

- Answering question 6 requires students to identify and explain the author's presentation of facts on two sides of an issue (RI.3.1,2,8; RI.4.1,2,8; RI.5.1,2,8).

MORE RESOURCES

PRIMARY SOURCES

Anglo-Saxon brooch, ca. 6th century (Metropolitan Museum of Art)

Equestrian statue of Charlemagne (probably), late Byzantine Empire, ca. 9th century (Louvre)

Silver coin minted during Charlemagne's reign, ca. 768 to 814 (British Museum)

Carolingian ivory plaque of Saint John the Evangelist, ca. 9th century (Metropolitan Museum of Art)

Leaf from Dominican manuscript, Martyrdom of Saint Peter, ca. 13th century (Metropolitan Museum of Art)

POETRY AND MUSIC

"Carmen Paschale," by Sedulius, medieval epic poem, written ca. 425 to 450 CE

ART AND ARCHITECTURE

Gothic sculpture of last judgment and coronation of the Virgin, France, ca. 1250 to 1270 (Metropolitan Museum of Art)

Statue of King Childebert I (Merovingian dynasty), France, ca. 13th century (Louvre)

USEFUL WEBSITES

History of Tintagel and connection to King Arthur mythology (English Heritage)

History of the Norman conquest of England (BBC)

History of the Tower of London (Historic Royal Palaces)

History of Notre Dame Cathedral (Notre Dame Cathedral)

The Renaissance: Thought Reborn and Made Beautiful

(ca. 1300 to 1648)
GRADES: 3, 4, 5

OVERVIEW

The Renaissance is distinguished by an intensified embrace of humanistic learning and a willingness to challenge inherited beliefs and practices, inspired by the study of ancient Greece and Rome. The newly invented printing press spread ideas widely. A new spirit of inquiry and questioning emerged—one that sometimes challenged the authority of the church and ushered in the Reformation. Despite the decline of feudalism in Western Europe, life remained hard for the peasant class, and this period also saw the introduction of African slavery by Europeans. Europe also "discovered" the New World, or, as we call it today, the Americas. Younger students will be introduced to the first major Renaissance painter, Giotto, through a close read of *Mario's Angels*. Older students will evaluate another great artist's extraordinary contribution through a close read of *Michelangelo*.

o o o

Interested in learning more about this time period? Read a more complete history in the "Era Summaries."

LEARNING EXPECTATIONS

Lower elementary: Students should understand that Europeans began looking at the world with fresh curiosity by the late Middle Ages. They looked back toward the Greeks and Romans to develop new arts and human-centered ideas during the period called the Renaissance. Looking outward, they started to explore the rest of the world. Division over the nature and power of the Catholic Church led to the Protestant Reformation.

Upper elementary: Students should know that late medieval interest in the wider world led to new study of the surviving achievements of the Greeks and Romans. This led to Europe's Renaissance, from which a new humanism developed. It challenged traditional ideas about church and state, and spurred novel, complex developments in the arts and in learning. Europeans also began to move physically outward as they sought to pioneer new routes to the riches of the East. In the process, they unintentionally discovered the Americas. Students should also understand that growing doubts about the power, legitimacy, and corruption of the Church sparked a rupture between Catholics and the new Lutheran Protestant movement—which severely divided Europe and brought centuries of violence.

SUGGESTED ANCHOR TEXTS

Michelangelo by Diane Stanley
Cathedral by David Macaulay
Joan of Arc by Diane Stanley
Journal of Inventions by Jaspre Bark
Leonardo: Beautiful Dreamer by Robert Byrd
Leonardo da Vinci for Kids: His Life and Ideas by Janis Herbert
The Renaissance in Europe by Lynne Elliott
How They Made Things Work in the Renaissance by Richard Platt
The Renaissance by Jane Shuter

FEATURED ANCHOR TEXT

MICHELANGELO BY DIANE STANLEY

This book was selected because it is a masterful artistic biography of one of the greatest artists in history. Although the book details the art and life of Michelangelo through beautifully created illustrations—overlaid in many cases with photographs of Michelangelo's actual works, it also teaches much about the history of the Renaissance. Students will learn about the profound impact of the Medicis and the various church leaders in the Italian city-states; they will come to understand the inextricably complicated relationship among wealthy patrons, church leaders, and artists, as well as about the effect that they had on Michelangelo's unique artistic development. Students will learn about the ways in which politics, religion, and art were entwined during the Renaissance. The book also includes a helpful author's note at the beginning and a bibliography at the end, encouraging students to use the special features of informational text to extend their knowledge of the given topic.

TEXT STUDY

The text-dependent questions require students to do a close reading as well as to analyze illustrations and author's style. Students also engage in meaningful word analysis work. Students must synthesize information across sections of this substantial informational text. The performance assessment and extension offer students a chance to convey what they have learned by formulating an opinion to be defended, citing evidence from the text, and conducting further research to compare what they learn from new research to what they learned in the anchor text.

Note: This book is not paginated in publication. We assigned the map adjacent to the author's note as page 1 and the author's note as page 2.

1. **Look closely at the cover of this book. What is the artist doing? How would you describe the image of the title? Notice the title page. What does this collection of illustrated features suggest about Michelangelo?**

    - The artist is looking up and painting with a paintbrush. The people he is painting look real, as if they were moving.

    - The title, *Michelangelo*, looks like it is carved in marble.

    - The title page shows an artist chipping away at a face while doing a sculpture.

    - Michelangelo was an artist who painted on ceilings, carved in marble, and created sculptures of humans.

2. **The root word of *Renaissance* means "birth." Gather ideas from the author's note on page 2 to explain how the Renaissance was a rebirth. Summarize these ideas into one sentence.**

    Note: Teachers might ask students to explain how adding the prefix re- changes the meaning of the word. Make sure they understand that the word means rebirth.

    You might also ask students to explore other words derived from the root word, for example, nascent.

    - Ideas from the author's note are as follows.
      - This period of time came after the Middle Ages, "when people began to rediscover the great achievements of their ancient past."
      - It was a time of "reawakening of learning and creativity."
      - It began in Italy, where archaeologists were uncovering ancient Roman ruins.
      - The rediscovery of buildings, sculptures, and writings of the ancient Greeks and Romans in science and philosophy inspired new thinking and new art.

    - During the Renaissance, people learned from the ancient Greek and Roman past to think creatively about their future in a rebirth of philosophy and art.

    Note: Sentences will vary.

3. **What simile does the author use to describe how many artists were in Florence during the Renaissance? How does the author support this figurative statement with details?**

    - She says that Florence was a place "where artists grew like wildflowers after a summer rain."

    - Maybe the author means that there were many, many artists in Florence during the Renaissance.

    - Maybe the author means that many artists sprung up quickly in Florence during the Renaissance because that is where artists were nurtured and encouraged, in the same way that rain makes flowers grow.

    - She supports her statement with the following details.
      - Florence was a center for the art of the Renaissance.
      - Patrons of the arts in Florence, such as the powerful Lorenzo de' Medici, paid artists to create works of art for them.

    Note: Teachers might help students understand the concept of patron, noting that there are still patrons of the arts today.
      - Giotto, Donatello Botticelli, da Vinci, and many others had come from Florence and excelled in art.
      - When someone bought a fake antique sculpture and wanted to find the person who made the beautifully crafted art piece, the first place they went was to Florence.

4. **According to pages 3 through 6, how did Michelangelo begin his art education?**

   - When Michelangelo's parents moved back to Florence, they sent him to live with his nurse, the wife of a stonecutter. He became very comfortable with the sounds of stonecutting, but he moved back to Florence with his family while he was still a baby.

   - When his mother died—when Michelangelo was about six—he returned to the stonecutters. It was probably during that time that he tried his hand at using a hammer and chisel to cut shapes out of stone. The author suggests that he might have gotten some lessons in stonecutting during this time. Eventually, he was an apprentice to a stonecutter and "already seemed to know how" to carve stone.

   - When Michelangelo was about ten, he loved to draw. His neighbor was an apprentice to a painter, Domenico Ghirlandaio. Michelangelo studied Ghirlandaio's drawings, acquired by his friend.

5. **An apprentice is "a person who works for another in order to learn a trade." Why did an artist, such as Ghirlandaio, need an apprentice to help in creating a fresco?**

   - When creating a fresco, the artist had to time the process correctly. He had to use water-based paint to create art on wet plaster. After the plaster was applied to a surface, the artist had only six hours to finish the art on that section of plaster.

   - The apprentices were the ones who made the brushes, mixed the paints, applied the plaster, and made the outline of the artist's figure on the wall using charcoal dust. They also filled in parts of the painting and painted areas too high for the viewer to see well.

6. **On pages 9 through 12, how does the author describe the effect that Lorenzo de' Medici had on Michelangelo's early life?**

   - De' Medici used his money to start a school for young sculptors. He hired the sculptor Bertoldo to be the master. De' Medici chose Michelangelo to be one of the students. It was during this time that Michelangelo learned on his own to work with marble, as the Greeks and Romans had done.

   - He invited Michelangelo to live in the palace as his son, giving him fine clothes to wear and an education. The author says that "at a most impressionable age, Michelangelo was suddenly thrown into the midst of the Medici circle, where poetry, science, philosophy, and art were subjects of dinner-table conversation . . ."

7. **According to the text, how did Michelangelo learn to create a lifelike human body from a lump of stone? How did his study affect the creation of the Pietà and David?**

   - According to pages 13 and 14, Michelangelo got permission to study anatomy at a morgue. "He spent hours dissecting bodies, memorizing the origins and insertions of the muscles, the positions of the tendons and veins."

   - On pages 17 and 18, the author says that the veins and tendons in Jesus's hands looked "more real than real." The reader can see in Jesus's upper arms, ribs, legs, and ankles how everything looks real and how utterly amazing that it is sculpted out of marble with a hammer and chisels.

   - According to pages 19 and 20, the author writes, "Michelangelo knew his anatomy so well that his David is astonishingly real." The reader can see the veins and tendons in the detailed hands as well as his chest muscles and chiseled face.

8. **Using a dictionary and the text on page 22, explain why the people of Florence called the painting of the new council chamber the "Battle of the Titans." How did the battle end?**

    - When you look up the word *titan* in the dictionary, it is defined as a word coming from Greek mythology that means "a person of enormous power or influence."

    - In this case, the persons of enormous talent were Leonardo da Vinci, an old man who was the "only man in Italy to rival him in fame" and Michelangelo. The idea of these two extremely talented men competing created the idea of an epic "battle" of art.

    - Leonardo was famous for his painting and looked down on people who were known for sculpting, like Michelangelo. Michelangelo knew Leonardo da Vinci looked down on him because da Vinci's opinion was that painting was a more "refined art."

    - The men were each given a wall mural to paint. Leonardo planned to paint a military scene with horses because he "drew horses beautifully." Michelangelo planned to draw a scene of soldiers surprised while taking a bath because he "was best at the human figure."

    - The battle ended with both withdrawing. Leonardo da Vinci tried a new method for painting frescos and it failed. Michelangelo got only as far as the sketch and was called away by Pope Julius II to Rome.

9. **How did the discovery of the Laocoon challenge Michelangelo's art in a new way? How did the discovery relate to the idea of the Renaissance as a time of rebirth?**

    - The Laocoon showed an ancient Trojan priest and his two sons writhing "frantically in a death struggle with two serpents." This *writhing* is defined as "twisting the body in pain." Michelangelo was challenged to think about how a sculptor could show this "extraordinary sense of movement" in contrast to the "calm elegance" of his Pietà and David sculptures.

    - "Inspired by this 'miracle of sculpture,' Michelangelo now threw himself into his work on the tomb" [of Pope Julius II]. In a sense, it was a "rebirth" for Michelangelo, too.

    - This Laocoon sculpture was a perfect demonstration of how the old work of the Roman Empire was reborn in the time of the Renaissance, inspiring the art of a master like Michelangelo.

10. **According to pages 26 through 28, how did Pope Julius cause a dispute between the city-states of Rome and Florence?**

    - When Michelangelo was in Rome, he was working for Pope Julius. Julius stopped paying Michelangelo for doing a huge marble tomb that he had commissioned, so Michelangelo sold what he had and returned to Florence.

    - Pope Julius wanted him back to Rome and sent three letters of request from him to return. Michelangelo refused to go and stubbornly stayed in Florence.

    - Finally, the council in Florence became afraid that Julius would invade Florence to take back Michelangelo. They convinced Michelangelo to go to Bologna "and beg the pope's forgiveness."

11. **What evidence does the author offer on page 28 that explains why Michelangelo resisted the idea of painting the ceiling of the Sistine Chapel?**

    - He considered himself a sculptor, not a painter.

    - He had little experience with frescos.

    - The task would take a long time and be "very uncomfortable."

    - Michelangelo was "afraid he would fail."

    Note: *Teachers may want to refer back to page 8 of this text to remember the difficulties Michelangelo faced when his ideas were different from those with whom he worked.*

12. **Using the information on pages 29 and 30, cite evidence that describes Michelangelo's four-year experience creating the panels on the ceiling of the Sistine Chapel.**

   - He worked, without assistants, to cover 5,800 square feet of ceiling with religious art.

   - He worked sixty feet up in the air, with his back arched like a bow and paint dripping on his face. He said, "my paintbrush all the day doth drop a rich mosaic on my face."

   - He was unhealthy, eating just enough to stay alive and working until he dropped into bed, dead tired every night, "with his clothes on, even to the tall boots."

   - He wrote to his brother, "I live here in great toil and great weariness of body, and have no friends of any kind and don't want any, and haven't the time to eat what I need."

13. **What did Diane Stanley mean by this statement on page 32: "To study the Sistine ceiling is to watch a genius learning how to paint"?**

   - If you know the order in which he painted the panels, from the flood to the creation, you can see how his painting changed.
     - In the first half, the figures are smaller. Michelangelo saw this when the scaffold was moved from one side to the other at the halfway point.
     - In the second half, he made the "figures much larger and the scenes simpler." He wanted people to be able to have a better view from the ground floor.
     - Stanley says that beyond altering the size and detail of the paintings, he also became more "confident and bold" in his style.

14. **How did the invasion of Rome by the King of Spain and the "Holy Roman Emperor" affect the Renaissance?**

   - Rome was destroyed; churches were burned and looted; and priests and nuns were murdered, along with thousands of citizens of Rome.

   - The Sistine Chapel became a stable.

   - Some historians believe it signaled the end of the Renaissance period of history.

15. **What two reactions to Michelangelo's painting of the Last Judgment in the Sistine Chapel does the author describe?**

   - One reaction was by Pope Paul, who "fell to his knees and prayed for mercy."

   - Others who saw it could only see the naked bodies in the fresco. Later they were covered with little draperies painted over the "shameful parts."

16. **Using pages 43 through 46 as reference, describe Michelangelo's work on St. Peter's from age seventy to age eighty-nine. What does his end-of-life work tell about him as a person?**

   - In 1547, Michelangelo was asked to work on St. Peter's as the chief architect. He worked for seventeen years on the task, not taking any form of payment.

   - Diane Stanley writes, "He did it for the good of his soul." Art, this challenging architecture in particular, nurtured his soul. He was motivated to work hard as he created beauty and the "crowning achievement of his remarkable life."

17. **What more is told of Michelangelo's character in the quote at the end of his life, how he "regretted 'dying just as I am beginning to learn the alphabet of my profession'"?**

   - This shows that he was always learning and developing his skills as an artist as he sculpted, painted, and designed architecture.

PERFORMANCE ASSESSMENT

Give students the following task:

- In your opinion, what was Michelangelo's greatest artistic contribution? Choose one of his art projects as your focus. Use evidence from this text and your own preferences about art to support your choice of artistic masterpiece and write an opinion essay.

Students should write a sentence that introduces their topic, use facts and definitions to develop points, and provide a concluding statement or section. At earlier levels, students may draw or dictate their informative/explanatory text and/or write a label, sentence, or series of related sentences. See standards for more details.

EXTENSION

Ask students to research other artists' depictions of David (for example, Donatello or Verrocchio) and write an informative/explanatory essay in which they compare the versions using evidence from the anchor text about Michelangelo's character as well as other research to explain why Michelangelo might have taken the approach that he did. For example, one key difference is that Michelangelo did not include the head of Goliath with his statue; the others did.

CONNECTIONS TO COMMON CORE STATE STANDARDS FOR ENGLISH LANGUAGE ARTS

- Question 1 addresses a number of related Common Core State Standards skills: the ability to consider and explain the illustrator's purpose, describe key illustrations, and synthesize the information gleaned from several illustrations to offer an opinion about what characteristics of the subject the illustrator was trying to convey (RI.3.2,3,7,8; RI.4.2,3,7,8; RI.5.2,3,7,8).

- Question 2 considers word analysis and etymology, as well as key details and concepts explained in the author's note, which students must summarize (RI.3.1,2,3,4,5,8,9; RI.4.1,2,3,4,5,8,9; RI.5.1,2,3,4,5,8,9).

- Somewhat similar to question 2, question 3 also asks students to consider the author's choice of words (or, in this case, a group of words—a simile) and its relevance to a key concept of the text. It asks students to identify the evidence the author uses to support the use of such figurative language (RI.3.1,2,3,4,8; RI.4.1,2,3,4,8; RI.5.1,2,3,4,8).

- Question 4 requires students to identify key details conveyed in the text (RI.3.1,2,3; RI.4.1,2,3; RI.5.1,2,3).

- Question 5 focuses students' attention on potentially new and important vocabulary and also asks them to identify key details and concepts in the text that relate to the words (RI.3.1,2,3,4; RI.4.1,2,3,4; RI.5.1,2,3,4).

- Question 6 addresses the way in which the author describes some key details about an important concept in the text (RI.3.1,2,3,8; RI.4.1,2,3,8; RI.5.1,2,3,8).

- Answering question 7 requires students to locate and relay important details from the text, conveyed over several pages (RI.3.1,2,3; RI.4.1,2,3; RI.5.1,2,3).

- Similar to questions 2 and 3, question 8 draws attention to a potentially new word and a figure of speech that is also a literary allusion. It asks students to explain why the author's choice of words helps to explain a key concept in the text. Students must also relay key details to demonstrate understanding (RI.3.1,2,3,4,8; RI.4.1,2,3,4,8; RI.5.1,2,3,4,8).

- Questions 9 and 10 demand that students synthesize information from several places in the text to understand a key turning point in Michelangelo's life and the impact of the Renaissance in general (RI.3.1,2,3; RI.4.1,2,3; RI.5.1,2,3).

- Questions 11, 12, 14, and 15 ask students to cite evidence from the text to explain an important event in the text (RI.3.1,2; RI.4.1,2; RI.5.1,2).

- Question 13 addresses students' ability to infer from an author's statement the impact of important details from the text and the greater significance of the central ideas she presents (RI.3.1,2,8; RI.4.1,2,8; RI.5.1,2,8).

- Questions 16 and 17 not only require students to cite details from the text but also to make an inference about the main subject of the text based on these details (RI.3.1,2,3; RI.4.1,2,3; RI.5.1,2,3).

- The performance assessment offers students an opportunity to convey their understanding of the text by writing an opinion essay, using evidence from the text to support their assertions (RI.3.1,2,3,9; RI.4.1,2,3,9; RI.5.1,2,3,9; W.3.1; W.4.1; W.5.1).

- The extension gives students a chance to learn more about other Renaissance artists' work and also the ability to relate that knowledge to what they have learned from the anchor text. They must cite evidence for their comparisons and contrasts from the anchor and other research texts (RI.3.1,2,3,6,7,9; RI.4.1,2,3,6,7,9; RI.5.1,2,3,6,7,9; W.3.2,7,8,9; W.4.2,7,8,9; W.5.2,7,8,9).

MORE RESOURCES

PRIMARY SOURCES

The Decameron of Giovanni Boccaccio, by Giovanni Boccaccio, ca. 1351 (The Gutenberg Project)

Gutenberg Bible leaf, printed ca. 1397 to 1468 (Ink and Blood Collection)

Text of Queen Mary I's speech at the Guildhall, 1554 (English History)

Queen Elizabeth I: Design for the obverse of the Great Seal of Ireland, ca. 1584 (British Museum)

POETRY AND MUSIC

Text of poems, speeches, and letters of Queen Elizabeth I

ART AND ARCHITECTURE

The Burghers of Calais, Rodin, 1884 to 1895, France

   Depicts scene from Hundred Years' War

USEFUL WEBSITES

The Black Death (The History Channel)

Martin Luther: The Reluctant Revolutionary (PBS)

Scrovegni Chapel official website

Large images of the frescoes of the Scrovegni Chapel

Americas North and South: The "New" World

(ca. 20,000 BCE to ca. 1500 CE)
GRADES: 3, 4, 5

OVERVIEW

The development of major population centers and advanced cultural patterns came relatively late to the Americas. Human migration into the continent from Asia was inhibited by the rise and fall of sea level. Geographical barriers often made interregional contact difficult. Inventions and improved farming techniques often spread slowly—if they spread at all. American civilizations ranged from loosely organized tribes to complex urban centers. Many would rise and fall by the time European explorers arrived—events that forever changed the world. *Lost City: The Discovery of Machu Picchu* gives lower elementary students insight into the mind of an explorer in Peru who discovered Machu Picchu. *The Ancient Maya* gives upper elementary students the background to analyze the impact of religion on Mayan civilization.

o o o

Interested in learning more about this time period? Read a more complete history in the "Era Summaries."

LEARNING EXPECTATIONS

Lower elementary: Students should understand that humans came relatively late to the Americas, migrating from Asia to establish tribal hunter-gatherer societies (these are the "Indians" that are probably most familiar to young students) and complex civilizations with urbanized empires in Central and South America.

Upper elementary: Students should know that humans migrated to the Americas—the last major continental area that humans settled—from western Asia. They should understand that many hunter-gatherer cultures existed across North America: settled cultures formed in the North American Southwest and ceremonial mound-building cultures arose in the east-central portions of the continent. There were many groups and local cultures that adapted to different climates and terrain according to location. Students should also understand that urbanized empires emerged in Central America, where the Maya developed a fully written language, and in South America. They should know that during the final centuries before European contact, the Aztecs and Incas established strong and culturally sophisticated militarist empires that imposed their powers on many neighboring peoples.

SUGGESTED ANCHOR TEXTS

The Ancient Maya by Jennifer Fretland VanVoorst
Aztec, Inca, and Maya by Robert Snedden
Aztec, Inca, & Maya by Elizabeth Baquedano
Birth of the Fifth Sun and Other Mesoamerican Tales by Jo Harper
Mesoamerican Myths by Anita Dalal
The Ancient Maya by Barbara A. Somervill
The Honey Jar by Rigoberta Menchu

FEATURED ANCHOR TEXT

THE ANCIENT MAYA BY JENNIFER FRETLAND VANVOORST

This book was selected because it is a topically organized, well-illustrated informational text about the fascinating features of the Mayan civilization and culture. The book is packed with facts that will shock the students, capturing their interest in an era when ball games had more at stake than a title or trophy. The author addresses aspects of the Mayan world: its order, its intellectual feats, the daily life of the people, and its eventual decline and fall. The text contains structural features of informational text that students may use to enhance their understanding: a timeline, a glossary, a bibliography, suggestions for further reading, and an index.

TEXT STUDY

The text-dependent questions address a variety of important aspects of informational text, including the role of structural features, author's purpose, the effect of illustrations, and the interpretation of author's phraseology, Many of them ask students to recall, summarize, or synthesize key historical details or concepts. The performance assessment enables students to discuss key details and therefore organize their thinking around these details before writing an informative/explanatory essay.

Be sure to discuss the organization of this text and review the table of contents before you begin with the questions. Students will need to note how the author is writing topically, going back at times to discuss similar ideas, but using a different lens, as explained by the chapter's titles.

1. **Using the title, front illustration, and back cover of the book, explain what you will learn while reading this book.**

   - From the title, we know we will be learning about the ancient Maya.
   - From the illustration on the cover, we know that the Mayans valued masks made of mosaics and valuable gems. In the shadow, we can also see a lizard or gecko, suggesting that the setting for this text is a tropical place.

- On the back of the book, we read that the civilization peaked 1,750 to 1,100 years ago. The Mayan culture centered on "pleasing their many gods" and that the book will include information about Mayan temples, written language, and a deadly serious ball game.

2. **According to page 5, what was the ultimate goal of the Maya as they played "pok-a-tok"?**

   - They wanted to please the gods, so the power of the gods would bring them "order, harmony, and plenty."
     - They wanted to please the rain god, Chak, so they would have rain.
     - They wanted to please the god of agriculture, Yum Ka'x, to "ensure a good harvest."
   - They wanted to bridge the gap between the natural and the supernatural.
   - By winning the game, they would be able to make the losers their slaves, prisoners, or possibly blood sacrifices for the gods.

3. **Describe the geographic location of the Mayan civilization. According to the map on page 8, what might have been the area where the civilization began?**

   - According to page 6, the Mayan civilization began on the Pacific coast of present-day Guatemala. Eventually it included land in "present-day southern Mexico, Belize, Guatemala, Honduras, and El Salvador."
   - Because the civilization began on the Pacific coast of Guatemala, it would have been near Kaminaljuyu.

4. **Why might the author have chosen to compare the European Dark Ages to the Mayan civilization on page 6?**

   - The author was probably trying to contrast the "stagnating" of "intellectual achievement in Europe" with "an amazing civilization an ocean away." The author went on to say they were studying the heavens, building amazing architecture, and "creating epic poetry."

   Note: *You may want to note the Eurocentric idea that European thought was always "leading the way" in history. This text suggests an important counterpoint to that thinking.*

5. **What were the four most well-known features of Mayan cities? What was the significance of each?**

   - According to page 7, Mayan cities had pyramids, palaces, plazas, and ball courts.
     - The pyramids were used as tombs for the dead and as bases for temples. The Mayans believed the pyramids gave the priests "closer proximity to the heavens."
     - According to page 28, the kings lived in large stone palaces, where they stayed most of the time. People saw the kings and the nobility "on public holidays and special events."
     - According to pages 4 and 5, the ball court was where the teams battled it out for slaves and prisoners, often used to appease the gods through death.

   Note: *The plazas are not explained in this text but would have been used for the performances and ceremonies in the city, surrounded by large architectural structures.*

6. **According to page 9, what was the king's role in the Mayan culture?**

   - The king ruled over a large city and the smaller cities nearby. His job was to serve the gods who gave him his power. The king had to follow the rituals in the Mayan belief system or the gods would not bless them with crops and food. He had to manage "an elaborate set of religious practices that kept order and prosperity in the Maya world."

7. **According to pages 10 and 11, what reasons does the author provide for the downfall of the Mayan civilization?**

    - Around 900 CE, things changed.
        - They stopped doing the stone carvings called the stelae.
        - They began leaving the cities.
        - They stopped believing the kings could stand between them and the gods.
        - Emphasis was placed more on trade than on religion.
    - By the mid-1500s, the Spanish had crushed the Mayan civilization.

8. **What does the author mean by "a well-ordered universe"?**

    - This was the underlying idea of the society in the Mayan culture. Everything needed to be in order and to be balanced for the world to be controlled and regulated.

9. **A culture may have an object represent a much greater idea. We might say the object symbolizes, or represents, a completely different idea. How did the "mighty Ceiba tree," pictured on page 15, symbolize the three worlds of the Maya?**

    - According to page 14, the tree lived in all three of the realms of the Mayan world.
        - The leafy top of the tree reached into the sky.
            - This was where the gods lived, in the upper world.
        - The tree grew on the earth.
            - This was the middle world.
        - The roots "plunged deep into the watery underworld."
            - This was called Xibalba, the "place of fear" where all of the dead lived.

10. **Using the text on page 13, give an example of a Mayan god who was "complex and contradictory."**

    - Gods could have different forms. When Itzamna was the creator, he was in the form of Hunab K'u. By contrast, when he was the god of writing and learning, he was Kukulkan.
    - Gods could also have different forms, sometimes animal and sometimes human. For example, Itzamna could be an old man without teeth, or as Kukulkan, he could be a feather-covered snake.

11. **Why might the author have repeated the description of the ball game, with more details, in this chapter?**

    - In this chapter, the author was telling about "a well-ordered universe." She was describing ways that the Mayan people pleased the gods through rituals and ceremonies requiring blood. Although she told of the Mayan people using animals and human blood without death, the games were a way to obtain humans to use in blood sacrifices.

12. **Describe the Mayan system of writing. On what materials did they write?**

    - They had one common writing system, even though they had twenty-five languages or dialects.
        - The written language was made up of seven hundred glyphs (symbols representing a word, a sound, or a syllable).
        - Reading the glyphs required reading in a zigzag fashion. The glyphs were written on pairs of columns, left to right, and then top to bottom.
    - The writing was used for telling stories on a variety of materials.
        - They carved stone columns with the hieroglyphics.
        - They painted the glyphs on pottery.
        - They wrote on deerskin.
        - They used thin paper bark to "fold like an accordion and make a book."

13. **According to the book's glossary, *codices* are "ancient manuscripts made of bark paper or animal skin." Discuss the three remaining codices and their role in identifying the point of view in history.**
    - The remaining codices tell the Mayan point of view of history. There are few because the Spanish missionaries burned the Mayan books when they conquered them in the 1500s.
    - The other information known about the Mayan civilization is from the Spanish point of view, very different from that of the people who were born into the culture and raised among its people.

14. **Why is the *Popol Vuh* important to the Mayans?**
    - It is a sacred (holy) book.
    - It tells the creation story.
    - It tells the story of the Hero Twins who, they believe, became the sun and the planet Venus.
    - Many of their customs and beliefs stem from the stories in this book.

15. **What were the two distinctive things about the Mayan numbering system?**
    - It had a zero in it, perhaps the first in the history of mathematics.
    - It was based on the number twenty.

16. **Why was the calendar important to the Mayan people?**
    - It was important for practical reasons.
      - The Haab, 365 days based on solar observations, helped to predict the times when they should plant and harvest crops.
      - The Chichen Itza pyramid was built with 365 steps from the bottom to the top of the platform.
      - The "Long Count" calendar lasted 5,128 years. This was a calendar that showed the kings where their reign fit into the timeline.
    - It was important for "mystical" reasons.
      - The Haab told them when to select lucky days for festivals.
      - The Haab told them which sacred days honored specific gods.
      - The "Count of Days," a calendar that repeated every 260 days, determined a person's personality and future.

17. **Describe the social classes of the Mayan culture.**
    - According to page 28, there were four social classes.
      - The top level included the kings, priests, scribes, and nobility.
      - The next level down was the "professional class" including "architects, merchants, warriors, and large landowners."
      - The third level down was the "commoners" including "craftspeople, small farmers, workers on large estates, laborers, and domestic servants."
      - The lowest level included the slaves.

18. **According to chapter 4, what made someone beautiful in the Mayan civilization? How do we know this to be true?**
    - A beautiful Mayan had a flat forehead that sloped back, crossed eyes, large noses, and decorated teeth. They also had piercings, tattoos, and paint on their bodies.
    - We can infer this to be true because of the carvings and paintings still left from the Mayan civilization; they probably based artistic works on the "beautiful" people.

19. **According to page 32, how did the Mayans use creative techniques to produce more crops on their farms?**

    - They used a "slash-and-burn" technique to make the soil more fertile. The farmers slashed rainforest plants during the dry season, allowing them time to dry. They later burned the plants to make ash, blended the ash with the soil, and created a new field with fertile soil.
    - They drained swamps and dug irrigation ditches, creating more land for crops.
    - They terraced fields on the sides of hills to make more-level cropland.

20. **From the illustrations and text on pages 34 and 35, tell how the Mayan people moved heavy loads.**

    - The Mayan slaves moved huge loads by having some of the slaves pulling the load with ropes and timber, similar to oxen. As they pulled, the load was rolled on logs. The slaves would have to pull the logs from the back and place them in the front as the load was pulled along.
    - The Mayan people used a "tumpline" placed across the forehead of the carrier to carry heavy things on wood frames on their backs. The strap across the forehead would help to balance the weight, supporting the heavy load.

21. **Using the information in chapter 5, create an annotated timeline for the decline and fall of the Maya.**

    - 800 CE: The Mayan civilization began to collapse. People left the cities possibly because of drought, war, disease, decline in trade, a natural disaster, or to farm new areas.
    - 900 CE: Southern Mayan cities decreased in size, and the northern cities prospered. Two cities in the Yucatan thrived: Chichen Itza and Uxmal.
    - 1221 CE: Chichen Itza and Uxmal were abandoned, but Mayapan became an important market city for trade.
    - 1440 CE: Mayapan fell due to warring families.
    - 1500s CE: Spanish soldiers, called conquistadors, came to seize the land of the Maya. They destroyed the villages with weapons and epidemics of European diseases.
    - 1502 CE: Christopher Columbus met some Maya in Honduras on his fourth voyage to the Americas.
    - 1542 CE: The Spanish created a capital city, called Merida, ending the Maya civilization in Mexico.
    - 1546 CE: The Spanish succeeded in taking over most of Mexico and Central America.
    - 1697 CE: The last Maya city in Guatemala was defeated.

PERFORMANCE ASSESSMENT

Create a cause-and-effect chart showing how the religion of the people affected the creation and development of the Maya civilization. Use this chart to generate ideas for the student writing.

Give students the following task:

- Write an informative/explanatory paragraph explaining the relationship between Mayan religious beliefs and the Mayan culture generally. Choose two or three activities in Mayan daily life that happened because of the people's effort to appease the gods.

Students should write a sentence that introduces their topic, use facts and definitions to develop points, and provide a concluding statement or section. At earlier levels, students may draw or dictate their informative/explanatory text and/or write a label, sentence, or series of related sentences. See standards for more details.

CONNECTIONS TO COMMON CORE STATE STANDARDS FOR ENGLISH LANGUAGE ARTS

- Question 1 directs students to use the structural features of this informational text, as well as cover illustrations, to preview the central ideas of the book (RI.3.5,7; RI.4.5,7; RI.5.5,7).
- Questions 2, 5, 6, 9, 10, 12, 14, 15, 16, 17, 18, 19, and 21 ask students to cite evidence from the text when recalling key details (RI.3.1; RI.4.1; RI.5.1)
  - Question 5 also pushes students not just to identify details but also to explain their significance.
  - Question 18 also asks students to make an inference.
  - Question 21 also requires students to create a timeline.
- Students must recall key details and synthesize information from a map and the text to answer question 3 (RI.3.1,2,5; RI.4.1,2,5; RI.5.1,2,5).
- Question 4 prompts students to consider the author's purpose in making a specific comparison (RI.3.1,2,8; RI.4.1,2,8; RI.5.1,2,8).
- Question 7 requires students to determine the details that an author provides to support key concepts or assertions (RI.3.1,2,8; RI.4.1,2,8; RI.5.1,2,8).
- Question 8 asks students to interpret the author's use of a particular phrase that relates to key historical information in the text (RI.3.4; RI.4.4; RI.5.4; L.3.5; L.4.5; L.5.5).
- To answer question 11, students must consider the author's purpose in repeating information from an earlier section of the text (RI.3.1,2,3,8; RI.4.1,2,3,8; RI.5.1,2,3,8).
- Question 13 requires that students recall key details and also that they consider various points of view of the historical information presented (RI.3.1,2; RI.4.1,2; RI.5.1,2).
- Question 20 asks students to glean information from illustrations and text (RI.3.7; RI.4.7; RI.5.7).
- The performance assessment gives students an opportunity to discuss and analyze as a group an important aspect of the Maya text and then to write an informative/explanatory or an opinion essay that addresses a specific question related to the class discussion or exercise (RI.3.1,2,3,5,8; RI.4.1,2,3,5,8; RI.5.1,2,3,5,8; W.3.2,9; W.4.2,9; W.5.2,9; SL.3.1; SL.4.1; SL.5.1).

MORE RESOURCES

PRIMARY SOURCES

Mayan sun god, ca. 8th century (Metropolitan Museum of Art)

Pueblo mesa architecture (Denver Public Library)

> *Photo taken in 1899*

Eskimo portrait (Library of Congress)

Head of a water deity, ca. 15th to 16th century (Metropolitan Museum of Art)

Incan silver figurine of a llama, ca. 15th century (Metropolitan Museum of Art)

POETRY AND MUSIC

Inuit throat singing, video (*National Geographic*)

USEFUL WEBSITES

Caribou migrating across the present Beringia (Encyclopedia Britannica)

Article on Nasca lines in Peru (*National Geographic*)

Europe's Global Expansion

(1492 to ca. 1700)
GRADES: 3, 4, 5

OVERVIEW

The Age of Exploration dawned as European nations, motivated by a vision of God, gold, and glory, explored the Americas. Intercultural contact led to the exchange of plants, animals, and foods between the New and Old Worlds. The expansion of European empires overseas, however, brought exploitation, disease, and death to native populations. Meanwhile, Europeans also ventured to Asia and India for trade and missionary opportunities. Their quest for new trade routes also led them to explore Africa—and expand a slave trade that would ultimately devastate the continent. Pairing *Pirates* with an informational text about Blackbeard helps younger students understand the famous English privateer-turned-thief. Older students who closely read *Hernando Cortés* will be able to join in an informed argument about whether the notorious Spanish conquistador can be considered a hero.

Interested in learning more about this time period? Read a more complete history in the "Era Summaries."

LEARNING EXPECTATIONS

Lower elementary: Students should understand that Europeans first ventured overseas in pursuit of gold, trade, and religious converts—that is, "God, gold, and glory." Soon, however, settlers went to forge new communities and societies. Students should know that expansion gradually moved from the Americas to Asia and often had negative consequences for native peoples.

Upper elementary: Students should understand that Europe's expansion into newly discovered lands led to the discovery of new crops, mineral wealth, and trade opportunities. It also had dire consequences for native peoples, especially in the Americas; the combination of brutal exploitation and unintentionally introduced diseases led to massive mortality and drastic societal changes. Students should know that Europeans traveled mainly to pursue commercial opportunities and religious conversions, but that some—particularly in the British colonies of North America—hoped to create new and better societies. Often, that involved the forcible removal of the native peoples. Students should realize that pursuit of coveted Asian trade goods gradually led to a strong European presence in India and East Asia, which would grow even more dominant in time. They should also understand that the evolving slave trade was a complex arrangement between Africans and Europeans and had a terrible impact on Africa.

SUGGESTED ANCHOR TEXTS

Hernando Cortés: Spanish Invader of Mexico by John Zronik
"Around the World with Captain Cook," *Calliope*, May 2002
"Early Explorers," *Cobblestone*, September 2011
LaMalinche: The Princess Who Helped Cortés Conquer the Aztec Empire by Francisco Serrano
Magellan's Voyage around the World by Cath Senker
Real Pirates: Over 20 True Stories of Seafaring Sculduggery by Claire Hibbert
"When Spice Ruled," *Calliope*, February 2006
Who Was Ferdinand Magellan? by Sydelle Kramer

FEATURED ANCHOR TEXT

HERNANDO CORTÉS: SPANISH INVADER OF MEXICO BY JOHN ZRONIK

This book was selected because of its detailed telling of the role of Spanish conquistadors as explorers, conquerors, and destroyers and transformers of civilizations. Wealth and fame motivated Cortés, and this text explains that important aspect of his character. The illustrations are vivid and the text also includes photographs of traditional Aztec art and architecture, examples of the codices, and reproductions of other artistic rendering of the events described. The text includes structural features of informational text, such as a table of contents, a glossary, an index, and a running timeline that borders many pages. Of particular interest in a world history set of lessons is the caveat at the end of the book that explains the drawback of studying this history as told exclusively by fame-seeking conquistadors through *probanzas*, or firsthand reports written by the conquistadors themselves.

TEXT STUDY

These text-dependent questions require close reading and the nimble examination of the various features of informational text here (for example, illustrations and insets with primary source material). Students must synthesize information across sections and make inferences about the effects of key events. Some questions here also help students understand characterization techniques in informational text.

1. **How does the text describe the Europeans' view of the world to their west before the 1500s?**

   - The western worlds were unknown to Europeans, sometimes shown on maps as "unknown, unexplored areas, if they were shown at all."

   - "Most Europeans did not know that North, Central, and South America existed."

   - "Many Europeans believed it was possible to sail westward across the Atlantic Ocean from Europe to Asia."

2. **According to page 4, what motivated Spanish explorers such as Cortés to go to the "New World"?**

   - Cortés went to the New World "in search of wealth and fame."

   - Fame came from conquering the people who lived in a place.

   - Once the conquistador was in charge of the land, he would set up a colony there in the name of the king or queen who had sent him. In this case, Cortés set up a colony in the name of the king of Spain.

   - "Gold, food crops, and other trade goods were sent from [the] New World colonies to Spain, making many Spaniards wealthy," suggesting that explorers saw the New World as a place where they could obtain wealth.

3. **What do you learn about the Aztec culture from the letter written by Cortés as shown on page 5 of the text? Support your conclusion about the culture with evidence from Cortés's letter.**

   - You learn more about the Aztec culture: its organization, its leadership, its dress, its wealth, and the Aztecs' pride in their capital city's construction.
     - Montezuma, the Aztec ruler, was an honored leader with two hundred lords who showed him respect by marching in strict formation around him, lining two sides of a walled street. He had two chiefs who walked beside him. The street itself was beautiful and very straight.
     - Touching him was not allowed; he was protected from Cortés's attempted hug by the lords who were with him.
     - The Aztecs came to meet Cortés in rich dress and no shoes.

   Note: *You may want to discuss the value in general of primary sources: in this case, a letter from the hand of the explorer himself, a powerful and insightful research tool for discovering what really happened in the sixteenth century.*

4. **According to page 6, what motivated exploration of the New World, and how did the discoveries by Christopher Columbus spark Spain's continued exploration of the New World?**

   - Near the end of page 6, the text says, "At the root of Spanish exploration was a quest for gold." We can infer that Columbus's conquests (described previously on this page) were successful in finding gold because other explorers followed quickly in his wake.

   - Although he was Italian, Columbus "sailed under the flag of the Spanish king and queen." He first visited "the Caribbean Islands of the Bahamas, Hispaniola, and Cuba."
     - Spain then claimed the Caribbean Islands, beginning with the island that now comprises Haiti and the Dominican Republic.
     - Ponce de Leon then claimed Puerto Rico and de Cuellar claimed Cuba.

5. **According to page 7, aside from gold and fame, what was another reason the Spanish wanted to go to the New World?**

   - They wanted to convert the native peoples to accept the religion of Christianity. They sent missionaries with the Spanish explorers. They were even willing to use force to convert them.

6. **According to pages 8 and 9, how did Cortés become wealthy?**

   - Cortés went to Hispaniola, Haiti, and the Dominican Republic of today in 1506. Similar to all conquistadors, he was given land and was allowed to tax the native peoples by requiring labor or goods to trade, but because colonists had already been there for twelve years, he moved on.

   - Cortés went to Cuba in 1511 and was granted land and slaves. He raised cattle on a farm, mined for gold, and became wealthy.

7. **According to pages 10 through 13, how did Cortés hear about the Aztec civilization?**
   - Cortés heard about the Aztecs from his journey to the Maya in Mexico. While he was traveling through the Mayan territory, one of the groups told him "of the great Aztec Empire to the west, and its capital city of Tenochtitlan."

8. **What can you infer about the native groups ruled by the Aztecs from the illustration and caption on the bottom of page 14? What information on page 15 adds to your knowledge of the native groups ruled by the Aztecs?**
   - The native groups were not necessarily loyal to the head of the Aztecs, Montezuma. They were deciding whether to side with the Spanish as they tried to take over the Aztecs.
   - The native groups were part of a defeated group of people because the Aztecs had conquered native groups of people to expand their own civilization.

9. **What do you notice about the geographical location of the capital city of Tenochtitlan as pictured and captioned on the bottom of page 15? Use the text on page 15 to add more understanding to your visual observations.**
   - The city is built on an island in a lake, Lake Texcoco. It looks like it is connected to the land by a long bridge. There are many buildings in this well-designed city.
   - The "long bridge" is a causeway connecting the city to the mainland. The buildings on the island were "pyramids, stone temples, and markets." They also had gardens in the city.

10. **Explain how the text describes the various classes of the Aztec people.**
    - According to page 16, there were slaves, peasants, and farmers at the bottom of the class ladder.
    - "Priests, warriors, and nobles were higher up." They had "finer homes" and more opportunities to be educated.

11. **According to page 17, how did the Aztec people keep their gods strong?**
    - They sacrificed humans. The illustration shows someone being killed to please the gods they worshipped.

12. **How does the text suggest that the religious beliefs of the Aztecs affected their view of Cortés?**
    - In their legends, "Quetzalcoatl" was a god who would someday return to rule their land. He was light-skinned and bearded. By coincidence, Cortés was light-skinned and bearded, so some of the priests believed that Cortés was Quetzalcoatl.

13. **According to the text, how did Cortés make sure his soldiers would come with him as he prepared to march on Tenochtitlan? How did he add to his numbers of soldiers?**
    - Cortés "caught wind" of a defection by some of his soldiers, who intended to sail back to Cuba. He stripped the boats of sails and anything useful, and "then destroyed most of his fleet."
    - According to page 19, Cortés's army fought a native group called the Tlaxcala. Cortés's army won and forged an alliance with them. They joined the effort to fight the Aztecs.
    - According to page 20, Cortés would attack native groups along the way to strike fear in other native groups so they would join him in the attack against the Aztecs.
    - According to page 21, Cortés went back to Veracruz, fought Spanish soldiers there, and convinced them to join his fight in Tenochtitlan.

14. **What did Cortés do with Montezuma after meeting him?**
    - According to page 20, Cortés allowed Montezuma to treat him as a guest and show him around the city, but eight days later, Cortés secretly took him prisoner and told him to act like he was still in charge.

15. **How did smallpox help Cortés?**
    - Smallpox was a disease brought over from Europe by explorers. Because the people in the New World had no immunities to this brand-new disease, thousands of them died or became very weak from it. This disease lessened the numbers of people Cortés needed to defeat.

16. **A siege means to surround an area in battle to cut off access to supplies. How did the Aztecs and the Spanish use a siege tactic in the war between them?**
    - The Aztecs cut off the causeway to the mainland and prevented the Spanish from leaving the island for supplies.
    - During the final battle, eighty days of fighting, the Spanish "cut off the Aztec's supply of food and water." The Aztecs surrendered August 13, 1521.

17. **How was Montezuma killed? How does the illustration on page 23 support the text?**
    - Montezuma's own people killed him when he went out on a balcony to talk to his people, trying to help the Spanish garner support from the native people. Someone threw a rock at Montezuma, and he later died.
    - The illustration shows Montezuma, in traditional Aztec dress, surrounded by Spanish soldiers, with a rock coming from the crowd to hit him in the head.

18. **How was Cortés rewarded for his victory over Tenochtitlan?**
    - He was given permission to rule the territory he had defeated.

19. **What happened to Tenochtitlan and its people after the Spanish conquest?**
    - The city was destroyed but rebuilt in a European style by the enslaved Aztecs.
    - "Catholic churches were built on top of ruined Aztec temples."
    - Some Aztecs were converted to Christianity, and the conquistadors moved on to conquer other areas. Aztec leaders were killed when they could not help the Spanish find gold.

20. **How did Europe change as a result of Cortés's discoveries in the New World?**
    - Wealth increased in all of Europe because of the "trade of gold, silver, tobacco, cacao beans, and other items." They also began to grow "corn, tomatoes, and chili peppers."
    - Mapmakers understood the coast of Mexico and nearby areas.
    - Cortés's exploration helped to build the knowledge in geography, specifically that North and South America were between Europe and Asia to the west.

21. **The word *distort* means to give a false meaning or to misrepresent what actually happened in an incident. According to page 31, how might the story of the Aztecs have been distorted in its telling?**
    - Conquistadors were the sources for the written history of the Spanish conquests. They were written with the hope of earning rewards from the king of their sponsoring country. They may have not stuck completely to the facts of what happened.

    Note: Teachers often tell students that history based on primary sources such as the probanzas, in this case, is more accurate than history simply passed down generation to generation. History might have been distorted for the personal gain of the explorers—from the very beginning of the reports sent back to Spain.

PERFORMANCE ASSESSMENT

On page 30 of this text, the author writes, "Hernando Cortés is an important figure in world history, but not a well-liked figure in present-day Mexico. He is remembered as the person responsible for the destruction of Aztec culture and way of life."

Give students the following task:

- Discuss this set of sentences and the rest of this page on Cortés's legacy. Use specific incidents from other parts of the text in your discussion. Choose one of the following statements to use as your topic sentence in an opinion essay:
    - Hernando Cortés is an important figure in world history and deserves to be called a hero.
    - Hernando Cortés is an important figure in world history, but does *not* deserve to be called a hero.

Students should write a sentence that introduces their topic, use facts and definitions to develop points, and provide a concluding statement or section. At earlier levels, students may draw or dictate their informative/explanatory text and/or write a label, sentence, or series of related sentences. See standards for more details.

CONNECTIONS TO COMMON CORE STATE STANDARDS FOR ENGLISH LANGUAGE ARTS

- Question 1 requires students to cite evidence asserted by the author in the text about key historical background information (RI.3.1,2; RI.4.1,2; RI.5.1,2).
- Question 2 requires students to cite evidence asserted by the author in the text about the motivations and actions of the main character in this text (RI.3.1,2; RI.4.1,2; RI.5.1,2; RL.3.3; RL.4.3; RL.5.3).
- Students must summarize, synthesize, and infer information to answer question 3. They must consider not only the information in the text but also that which is highlighted in the primary source inset on the same page (RI.3.1,2,3,6; RI.4.1,2,3,6; RI.5.1,2,3,6).
- Question 4 asks students to make inferences based on details that they must also identify in the text (RI.3.1,2; RI.4.1,2; RI.5.1,2).
- Questions 5 through 7, 10 through 16, and 18 through 20 require students to identify key details and concepts in the text (RI.3.1,2; RI.4.1,2; RI.5.1,2)
    - Questions 13, 15, 16, 19, and 20 also require students to synthesize information across sections of the text and make connections among details and concepts (RI.3.3; RI.4.3; RI.5.3).
    - Question 16 also addresses academic vocabulary. Students must understand the word to answer the question (RI.3.4; RI.4.4; RI.5.4; L.3.4; L.4.4; L.5.4).
- Students must synthesize information from the text and the illustrations to answer questions 8, 9, and 17 (RI.3.1,2,3,7; RI.4.1,2,3,7; RI.5.1,2,3,7).
- Question 21 not only asks students to explain key details but also asks them to consider how history may be presented from various viewpoints (RI.3.1,2,3,6; RI.4.1,2,3,6; RI.5.1,2,3,6).
- The performance assessment helps students organize information from the text to write an opinion essay in which they must take a position and defend it with evidence from the text (W.3.1; W.4.1; W.5.1).

MORE RESOURCES

PRIMARY SOURCES

Treaty of Tordesillas, signed 1494 (General Archive of the Indies)

Photo of handwritten notes by Christopher Columbus on Marco Polo's "Le Livre des Merveilles," 15th century (Wikipedia)

Wooden ceremonial shield with mosaic inlay, Aztec, ca. 15th to 16th century (British Museum)

Map of South America, drawn 1562 (World Digital Library)

General History of the Things of New Spain: The Florentine Codex, by Fray Bernardino de Sahagún, published 1577 (World Digital Library)

A *Briefe and True Report of The New Found Land of Virginia*, 1590 (Gutenberg Project)

ART AND ARCHITECTURE

Seated Portuguese figurine, Nigeria, 18th century (Metropolitan Museum of Art)

USEFUL WEBSITES

English translation of the Treaty of Tordesillas (Yale Law School, Avalon Project)

The map that named America (Library of Congress)

Account of the discovery of North America from the "Saga of Eric the Red" (Bartleby.com)

The Revolutionary Roots: The Modern West

(ca. 1600 to 1800)

GRADES: 3, 4, 5

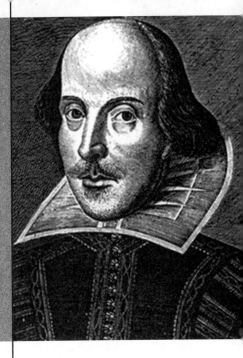

OVERVIEW

The seventeenth century was a time of enormous change in Western Europe. The feudal system had long since collapsed and given way to greater social mobility. The era was also marked by agricultural advancements, a rapidly growing population, bigger cities, and greater individual prosperity. A revolutionary spirit led to battles for liberty in Europe. Many of these struggles, notably the English civil wars and the French Revolution, were marked by great savagery and claimed an enormous number of lives. It was also the spirit that led to the independence of the United States of America from Great Britain. Younger students will read *Peter the Great* and learn how the celebrated Russian leader changed his country. Older students will explore how Galileo changed the world with his ideas by reading *Starry Messenger*.

o o o

Interested in learning more about this time period? Read a more complete history in the "Era Summaries."

LEARNING EXPECTATIONS

Lower elementary: Students should understand that as European society modernized—and began to more closely resemble our modern-day—people became more and more ready to challenge long-held ideas about royal power, religion, and science. As more people pushed to make their voices heard in government, change came—sometimes with revolutionary consequences.

Upper elementary: Students should understand that European nations moved unevenly toward a more modern commercial society—sometimes, as in Peter the Great's Russia, under deliberate pressure from the state. Students should also know that an increasing foment of thought contributed to major scientific advances and to novel ideas about religion, government, and freedom. As more people gained wealth and social status, there was a greater willingness to challenge long-standing ideas about royal power and popular obedience. In England, such ideas led to civil war by the seventeenth century and weakened the monarchy. In America, British ideas of rights (which had developed through the colonies' long experience of virtual self-rule) led to democratic revolution in the 1770s, because Britons seemed to deny the colonies the rights they themselves enjoyed. In France, vibrant ideas emerged during the Enlightenment—but government remained autocratic and left grievances to fester until they exploded in France's violent revolution of the 1780s to 1790s.

SUGGESTED ANCHOR TEXTS

Starry Messenger: Galileo Galilei by Peter Sis
Discovering Nature's Laws: A Story about Isaac Newton by Laura Purdie Salas
Galileo's Telescope by Gerry Bailey and Karen Foster
I, Galileo by Bonnie Christensen
Isaac Newton by Anne Marie Sullivan

FEATURED ANCHOR TEXT

STARRY MESSENGER: GALILEO GALILEI BY PETER SIS

This book was selected because it renders a detailed account of Galileo's life and scientific accomplishments through captivating illustrations and text. The book also conveys key information in captions, sidebars, and insets, helping students to understand how to navigate a complex informational text and extract key details and concepts from these structural features.

TEXT STUDY

These text-dependent questions help students examine text and intricate illustrations to infer an author's purpose and identify and explain important details and concepts in this informational text. Students also examine diction and figurative language. The performance assessment and extension give students opportunities to convey their understanding of key details and concepts through opinion and informative/explanatory writing.

1. **Look closely at the title and cover illustration of this book. What details do you notice that offer hints about Galileo's interests?**

   - The cover illustration depicts a man looking through some kind of telescope up at the night sky; we learn later in the book that Galileo was very interested in the sky, the moon, and the planets.

   - The title of the book is *Starry Messenger*, which tells us that the book might be about someone interested in stars.

   - Galileo's clothing looks like he lived long ago, when men still wore long robes, indicating he may have been a pioneer in his field.

   - Galileo is standing in a cave created by people, covered with the images of old beliefs about the constellations. He seems to have punched out a place to see into the sky with his telescope, exploring for discovery.

2. **Look closely at the illustration on page 1 of the text. What seems strange about the Earth as pictured in the illustration? How does the writing at the upper right-hand side of the drawing help to explain the illustration?**

   - The sun is revolving around the Earth.

   - The Earth is in the center of the revolving planets.

   - The constellations are revolving around the Earth.

     Note: Teachers may need to pause to discuss or explain the word constellation.

   - It looks like an illustration of an old-fashioned idea about how the planets and the stars work because the bearded man (standing in a robe in front of the columned building on the lower left) looks like someone who lived long, long ago.

   - The writing at the upper right-hand side of the drawing says "the earth stands still" giving a title to the illustration and suggesting that whoever drew this picture didn't think that the Earth rotated around the sun.

3. **According to the text on page 1, what did people believe about the Earth's position in the universe? According to the midsection of the page, where might they have gotten this idea?**

   - People believed the Earth was in the center of the universe.

   - The author wrote, "They just followed tradition."

   - They believed "the sun and the moon and all the other planets revolved around it."

   - The timeline and drawing in the midsection of the page suggests that there are three men who may have taught this idea: Eudoxus, Aristotle, and Ptolemy.

     Note: Point out "The Ptolemaic System" caption at the top of the page.

   - A verse from the Psalms is also quoted in the midsection: "God fixed the Earth upon its foundation, not to be moved forever," introducing the notion that the Bible may have been a source for people's beliefs about the Earth's position in the universe.

4. **According to page 2, what did "one man" wonder about the Earth? Why didn't he boldly announce his ideas to the world? After considering the text features and illustration, who do you think the man described in the text is?**

   - The text says that the man wondered if maybe "the earth and the other planets move around the sun."

   - He probably didn't announce his ideas to the world because "he knew he could not prove they were true." Even though he had made observations by looking closely at the universe, he had no way of proving that he was right.

   - Considering the timeline and the illustration together, we can guess that it was Copernicus who said this because the title of the illustrations on pages 2 and 3 (in which the Earth actually does appear to be moving around the sun) is "The *Copernican* System–The Earth Moves."

5. **How do the illustrations on pages 2 and 3 enhance the account in the text?**

   - The crowned but blindfolded woman does not see the winged cherub twirling the world around like a globe on a stand.

   - In the bottom right-hand corner, a man is reading and studying something, and "death," as portrayed by a skeleton in a black robe, seems to be coming after him, suggesting that it may be the man described in the text, who didn't have enough time on the Earth to prove his theory that the Earth moves.

     Note: To answer questions 4 and 5, teachers will need to help students track and understand the implied relationships across text and illustrations.

6. **Using the regular text and the circular writing on page 4, summarize the information into one sentence about Italy. Do the illustrations on pages 4 and 5 support your sentence?**

   - Although Italy was a country filled with creative people in many city-states, the Catholic Church was the major religion and influence.

     Note: *Answers may vary, of course, but the sentence should suggest that Italy was a Catholic country of city-states where many talented (that is, "artistic" and so on) people lived.*

   - The illustrated map shows the different city-states. Around the frame of the map is a key showing the different kingdoms in Italy. The church leader is shown in Rome.

     Note: *Sentences should be consistent with this information.*

7. **Look closely at the illustration on pages 6 and 7. What do you notice about each of the babies? Which baby seems unique? How does the illustration support what the text says?**

   - The text says "a little boy was born with stars in his eyes. His parents named him Galileo."
     - On each baby blanket in the illustration is an image of what the child will be as an adult.
     - One of the babies is wrapped in a blue blanket covered in white stars.

8. **According to the clues on page 6, how did the author tie the words of Shakespeare to Galileo?**

   - Shakespeare and Galileo were both born in 1564.

   - Sis illustrated Galileo differently than all of the other babies on the page, showing he was different and a "star" from birth.

   - The vertical quotation by Shakespeare reads, "Be not afraid of greatness: some are born great, some achieve greatness, and some have greatness thrust upon them."
     - The Shakespeare quotation appears to caption the illustration of this baby destined to be great.

9. **How does the illustration on pages 8 and 9 support the author's claim that Galileo "was more curious than most and stars were always on his mind"?**

   - The illustration shows children playing many different kinds of games. They are flying kites, playing with toy horses, and rolling hoops among many other activities. In the upper-left quadrant, one boy is drawing bright blue stars in the dirt in an illustration that is otherwise entirely yellowish-white.

     Note: *Sis's illustration may be an homage to Pieter Brueghel the Elder's* Children's Games, *painted in 1560.*

10. **According to the "S-shaped" writing on page 8, what was the downside of life in the beautiful cities during Galileo's childhood?**

    - They used candles for light and had nothing to keep their food cold.

    - The "streets were open sewers."

    - People died of diseases such as typhoid and the bubonic plague.

11. **How does the author use the word *star* in a different way on page 10? How does the illustration support this meaning of the word *star*?**

    - The author uses the word *star* to describe how other people were talking about Galileo. "Galileo is our star," the people would say. It means that he is set apart or distinguished as someone special.

    - When looking at the sea of people in the illustration, Galileo is seen robed in stars and looking up to the stars. Everyone else in the mob is amused by his experiments and demonstrations.

12. **What is Galileo demonstrating from the Leaning Tower of Pisa, described in the text and pictured on page 11?**

    - He was proving that Aristotle was wrong; his experiment, according to the text, came to be known as "The Law of Falling Objects." He dropped two balls of unequal weight from the Leaning Tower of Pisa; the balls fell at the same speed, even though each ball weighed different amounts.

      Note: *Teachers may want to highlight some of the vocabulary:* observer, experimenter, imparter of knowledge.

13. **Look closely at the three scenes featured in the illustration on pages 10 and 11. What does each scene show us about Galileo's growing knowledge of science?**

    - The first scene shows Galileo observing.
    - The second scene shows Galileo experimenting.
    - The third scene shows Galileo speaking, sharing his discoveries with others.

14. **According to pages 12 and 13, how did Galileo find a different use for this "new instrument"?**

    - Galileo took an instrument used to see things far away, a spyglass, and turned it up toward the sky. He used it like the telescope we use today.

15. **Summarize the observations made from Galileo's telescope, as described in the illustrations and captions on pages 14 and 15.**

    - Galileo used his telescope to observe the moon and its phases. He found that although the moon is beautiful to see at night, it was "rough and uneven" and covered with mountains, valleys, and "chasms."

16. **How does the text on page 14 help the reader to learn where the book title originated?**

    - The text says that Galileo published his work in a book titled *The Starry Messenger*.

17. **According to the illustration on page 17, what other object in the sky was viewed and studied by Galileo?**

    - With his telescope, Galileo viewed the sun and drew the sunspots.

18. **Citing evidence from the text, explain how Galileo's knowledge spread throughout the world.**

    - According to the caption on page 18, Galileo moved to Florence to become "Chief Philosopher and Mathematician to the Medici court."
    - According to page 19, all of the kings and princes of Europe received a gift of a telescope and Galileo's book.
    - According to page 20, many people across the world learned about his work because his book was "translated into many languages, including Chinese."
    - According to page 20, his book was presented at a book fair in Frankfurt (Germany).
    - According to page 21, people celebrated his ideas and discoveries "with statues and parades and spectacular events."

19. **According to pages 22 and 23, why were Galileo's popularity and fame a problem?**

    - Galileo had gone against what the religious leaders, the Catholic Church, believed about the Earth being the center of the universe.
    - The Church began to worry that he was too popular.

      Note: *According to the writing in the illustration on page 23, Galileo was boldly stating that the sun was the center and that the Earth rotated and revolved around the sun. Note how Galileo is being summoned to the menacing beast creating a door in the cavernlike room and tower.*

20. **How does the illustration on page 25 show the change in Galileo's world? How does the text express the change?**

    - Galileo looks as if he is locked into a cell of some kind, a fearful place with scary creatures, and flames with faces are on the walls. A huge snake, wrapped around the room, is poised to attack him. In previous pages, the colors were bright and showed him surrounded by people who admired him. Now he is completely alone.

    - The light continues to shine on him, perhaps highlighting who he is and what he stands for.

    - The text says that Galileo was afraid and that he knew that other people had been tortured and punished for the same kind of offense.

21. **On page 26, what did the author mean by "the stars had left his eyes"? What is significant about the placement of Galileo in the illustration on page 27?**

    - When Galileo was judged in the court, he was not allowed to persist in his exploration of the universe and think about the stars. The phrase "the stars had left his eyes" is a figurative (versus literal) description of Galileo's sadness or disappointment.

      Note: If necessary, teachers should review the difference between literal and figurative language.

      The cursive note at the top of page 26 says that Galileo was convicted of believing something different from what the church leadership believed about the Earth, which helps explain his position alone in "the Pope's court."

    - Galileo is in the center (like the Earth) with the sun and planets rotating around the Earth, as the Church's teaching held. Note how similar this arrangement of figures is to the illustration of the Earth on page 1.

22. **Even though Galileo was locked in his house, how does the text suggest that Galileo stayed focused on the stars?**

    - According to page 28, he thought about the "wonders of the skies and the mysteries of the universe." He kept passing on his ideas to other people.

      Note: Notice the way that Galileo is again in the center with planets surrounding him as he makes a star with a stick—thinking of the skies again. His continued study is evident by the adult work posted on the walls.

23. **The word *pardon* means to be forgiven with the penalty taken away. Why did the church leaders pardon Galileo three hundred years later?**

    - The Church finally acknowledged that he was "surely and absolutely right."

24. **View the inside cover pictures at the beginning and end of the book. How are the two seemingly similar illustrations different?**

    - In the first illustration, Galileo appears to be in the tower viewing the stars. The architecture is from his era. The borders show ancient scenes of the pyramids in Egypt, early ships, and ancient battles.

    - In the second illustration, there appears to be someone still looking through a telescope but in a modern city, possible New York City. The illustrations show a more modern view of the world with a hot air balloon, a jeep on safari, an airplane, and a train.

      Note: You may want to discuss how space still holds its mysteries, waiting to be studied by someone who is curious and has a telescope.

PERFORMANCE ASSESSMENT

Give students the following opinion-based question to answer using evidence from the text and illustrations.

- Do you think it was important for Galileo to be "pardoned" three hundred years after he died? Support your opinion with two or three pieces of evidence from the text.

Students should write a sentence that introduces their topic, use facts and definitions to develop points, and provide a concluding statement or section. At earlier levels, students may draw or dictate their informative/explanatory text and/or write a label, sentence, or series of related sentences. See standards for more details.

EXTENSION

Ask students to do some research into the role of the Medici family in Galileo's work (mentioned on page 20). Note this powerful family's support of Galileo's study. Have students create an illustrated timeline of the Medici family's contribution to science and art from Galileo through Michelangelo and write a brief informative/explanatory essay that summarizes the Medici family's role and how important they were to Galileo's work.

Ask students to be sure to introduce the topic clearly; develop the topic with facts, details, and examples; link ideas; use precise language and domain-specific vocabulary; and provide a concluding statement. See standards for more detail. At earlier levels, students may write a coherent paragraph that summarizes the main topic and key details.

CONNECTIONS TO COMMON CORE STATE STANDARDS FOR ENGLISH LANGUAGE ARTS

- Question 1 prompts students to consider the illustrations and the text of a cover to infer the potential topics or central ideas addressed in the text to come (RI.3.1,7; RI.4.1,7; RI.5.1,7).

- Similar to question 1, question 2 also prompts students to consider the illustrations and the text to infer key information; specifically, it asks students to determine how the text helps explain the illustration (RI.3.1,7,8; RI.4.1,7,8; RI.5.1,7,8).

- Questions 3 and 9 ask students to synthesize important details from the text and inserts (a timeline and a quotation) and to cite evidence for their assertions (RI.3.1,2,3; RI.4.1,2,3; RI.5.1,2,3).

- To answer question 4, students must make some difficult inferences about the implied relationship among the information in the timeline, in the text, and in the illustration (RI.3.1,2,3,5,7,8; RI.4.1,2,3,5,7,8; RI.5.1,2,3,5,7,8).

- Similarly, to answer question 5, students must also make some difficult inferences about the implied relationship between the information in the text and in the illustration (RI.3.1,2,3,7,8; RI.4.1,2,3,7,8; RI.5.1,2,3,7,8).

- Questions 6 and 15 require students to glean information from the text and illustrations and summarize it (RI.3.1,2,3,7; RI.4.1,2,3,7; RI.5.1,2,3,7; W.3.2,9; W.4.2,9; W.5.2,9).

- Questions 7 and 20 require students to examine the illustration closely and read the text closely to note the relationship between the two (RI.3.1,2,3,7; RI.4.1,2,3,7; RI.5.1,2,3,7).
- Question 8 asks students to make connections among the ideas presented in several sections of the text (RI.3.1,2,3; RI.4.1,2,3; RI.5.1,2,3).
- Questions 10, 12, 14, 16, 18, 22, and 23 ask students to identify important details, citing evidence from the text (RI.3.1,2,3; RI.4.1,2,3; RI.5.1,2,3).
  - Question 12 also requires that students compare the information in the text to that in the illustration (RI.3.7; RI.4.7; RI.5.7).
- Question 11 addresses the author's choice of words and the multiple meanings of a word (RI.3.4,8; RI.4.4,8; RI.5.4,8; L.3.5; L.4.5; L.5.5).
- Questions 13 and 17 ask students to explain events that some of the illustrations describe (RI.3.7; RI.4.7; RI.5.7).
- Question 19 requires students to make connections among key details and concepts presented in the text (RI.3.1,2,3; RI.4.1,2,3; RI.5.1,2,3).
- Question 21 addresses the author's use of figurative language as well as how it relates to the illustration (RI.3.4,7,8; RI.4.4,7,8; RI.5.4,7,8; L.3.5; L.4.5; L.5.5).
- Question 24 asks students to compare the inside cover pictures of the text (RI.3.7; RI.4.7; RI.5.7).
- The performance assessment enables students to develop and present an opinion on an important aspect of the text, using evidence from the text (RI.3.1,2,3; RI.4.1,2,3; RI.5.1,2,3; W.3.1,9; W.4.1,9; W.5.1,9).
- The extension gives students a chance to research a topic discussed in the text and convey their understanding of the new information in a timeline and an informative/explanatory text (RI.3.1,2,3,6,9; RI.4.1,2,3,6,9; RI.5.1,2,3,6,9; W.3.2,7,9; W.4.2,7,9; W.5.2,7,9).

MORE RESOURCES

PRIMARY SOURCES

Seals and insignias of the East India Trading Company (Columbia University)

Title page of *Hamlet*, First Quarto, 1604 (The British Library)

Petition of Right, 1628 (Luminarium: Encyclopedia Project)

Early King James Bible, printed 1630 (Newberry Library, Chicago)

De revolutionibus orbium caelestium, Nicolaus Copernicus, 1543

    Includes first-published diagram of heliocentric cosmology

Illustration: "The Arrest of Robespierre, the French Revolutionary Leader" (Heritage History)

POETRY AND MUSIC

"The Doubt of Future Foes," Queen Elizabeth I (Luminarium: Anthology of English Literature)

"La Marseillaise," the French National Anthem, 1792 (National Anthems)

    Includes history of composition, lyrics, translation into English, and playable track

ART AND ARCHITECTURE

Sculptural portrait of Peter I (Peter the Great), 1723 (State Heritage Museum, Russia)

Drawings of young Louis XIV, ca. 1645

"Liberty Leading the People" by Eugène Delacroix, 1830 (Louvre)

The apprehending of Guy Fawkes by Sir Thomas Knevet, printed 1802 (British Museum)

USEFUL WEBSITE

The Gunpowder Plot (BBC History)

The Industrial Revolution: Nationalism Unites

(1790s to 1880s)

GRADES: 3, 4, 5

OVERVIEW

Napoleon's early nineteenth-century conquests destabilized Europe's old political regimes and helped spread revolutionary ideas, despite his ultimate defeat. Simultaneously, nationalism was directing cultural and ethnic loyalties to new states and new borders. During this time, industrial revolution was also changing life for millions. Labor shifted from rural to urban areas and factories displaced skilled artisans. The dislocation of workers, as well as agricultural crises, spurred emigration from Europe, particularly to the United States. Lower elementary students gain biographical information from *Louis Pasteur* so that they can explain how the famous scientist improved our world. *Marie Antoinette* gives upper elementary students biographical details needed to explain how her extravagant lifestyle sparked the ire of starving French peasants.

○ ○ ○

Interested in learning more about this time period? Read a more complete history in the "Era Summaries."

LEARNING EXPECTATIONS

Lower elementary: Students should know that during and after Napoleon's conquests of Europe, new ideas changed the way people viewed government and power. At the same time, the rise of industrial factories changed the way people lived and worked. Old political regimes became more vulnerable as more people demanded change. Students should know that such popular pressures, together with conquests and repeated revolutions, remade the map of Europe and began to shape the world as we know it today.

Upper elementary: Students should understand that Napoleon's conquests helped destabilize Europe's old political regimes and helped to spread new revolutionary ideas—especially as the growing Industrial Revolution fundamentally changed European society, spurring increased demands by laborers and by the growing middle class. They should also understand that nationalism—the belief that people of the same ethnic group and language should be united in a single, independent nation—became a rising force in nineteenth-century Europe. Old regimes and old borders were challenged, and the unification of Italy and Germany completely changed Europe's balance of power. Students should also realize that the era's dramatic climate of change also profoundly affected the sciences and the arts.

SUGGESTED ANCHOR TEXTS

Marie Antoinette: "Madam Deficit" by Liz Hockinson
Journal of Discovery by Peter Riley
"Potatoes Rot: Famine Plagues Ireland," *Calliope,* April 2006
Revolution News, A.D. 1770–Today by Christopher Maynard

FEATURED ANCHOR TEXT

MARIE ANTOINETTE: "MADAM DEFICIT" BY LIZ HOCKINSON

This book was selected because it is a well-written narrative history illustrated with a variety of descriptive photographs and other illustrations, including drawings and reproductions of paintings. It also includes informative sidebars, fact-filled captions, a timeline, and other structural features of informational text that make this a fascinating and easy-to-follow (if not challenging) text. The text is rich with figurative and humorous language, making it a compelling book for students at this level.

TEXT STUDY

These text-dependent questions range from asking about key details and related concepts to author's style and purpose. They encourage students to interpret figurative language, infer information, and synthesize information from a variety of places in the text. The performance assessments require students to reread closely, to make inferences from key details in the text, and to cite evidence as they convey their understanding of the text in informative/explanatory essays.

1. **Look closely at the illustration on the cover of the book. What are the objects chosen by the illustrator to place around the drawing of Marie Antoinette?**

   - She is holding a piece of cake on a china plate.
   - There are pearls and a lace mask.
   - There is a photograph of a beautiful European building positioned on the edge of a large pool of water. There is a statue of children in the foreground of the photograph.
   - There is a guillotine.

2. **According to page 1, what are the four words that made Marie Antoinette famous? What other details about her does the author include that offer hints about her character?**

   - She said, "Let them eat cake."
   - The other details on this page that offer hints about her character are as follows.
     - She was excited about becoming a queen in France but "had no interest in politics."
     - She wanted to be a queen because she wanted to have a "grand life."
     - Her people would starve and she would live decadently.
       - In this case, decadently means self-indulgent, having whatever she pleased because she was the queen.

3. **Using the caption and the details in the photograph, describe the place pictured on page 2.**
   - The place pictured in the photograph is the palace of Versailles, just outside Paris in France; at the time, it was considered the largest palace in Europe.
   - When Marie was queen, she lived there with five thousand people and two thousand horses.
   - Although the royal apartments were fine, the other rooms were "small, dirty, and smelling." They used chamber pots for toilets and tossed the refuse out the window.

4. **According to pages 3 through 5, what was Marie's childhood like?**
   - She was the fifteenth of sixteen children in "one of the most important royal families of Europe in the middle of the eighteenth century."
   - She grew up in a beautiful palace in Vienna, Austria.
   - The text says (on page 5) that "Marie's childhood was like a fairy tale."

   Note: Teachers might pause here to discuss the use of this simile and ask students to be ready to interpret this figurative language after reading the full description of her childhood.

   - She was spoiled, usually allowed to do what she loved.
   - She was not given a good education and could barely read or write.
   - Her mother was determined that she and her eleven sisters would marry royalty, for the purpose of creating "alliances for Austria."

5. **On page 6, the day Marie Antoinette is handed over to France is described as a day "that thunder rumbled in the nearby Black Forest during the ceremony and that Marie wept bitterly." Why might she have wept?**
   - She was leaving everyone and everything she had ever known in Austria.
   - She was marrying someone she did not know; her parents had arranged her marriage.
   - People had just made her change out of her Austrian clothes, every stitch of them, into French-designed royal clothing.
   - She was entering France and would never be able to live in Austria again.

   Note: You may want to skip the last nine lines of the text on page 6 if you are teaching this lesson to students for whom this is too much information.

6. **According to the text, why did Marie Antoinette once complain with these words, "I put on my rouge and wash my hands in front of the whole world"?**
   - According to page 8, "Each day, thousands of commoners were allowed to crowd into the palace to watch the Royals' every move, including the eating of meals."
   - She was tired of "the gaggle of courtiers" who were "pushing each other out of the way to assist the Dauphine and acquire royal favor."

   Note: Teachers might examine the use of the phrase gaggle of courtiers, making sure students know what each of these words means and discuss why the author might have chosen this image to describe these people.

   Teachers might examine the masculine and feminine French nouns, Dauphin and Dauphine.

7. **Why did the author compare what the Austrians ate at a meal to what the French ate at a meal?**

   - The author might have been trying to emphasize how very different life was for Marie Antoinette when she came to France.
     - She had been accustomed to eating simple meals, whereas the French meals were much more extravagant.
     - The text says that she continued to eat small amounts of food and to eat food that was not rich. By including this detail, the author may have been trying to underscore how single-minded Marie was, that she would not change her habits to suit the citizens of her adopted country, France.

8. **Tell the history of the croissant.**

   - The croissant was invented in Vienna, Austria, after the Austrians defeated the Turks. The Turks had a crescent, a symbol of Islam, in their flag. A baker designed the croissant in the shape of the crescent to celebrate the victory.
   - Marie Antoinette loved them in Austria and brought the idea to France, where they became very popular.
   - Today, people believe the origin of the croissant is French.

9. **Use evidence from the text to explain how Marie's appearance in public exhibited her extravagance.**

   - She wore formal gowns and thick makeup on her face.
   - Her hair was put up in three-foot-high piles, with "plumes, jewels, flowers, and woven-in miniatures depicting current events or pastoral scenes."
   - Her shoes were many and decorated with jewels.
   - Her perfume was made especially for her.

10. **Describe the French people's response to the coronation of King Louis XVI.**

    - The people were "jubilant" and celebrated with "volleys of artillery."
    - The king and queen were popular with the people.

11. **On page 12, the author quotes a French historian who wrote, "She as yet knew nothing of the crown but its flowers." The author then wrote, "Soon, she would come to know the crown's full weight." What do these two statements mean?**

    - At the beginning of the reign, the queen knew only of the happiness and celebration (the "flowers") that came with being queen. The author has just described the happiness of the crowd at the coronation and the popularity of the new king and queen, supporting the idea of flowers.
    - Later in her reign, she would know the pressure and the hardships ("the crown's full weight") of being royalty.

12. **According to page 14, what were the problems in France?**

    - They were helping the Americans with the Revolution and were "bleeding money." This means that they were spending more money than they could afford to spend. They were about to have nothing and owe too much.
    - The taxes were heavy on the people who were working, "while the aristocrats lived large and tax-free."

    Note: Teachers might want to ensure that students know the meaning of aristocrat, *an academic vocabulary word. Students could work with context clues and the dictionary (to examine etymology). They might also examine different forms of the word as different parts of speech (for example, aristocracy, aristocratic).*

- Food was scarce because of a bad harvest.
- The winter was hard, leaving people cold and hungry.

13. **How did the new queen react to all of the problems in France?**
    - She is quoted as saying, "Let them eat cake."
    - She completely ignored the needs of the people in her country while she was "living it up" as the new queen.
        - While her people were suffering, she was wearing a new gown with diamonds and gems every time she went out.
        - According to page 18, she stayed busy with the theater, the opera, going to balls, gambling, riding a donkey around, and pampering her dog.
        - She had her own palace and had a "fake country village" built to play in with her friends.
        - She laughed a lot, and that wasn't proper for royalty.

14. **Although the "let them eat cake" statement is probably not truly a quotation from Marie Antoinette, why did it stick to her legacy?**
    - According to page 14, she was known for her "notorious excess," meaning that her taste and extravagant lifestyle made it believable that it was she who said it.

15. **How did the queen change after she had children? Did this change people's opinion of her?**
    - According to page 21, she calmed down. She went to fewer parties, she wiped off the heavy makeup, and she dressed more simply in private.
    - People's opinion did not change. They had seen too much, and her reputation was fixed.

16. **To revolt means to rise up against authority. According to pages 22 and 23, what were the signs that the people were revolting against the government?**
    - The people now hated the queen. They called her "Madame Deficit" because she was so careless with money.
    - Pamphlets were created that openly made fun of the king and queen.
    - There were riots in Paris, with people demanding more rights.
    - The people were hungry and they had found weapons.
    - "They demanded an end to the monarchy. France was in revolution."

    Note: Teachers might want to ensure that students know the meaning of these academic vocabulary words.
        - Students could work with context clues and the dictionary (to examine etymology and the meaning of roots and affixes).
        - They might also examine different forms of the words as different parts of speech (for example, monarch; revolutionary—adjective and noun, and revolve).
        - They might use knowledge of root words to explore and track words with the same root (for example, monochromatic, monogamy; revolver).
    - The revolutionaries put thousands of people in prison and constructed a guillotine in Paris.

17. **According to page 25, what were the women demanding when they marched into the palace where the king and queen were living? Why is this demand an important fact in this story?**
    - They demanded flour.
    - The queen was known for living extravagantly while her people had nothing, not even the flour to make the most basic food—bread—to eat.

18. **What happened to the king and queen?**
- They were first put in prison.
- They were individually tried in court.
- They died by the guillotine.

PERFORMANCE ASSESSMENTS

1. Review with students that, according to this book, the French Revolution was caused in part by hungry people's anger at the king and queen who feasted. Have students use evidence gathered in the text-based questions to complete the following writing task:

- Write an informative/explanatory essay describing Marie Antoinette's role in the French Revolution. Be sure to use specific details as you describe her extravagance at a time when the people were starving and poor.

Students should write a sentence that introduces their topic, use facts and definitions to develop points, and provide a concluding statement or section. At earlier levels, students may draw or dictate their informative/explanatory text and/or write a label, sentence, or series of related sentences. See standards for more details.

2. Revisit the first question in the text study. Give students the following task:

- Write an informative/explanatory essay describing the author-illustrator's choices of images for the cover of the book. Tell why each image was chosen and how it relates to Marie Antoinette.

Students should write a sentence that introduces their topic, use facts and definitions to develop points, and provide a concluding statement or section. At earlier levels, students may draw or dictate their informative/explanatory text and/or write a label, sentence, or series of related sentences. See standards for more details.

CONNECTIONS TO COMMON CORE STATE STANDARDS FOR ENGLISH LANGUAGE ARTS

- Question 1 asks students to analyze an illustration by considering why the illustrator chose to include certain objects (RI.3.7; RI.4.7; RI.5.7).

- Students must make an inference about key concepts in the text from details provided by the author to answer questions 2, 6, 16, and 18 (RI.3.1,2; RI.4.1,2; RI.5.1,2).
  - Question 6 also addresses the interpretation of a quotation from the main character and asks students to cite evidence for why the author chose to use this quotation (RI.3.1,2; RI.4.1,2; RI.5.1,2).
  - Students might also interpret figurative language in question 6 and debate whether the metaphor is apt or not (RI.3.4,8; RI.4.4,8; RI.5.4,8; L.3.5; L.4.5; L.5.5).
  - Students might also examine the etymology and various forms of academic vocabulary words when answering question 16 (RI.3.4; RI.4.4; RI.5.4; L.3.1(a); L.3.1(c); L.3.1,4; L.4.1,4; L.5.1,4).

- Question 3 prompts students to synthesize information from a photograph and its caption to describe a pictured place in the text (RI.3.1,5,7; RI.4.1,5,7; RI.5.1,5,7).

- Questions 4 and 14 ask students to identify and explain key details in the text that relate to important concepts (RI.3.1,2; RI.4.1,2; RI.5.1,2).
  - Students might also interpret figurative language and debate whether the simile is apt or not (RI.3.4,8; RI.4.4,8; RI.5.4,8; L.3.5; L.4.5; L.5.5).
- Question 5 requires students to cite evidence when making an inference from details offered in the text (RI.3.1; RI.4.1; RI.5.1).
- Question 7 addresses the author's intent. Students must suggest why certain details are included in the text (RI.3.8; RI.4.8; RI.5.8).
- Questions 8, 9, 10, 12, 13, 15, 17, and 18 require students to track and explain key details from the text (RI.3.1,2; RI.4.1,2; RI.5.1,2).
- In order to answer question 11, students must interpret a metaphor by using details from the text to explain its meaning (RI.3.1,2,4; RI.4.1,2,4; RI.5.1,2,4; L.3.5; L.4.5; L.5.5).
- Students must interpret a quotation and make a judgment about why it may have been attributed to one of the main characters in the text when answering question 14 (RI.3.1,2,3,8; RI.4.1,2,3,8; RI.5.1,2,3,8).
- The performance assessments require students to reread closely, to make inferences from key details in the text, and to cite evidence as they convey their understanding of the text in informative/explanatory essays (W.3.2; W.4.2; W.5.2).

MORE RESOURCES

PRIMARY SOURCES

The Rosetta Stone, dated 196 BCE, discovered 1799 (British Museum)

Print of Emperor Napoleon, ca. 1830 (British Museum)

Irish passengers immigrating to America (Library of Congress)

Grammar book for children, published 1824 (The British Library)

Original manuscript of *Alice in Wonderland*, Lewis Carroll, 1862 (The British Library)

Guide to ladies' fashion and etiquette, 1811 (The British Library)

POETRY AND MUSIC

"To the Column," poem by Victor Hugo, 1830

> *Celebrates the memory of Napoleon*

ART AND ARCHITECTURE

"The Emperor Napoleon in His Study at the Tuileries," Jacques-Louis David, 1812 (National Gallery of Art)

USEFUL WEBSITES

1820–1860: The Age of the Factory (Spinning the Web: The Story of the Cotton Industry)

Primary sources on Irish immigration to America (Library of Congress)

The Belgian Revolution (Rijks Museum)

> *Includes a brief history, art, and artifacts*

Modern Imperialism: A Race of Conquest and Supremacy

(ca. 1790s to 1900)
GRADES: 3, 4, 5

OVERVIEW

European nations competed fiercely for imperial dominance overseas. They sought control over trade and raw materials, and new markets for capital. They imposed harsh rule on the colonies they created, often accompanied by virulent racism. Britain expanded its empire into East Asia, Australia, and India, though rebellions in the Americas caused the decline of British, French, and Spanish colonization there. Most of the African continent was parceled out by several European nations, and in the Belgian Congo alone the oppression claimed the lives of millions of natives. Students in lower grades will read *Samurai* and then prepare a digital informative presentation on a particular aspect of Samurai life. After a close reading of *The Slave Trade*, older students will deliberate to find one word to describe the worldwide system of enslavement.

o o o

Interested in learning more about this time period? Read a more complete history in the "Era Summaries."

LEARNING EXPECTATIONS

Lower elementary: Students should understand that European nations competed with each other for new sources of raw materials and trade opportunities. To that end, the various powers colonized much of the world during the course of the nineteenth century. Students should also understand that the West was able to carry out its imperialist plans because of its superior military technology, despite resistance from Asian and African peoples.

Upper elementary: Students should understand that Western imperialism accelerated dramatically in the nineteenth century. In Japan, European powers used naval threats to force its markets open—and inspired the Japanese to modernize and seek their own colonies. In China, European powers went to war to force the Chinese government to allow free trade in opium and other goods. The result was the near collapse of Chinese sovereignty and the division of the country into European spheres of power. Colonial expansion in Africa was extraordinarily rapid: in just twenty years, European powers increased their holdings from a handful of coastal enclaves to encompass most of the continent—and they often imposed brutal and exploitative rule.

SUGGESTED ANCHOR TEXTS

The Slave Trade by Melody Herr
Commodore Perry in the Land of the Shogun by Rhoda Blumberg
Manjiro: The Boy Who Risked His Life for Two Countries by Emily Arnold McCully
Shipwrecked! The True Adventures of a Japanese Boy by Rhoda Blumberg
The Tree of Life: Charles Darwin by Peter Sis

FEATURED ANCHOR TEXT

THE SLAVE TRADE BY MELODY HERR

This text was selected because it tells the story of the slave trade from a world history perspective. Instead of simply telling the story from the American point of view, it tells of the rich cultures of Africa, the tragic participation in slavery of the Africans themselves—long before it came to the Americas—the ruthless ways of the Europeans, and the ultimate devastation to the slave and the mother cultures. The illustrations are perfectly matched to the text, containing a mix of ancient illustrations and photographs of primary sources. The book also exhibits many useful structural features of informational text that help steer students through it and provide additional information (for example, a table of contents, subtitles under chapter titles, insets, maps, a timeline, a glossary, an index, and suggestions for further reading).

TEXT STUDY

These text-dependent questions address a wide variety of literacy skills and also focus on key historical content. Students must analyze text, illustrations, photographs, insets, and captions to summarize and synthesize information and to determine cause and effect, as well as other relationships among concepts. They examine vocabulary and author's craft. The performance assessment and extension offer students opportunities to synthesize and enhance their understanding of key concepts and render their understanding in informative/explanatory essays.

1. **Using the text on page 4 and the map on page 5, explain what kingdoms there were in Africa in the 1400s.**

   - There were three main kingdoms in Africa.
     - The Songhay Kingdom was in the northwest part of Africa.
       - It was "the last of the great West African kingdoms."
       - The kingdom was a trade center for salt and gold.
       - Timbuktu was a "center for learning," attracting people from far away to study "philosophy and science."
     - The Benin Kingdom was on the west coast of central Africa, near the mouth of the Niger River.
     - The Congo Kingdom was near the mouth of the Congo River on the west coast of Africa, farther south than the Benin Kingdom.

2. **According to page 4, how did European trade with Africa change around 1440?**

    - European traders had been content to trade for ivory and gold. In 1440, they began to want to "buy workers." This "trade in human beings" continued for 420 years.

3. **How does the text on pages 6 and 7 describe how the Portuguese were received differently in East Africa than in West Africa?**

    - In East Africa, the Portuguese were not welcomed because the East African and Arab traders did not want them to interfere with their trading business, which was already established.

    - In West Africa, the Portuguese were welcomed. The text says, "The Congo king invited missionaries to his court. He converted to Christianity. He also adopted European dress, manners, and laws." West Africans studied in Portuguese schools. The cooperation "went both ways"; the text says, "In exchange for cloth, metal tools, and other European goods," the Portuguese received "copper, ivory, and gold."

    - On page 6, an illustrated map shows the "East African coastline in the 1500s." It shows the cities that were thriving because of all of the trade along the coast.

    - On page 7, the East African trade disputes led to the building of Portuguese forts along the coast. These forts were photographed and still stand today.

4. **According to page 8, how did Christopher Columbus's discovery of the new land in the Americas affect the people of Africa?**

    - Although the Western slave trade began with the Portuguese and the West African prisoners of war (page 4), the discovery of this new continent made the hunger for slave labor grow. On page 8, the author wrote, "with so much work to be done in this new land, slaves were in higher demand than usual."

5. **How did the colonists in the New World affect the need for slave labor?**

    - According to page 9, the colonists in the Caribbean and South America were raising sugar cane and mining for gold. They could not do all of the labor themselves. When they tried to use people native to the Americas, they died of European diseases. They decided they needed slave labor.

6. **According to the text on page 10, what is slavery?**

    - The author defines slavery as "one person—the owner" treating "another person—the slave—as property."

    - The author describes the horrible effect that having no rights has on a human being: "Everything, including their clothes, their food, even their children, belonged to their owners. Slaves had no rights and could be tortured and beaten by their owners."

    - The text says, finally, "Slaves were not even considered human beings."

7. **According to page 11, how did the slave trade expand in 1518?**

    - In 1518, the slave trade extended to the colonies in the Americas, directly from Africa. Eventually, over four hundred years of trade, more than twelve million Africans were enslaved in the Americas.

8. **According to the author, how were indentured servants different from slaves? Why did the British colonies eventually turn to slavery instead of the original system of indenturing shorter-term labor?**

    - According to the glossary and to the text on pages 13 and 14, an indentured servant sold "his or her labor for a certain amount of time," often in exchange for passage to the colonies. Slaves were people who were sold permanently to others and forced to work; they had no choice in the selling of their labor.

- According to page 14, there were simply not enough workers to keep up with the demand for labor on tobacco and rice plantations. People no longer wanted to work as servants in the fields, so between 1600 and 1750, colonists "began turning to slavery as an answer to the worker shortage."

9. **According to pages 16 and 17, which Europeans were involved in the slave trade with Africa? Why did they call the slave route a *triangle*?**

   - The British, the Dutch, the French, and the Portuguese.

   - The slave trade was called a "Trade Triangle" because the British trade route had three main stops.
     - The trip began in Britain with a load of "cloth, tools, guns, metal bars, jewelry, and other factory-made items."
     - It sailed to a West African port to trade the British items for "enslaved men, women, and children."
     - The ship then sailed to America with the load of slaves to be traded for various items, as seen on the map on page 17. The items included fish, flour, livestock, sugar, rice, silk, indigo, tobacco, lumber, whale oil, and furs.

10. **A justification means an explanation or argument that defends an act or belief. How do the photograph and its picture caption on page 19 relate to one point in the European justification of slavery, as described in the paragraph at the top of the page?**

    - Europeans scholars "claimed that Africans were less intelligent" than Europeans and asserted therefore they should be ruled by the European masters.

    - The illustration at the bottom of page 19 shows the "Great Zimbabwe," built before the slave trade began. The Great Zimbabwe is a great cultural achievement that people believed could not have been created by Africans themselves, but by other ancient people who settled there. African people created it, and it exhibits the high level of creative intelligence in the people of this culture.

    Note: If your students are interested in more information on this story of culture, see this article on the Great Zimbabwe on a BBC website.

11. **How does the true story of Ayuba Suleiman Diallo (page 21) illustrate the task of "Gathering Slaves" and "Searching for More Slaves"?**

    - Just after this educated Muslim merchant sold his slaves in West Africa, he was captured and sold as a slave. He was sent to Maryland to work as a slave on a tobacco farm.

12. **How did the desire for guns act as fuel to the slave trade?**

    - The African rulers wanted guns to protect their people and to attack their enemies.

    - When they attacked enemies with the guns, and then took prisoners, the prisoners became the slaves they would trade for more guns.

13. **How do the pyramids of Giza relate to the slave trade?**

    - On page 23, the author was making the point that slavery may have been part of the early history of the African culture. For example, even the building of the most famous structures in Egypt, such as the pyramids of Giza, may have been built by slaves.

14. **According to pages 24 and 25, how does the author build her case that this triangular trade was a new and different kind of slavery?**

    - The author explains how and why the slave trade changed as it grew beyond Africa's borders.

- She first tells how the European slave trade expanded slavery significantly beyond Africa's borders, involving businessmen and royal charters to independent traders.
- African slaves had previously been considered "enemies or social outcasts."
- The Europeans, who came to trade, thought of the slaves as "trade goods."
- The colonists thought of them as "work animals."
- Among the Africans, the slaves were still valued as people even though words such as *enemy* and *outcast* were used to describe them. But with the Europeans they were *goods* and *animals*, simply objects to be owned.

15. **Using the text and illustrations on pages 26 through 33, describe the journey of the African slaves from their African home to their new life in a colony.**

- Slaves, captured during a war or kidnapped, were walked in single file, chained, until they reached the coast.
- They were imprisoned at the trade post until a ship could come, staying in a "dungeon-like prison" or a pen.
- Slaves were packed as cargo into ships, as seen in the illustration on page 29.
- They spent fifty to eighty days on the westbound ship, if the wind blew strong enough to get them across the Atlantic. Space was tight and food became scarce. Disease spread rapidly because of close quarters and filthy decks. Ten to 20 percent died.
- They were cleaned up and fed in the Americas and then sold. As soon as they were sold, they were branded.

  Note: *Teachers may wish to do some word analysis work here with the word* branded, *considering its etymology, its various related forms and functions as various parts of speech, its root and affixes (for example,* brand–*the verb with multiple meanings,* brand–*the noun, the participial adjective, or past-tense verb* branded, *as here).*

16. **According to pages 34 and 35, how did the slave trade ultimately affect peoples and culture in Africa?**

- Families and communities were devastated by the loss of men in their families and villages. They lived in "grief and fear."
- Kings and queens tried to protect their people by allowing only war captives to be taken or by building walls around their cities.

17. **Using the text, insets, and illustrations on pages 36 through 41, explain some of the ways in which slaves rebelled, won their freedom, and later built their own lives in the Americas.**

- Slaves sometimes revolted on ships (inset, page 36).
- Slave rebellions started early in the Americas, with one particularly effective rebellion in South Carolina in 1739, according to page 36.
- Some slaves escaped. "Runaway slaves–called **maroons**–built villages deep in jungles, swamps, and mountains."
- "In the Americas," the author asserts on page 38, "slaves from different societies blended their traditions and incorporated European traditions."
- She describes one slave who purchased his freedom "by cutting wood, raising watermelons, and fishing for lobsters," gradually earning enough money to buy his family.

18. **Describe how the author ends her "story" about slavery on pages 42 to 43. Why do you think the author chose to end the book this way?**

   - On these two pages, the author tries to recap the tragic story of slavery but also to offer some hope when, for example, on page 42, she says, "But the slave owners could not chain Africans' hearts and minds."

   - She notes a proverb from the Congo "that says, 'No matter how long the night, the day is sure to come.'"

   - She ends by saying that many people, both enslaved and free, "fought bravely to win their freedom, stop the slave trade, and eventually end slavery."

   - Perhaps the author offers these positive sentiments to remind the reader that ultimately the terrible practice of slavery came to an end.

PERFORMANCE ASSESSMENT

Give students the following task:

- Choose one word to describe the worldwide slave trade. Write an informative/explanatory essay supporting your descriptive word choice with evidence from this text.

Students should write a sentence that introduces their topic, use facts and definitions to develop points, and provide a concluding statement or section. At earlier levels, students may draw or dictate their informative/explanatory text and/or write a label, sentence, or series of related sentences. See standards for more details.

EXTENSION

Have students research the Great Zimbabwe or the Songhay Kingdom and then write an informative/explanatory essay describing two or three cultural features of these advanced African societies.

Ask students to be sure to introduce the topic clearly; develop the topic with facts, details, and examples; link ideas; use precise language and domain-specific vocabulary; and provide a concluding statement. See standards for more detail. At earlier levels, students may write a coherent paragraph that summarizes the main topic and key details.

CONNECTIONS TO COMMON CORE STATE STANDARDS FOR ENGLISH LANGUAGE ARTS

- Question 1 asks students to synthesize information from maps and the text to identify key details related to important concepts (RI.3.1,2,5; RI.4.1,2,5; RI.5.1,2,5).

- Students must identify key details that support a main idea in order to answer questions 2, 6, 7, 12, and 15 (RI.3.1,2; RI.4.1,2; RI.5.1,2).
  - Question 15 also addresses language standards about grammar and vocabulary development, asking students to examine etymology, word parts, parts of speech, and the relationship among the various forms of the word (L.3.1(a); L.3.4,5; L.4.4,5; L.5.4,5).

- Question 3 requires students to cite evidence from the text to support a comparison that the author makes between two different phenomena (RI.3.1,2,3; RI.4.1,2,3; RI.5.1,2,3).

- Questions 4, 5, and 16 ask students to explain cause and effect among important events by tracking key details (RI.3.1,2,3; RI.4.1,2,3; RI.5.1,2,3).
- Questions 8 and 9 address the definitions of key academic vocabulary words and ask students to cite evidence from the text that defines and explains the terms (RI.3.1,2,3,4; RI.4.1,2,3,4; RI.5.1,2,3,4).
  - Question 9 also addresses the interpretation of figurative language and the consideration of illustrations to enhance understanding (RI.3.5; RI.4.5; RI.5.5; L.3.5; L.4.5; L.5.5).
- To answer questions 10, 13, and 17 students must synthesize information from the text insets, photographs, and captions (RI.3.1,2,3,5,7; RI.4.1,2,3,5,7; RI.5.1,2,3,5,7).
- Question 11 requires students to explain the relationship between two sections of text—subsections of a chapter in the text and a related story, told in a nearby inset (RI.3.1,2,3,5; RI.4.1,2,3,5; RI.5.1,2,3,5).
- Question 14 asks students to track one of the author's arguments, describing how she presents evidence to support her assertion that the people involved in the slave trade shifted as slavery expanded globally (RI.3.1,2,3,5,8; RI.4.1,2,3,5,8; RI.5.1,2,3,5,8).
- Question 18 prompts students to consider why the author chose to end the book in a certain way, citing evidence from the text (RI.3.1,2,3,8; RI.4.1,2,3,8; RI.5.1,2,3,8).

MORE RESOURCES

PRIMARY SOURCES

Map of British Empire, 1897 (British Empire)

King's Navy Crackers, advertisement (British Empire)

Victorian advertisement for dolls and toys, 1886 (The British Library)

Scene from the Patna opium factory, from the London weekly magazine, 1882 (The British Library)

Revolutionary France and Haiti resources, 1787–1804 (Newberry Library, Chicago)

USEFUL WEBSITES

Toussaint L'Ouverture biography (History Wiz)

Reenactment video of slavery debate in UK Parliament on February 23, 1807 (YouTube)

The Victorian vision of China and Japan (Victoria and Albert Museum)

    Article with photos of items in the museum collection

National Rivalries: The Eruption of Global Conflict

(1880s to 1918)

GRADES: 3, 4, 5

OVERVIEW

While European colonial expansion exploded in Asia and Africa, powerful new nations and strong political rivalries emerged within Europe itself. Tensions between the Axis and Allied alliances mounted until the assassination of Archduke Franz Ferdinand finally triggered World War I. Innovations in weaponry, including warplanes, poison gas, submarines, and heavy artillery, caused horrific damage on the battlefield. Civilian casualties were vast. *The Donkey of Gallipoli* gives lower elementary students insight into World War I through the eyes of a brave British soldier. Upper elementary students delve deeper into the Great War through a close reading of *Where Poppies Grow* and the celebrated poem "*In Flanders Field,*" leading them to craft a written explanation of the significance of the poppy to soldiers during the devastating war.

○ ○ ○

Interested in learning more about this time period? Read a more complete history in the "Era Summaries."

LEARNING EXPECTATIONS

Lower elementary: Students should understand that Europe's great powers quarreled over who controlled what abroad—even as they pushed at each other for advantages in Europe. The final result was a devastating war that drew in much of the world. Students should also know that science and technology made enormous strides during this period, starting to create the world we would recognize—and making the war far more deadly than any that had come before it.

Upper elementary: Students should understand that rivalries among Europe's imperial powers reinforced the strains caused by the rising power of Germany, finally dividing Europe into armed rival camps. They should know that rising conflicts in the ever-unstable Balkans provided the spark: the 1914 assassination of the heir to the Austro-Hungarian throne by Serbian nationalists threw Austria and its ally Germany against Russia, France, and Britain. The result was the incomprehensible devastation of the First World War. Students should also understand that rapid developments in science and technology—such as electricity, X-rays, automobiles, and radio—helped create a more modern world and escalated the terrible violence of the war.

SUGGESTED ANCHOR TEXTS

"In Flanders Field" by John McCrae
Where Poppies Grow: A World War I Companion by Linda Granfield
Archie's War: My Scrapbook of the First World War, 1914–1918 by Marcia Williams
In Flanders Field: The Story of the Poem by John McCrae by Linda Granfield
In the Trenches in World War I by Adam Hibbert
One Boy's War by Lynn Huggins-Cooper

FEATURED ANCHOR TEXTS

"IN FLANDERS FIELD" BY JOHN MCCRAE
WHERE POPPIES GROW: A WORLD WAR I COMPANION BY LINDA GRANFIELD

This book was selected because of its unique roots in a poem named "In Flanders Field" that recalls the memory of those who fought for freedom in the First World War, often called "The Great War." The illustrations, photographs, and reproductions of primary sources—all beautifully interwoven with text—tell the story of a war that was characterized by new technology that led to massive casualties and fatalities, ranking it among one of the deadliest wars in history. The goal of the author, made clear at the beginning of the text, is to challenge the reader to think deeply about the people who sacrificed their lives so that their descendants could enjoy freedom. In addition to its rendering of the details of the course of the war, the text also discusses many varied aspects of the war, including technology, the treatment of animals, the role of nurses, communication between soldiers and loved ones at home, espionage, and folklore from the war. These varied topics and perspectives make the multifaceted aspects of the war come alive for students. The author's style is engaging, asking questions of the readers that draw them in to the heart of this story.

TEXT STUDIES

These text-dependent questions offer students a chance to examine poetry, primary sources, and other features of this unusual text, such as fact-filled captions to build a rich understanding of the causes, course, and effects of the First World War. Students examine diction, interpret metaphors, and synthesize information from many perspectives in this informational text. Informative/explanatory writing and narrative writing are possibilities for the performance assessment or extension.

"In Flanders Field" by John McCrae

You may want to begin this study with multiple readings of "In Flanders Field" by John McCrae. Written by a Canadian medical officer during the First World War, this was the most popular poem of the Great War. The title of this informational text is taken from the imagery in the poem. This book was also written from a Canadian point of view.

Where Poppies Grow: A World War I Companion by Linda Granfield

1. **According to pages 4 and 5, what were the causes of the "Great War"?**
    - Germany and other European nations "craved more power."
    - France and others "wanted revenge for past wrongs."
    - Britain "feared Germany's growing fleet and industrial power."
    - The heir to the Austro-Hungarian throne was murdered.
    - Germany moved into the neutral country of Belgium.

2. **What does the author mean by the death of the heir to the Austro-Hungarian throne being the "spark that lit this ready tinder?"**
    - The author is comparing "ready tinder," which easily catches fire, to the people being "primed for war." As discussed in the first question, people in different countries were ready for a war to start. It was easy for one event (a spark) to start the war. The text says, "People were primed for war." When the heir to the Austro-Hungarian throne was murdered in June 1914, the war began.

3. **What might the illustrator be trying to show in his choice of the two photographs for page 4?**
    - The illustrator seems to be emphasizing the part of the first paragraph of page 4 that discusses how young many of the soldiers were. The text says, "no one knew that millions of young men and women would die before the conflict ended in 1918."
      - According to the caption of the eighth-grade graduation, the illustrator was showing how some of the male students would enlist in the war, never to return for a class reunion.
      - According to the caption accompanying the picture of the boy, this is a boy who joined the army, claiming to be 18. The boy obviously looks much younger.

4. **In the last paragraph of page 5, what is the author persuading the reader to consider?**
    - The author asks the reader to look at the faces in the old photographs from this era, pause, "and consider who they were."
    - Consider how "their faces are our faces, their deeds our inheritance."
    - The author seems to be asking the reader to consider the sacrifices made by the people in the photographs, the people who gave their lives to fight for what was right. We have inherited the results of their good deeds.

5. **Describe the training before heading into the Great War.**
    - According to pages 6 and 7, men had to train for a new vocation after they enlisted to fight in the war. They learned many new skills.
    - They learned to wear properly the uniform of the army.
      - They learned to cover the color in their kilts with "khaki," the "dust-colored" camouflage for the battlefield or forest.
    - They learned to take care of and carry their seventy-five pounds of a supply kit, ammunition, and weapons.
    - They enhanced their physical fitness by climbing walls.
    - They learned to dig trenches, a skill needed for the fighting in France.
    - They learned to be a soldier by studying a 250-page training manual.

6. **According to page 9, what was the key to success in battle?**

- The picture caption reads, "The main essential to success in battle is to close with the enemy, cost what it may." The soldiers could not be trained to stand back, but to go toward the enemy line and to engage in battle, without a thought of saving themselves.

7. **Describe the Allied "trenches" system in Flanders, as explained on page 10 of the text.**

- The trenches were on the Western Front of the Great War. There were three lines of trenches: "the front line, the support line, and the reserve line."
  - The front line of trenches was near the line of engagement, close to the enemy. Each other line was farther back, but soldiers were able to communicate and move between and through tunnels.

    Note: Teachers might pause to ensure that students understand the use of the word engagement *in this context, examining other forms of the word, its etymology, and its root and affixes (for example,* engage, engaging, engaged*).*

  - The trenches were six feet deep and lined with metal or sandbags.
  - There were wooden boards on the ground to keep the men's feet out of the gathered water and mud.
  - There was a "firing step" from which a soldier fired across "no man's land" toward the enemy in their system of trenches.

    Note: Teachers might want to extend the word study of engagement *to the word* entrenchment, *examining other forms of the word, its etymology, and its root and affixes (for example,* entrench, entrenched, entrenchment*).*

8. **According to pages 16 and 17, what were some of the new technologies used in the First World War?**

- The troops used line telegraphs and field telephones relayed through buried cables to communicate.
- Army tanks were first used during the First World War.
- Poison gas was used and a Canadian invented the gas helmet. Later a "small box respirator" prevented death from the poison gases.

9. **How was the sinking of the luxury liner *Lusitania* related to the war as a cause and an effect of the war for Americans?**

- The German side of the Great War used "U-boats," or submarines, to blow up the Allied ships. As an effect of this tactic, a U-boat blew up the *Lusitania*, killing over one thousand people.
- The attack on the *Lusitania*, which carried U.S. citizens, partially caused the American decision to join the Allies' cause.

10. **What was the purpose of the "dazzle ships"?**

According to page 19, the crazy painting of the British ships confused the enemy U-boats as they tried to aim at the ship above them in the water. The different designs made the boats appear as fewer, smaller ships, an optical illusion to the attacker.

11. **How did the role of planes change during the First World War?**

- According to page 20, the planes were first used for three purposes.
  - They flew to determine the location of the enemies.
  - They flew to make maps.
  - They flew to take photographs.
- Later both Allied and German planes became weapons, "attack machines in the air."

- This change is further illustrated by the caption accompanying the photographs of the dual uses of the German Zeppelins. They were used first as a means for romantic travel in the air for passengers. During the war, they carried bombs.

12. **According to this text, what was propaganda? What are some of the examples of propaganda seen on pages 24 and 25?**

- On page 24, the author defines *propaganda* as "information sent out to help or damage a cause." It was an attempt "to change the emotions and opinions of people." Propaganda was seen in multiple forms: "posters, paintings, songs, and literature."

   Note: *Teachers might want to discuss the meaning of the word* propagate *as the origin of the word* propaganda.

- The caption notes that these images provoked "emotional responses designed to boost morale and commitment to the war effort."

- There are multiple examples of propaganda in this section of text.
   - We see a reproduction of a page from a children's book that appeals to one's sense of patriotism by discussing the symbolism of the colors in the flag: red, white, and blue.
   - The "Woodrow Wilson and flag" image appeals to Americans' love for their flag and underscores the president's support for the war.
   - One postcard shows a German soldier feeding a baby, whose mother he had killed. It was designed to make the French hate the Germans.
   - One painting shows a drunk German soldier, lying on a bed, reminding the French that the German army often commandeered, or took over, houses for their own use.

13. **According to pages 32 and 33, how did John McCrae's poem actually help the war effort?**

   Note: *This poem is a sonnet. Teachers may choose to pause and explain this form of poetry.*

   Be sure to have students read and analyze the poem, if there is time, but especially the final stanza.

- One caption explains that the poem was published in a popular magazine early in the war and that it became the most popular poem of the war. We can infer that reading it inspired others to fight in or at least support the war.

- Another caption explains that the final stanza's "call-to-arms" was used to recruit more soldiers.

- Those same words were used to raise "victory loan bonds" in Canada, raising four hundred million dollars.

14. **According to pages 38 and 39, how did animals help with the war effort?**

- Horses were used for transportation by European troops.

- Pigeons were used to carry cameras that photographed the enemy troops. They were also used to carry messages.

- Although dogs were enjoyed as a comfort from home, they also were trained to carry messages, to act as guards, and to locate wounded men.

   Note: *Be sure to share with children the A. A. Milne inspiration for Winnie the Pooh as related to the Canadian soldier's pet bear.*

15. **Why might the author have chosen to include the sections, "Dear Cora . . ." and "Dear Amy"?**

- The author may have been returning to her technique at the beginning of the text, where she asked the reader to consider the cost of freedom to real people.
   - The "Dear Cora" section was about a real soldier, part of a family, who died in the Great War.
   - The "Dear Amy" pages were about a soldier who was weakened by poison gas before returning to his family.

16. **Describe how the poppy flower became a symbol for remembering.**
    - According to page 44, the war ended on Armistice Day, "at the 11th hour of the 11th day of the 11th month" in 1918.
    - The poppy flower had been a symbol to the soldiers in Flanders Field of loss and accomplishment.
    - Because of the flower's prominence in the McCrae poem, a woman from Georgia decided the "Flanders poppy" should become the "memorial flower."
    - "Poppy mania" spread all over the world, representing "the remembrance of life, sacrifice, and honor."

PERFORMANCE ASSESSMENT

Give students the following task:

- Write an informative/explanatory essay explaining the symbolism of the poppy from the First World War. Use evidence from the text to support the ideas of "life, sacrifice, and honor."

Students should write a sentence that introduces their topic, use facts and definitions to develop points, and provide a concluding statement or section. At earlier levels, students may draw or dictate their informative/explanatory text and/or write a label, sentence, or series of related sentences. See standards for more details.

EXTENSION

Have students create an illustrated picture book using the poem "In Flanders Field" as their text.

CONNECTIONS TO COMMON CORE STATE STANDARDS FOR ENGLISH LANGUAGE ARTS

- Questions 1, 5, 7, 8, 9, 10, 11, 12, 14, and 16 ask students to explain key details from the text that are related to its central ideas (RI.3.1,2; RI.4.1,2; RI.5.1,2).
  - Question 9 also asks students to make connections among events and details, considering cause and effect (RI.3.3; RI.4.3; RI.5.3).
  - Question 12 also requires students to examine the meaning of academic vocabulary words and to explain the significance of the reproductions of primary sources (RI.3.4,7; RI.4.4,7; RI.5.4,7; L.3.4; L.4.4; L.5.4).
- Question 2 requires students to interpret a metaphor that relates to key historical content (RI.3.1,2,4; RI.4.1,2,4; RI.5.1,2,4; L.3.5; L.4.5; L.5.5).
- Using the photographs and their captions in conjunction with the actual text on the first page, students must infer the illustrator's purpose in choosing to include certain photographs at the outset of the text in order to answer question 3 (RI.3.5,7,8; RI.4.5,7,8; RI.5.5,7,8).
- To answer question 4, students must analyze the author's style and purpose (RI.3.6,8; RI.4.6,8; RI.5.6,8).

- Students must draw information from the caption to answer question 6 about a key detail (RI.3.1,5; RI.4.1,5; RI.5.1,5).

- Question 13 asks students to explain the relationship between the theme and import of a poem about the war and the war effort at home, as described in the text and captions. It asks students to examine the poem, written by a medical officer during the war, which offers students a firsthand account of events (RI.3.1,2,3,5,6; RI.4.1,2,3,5,6; RI.5.1,2,3,5,6).

- Question 15 addresses the author's purpose and her decision to include certain information (RI.3.1,2,3,8; RI.4.1,2,3,8; RI.5.1,2,3,8).

- The performance assessment gives students a chance to explain the symbolism of the title by citing evidence from the text in an informative/explanatory essay about the main idea of the text (RI.3.1,2,3,4,8; RI.4.1,2,3,4,8; RI.5.1,2,3,4,8; W.3.2,9; W.4.2,9; W.5.2,9).

- The extension enables students to interpret and illustrate the poem in a narrative essay ("picture book") and simultaneously convey their understanding of the text (RL.3.1,2,4; RL.4.1,2,4; RL.5.1,2,4; RI.3.1,2,3,4; RI.4.1,2,3,4; RI.5.1,2,3,4; L.3.5; L.4.5; L.5.5; W.3.3,9; W.4.3,9; W.5.3,9).

MORE RESOURCES

PRIMARY SOURCES

Boer soldiers fight in trenches during the Boer War, 1899–1902 (Encyclopedia Britannica Kids)

"Spain to Use Privateers; An Official Decree Declares That She Is Determined to Reserve This Right," Headline, April 24, 1898 (*New York Times*)

Images from the Philippine-U.S. War (Historical Text Archive)

Propaganda of the Russo-Japanese War (MIT–Visualizing Cultures)

The *Black Ship Scroll*, 1854 (MIT–Visualizing Cultures)

Teddy Roosevelt's Nobel Peace Prize speech, 1910 (Nobel Prize)

HMS *Dreadnought*, 1906 (Naval History and Heritage Command)

The Bolsheviks storm the Winter Palace, 1917 (Eyewitness to History)

The Sinking of the Titanic, 1912 (Eyewitness to History)

Letters home from a soldier in the First World War (Letters Home from the War)

First World War eyewitness accounts (Eyewitness to History)

POETRY AND MUSIC

"The Hills of Manchuria," Russian folk song (Stanford University)

"War Sonnets" by Rupert Brooke, WWI poetry (Emory University)

USEFUL WEBSITES

The Road to War: The Triple Alliance (BBC)

Photos of the Great War (Great War Primary Documents Archive, Inc.)

Depression after Versailles: The Rise of Totalitarian Powers

(1919 to 1930s)
GRADES: 3, 4, 5

OVERVIEW

The plans to end World War I had humanitarian intentions, but the desire for vengeance on Germany made the Treaty of Versailles a settlement that heavily favored the victors. From a destabilized Europe, the new phenomenon of totalitarianism emerged in the regimes of Hitler and Stalin. Japanese nationalists moved to reclaim dominance in Asia. Meanwhile, scientists discovered how to unleash atomic energy and create weapons of hitherto unimagined destruction. Closely reading *On a Beam of Light* lets K–2 students explain how the famous scientist unlocked scientific mysteries. Older students will understand Communist Russia through a close read of an informational article about Stalin and the novel *Breaking Stalin's Nose*. They will then defend an opinion about whether Stalin was "an enemy of the people."

○ ○ ○

Interested in learning more about this time period? Read a more complete history in the "Era Summaries."

LEARNING EXPECTATIONS

Lower elementary: Students should know that the First World War left Europe badly divided, with defeated Germany and its allies deeply embittered by the Allies' harsh peace terms. They should understand that extremists, who opposed basic ideas of human freedom, used that anger and the economic crisis of the Great Depression to seize power—especially in Germany, where Adolf Hitler's dangerous Nazi Party took control. Other oppressive regimes, particularly Stalin's brutal one in the Soviet Union, also menaced their own people with murder and terror. Meanwhile, rapid scientific advancements enriched people's lives—but they would also make future wars much more dangerous.

Upper elementary: Students should understand that post-war chaos and alarm over Russia's Communist revolution helped promote the rise of authoritarian, anti-Communist Fascism in Italy; in Germany, anger over the humiliating Treaty of Versailles fueled the rise of Hitler's Nazi Party, which rose to power as the widespread despair of the Great Depression increased the people's desperation. In the Soviet Union, Stalin used state-sponsored terror and probably even deliberately engineered a massive famine to ruthlessly control the nation. Students should understand the racial obsession of the Nazis and the dire consequences it entailed for Jews, Slavs, and others. Students should also realize that the rapidly changing world of science gave free and totalitarian governments new tools, quickly advancing technology and making war more dangerous. They should also be aware that Nazi distortions of these new sciences helped bolster their warped ideas of racial purity.

SUGGESTED ANCHOR TEXTS

"Joseph Stalin (1879–1953)" by BBC History
Breaking Stalin's Nose by Eugene Yelchin
Albert Einstein and Relativity for Kids: His Life and Ideas with 21 Activities and Thought Experiments by Jerome Pohlen
Bomb: The Race to Build and Steal the World's Most Dangerous Weapon by Steve Sheinkin
Marie Curie: A Photographic Story of a Life by Vicki Cobb

FEATURED ANCHOR TEXTS

"JOSEPH STALIN (1879–1953)" BY BBC HISTORY
BREAKING STALIN'S NOSE BY EUGENE YELCHIN

The BBC article about Joseph Stalin gives students essential background information about the Soviet leader, which helps students to understand the setting of the novel *Breaking Stalin's Nose*. The informational text is also filled with essential vocabulary words such as *Marxist* and *purges*, giving students another opportunity to discuss the meanings of these words in a compelling context. Students can also use the article as a source for any timeline or biography work they might do as a part of their study on Communist Russia.

The book was chosen because it is a Newbery Honor book and tells the story of Soviet Communism from the viewpoint of a young boy living through its early years. Throughout the book, the reader sees how Sasha, the young boy, has been duped by the propaganda from the Soviet regime. By prefacing this text study with an examination of an informational article on Stalin, students will read *Breaking Stalin's Nose* with newly formed background knowledge to compare the "real Stalin" with the Stalin Sasha refuses to see.

TEXT STUDIES

These text-dependent questions help students examine—and appreciate the differences between—events as told objectively in an informational article and as told through the eyes of a young child narrator of a novel. The questions focus on students' ability to track details and relate them to main ideas, examine important academic vocabulary words, recognize irony (although that term is not used here), and synthesize information from both texts in order to form an opinion on the topic and render that opinion, using evidence from the texts, in an opinion essay.

"Joseph Stalin (1879–1953)" by BBC History

1. **According to the italicized introduction to the BBC article on Joseph Stalin, what are the words and phrases used to describe him and his rule?**

    - The words and phrases used to describe Stalin and his rule are as follows.
      - "one of the most powerful and murderous dictators in history"
      - "supreme ruler of the Soviet Union" for twenty-five years
      - "regime of terror"
      - "caused the death and suffering of tens of millions"

2. **Communism is a system of organizing society with property held in common and actually owned by the community or the state. Someone who believes in Communism is called a Communist. How does the article describe Stalin's participation in the Communist party and how did his activism in the party help him later?**

    - He "rose through the ranks of the party," and in 1922 was named the general secretary of the party, "a post not considered particularly significant at the time but which gave him control over appointments and thus allowed him to build up a base of support."

3. **"Collectivization of agriculture" is "collective farming." In the Soviet Union, under Stalin, peasant farm owners were required to combine their farms and farm them in community, supervised by the state. Using other evidence in this article, what might the text mean by this "collectivization" costing "millions of lives"?**

    - The reader can infer from the text description of Stalin being a murderous dictator and his "regime of terror" that he probably forced people to put their farms together as true Communists or he killed them.

      Note: This idea can be explored further with research. The goal here is simply for students to see that the phrase cost millions of lives is connected to the Communist idea. This will give background knowledge for the students to note the required communal living and the fear of Stalin in the historical fiction.

      Teachers may choose to study the word collectivization: its etymology, its related word forms—including their parts of speech—and its root and affixes, in order to appreciate the concept of collectivism (for example, collect, collection, collector, collectively).

4. **According to this article, what was the "Great Terror of the 1930s"? What was the effect of these purges?**

    - The Great Terror of the 1930s was a time when Stalin executed thousands of people, thought to be "enemies of the people." He also exiled "millions to the gulag system of slave labor camps."

    - When Stalin "purged" the people who were enemies within his ranks, he caused his army to be depleted, or decreased, to the point that he struggled to defend his country.

      Note: Teachers may choose to study the word purge: its etymology, its related word forms—including their parts of speech—and its root and affixes, in order to appreciate its use in this context (for example, purger, purgatory, expurgate).

5. **What does this article mean when it says, "The human cost was enormous, but was not a consideration for him"?**

    - This means that Stalin did not really care about the human lives that were lost under his rule.

Breaking Stalin's Nose by Eugene Yelchin

Chapters 1 through 6

1. **According to chapter 1, why was Sasha, a Communist child, writing a letter to Stalin? How does he feel about the children growing up in a Capitalist country, a country where people are able to own their own land and make personal profit?**

   - Sasha was writing to thank Stalin for his life and to make some promises.
     - Sasha was writing to thank Stalin for his happy childhood and for the opportunity to be a "Young Pioneer."
     - He promised Stalin to exercise, to "forge" his Communist character and to be "vigilant."
   - Sasha pities the children who grow up in Capitalism.
     - Their lives are hard.
     - They won't see dreams come true.

   Note: *Teachers may choose first to examine the word* capitalist: *its etymology, its related word forms—including their parts of speech—and its root and affixes, in order to appreciate its use in this context (for example,* capitalism *and* capital, *used as a noun and as an adjective).*

2. **According to chapter 2, how do Sasha's living arrangements show more about Communist beliefs?**

   - There are forty-eight "hardworking, honest Soviet citizens" sharing a kitchen and one toilet, living together in one communal apartment.
   - Sasha makes the point that everyone who lives in the apartment is equal and there are no secrets.
   - They have bookshelves with books about Stalin.
   - Their living shows an attitude of "we" instead of the capitalist attitude of "I."
   - They line up and sing patriotic songs together in the morning.

   Note: *You will want to review the definition of* Communism *in question 2. These facts about the living arrangements illustrate the lack of individual ownership and the power of the communal attitude. The limited reading and the commitment to patriotism show an almost godlike worship of their leader.*

3. **What does the reader learn about the secret police in chapter 3? How does Sasha feel about the carrot, and how does he relate it to Capitalism?**

   - The reader learns that the job of the secret police is to "unmask the disguised enemies 'infiltrating'" the borders of the Soviet Union. The reader learns that Sasha's father is in the secret police, working for Stalin. The reader learns that Stalin regarded a secret policeman as an "iron broom purging the vermin from our midst."
   - Sasha regards the carrot as a treat he enjoys only "now and then," showing that he doesn't have a lot of food to eat. He thinks that children who live in Capitalist countries do not have carrots and probably have "never even tasted" one.

4. **How does the reader know that the people in the apartment fear Sasha's dad?**

   - At the beginning of chapter 4, Sasha comments that people in the apartment stop talking when his dad walks in. Sasha then comments about how the people "look like they are afraid," but he knows "they are just respectful."
   - At the end of the chapter, his dad knocks on the wall, signaling silence, and the music stops immediately. Again, Sasha comments about how people respect his dad, but the reader knows the man is really afraid of his dad, a secret policeman.

- Throughout this chapter, the reader sees what Sasha does not. His father is a secret policeman, and people are terrified of what he could do to them. They do not "respect" him so much as they fear him.

5. **Describe the behavior of Stukachov in chapter 4.**

- Stukachov kept following Sasha and his dad.

- When Sasha and his dad went into their spacious room, Stukachov looked into the room.

- Sasha's dad did not trust Stukachov and warned Sasha not to trust him.

6. **From what you know about Stalin from the informational article, is Sasha correct to think in chapter 5, "nothing could happen to my dad: Stalin needs him"? What does this show you about Sasha?**

- Sasha is not right to believe his dad is safe from Stalin. According to the article, during Stalin's reign of terror, he was constantly looking for enemies of the state within his ranks. He exiled or murdered so many people during this period that he did not have enough men to have a full army.

- Sasha believes what the State has taught him about Stalin. His blind trust in Stalin is the reason he believes his dad is safe and that his dad is respected, not feared.

7. **According to chapter 5, why was Stukachov following Sasha and his dad around in the apartment?**

- Stukachov had turned Sasha's dad into the authorities and was planning to move into the large room in the apartment.

8. **According to chapter 6, what will happen to Sasha now that his father is gone?**

- According to pages 27 and 31, he will come under the care of the State and go to an orphanage.

Chapters 7 through 10

9. **Gather evidence from chapters 7 through 10 that illustrates Sasha's opinion of Stalin.**

- Sasha believes that Stalin is a caretaker of his people.
  - "Stalin is busy; he has to take care of all of us, millions all over the country" (page 32).

- When Sasha imagines telling Stalin about his dad's arrest, he imagines Stalin will consider releasing him as an emergency.
  - "Special unit! Emergency! Wrench Zaichik's dad from the traitors' claws!" (pages 35–36).
  - "As soon as Stalin finds out, my dad is coming back" (page 40).

- Sasha has so much respect for Stalin, he sets aside the stack of papers with Stalin's picture on the front, not using those to make a bed (page 43).

- Sasha holds out hope that Stalin cares deeply about his dad's release.
  - "Tomorrow everything will be better. Tomorrow Stalin will rescue my dad" (page 45).

Note: You may want to lead a point-of-view discussion with the class, contrasting the informational article's description of Stalin as a leader of the Soviet people and Sasha's viewpoint as a young citizen under his leadership.

Chapters 11 through 13

10. According to these chapters, who are those considered by the Soviet citizens as "enemies of the people"?

- On page 48, Sasha is called "Amerikanetz" because of his mother. Sasha's father had warned him never to tell anyone that his mother was an American because Americans were considered enemies of the people. When Sasha hears, "Death to the enemy of the people!" he is even more afraid that more students know he is part American.

- On page 49, "Four-Eyes" was the student they were calling as "enemy of the people." He is the only Jewish student in class and his parents were arrested earlier in the year.

- On page 52, Sasha was called a "traitor" because he was not willing to join in the bullying of "Four-Eyes," which would have proven his loyalty to "the people." Anyone who did not join them was "against them."

  Note: There could be an interesting discussion regarding the teacher's comment on page 60 about those "who vote against the majority." Was the teacher implying those who have their own opinion are also enemies of the people?

Chapters 14 through 16

11. According to chapter 16, how does Sasha imagine things will go if he is discovered as the person who accidentally broke the statue's nose? According to the text thus far, why does Sasha think so much will happen as a result of a mere accident?

- Sasha imagines that a whole chain of events will happen if he is found out.
  - He will "never become a Pioneer."
  - He will be reported to State Security for doing "an act of terrorism."
  - Everyone will find out who did it, and he will be arrested.
  - He will become "an enemy of the people" because he has "defaced a sacred statue of Stalin."

- Although Sasha says he believes that Stalin wants the best and is a protector of his people, this reaction shows that Sasha now lives in fear of being on the wrong side of Stalin's favor.

Chapters 17 through 30

12. Consider this quotation from chapter 24: "when we blindly believe in someone else's idea of what is right or wrong for us as individuals, sooner or later our refusal to make our own choices could lead to the collapse of the entire political system. An entire country. The world, even." How did Sasha finally show that he could make his own choice?

- He refused to renounce his father (page 134).

- He chooses to run from being a Pioneer (page 141).

PERFORMANCE ASSESSMENT

Give your students the following task:

- In your opinion, was Sasha "an enemy of the people" at the end of the story? Support your opinion with at least two pieces of text evidence.

Students should write a sentence that introduces their topic, use facts and definitions to develop points, and provide a concluding statement or section. At earlier levels, students may draw or dictate their informative/explanatory text and/or write a label, sentence, or series of related sentences. See standards for more details.

CONNECTIONS TO COMMON CORE STATE STANDARDS FOR ENGLISH LANGUAGE ARTS

"Joseph Stalin (1879–1953)" by BBC History

- Question 1 asks students to identify key words and phrases in an introduction that relate to larger important historical concepts in the article to follow (RI.3.1,2,4; RI.4.1,2,4; RI.5.1,2,4).

- Question 2 addresses an important academic vocabulary word and asks students about some key details from the text related to the term (RI.3.1,2,3,4; RI.4.1,2,3,4; RI.5.1,2,3,4; L.3.4; L.4.4; L.5.4).

- Question 3 asks students to examine and analyze an important historical term (academic vocabulary) as well as some related grammatical concepts; they must use this knowledge to glean and infer more information from the text (RI.3.1,2,3,4; RI.4.1,2,3,4; RI.5.1,2,3,4; L.3.1,4,5; L.4.1,4,5; L.5.1,4,5).

- Question 4 also asks students to examine and analyze an important historical term (academic vocabulary) as well as some related grammatical concepts. They must also explain the effect generated by the phenomenon referred to through the use of the term (RI.3.1,2,3,4; RI.4.1,2,3,4; RI.5.1,2,3,4; L.3.1,4,5; L.4.1,4,5; L.5.1,4,5).

- Students must use knowledge from the text to interpret a quotation from the article to answer question 5 (RI.3.1,2,3; RI.4.1,2,3; RI.5.1,2,3).

Breaking Stalin's Nose by Eugene Yelchin

- To answer question 1, students must examine an academic vocabulary word and be able to understand and explain it in the context of events described in the text. They must also identify key details and explain their relationship to the main ideas in the text (RI.3.1,2,3,4; RI.4.1,2,3,4; RI.5.1,2,3,4; L.3.1,4; L.4.1,4; L.5.1,4).

- Questions 2, 3, and 11 require students to track key details and explain how they support a main idea (RI.3.1,2,3; RI.4.1,2,3; RI.5.1,2,3).

- Question 4 asks students to note the differences between how events are perceived differently by the storyteller on the one hand and the readers on the other (RI.3.1,2,3,6; RI.4.1,2,3,6; RI.5.1,2,3,6).

- Questions 5, 7, 8, 10, and 12 require students to track key details in the text (RI.3.1,2; RI.4.1,2; RI.5.1,2).

- Question 6 gives students a chance to compare details from the informational article to events and characters' attitudes in the historical narrative. Students must synthesize information from both texts in order to recognize the dramatic irony here (students don't necessarily have to be introduced to this term now) and explain the character's beliefs (RI.3.1,2,3,6; RI.4.1,2,3,6; RI.5.1,2,3,6; RL.3.3; RL.4.3; RL.5.3).

- Question 9 is similar to question 11 in that it gives students a chance to compare the informational article to events and character's attitudes in the historical narrative; in this case, the question focuses more on the contrast in points of view (RI.3.1,2,3,6; RI.4.1,2,3,6; RI.5.1,2,3,6; RL.3.3; RL.4.3; RL.5.3).

Performance Assessment

- The performance assessment enables students to synthesize information from two types of texts to formulate an opinion and present it in an opinion essay, citing evidence to support their assertions (RI.3.1,2,3,6,8; RI.4.1,2,3,6,8; RI.5.1,2,3,6,8; W.3.1,9; W.4.1,9; W.5.1,9).

MORE RESOURCES

PRIMARY SOURCES

President Wilson's Fourteen Points, 1918 (The World War I Document Archive)

League of Nations photo archive

Photos of Mustafa Kemal Ataturk (Wikimedia Commons)

Portrait of Josef Stalin, 1936 (Josef Stalin Archive)

Weimar Republic notes used as wallpaper, 1923 (Ludwig von Mises Institute, U.S.A.)

Election results in Germany, 1924–1933 (Rise of Fascism in Germany Index)

USEFUL WEBSITES

Versailles official website (Chateau de Versailles)
    Includes history, photography, and collection info

The Ending of World War One and the Legacy of Peace (BBC History)

Rise of the Nazi Party timeline (A Teacher's Guide to the Holocaust)

Einstein for Kids

Global Calamity: Appeasement Fails and Global Conflict Returns

(mid-1930s to 1945)

GRADES: 3, 4, 5

OVERVIEW

Fascist movements that emerged in Europe lured the masses through propaganda filled with hatred for invented enemies and with the expectation of conquest and prosperity. Alliances shifted throughout World War II, and war raged until the United States and its allies defeated the German-Italian-Japanese Axis in 1945. But victory came at an enormous cost: an estimated eighty million people died, entire cities were devastated, and weapons appeared that had the potential to destroy the entire planet. Younger students who closely read *Always Remember Me* will gain insight into how life changed for German Jewish families because of World War II. *Remember World War II* deepens student understanding of the worldwide conflict through primary sources that document daily life during World War II.

o o o

Interested in learning more about this time period? Read a more complete history in the "Era Summaries."

LEARNING EXPECTATIONS

Lower elementary: Students should understand that Europe's dictatorial Fascist regimes steadily became a greater threat to their neighbors in the 1930s. Hitler's Nazi Germany believed the German people were superior to all others, and he was set on making them masters of the world. Students should know that international attempts to appease the Nazis by agreeing to their demands failed and only led Hitler to make more demands. Nazi aggression finally sparked a catastrophic global war that witnessed previously unseen atrocities.

Upper elementary: Students should understand that the Fascist regimes in Europe—Germany and Italy—and the militarist nationalists in Japan became a growing threat to world peace in the 1930s. Germany and Japan especially viewed themselves as inherently superior people and looked to rule huge stretches of the world. Hitler, determined to make the Germans Europe's master race, was the most immediate threat. The Western democracies tried to deal with him through appeasement, agreeing to his demands in the hopes that he would be satisfied. But by 1939, it was clear that there was no limit to Hitler's ambitions: the more he was allowed to take, the more he would demand. War finally erupted, and Hitler swept across Europe, unleashing systematic atrocities and exterminations on a scale that had never been seen before. Hitler's invasion of the massive Soviet Union began to bog down in 1941. Nationalist Japan, which was determined to take full control of the Pacific, brought the powerful United States into the war. At an enormous cost, the Allies finally defeated the German-Italian-Japanese Axis.

SUGGESTED ANCHOR TEXTS

Remember World War II: Kids Who Survived Tell Their Stories by Dorinda Makanaonalani Nicholson
Irena's Jars of Secrets by Marcia Vaughan
Living through World War II by Andrew Langley
Rose Blanche by Roberto Innocente
The Grand Mosque of Paris: A Story of How Muslims Rescued Jews during the Holocaust by Karen Gray Ruelle
The Great Skating Race by Louise Borden
The House Baba Built by Ed Young
World War II for Kids: A History with 21 Activities by Richard Panchyk

FEATURED ANCHOR TEXT

REMEMBER WORLD WAR II: KIDS WHO SURVIVED TELL THEIR STORIES BY DORINDA MAKANAONALANI NICHOLSON

This book was selected because it tells the story, from multiple viewpoints, of the Second World War as the war evolved to include more and more countries. The strong informational text is seamlessly interwoven with various children's vivid accounts of the war. Photographs, maps, and a wide variety of primary sources lend depth and credibility to this text. The story of war is told in three sections: the beginning of the war in Europe, the coming of war to the Pacific, and the home front in America. In this world history–focused lesson, we chose to focus on the events in Europe and the Pacific.

TEXT STUDY

The Second World War is not an easy topic to teach children. It is filled with the horrors of intolerance, torture, and death. You will want to select from among these passages the ones most appropriate for your students based on what your students can handle. The featured anchor text makes selective passage choice possible and still is able to convey the key events of the war to the students. The text also exhibits the efficacy of many useful structures of informational text, such as an introduction from Madeleine Albright (former secretary of state), a table of contents, maps, an epilogue, an annotated timeline, postscripts about where the children are today, a bibliography, and an index. We have written questions for many passages, some of which you may choose to skip or modify based on your own priorities and students' needs.

These text-dependent questions and performance assessments represent multiple opportunities for students to analyze and compare primary and secondary sources about the Second World War. They are asked to evaluate structural features of informational text, to track details and relate them to main ideas, to recognize cause-and-effect relationships, and even to interpret characters' actions, as in a literary text.

1. **Look closely at the cover of the book. How are the title and subtitle of the book related to the cover illustration?**

   - The title of the book is *Remember World War II*. The cover photograph shows early models of cars driving in a bombed-out neighborhood, filled with debris and destruction.

   - The subtitle of the book is *Kids Who Survived Tell Their Stories*. The photograph shows children sitting on a log, looking out at the devastation in a neighborhood, perhaps a neighborhood where they lived.

2. **According to Madeleine Albright's introduction, why was she "lucky"? What did she learn sixty years later that made her realize how fortunate she really was?**

   - According to the text on page 9, Albright was lucky because she was able to escape Czechoslovakia a year after Hitler had invaded her home country. She was able to live in England while her father worked for his home government.

   - When she was the U.S. secretary of state in 1997, she learned that she was Jewish and that three of her "grandparents and numerous other family members had perished in Nazi death camps."

Chapter 1, "World War II Begins in Europe"

3. **According to the caption below Hitler's photograph on page 10, how did Hitler find so many followers among the German people? What is the effect of calling him "the most dangerous man in Europe"?**

   - Hitler was a "brilliant speaker."
     - His speaking style was to begin slowly and quietly and offer simple solutions for the problems in the country. He then became more passionate and his voice "raised into a full fury."
     - He planned his gestures to pull people into "adoring submission."

   - The closing comment about Hitler being "the most dangerous man in Europe" makes the reader think about how his speaking style was deceptive, fooling people into trusting someone who would eventually cause them harm.

4. **According to page 11, how does the author describe Germany in 1933? What did Hitler say to give the German people hope?**

   - Germany was bitter and angry over the Treaty of Versailles, ending the First World War. They were poor, "food was scarce," and they had "lost hope."

   - Hitler made promises to the people of Germany.
     - He promised to regain the areas of land lost in the war.
     - He promised to create jobs.
     - He promised to have plenty to eat.

5. **How did young Olga Held's account of the Nazi parade in Nuremberg support the idea that Hitler's tactics were dangerous but also that they were resonating with the German people?**

  - Hitler's tactics were resonating with the German people, as demonstrated by the tremendous admiration he seemed to inspire.
    - She describes thousands of people "hailing" Hitler with a stiff-armed salute as he rode into the parade grounds, showing how he had become a person of great stature in their country.

      Note: Look at the people's faces in the photograph on page 12.

    - Olga described his blue eyes as "piercing," showing her admiration of the way he looked in person.
    - She also had an elated response to the fact that Hitler shook her hand, saying she was thrilled and boasting, "Our führer shook hands with me."
    - The entire description suggests that the crowds were caught up in—and fueled by—the excitement that his presence engendered.

  - Olga's father's response to her excitement suggests that he found the enthusiasm of the crowd to be very dangerous. In response to her "boasting" about Hitler shaking her hand, her father "just looked down at me and didn't say one word."

  - We can infer that her father was disdainful, or at least suspicious, of Hitler's dangerous ideas and beliefs.

6. **According to the picture caption on the bottom of page 12, why did Hitler target Jewish people as enemies?**

  - Hitler "believed his followers were part of a superior master race called Aryans."

  - Hitler blamed Germany's problems on the Jewish people.

7. **According to page 13, what was the event that caused the "night of broken glass" or *Kristallnacht*? What happened on that night? How did Hitler exploit this event?**

  - A Jewish teenager named Herschel Grynszpan killed a German diplomat in revenge for the way his parents were mistreated. They had been living in Germany, but because of their Jewish ethnicity, they were sent back to Poland.

  - On November 9, 1938, all of the Jewish people, their homes, their businesses, and their synagogues were attacked. There was so much broken glass, they called it "crystal night" or the "night of broken glass."

  - Hitler used this event to encourage a night of attacks across the whole country of Germany, punishing all of the Jewish people for the act of that one young man.

8. **What does Hedi's narrative, on page 14, add to the informational telling of the attacks on the Jewish people?**

  - Hedi's story tells how this hatred toward Jews was experienced in a Jewish family. Her story makes it personal and detailed.
    - The Nazis broke all of the windows and furniture in their apartment when they came to seize her father.
    - The Nazis took Hedi's father and uncle and marched them through the streets in pajamas and chains. Hedi never saw them again.
    - She adds the poignant detail about her mother hanging out the window with her to call to the father and let him know that mother and daughter were "safe" together, but that they never knew if he had heard them.
    - Hedi lived in such fear that she could not sleep by herself or use the bathroom alone.
    - She was sent away to England, along with ten thousand other children, to live in foster care until the war was over. She never saw her parents again.

9. **How do the stories of Jirina, Fred, Solange, and Olga add to the multiple viewpoints of this period of history?**

- Each of these young people tells a story from a differing viewpoint. It helps to see how various groups of people of distinct ethnicities in different countries all experienced the war, because it progressed in a variety of ways.
  - Jirina lived in a Czechoslovakian village, which was taken over by Nazi soldiers after all of the Jewish neighbors had been sent away. Her story shows how villages and people were affected by the Nazi invasion of Czechoslovakia in March 1939.
  - Fred, training to be one of the German "Jungvolk," was returning from a training mission with others when they were told to return home immediately. His story tells of the German youths' "programming" to be loyal to Hitler and the beginning of the war in September 1939.
  - Solange tells of the failed attempt to flee her village in Belgium and escape to France. When she and her family returned home, they had to share their home with Nazi soldiers. Her story tells how the Nazi invasion and Belgium's surrender affected the people of Belgium in May 1940.
  - Olga tells the story from the German point of view, because she was told to work twelve hours a day on a farm picking hops. Her story tells how the absence of men to work on the farms caused children like Olga to help carry the load of work on the home front of Germany.

10. **According to pages 22 through 24, what happened to Hedi's parents back in Kippenheim, Germany?**

- The Jewish people, including Hedi's parents, were "forced from their homes into drab army trucks with German soldiers standing guard."
- Her parents were sent to a camp in France on October 22, 1940.
- Both parents ended up being sent to Auschwitz in 1942. They died there in the death camp.

11. **Lilly's story helps the reader to understand the differences among the ghetto, the death camp, and a slave labor camp. Explain the differences among each of these from the evidence in Lilly's story on pages 24 through 26.**

- According to page 24, the ghetto was "a confined area" in one section of town where the Jews were forced to go before they were deported to the camps. People in this particular ghetto would have to sleep in barracks. People would work in the brick factory. Some families would leave in trucks and never return.
- People would travel by train, layered on one another, to Auschwitz, a death camp. Inhumanly treated from the time they arrived, they were cold and hungry until they met death in the gas chambers.
- The slave labor camp was a place where the stronger workers from the death camp would go to work. In this case, the workers were making ammunition for the German army. The workers were not free, but they did not face certain death.

12. **According to pages 26 and 27, what was important about D-Day?**

- D-Day, June 6, 1944, was the day "Hitler's Europe" was invaded. The Allied forces landed on the beach in Normandy, France.
- D-Day began the saving of Paris, France. The Allies were able to arrive early enough and strong enough to save Paris from the burning about which Hitler had warned.

13. **According to pages 27 through 29, what events led to the end of the war in Europe?**

- The Battle of the Bulge in December 1944 ended with 120,000 to 200,000 of Hitler's best soldiers gone. He had run out of soldiers with which to replace them.

- In February 1945, the Allied forces advanced to Berlin. Hitler realized the war was over and refused to surrender. He committed suicide. His Secret Service and the Hitler Youth fought to the end. Russia flew the Soviet flag from the top of the German Parliament in victory.

Chapter 3, "War Comes to the Pacific"

14. **The Japanese attack on Pearl Harbor, an American port, occurred in Hawaii on December 7, 1941. How does each child add a unique perspective to the account of the attack on Pearl Harbor?**

- Thompson was American born and his father was born in Japan, but living in Hawaii. Father and son were fishing nearby when they heard the swarm of Japanese planes speeding toward them. It was hard to be Japanese in a place that Japan had attacked. They were immediately evacuated to a sugarcane field and guarded by American soldiers.

- Judy was the daughter of a Navy carpenter stationed in Hawaii. Her father had to go to work immediately and she was given the assignment to watch for enemy paratroopers. They had to live in total blackout, ready to fight the Japanese in case they invaded. The main text explains how life changed after the attack, and Judy adds details, such as the fact that they had to know how to go into shelters during a possible air raid, how to put on gas masks, and how to execute other safety routines in case of attack. Eventually Judy, her mom, and her sister were evacuated to mainland America.

- Joy describes what it was like to be a British family living in the Philippines during a very similar attack two days after Pearl Harbor. She tells how the Japanese took her house for their headquarters, allowing them to take only one suitcase for the family when they left. The photograph on page 39 shows the crowded quarters where the men had to stay at the university after the invasion. They were prisoners of war for two years until the Americans liberated them.

   Note: You may want to discuss how all the families were evacuated from their homes as a result of Japan's attacks, but all for different reasons.

15. **According to pages 41 through 43, what "end-of-war" events happened in Japan from March to September 1945?**

- After the United States was able to capture Saipan and other islands in the Pacific, American planes were close enough to Japan for air raids to begin.

- People in Japan had to be prepared for daily bombings, learning to hide in bomb shelters, prepared with food, water, and identification.

- The first atomic bomb was dropped on Hiroshima and three days later another was dropped on Nagasaki.

- On August 15, 1945, V-J Day, the Japanese emperor "said it was time for Japan to surrender."

- The Japanese surrender was signed on September 2, 1945.

PERFORMANCE ASSESSMENT

Give students the following task:

- Choose two firsthand accounts in the text and write an informative/explanatory essay about how these primary sources enhance your understanding of the facts about the war, as described in the main text. Tell students to use at least two specific examples of stories that add suspense, emotion, or even just more descriptive detail to the standard accounts of events. They should include quotations from the accounts to support their assertions.

Students should write a sentence that introduces their topic, use facts and definitions to develop points, and provide a concluding statement or section. At earlier levels, students may draw or dictate their informative/explanatory text and/or write a label, sentence, or series of related sentences. See standards for more details.

EXTENSIONS

1. Have students choose one of the main events that happened in the European or Pacific front of the Second World War. They should research the event, studying its causes and effects and then write an informative/explanatory essay discussing the causes and effects of the event.

2. Have trios or small groups of six or nine students practice and perform this dramatic reading about children in war. The first paragraph of the introduction by Madeleine Albright, on page 9, is the text of this reading.

READER 1:	To a child growing up in a time of war
ALL:	the abnormal
READER 2:	is the only reality one has experienced.
ALL:	This is what life is like:
READER 1:	to spend your evenings in a bomb shelter
READER 2:	to fear thunder in the sky
READER 3:	to move about from place to place
READER 1:	to watch adults for signs of reassurance or warning
READER 2:	to listen for clues to what is really going on
READER 3:	to have loved ones disappear
READER 1:	to be told you are brave
READER 2:	when you are only bewildered
READER 3:	to hope for a return to the real normalcy
ALL:	you have never known.

CONNECTIONS TO COMMON CORE STATE STANDARDS FOR ENGLISH LANGUAGE ARTS

- Students must analyze and explain the relationship among various structural features of this informational text to answer question 1 (RI.3.5,7; RI.4.5,7; RI.5.5,7).

- Question 2 requires students to read the introduction closely and make inferences based on the details offered there (RI.3.1,2,3,9; RI.4.1,2,3,9; RI.5.1,2,3,9).

- Questions 3 and 6 ask students to glean information from a caption to understand some of the main ideas of this text (RI.3.5; RI.4.5; RI.5.5).

- To answer questions 4, 10, 11, 12, 13, and 15, students must track key details and relate them to main ideas in the text (RI.3.1,2; RI.4.1,2; RI.5.1,2).
  - Question 11 also asks students to cite evidence from the text to support assertions (RI.3.1; RI.4.1; RI.5.1).
  - Question 13 also asks students to explain the cause and effect of events that led to the end of the war (RI.3.3; RI.4.3; RI.5.3).

- To answer question 5, students must track key details and relate them to main ideas in the text, with an emphasis on interpreting characters' words and actions, as in a literary text (RI.3.1,2,6; RI.4.1,2,6; RI.5.1,2,6; RL.3.3; RL.4.3; RL.5.3).

- Question 7 requires students to identify key details as they relate to one another and to main ideas in the text, including the recognition of cause and effect (RI.3.1,2,3; RI.4.1,2,3; RI.5.1,2,3).

- To answer questions 8 and 9, students must track key details and relate them to main ideas in the text, with an emphasis on interpreting characters' words and actions, as in a literary text, and on explaining how they contribute to the reader's overall understanding of these multidimensional events (RI.3.1,2,3,6; RI.4.1,2,3,6; RI.5.1,2,3,6; RL.3.3; RL.4.3; RL.5.3).

- Question 14 prompts students to recognize the ways in which firsthand accounts from different perspectives contribute to our overall understanding of key historical events (RI.3.1,2,3,6; RI.4.1,2,3,6; RI.5.1,2,3,6).

- The performance assessment not only enables students to reread the text closely but also reinforces their understanding of the ways in which primary source accounts enhance our understanding of history (RI.3.1,2,3,6,8; RI.4.1,2,3,6,8; RI.5.1,2,3,6,8; W.3.2,9; W.4.2,9; W.5.2,9).

- The extensions give students opportunities to conduct further research and convey their understanding of the causes and effects of specific events in an informative/explanatory essay or to immerse themselves in an important account of the war and perform the account, committing it to their memory in a significant way (W.3.2; W.4.2; W.5.2).

MORE RESOURCES

PRIMARY SOURCES

Italian Fascist propaganda (Italian Life under Fascism)

Salute to women in war work, British Paramount News, 1943 (Imperial War Museum, London)

Royal Navy during the Second World War (Imperial War Museum, London)

Yalta Conference photos, 1945 (California Connection)

Photos of Benito Mussolini (World War 2 Diaries)

Photos of Axis military leaders (The History Channel)

History features: London Blitz (The History Channel)

Neville Chamberlain meeting with Hitler and Mussolini, 1938 (Wikimedia Commons)

Winston Churchill speech, "We shall fight on the beaches," 1940 (YouTube)

Text of Winston Churchill's speech, "We shall fight on the beaches," 1940 (Winston Churchill Centre)

USEFUL WEBSITES

Winston Churchill for kids (Ducksters)

Children of World War 2 index (BBC Primary History)

World War II audio clips (BBC School Radio)

Includes sounds of air raid sirens, famous speeches, interviews with survivors, radio programs with songs and music, and context and photos about the clips

Pacific War timeline (World War 2 Diaries)

Post-War World: An Iron Curtain Divides the Globe

(1945 to 1960s)

GRADES: 3, 4, 5

OVERVIEW

Barely six months after the end of World War II, Winston Churchill declared that an "iron curtain" had descended across Europe. A dangerous Cold War between the United States and Russia began. Tension over the founding of Israel led to war with the surrounding Arab nations. China, Vietnam, and later Cambodia and Laos established Communist governments, often killing staggering numbers of their own citizens in order to consolidate power. Younger students will read *Red Kite, Blue Kite* and explore the symbolism of the kite that sustains the connection between a father and his son during the displacement and chaos of Chinese Cultural Revolution. Older students will draw on the history of South African Apartheid to understand the segregated culture in which the novel *Journey to Jo'Burg* takes place.

o o o

Interested in learning more about this time period? Read a more complete history in the "Era Summaries."

LEARNING EXPECTATIONS

Lower elementary: Students should understand that the Communist Soviet Union and the Western democracies set their enormous differences aside in order to fight their common enemy, Germany, during the Second World War. When they defeated Germany and the war ended, conflict between the Soviets and the United States intensified. Students should know that the Cold War, the tense rivalry between the two nuclear-armed superpowers and their allies, dominated world affairs for decades.

Upper elementary: Students should understand that the uneasy alliance between the Communist Soviet Union and the Western democracies was solely driven by the mutual necessity of defeating Hitler's Nazi threat. It quickly collapsed after the war ended in 1945. As the Soviets seized control of Eastern Europe, the two blocs divided Germany between themselves. Both were soon armed with nuclear weapons, and a tense standoff—the Cold War—emerged by the late 1940s. Both sides sought to expand alliances; the West aggressively tried to block Communist expansion around the world, and the Soviets helped bring China into the Communist sphere. Unable to fight directly without risking nuclear war, the superpowers fought proxy battles in Korea, Vietnam, and elsewhere. Each tried to impress nonaligned developing nations and fought hard to win public relations battles such as the race to land on the moon.

SUGGESTED ANCHOR TEXTS

"Lesson on Discrimination Based on Race" by United Nations Cyber School Bus
"Apartheid Timeline" by United Nations Cyber School Bus
Journey to Jo'Burg: A South African Story by Beverley Naidoo
Mao and Me by Chen Jiang Hong
Red-Scarfed Girl: A Memoir of the Cultural Revolution by Ji-li Jiang
The Wall by Peter Sis

FEATURED ANCHOR TEXTS

"LESSON ON DISCRIMINATION BASED ON RACE" BY UNITED NATIONS CYBER SCHOOL BUS

"APARTHEID TIMELINE" BY UNITED NATIONS CYBER SCHOOL BUS

JOURNEY TO JO'BURG: A SOUTH AFRICAN STORY BY BEVERLEY NAIDOO

This text was chosen for this era because it tells a black African child's viewpoint of a terrible time in South African history—Apartheid. By interweaving the timeline created by the United Nations in the paired informational text with the fictional story of Naledi and Tiro, this period of history comes to life. The young characters in the story exhibit a wide range of emotion and are also courageous in a coming-of-age journey from their village to Johannesburg. The map helps the reader to understand the geographical journey of the children. The glossary brings clarity to the terms and Afrikaans language.

TEXT STUDIES

This set of text-dependent questions enables students to analyze and compare a literary treatment of events also described in an informational text. Students use an annotated timeline to help put events in the story in context. Students examine academic vocabulary terms in the context of events in the story and cite evidence to support their understanding of events. The performance assessment gives students an opportunity to convey their understanding of events in the story as it relates to their understanding of real-life events described in an annotated timeline.

"Lesson on Discrimination Based on Race" by United Nations Cyber School Bus

In preparation for this lesson, you may want to make student copies of the "Introduction to Apartheid" part of this material. The lesson suggests having students work in groups on the timeline sections to determine whether the event describes an act of discrimination, an act of resistance, or some of both. Although this is a very valuable activity, we are going to use the timeline simply as a timeline of information in this study preparing students to see how these events, beginning in 1651, inspired the Soweto uprising of 1976, featured in the novel, *Journey to Jo'Burg: A South African Story*.

"Introduction to Apartheid" and "Lesson on Discrimination Based on Race" by United Nations Cyber School Bus

1. **Apartheid is defined in this article as "apartness." How did Apartheid separate people into groups?**
   - Apartheid was a system that legally separated "South Africa's whites from the blacks, Asians, and people of mixed race."

     Note: *Teachers may choose to study the root word* apart: *its etymology, its related word forms—including their parts of speech—and its root and affixes, in order to appreciate the use of the word* apart *in this context (for example, Apartheid, apartment, or related idioms such as tell apart, fall apart, or take apart).*

2. **According to the introduction of this article, how did this system of discrimination begin? How does the timeline, selection 1, add details to this onset of discrimination?**
   - This discrimination against the original inhabitants of Africa began with the Dutch and English colonization in the 1600s.
   - The timeline shows how the Dutch settled in 1651, seizing the land by force as the Boers, or Dutch farmers, seized the pastureland on which the Africans depended for their livelihood. Because their cattle and sheep had no land, the Africans were forced to begin working for the Dutch.

3. **How did diamond mining help to solidify this discrimination?**
   - According to the timeline, diamond mining began in 1867. The native Africans, because they were black, were treated unfairly as this industry grew.
     - Africans were given the most dangerous jobs.
     - They were paid "far less than white workers."
     - They were housed "in fenced, patrolled barracks."
     - They were prevented from any kind of organizing for change by the "constant surveillance" by the whites.

Journey to Jo'Burg: A South African Story by Beverley Naidoo

Note: In these questions related to the novel, students are asked to refer to the timeline. You may want to cut the timelines into the suggested selections and have pairs of students refer to their assigned selection instead of perusing the whole body of work.

1. **According to chapter 1, how does the reader know that Naledi and Tiro's family lives in poverty? According to the events described in the timeline, why might they be so poor?**
   - The poverty of Naledi and Tiro's family is seen in a number of ways.
     - On page 1, Naledi knows her sister cannot go to the hospital because they "had no money to pay a doctor."
     - On page 2, the text says that she "tightly clutched the coins in her hand" to pay for the water at the village tap.
     - On page 4, it says they do not even have money to send a telegram to their mother.
     - On page 5, when asked about food for the journey, they replied, "Oh, we'll find something." They had a friend give them two sweet potatoes and commented on how she was a good friend to do that.
   - According to the timeline, the wages of the Africans were well below the whites because of South African policies.

- ○ Since 1867, the Africans were given the most dangerous jobs in the diamond mines and were paid the least.
  - ○ By 1939, whites were paid five times what Africans were paid.
  - ○ By 1946, whites were paid twelve times what Africans were paid.
- According to the timeline, finding jobs was generally a problem for the Africans in South Africa. In the 1920s, Africans were fired from jobs and the jobs were given to whites.

2. **According to page 8, the grown-ups were always talking about "passes." For what activities was a pass required? How does the timeline lend more insight into the passes?**

- According to page 8, the passes were required to visit a place or to change your job. If you didn't have a pass, you could be arrested and sent to a prison farm.

- According to the timeline, there were two acts passed that mentioned needing passports or passes.
  - ○ The Bantu Homelands Act of 1951 stripped the Africans of their citizenship in South Africa. Therefore, they were only citizens of the areas reserved for blacks. They had to have a passport to go to other areas of South Africa.
  - ○ The Abolition of Passes and Coordination of Documents Act of 1952 actually required all Africans "to carry identification booklets with their names, addresses, fingerprints, and other information." These booklets were called passes. The timeline entry said, "Between 1948 and 1973, over 10,000,000 Africans were arrested because their passes were 'not in order.'"

3. **How does the map in the front of the book help the reader to follow the journey?**

- The map shows the journey from the village where they live to their destination in Johannesburg.
- The reader sees where the hospital is located.
- The map shows the areas within the city of Johannesburg.
- The legend of the map shows how the children traveled to the city and back home again.
- The legend also shows the distance in miles and kilometers.

4. **How does the story of the boy on the orange farm in chapter 3 illustrate the early Boer attitude of white domination over blacks?**

- When the boy at the farm warned the children *not* to eat the oranges, he described the owner of the farm as white. He said that he, the black boy who worked on the farm, was allowed to *pick* the oranges, but he was not allowed to *eat* the oranges.

- He also referred to the little bit of food given to the farm workers as *pap*. Defined as cornmeal porridge in the glossary, he said, "I brought you a little pap. I'm sorry, but that's all we get here most days."

5. **According to pages 20 through 33, Naledi and Tiro were not allowed to stay with their mother in the city of Parktown. According to the timeline, what might be the cause of the children having to live apart from their mother?**

- In 1951, the Group Areas Act was passed. It set aside certain areas for the "whites, coloreds, and native" to live. The native, or African/black, were not allowed to live in the areas set aside for the whites.

- Their mother worked for a white family in a white area. According to the Group Areas Act, her black children could not live there with her.

6. **According to page 22, how does the story of their father's illness and death connect to the timeline?**

   - Their father's illness came from working deep in the mines. From 1867, the Africans were given the jobs in the mines that were most dangerous.

7. **What was the problem faced by the man in chapter 8? How did Tiro try to solve the problem? How did the son respond?**

   - According to page 37, a father had left his passbook at home. The police were doing a "pass raid," which meant that they were stopping all of the Africans and checking to see that they had their passbooks with them.

   - Tiro ran to the man's house and asked the boy for his father's passbook. They all ran back with the passbook, but missed the van already on its way to the police station.

   - The son was so angry that he threw a stone at the van. He also cried out, "I'll burn this one day!"

8. **According to the 1952 and 1960 entries in the timeline, how did people protest the requirement to carry passes? How did the government respond to their protests?**

   - African people burned their passes in protest.

   - In Sharpeville in 1960, a large number of blacks refused to carry the passes.

   - The government fined people, sent them to prison, and whipped them. Sixty-nine people died and 187 people were wounded. African political organizations were banned from then on.

9. **Grace's story of her brother Dumi is told on pages 44 through 48. How does his story match up to the events on the timeline?**

   - Dumi was involved in a 1976 student rebellion against the government teaching them "only what the white government wanted them to know."
     - They were marching in rebellion and carrying signs.
     - The police responded with guns, tear gas, and even tanks.
     - People became angrier and began throwing stones, burning schools, and burning government buildings.
     - Dumi was arrested, and then finally disappeared completely.
     - Much later, they received a letter from him, but they never again heard from him.

   Note: According to page 35, the family lived in Soweto.

   - This fictional event seems to match up with the Soweto uprising in 1976. The people were demonstrating against "discrimination and instruction in Afrikaans, the language of whites descended from the Dutch. A student leader named Steven Biko was beaten and left to die in jail."

10. **On page 49 of the novel, Naledi was pondering the meaning of the word *freedom*. What were the areas of her life that she considered might be affected?**

    - She wondered if she would be free to live with her mother.

    - She wondered if she would be free to go to "secondary school."

    - She wondered if being free would affect what she actually learned in school.

11. **One of Grace's comments about education was that children were taught "rubbish" in school. According to page 54, what was wrong with the education offered to the black children in South Africa?**

    - Black children were only taught how to be servants.

12. **How did Naledi's thoughts about education become more solid on page 72? How did this thinking spur her on for change?**

   - She finally understood what was wrong with her own education.
     - She was being taught to write letters with the goal of getting a job as a servant.
     - She was taught to write about how she was good at "cooking, cleaning, washing, and gardening."
     - She was taught to sign her letters, "Yours obediently."
   - She considered becoming a doctor, a person who would help her family and her village to be healthier. She also decided to begin talking with the older students at her school about the need for change in education.

13. **According to page 73, how did Naledi find good in the hard journey to Jo'burg?**

   - Her sister's life was saved.
   - She found out how life worked in South Africa during the time of Apartheid. She understood it and was ready to act on it.

PERFORMANCE ASSESSMENT

Discuss with students how throughout this set of questions, they have seen how the author of a novel based her fictional story on real events in history. Give students the following task:

- Write an explanatory/informative essay focused on two or three events from the timeline. Explain how the author created a story based on those two or three events.

Students should write a sentence that introduces their topic, use facts and definitions to develop points, and provide a concluding statement or section. At earlier levels, students may draw or dictate their informative/explanatory text and/or write a label, sentence, or series of related sentences. See standards for more details.

CONNECTIONS TO COMMON CORE STATE STANDARDS FOR ENGLISH LANGUAGE ARTS

"Introduction to Apartheid" and "Lesson on Discrimination Based on Race" by United Nations Cyber School Bus

- Question 1 asks students to cite evidence from the text to help explain a key concept and an academic vocabulary term (RI.3.1,2,4; RI.4.1,2,4; RI.5.1,2,4; L.3.4; L.4.4; L.5.4).

- Question 2 asks students to cite evidence from the text to help explain a key concept from the text. It also requires students to understand how a timeline enhances their understanding of events (RI.3.1,2,5; RI.4.1,2,5; RI.5.1,2,5).

- Question 3 asks students to cite evidence from the text to help explain a key concept from the text (RI.3.1,2; RI.4.1,2; RI.5.1,2).

Journey to Jo'Burg by Beverley Naidoo

- Questions 1 and 2 ask students to cite evidence from the text to help explain a key concept from the text. They also require students to understand how a timeline enhances their understanding of events (RI.3.1,2,5; RI.4.1,2,5; RI.5.1,2,5).

  Note: *For questions 1 and 2, the applicable standard is now called Literary (RI.3.1,2,5; RI.4.1,2,5; RI.5.1,2,5).*

- To answer question 3, students must glean information from a map (RI.3.7; RI.4.7; RI.5.7).

  Note: *We have cited an informational text standard because there is no standard for literature that addresses the use of maps or other structural features for these grade levels.*

- Question 4 addresses how one example of a phenomenon described in the book exemplifies a larger concept (RI.3.1,2,3,5; RI.4.1,2,3,5; RI.5.1,2,3,5).

- Answering questions 5, 6, 8, and 9 requires students to understand how a timeline enhances or relates to their understanding of events described in the story (RI.3.1,2,5; RI.4.1,2,5; RI.5.1,2,5).

  Note: *We have cited an informational text standard because there is no standard for literature that addresses the use of timelines or other structural features for these grade levels.*

- Questions 7, 11, 12, and 13 require students to cite evidence from the text when summarizing events (RI.3.1,2; RI.4.1,2; RI.5.1,2).

- Question 10 asks students to cite evidence from the text to help explain a key concept and an academic vocabulary term (RI.3.1,2,4; RI.4.1,2,4; RI.5.1,2,4; L.3.4; L.4.4; L5.4).

- The performance assessment gives students an opportunity to convey their understanding of events in the story as it relates to their understanding of real-life events described in an annotated timeline (RL.3.1,2,3,5; RL.4.1,2,3,5; RL.5.1,2,3,5; RI.3.5,9; RI.4.5,9; RI.5.5,9; W.3.2,9; W.4.2,9; W.5.2,9).

MORE RESOURCES

PRIMARY SOURCES

American Ballet Theatre performs in U.S.S.R., 1960 (Library of Congress)

Sputnik 1, first artificial satellite, launched 1957 (NASA)

NATO photos (NATO official website)

Berlin Wall: Kennedy's speech, 1963 (Encyclopedia Britannica)

Portrait of Mao Zedong (Wikimedia)

Korean War images (Eisenhower Presidential Library)

USEFUL WEBSITE

Revelations from the Russian Archives (Library of Congress)

The Cold War Thaws: Uneasy Cooperation between Nations

(1960s to Present)
GRADES: 3, 4, 5

OVERVIEW

In the 1980s, the Western powers renewed their mission to oppose Communism, and the Cold War ended by the early 1990s with the collapse of the Soviet Union. But the world witnessed uneven economic development in Africa, along with devastating famines and civil wars, ruthless dictatorships in Central and South America, and strain between Islamic traditionalism and Western modernity. At the same time, economic globalization demanded that nations cooperate with one another more closely than ever before. *Nasreen's Secret School* shows younger students the barriers to education girls in Afghanistan faced under Taliban oppression. *Hands around the Library* illustrates the importance of the Alexandria library to the Egyptian people, leading older students to understand and explain why the Egyptian people carefully protected this world-renowned landmark during a time of civil unrest.

○ ○ ○

Interested in learning more about this time period? Read a more complete history in the "Era Summaries."

LEARNING EXPECTATIONS

Lower elementary: Students should understand that the nuclear dangers of the Cold War drove the major world powers to improve diplomatic ties in the 1970s, which reduced tensions. However, the West's aggressive push to thwart Communism in the 1980s forced a new arms race that the Soviets could not afford—and helped to drive internal reforms in the Communist world that ended the Cold War by the early 1990s. Students should know that as people have struggled over the future since the Cold War ended, fresh political, economic, and religious tensions have gripped the world.

Upper elementary: Students should understand that the dangerous tensions of the Cold War, especially the constant risk of nuclear war, helped spur diplomacy and reduce global tensions between the superpowers in the 1970s. For the first time, the United States and the Soviet Union agreed to limit the increase of their nuclear arsenals, and the United States opened diplomatic ties with Communist China. In the 1980s, a fresh determination by the Western powers to take a tough line and overpower Communism led to a military buildup that the sputtering Communist economies could not match. Students should understand that the West's anti-Communist program helped spur internal reforms in the U.S.S.R. and Eastern Europe that ended the Cold War by the early 1990s. Students should realize that since then, higher degrees of international cooperation and economic globalization have bound many nations more tightly together. At the same time, these changes have come at a heavy price. As some amass great wealth through global trade, the pressure to keep costs low has led to low wages and increased poverty for many others. Students should also understand that since the Cold War ended, new global tensions have arisen– particularly between the dominant Western powers and an Islamic world that is suspicious of Western power and social modernity. Today, many differ bitterly over who will lead the world forward.

SUGGESTED ANCHOR TEXTS

Hands around the Library: Protecting Egypt's Treasured Books by Karen Leggett Abouraya
Afghan Dreams: Young Voices of Afghanistan by Tony O'Brian and Mike Sullivan
Muhammad's Journey: A Refugee Diary by Anthony Robinson and Annemarie Young
Nelson Mandela by Kadir Nelson

FEATURED ANCHOR TEXT

HANDS AROUND THE LIBRARY: PROTECTING EGYPT'S TREASURED BOOKS BY KAREN LEGGETT ABOURAYA

This book was selected because of the full-circle history this true Egyptian story presents, from the land of the first civilization to the most recent period of world history. The beautiful paper collages illustrate perfectly the masses of diverse people gathered for one purpose: the trumping of democracy and freedom. The focus on the library as a center for the free exchange of ideas, whether through the gathered people themselves or the written ideas in books, demonstrates to students the role of knowledge in political and social change. The book contains many photographs of the protests, captioned with good information. It also contains useful background information, translations of Arabic words (to help students read the protest signs), suggestions for further study, and an author's note that describes the inspiration for the motifs used in the books and their connection to the protest.

TEXT STUDY

These text-dependent questions address not only the content and craft of the text itself but also the content in the significant author's note, which contains related information. Students must compare the two texts on the same topic. Students are also asked to cite evidence from the text regarding key details as they relate to main ideas, to evaluate the efficacy of primary sources (such as photographs), and to interpret the author's choice of words and phrases. The performance assessment prompts students to think about what symbols are and to explain their understanding of the 2011 protest in that context in an informative/explanatory essay.

1. **On page 1, what does the author mean by, "Once upon a time, *not* a long time ago"?**
   - Usually when a story is told with "Once upon a time" the story is an old story and people do not know when the telling of the story began.
   - In this book, the beginning of this crisis of freedom may not be exactly known, but this story happened recently.

2. **On page 1, what is the evidence that the people's freedoms have eroded?**
   - The text says that people's emotions ranged from sad to angry because they had lost three freedoms.
     - They lost the freedom to speak freely.
     - They lost the freedom to vote for the person they wanted.
     - They lost the freedom to gather in groups.

3. **Cite evidence from the text to explain why the Alexandria Library is so important to the people of Egypt?**
   - The Alexandria Library is where people heard about the freedoms that were enjoyed in other parts of the world.
     - They learned about freedom from the books in the stacks.
     - They learned about freedom from the Internet.
     - They learned about freedom from the people they met in the library, talking in whispers.

4. **Why were the young people of Egypt marching in the streets?**
   - The young people want to "let their voices be heard."
   - They want other people to follow them.

5. **According to pages 5 and 6, what were the signs that the marching was becoming violent? Why was this frightening the narrator of this account?**
   - Protestors had "acted in anger" through parts of the city.
     - They had set fire to cars.
     - They had set fire to a police station.
   - The narrator is also marching in Alexandria and the marchers are moving toward the beloved Alexandria Library. According to page 7, she has strong reasons for her fear of losing it.
     - The present library is built "on the ashes of the ancient, famous one."
     - The library itself is the "most beautiful modern building in all of Egypt."
     - The stories of ancient Egypt are housed there and kept alive "in the books, and in the carved stone, and shimmering glass of the building itself."
   - The library was a place of freedom for the people who were not free outside its walls.

6. **Cite evidence from pages 8 and 9 that shows how the narrator described the people who were making the loud sounds. How did the author show, on page 9, that the marchers were a great moving force?**
   - The narrator wondered about the emotions and character of the people who were pounding their feet and shouting; she didn't know if they were still just loudly, marching for freedom, or if they "were so angry that they would hurt each other, hurt me, or hurt our library!"
   - The author used a simile to describe the way in which the crowd of thousands seemed unstoppable. She said, "Thousands of us were marching for freedom, as if caught on a wave from the Mediterranean Sea."

   Note: Teachers might want to review similes, if not already covered, and their effect on the reader.

7. **According to page 9, what was the library director's only hope for saving the library? Why?**

   - His only hope was in "the will of the people," as he reminded them of the building filled with "treasures." In other words, he was hoping the people would choose not to destroy the library.

   - He knew he had no other choice. He was powerless to stop the "wave."
     - He had no power to protect the library with locked gates, because it had no gates.
     - He knew the doors were made of glass and offered little protection if the marchers wanted to attack.

8. **Describe the scene as the marchers came closer to the library. According to pages 11 through 18, what happened to break the focus from the surging crowd?**

   - The crowd grew into a tighter, moving formation. The author uses the word *surged*, meaning "a strong, wavelike, forward movement, rush, or sweep." The crowd was first in front of the library and then moved up on the steps.

   - A young man, as seen in the illustration and told in the text, broke out from the surging crowd and raced up the steps "and took hold of the director's hand!"
     - A young girl took the director's other hand, and others joined the boy, holding hands with Dr. Serageldin (the director). More people joined the chain of hands, until the people were stretched around the library and "reaching toward the sea."
     - The people spread a huge Egyptian flag across the steps of the library, as people expressed their love for their home, crying, "We love you, Egypt."

9. **According to the narrator, why was that day such an important day in the history of Egypt?**

   - The world had seen the Egyptian people recognize the value of the library and choose to protect it by holding hands around it.

   - The world heard the words of the library director as he thanked the demonstrators for choosing not just to spare the library but also to protect it.

   - The stories stored in the library had been protected, "holding all of our stories," says the narrator, preserved for future generations.

10. **How do the photographs and captions on pages 25 and 26 add to the credibility of the story?**

    - The photographs are primary sources, showing the hand-holding protection of the library actually happened not so long ago.

    - A photograph of the huge flag shows its being held by hundreds of people. Another photograph shows demonstrators holding hands and their signs.

    - The photograph of the demonstrators on the bottom of page 26 shows the huge number of people who were marching.

    - The captions add more information, such as the name of the Egyptian president, Hosni Mubarak, who resigned at the end of the eighteen days of demonstration.

    - The photographs and captions illustrate the beauty and unique appearance of the library itself.

11. **Use the information on page 27 to describe the origins of the Great Library of Alexandria.**

    - Alexandria was a port city with ships coming in and out of the port. About 2,300 years ago, the king of Egypt, Ptolemy, decided he wanted "to collect all the knowledge of the world in one place." He built a library in Alexandria. He required his scribes to copy all of the scrolls carried on ships from all over the world. The copies of the information, scribed on papyrus scrolls, were then placed in the library.

12. **Why was the ancient library important through the years of its existence?**
   - It was a center for learning from 400 BCE until 300 BCE.
     - The text says it was a place "where great thinkers, scientists, mathematicians, and poets came to study and share ideas."

13. **What are the theories about the ancient library's disappearance?**
   - There are two main theories about how the ancient library disappeared.
     - One theory says that Julius Caesar, of Roman Empire fame, burned the Egyptian ships in the Alexandria harbor, and that the fire spread to the library and it burned down.
     - Another theory suggests that either Christian or Muslim leaders burned books "that did not agree with what they believed."

14. **How is the modern library similar to the ancient library?**
   - Both libraries were named *Bibliotheca Alexandrina*, derived from Latin.
   - Both libraries are holding the knowledge of the world.
     - The old library used its port to collect the knowledge that was placed in the library.
     - The new library is shaped in a circle to represent the sun shining on the whole world. The stones around the outside of the library are covered with letters or signs from five hundred different alphabets.

15. **According to page 28, what did the demonstrators of 2011 want to accomplish?**
   - They wanted the president of Egypt to resign.
   - They wanted to enjoy a democratic form of government.

16. **According to the author's note on page 30, what is the message of this book?**
   - She believes that children should be "taught, from the time they are born, to love books and to hold hands around the world." She illustrates this message with the idea of children holding hands across borders with "barbed wire fences and stone walls."

PERFORMANCE ASSESSMENT

Give students the following writing task:

- Write an informative/explanatory essay explaining how the Alexandria Library was a symbol that needed to be fiercely protected during the demonstrations of 2011. Use evidence from the text, gathered in the questions, to describe why the library was important to the Egyptian people and why it needed to be protected for the Egyptian people.

Teachers might want to introduce or review the concept of *symbol*, noting the word's etymology, related forms (and various parts of speech), and its root and affixes (for example, *symbolic, symbolize, symbolically*).

Students should write a sentence that introduces their topic, use facts and definitions to develop points, and provide a concluding statement or section. At earlier levels, students may draw or dictate their informative/explanatory text and/or write a label, sentence, or series of related sentences. See standards for more details.

CONNECTIONS TO COMMON CORE STATE STANDARDS FOR ENGLISH LANGUAGE ARTS

- Question 1 asks students to interpret the use of a phrase used by the author to introduce the text (RI.3.1,5,8; RI.4.1,5,8; RI.5.1,5,8).

- Questions 2, 3, 4, 7, 8, and 9 require students to cite evidence and key details that support a main idea (RI.3.1,2,3; RI.4.1,2,3; RI.5.1,2,3).

- Question 5 asks students to identify some key details and explain them in the context of events described in the book and how they affected the narrator (RI.3.1,2,3,5,6,8; RI.4.1,2,3,5,6,8; RI.5.1,2,3,5,6,8).

- Question 6 requires students to cite evidence from the text to explain the effect of the author's vivid descriptions (RI.3.1,2,8; RI.4.1,2,8; RI.5.1,2,8).

- Question 10 addresses the role of (primary source) photographs in adding credibility to the story (RI.3.5,7; RI.4.5,7; RI.5.5,7).

- When answering questions 11 through 16, students must read another text on this topic in the form of the author's note at the end ("Alexandria Then and Now"). They must cite evidence from this text to describe details, events, and history related to the story (RI.3.1,2,3,6; RI.4.1,2,3,6; RI.5.1,2,3,6).
  - Questions 12 and 13 also ask students to cite other details from the author's note (RI.3.1,2; RI.4.1,2; RI.5.1,2).
  - Question 14 also requires students to compare information from this note to what they learned in the text (RI.3.3; RI.4.3; RI.5.3).

- The performance assessment prompts students to think about what symbols are, how the library at Alexandria was a symbol that needed to be protected, and then to explain their understanding of the protest of 2011 in an informative/explanatory essay (RI.3.1,2,3,4,8; RI.4.1,2,3,4,8; RI.5.1,2,3,4,8; W.3.2,9; W.4.2,9; W.5.2,9).

MORE RESOURCES

PRIMARY SOURCES

"From the Archives: President Nixon Announces the End of the Vietnam War," 1973 (NBC Nightly News)

Text of the Camp David Accords (Israel Ministry of Foreign Affairs)

Margaret Thatcher and George Bush joint press conference on Iraqi invasion of Kuwait, 1990 (Margaret Thatcher Foundation)

Biography on Mikhail Gorbachev (PBS: *American Experience*)

World Trade Center bombing article, 1993 (BBC News)

USEFUL WEBSITES

Witnessing Tiananmen: Clearing the square, 2004 (BBC News)

America's Day of Terror, 2001 (BBC News)

Includes official reports, audio, video, eyewitness reports, timelines, and so on

Era Summaries

The last significant human settlement waves were into the Arctic after the glaciers retreated about five thousand years ago and the isolated islands of the Pacific about two thousand years ago.

PALEOLITHIC SOCIETIES AND THE EMERGENCE OF HUMAN CULTURE

Hominins began using stone tools at least 2.6 million years ago; the achievement marked the advent of the long era that anthropologists and archaeologists call the Paleolithic period, or Old Stone Age (commonly dated from circa 2.6 million years ago to circa 8000 BCE). This enormous period began with the first tool-making hominins, long before modern humans evolved. It continued until the eve of agricultural settlement, which occurred in the comparatively recent past.

For most of the vast Paleolithic period, human species lived as hunter-gatherers: they depended on wild game and naturally occurring resources such as wild plants and fish. Our distant ancestors, who lived at least 1.5 million years ago, already showed evidence of strong familial and social relationships—the roots of human community. Recent evidence suggests that hominins were making and using fire at least a million years ago.

Although they had not yet formed permanently settled communities, modern humans—*Homo sapiens*—quickly demonstrated an aesthetic sense by producing ornaments and creating intricately worked tools. People were carving simple geometric patterns at least seventy-five thousand years ago. Complex works of art, such as small portable sculptures and figural paintings in caves and rock shelters, were created in Europe, Africa, and Australia at least thirty-five thousand years ago. Music is another ancient art form: sophisticated flutes have recently been found and dated to more than forty thousand years ago.

It seems that early humans also developed a variety of religious beliefs. The fact that they generally buried their dead suggests that they probably had some belief in an otherworld or afterlife. It is also likely that much early art reflected religious beliefs and practices, which probably focused—as the art did—on the animals that dominated the landscape and on which humans depended for their survival. (Such trends were not unique to *Homo sapiens*: Neanderthals also appear to have buried their dead, though in less elaborate form. They also made fine tools for tens of thousands of years and produced at least some ornamentation.)

Wild wolves adapted to the presence of humans and seem to have evolved into domestic dogs at least thirty-five thousand years ago, exploiting the animal carcasses that human hunting produced and the shelter offered by human dwellings. The relationship between the two marked the first major partnership between humans and another species, long before the domestication of livestock. Some experts argue that by helping humans hunt and later helping to control livestock and vermin populations, dogs played an important role in human development.

THE AGRICULTURAL REVOLUTION

As the last major ice age ended about twelve thousand years ago, plant life grew more rich and diversified. Wild crops of cereals, peas, and beans thrived in the warmer climate, and the abundant food sources enabled the human population to grow into the millions. People no longer needed to move to find resources, so they abandoned their nomadic lifestyle and established stable villages. They built permanent structures, including stone temple complexes. This transitional period away from the hunter-gatherer lifestyle is known as the Mesolithic period, or Middle Stone Age.

Contrasted with the long span of the Paleolithic, the transitional Mesolithic period was brief. Humans soon made the monumental shift from depending on wild plants to deliberately planting and selectively hybridizing crops—thus manipulating the food supply and ushering in the revolutionary birth of agriculture. The first active agriculture appears to have emerged by 8000 BCE (ten thousand years ago), in West Asia's Fertile Crescent: an area with favorable growing conditions stretched along the Tigris and the Euphrates Rivers in modern-day Iraq (the region historically called Mesopotamia, which means "between the rivers"), and down the Mediterranean coasts of the modern-day nations of Syria, Lebanon, and Israel.

From the Fertile Crescent, agriculture eventually spread into Europe, Central Asia, and North Africa. Farming's scope and sophistication gradually grew as planting and harvesting techniques improved. Irrigation—creating ducts and channels to supply water to people's crops—also enabled people to cultivate what would have been less-hospitable areas.

Around the world, human society was changing quickly. Although agriculture appeared first in the Fertile Crescent, it developed in other areas at nearly the same time. The cultivation of rice seems to have emerged independently in northern China around 7000 BCE (although limited communication between Mesopotamia and China may have occurred). Meanwhile, the peoples of the Americas were entirely isolated from the rest of the world; agricultural practices began there around 6500 BCE.

The widespread adoption of planned agriculture marked the dawn of the Neolithic period, or New Stone Age. Mesolithic communities had been able to hunt wild game, but settled communities now began to keep and selectively breed animals for food and work. The domestication of species for livestock followed the Agricultural Revolution—primarily in West Asia but also in Europe and East and South Asia.

Although settled agricultural lifestyles were soon widespread throughout the world, they were not universal. In some areas and cultures, hunter-gatherer lifestyles remained dominant or coexisted alongside limited agriculture. For instance, many peoples in North America settled and raised crops for part of the year and migrated and hunted at other times. In Australia, aboriginal peoples maintained a hunter-gatherer lifestyle until modern times.

TECHNOLOGY, TRADE, AND THE RISE OF SETTLED COMMUNITIES

As farming spread, settled human societies rapidly became more sophisticated. Early Neolithic communities formed progressively larger villages near valuable natural resources: stone for tools and monuments, water for irrigation and fishing, and rich soil for farming. New technologies developed, and societies formed increasingly complex ritual practices. Meanwhile, traditions passed down between generations facilitated the emergence of distinct local and regional cultures.

Natural clays used to make pots were another important resource. Pottery, a very ancient innovation (in China, evidence of pottery dates twenty thousand years back), became more widespread in many regions after about 7000 BCE. People used pots to carry water greater distances, stored goods in pottery vessels during harsh winters, and transported goods in pottery containers to trade with other groups. After the potter's wheel was invented sometime after 4000 BCE, pottery production became even more efficient and practical.

In another very important development, Neolithic peoples began to move beyond stone and experiment with a new technology: metal. Simple metallurgy allowed them to shape natural copper deposits into tools such as axes before 5000 BCE; smelting technology, which enabled copper to be extracted from ore, emerged by the early fifth millennium BCE. Pure copper is a soft metal and thus difficult to keep well-shaped or sharpened. In many ways, stone tools were actually superior—tools made from hard-to-find copper often had more to do with status than utility. Nonetheless, the beginnings of metalworking were a crucial development, laying the technological groundwork for the Bronze and Iron ages that would follow.

Even before the Mesolithic and Neolithic periods, different groups had traded over long distances for goods they lacked: for instance, a coastal people would trade shells to an inland group that had access to high-quality flint for making tools. As settled communities grew larger during the Neolithic period, long-distance trade expanded and became more organized. Broad regional economies developed as people exchanged raw materials such as copper and flint for agricultural products and livestock. Crops that flourished in one area were traded for those that grew better somewhere else. Soon communities and regions specialized in particular crops and developed more distinctive cultures.

Increasingly organized communities also became more stratified: political, military, and religious elites gained greater power. Large-scale stone communal structures had already begun to appear in the Mesolithic, but now communities had larger labor forces with clear central authority and more unified aims, driven by shared religion and culture. By the fourth millennium BCE, structures such as temples and megalithic monuments were more widespread and sophisticated. Elaborate burials reflected the growing status and wealth of kings, chieftains, and priests.

ERA 2: CIVILIZATIONS EMERGE: THE POWER OF WORDS AND OF BRONZE (CA. 3500 BCE TO CA. 1000 BCE)

THE FIRST CITIES: MESOPOTAMIA, EGYPT, INDIA, AND CHINA

Some Neolithic communities gradually began to expand. Major river valleys offered naturally fertile soil and accessible water; people used water sources to build irrigation systems, which thus opened more land to crops. As populations grew denser, the world's first true urban centers emerged. These cities were larger than villages and had far more complex architecture. Early cities also created impressive, sometimes massive, works of art.

Organized, larger-scale farming led to crop surpluses—and for the first time, securing food did not demand the work of every community member. In the urban centers, some people ventured beyond agriculture. Craftspeople, artisans, and trades people appeared; as city-states began to fight over resources and territory, professional soldiers and commanders were recruited. A new class of wealthy elites began to emerge. State-sponsored religious systems also developed. The worship of many gods centered in elaborate temple complexes; religious texts offered tales of the world's creation through wars among the gods—tales that would later strongly influence early Greek mythology. Priests gained prominence as their temples became wealthy and socially influential. Kings assumed unprecedented power, ruling through bureaucratic government systems and powerful elite classes.

The wealthy and powerful needed others to work their lands and to build and maintain their temples and palaces. Labor was increasingly forced from slaves, who were often captives taken in war. The concept of owning other people as forced laborers was already ancient, but the rise of wealthy social elites—and their heavy labor needs—made slavery a major institution. Slavery would remain a constant in many cultures around the world for much of later human history. Although the practice is technically illegal everywhere, it persists in some regions even today.

The first cities (such as Ur, Uruk, Nippur, Kish, and others) appeared circa 3500 BCE among the Sumerian peoples of southern Mesopotamia, between the Tigris and Euphrates Rivers in what is now Iraq. These cities were marked by planned urban settlement and large, communally built public structures—particularly temples on tall, imposing terraced platforms called ziggurats. Early urbanization largely developed around the ziggurats. Rulers lived in palaces and other elites enjoyed elaborate residences. The first sophisticated plumbing and sewage systems were developed and even served private homes.

In the Nile Valley, Egypt began to urbanize several centuries later. Many Egyptians continued to live in farming villages along the Nile River. Although it was surrounded by desert, the river's annual floods and the rich silt they left behind made the valley fertile and excellent for farming. But cities also emerged, centered on temple complexes and palatial royal residences.

Early urban culture also developed in the Indus River Valley, in present-day Pakistan, where highly organized, well-planned cities appeared circa 2500 BCE. Major Indus Valley cities included Harappa and Mohenjo Daro. Built on carefully laid-out grid patterns and atop brick platforms to overcome the region's frequent floods, these cities featured elaborate ritual baths and sophisticated plumbing systems. In China, urban civilization emerged from Neolithic cultures along the Yellow River sometime after 2000 BCE, as rulers and priests concentrated their power and wealth.

STATES OF THE EARLY BRONZE AGE

The late Neolithic period—the period immediately before bronze was created—is sometimes called the Copper Age. However, pure copper was too soft (and for a long time, too scarce) to make practical tools and weapons. Although copper objects were prized and traded as symbols of status, stone remained dominant for practical tools such as spear points and arrowheads. The invention of bronze, an alloy of copper and tin, was a major technological breakthrough: it was harder and stronger, and ushered in a new age as metal finally began to displace stone.

Bronze first appeared by the middle of the fourth millennium BCE, but its use became widespread only as urban civilization developed. Organized labor was needed to mine the necessary copper and tin; advanced metallurgical techniques were necessary to extract the metals from natural ores, and sophisticated workshops were necessary to turn out bronze goods in large quantities. The concentrated skills and large labor forces of the first cities enabled bronze technology to become dominant, and the Bronze Age truly began.

In Mesopotamia, the early Sumerian cities formed into individual city-states that generally had their own rulers. Sumerians shared a common language and culture, but relations between such states were complex: trade and warfare were common between different city-states. Starting in the later third millennium BCE, several city-states—including those of newly arrived Semitic peoples as well as of Sumerians—established wider spheres of power through conquest, assimilation, and economic strength.

Along the Nile, Egypt had long been divided between two kingdoms called Upper and Lower Egypt (these were named for the direction of the Nile's south-to-north flow, so Upper Egypt was in the south and Lower Egypt was in the north). The two kingdoms were united circa 3000 BCE by the pharaoh Narmer, and their two crowns combined into one. The pharaohs became exceedingly powerful kings and were soon able to organize vast manpower and resources to construct enormous pyramids over their tombs. The unified Egypt gained wealth and military power and developed an artistically sophisticated culture.

The cities of the Indus Valley were most likely never united under a single ruler. However, they resembled each other closely in culture and were tied together by commerce. The Indus urban centers also had a trading relationship with the Mesopotamian city-states—offering one of the first examples of long-distance trade between advanced civilizations.

At least at times, China's early city-states were apparently unified under powerful dynastic kings. According to ancient Chinese historians, the first large Bronze Age kingdom was the Xia. Though it was long considered mythological, some scholars now argue that early tombs with elaborate bronze ritual objects belonged to an actual Xia state. Archaeological finds show that the powerful Shang state—identified by the ancient sources as the Xia's successor—controlled a wide area in the second millennium BCE, when bronze technology had already become widely established.

THE INVENTION AND IMPACT OF WRITING

The earliest ideas were preserved only by word of mouth. Writing was a crucial development of the first civilizations, one that transformed human history. For the first time, people could keep permanent records and pass ideas to later generations. Literature was freed from the constraints of memory and oral performance.

Writing also revolutionized government. The rulers of new and growing urban centers were able to create written legal codes and keep track of resources, populations, and taxes. Indeed, the need for such record keeping spurred the appearance of writing in at least some areas. Many early civilizations were meticulously bureaucratic: methodical lists were kept of goods, slaves, property, and taxes. Mathematics—especially arithmetic and geometry—also appeared early in literate civilizations: such skills enabled people to define property lines, plan buildings, and keep accurate records.

Writing probably first emerged among the Sumerians in Mesopotamia around 3000 BCE, most likely because they needed to record commercial accounts, make property transactions, and keep administrative records. A system of ideograms (or pictures that represent ideas) gradually developed into a system of abstract, stylized characters called cuneiform. These characters represented syllables of spoken language and were created by pressing a wedge-shaped stick into clay. Eventually, this writing system was used to record several different languages across West Asia.

Beyond commercial and bureaucratic records, writing allowed people to create works of literature. The richly imaginative *Epic of Gilgamesh*, containing tales of a legendary ruler from the early urban era, was composed in Sumer during the third millennium BCE. It is thought to be the oldest written narrative in the world. Hammurabi, ruler of the city-state of Babylon in Southern Mesopotamia, created the first known written legal code in the world around 1770 BCE; the Code of Hammurabi was publicly displayed on impressive stone steles (large upright slabs).

The Egyptian writing system appeared at roughly the same time as the Sumerians'. Scholars debate whether the Egyptians independently invented it or if they borrowed the concept of written language from Mesopotamia. Their system also began with the use of ideograms, and their pictorial symbols developed into an elaborate, beautifully artistic method of writing Egyptian syllable sounds.

The Egyptian script, called hieroglyphics, was written in ink on paperlike papyrus and carved in stone on monuments and temples. Egyptians recorded royal conquests and triumphs, bureaucratic accounts, and religious myths and practices—including the elaborate rituals to ensure life after death. Specially trained scribes were literate; most others were not, but private letters and poetry also survive. The Rosetta stone, which French soldiers uncovered in Egypt in 1799, preserved a late Egyptian text that was written after the Greek conquest of Egypt. The artifact bore the same text in both Egyptian and Greek; the Greek text was easily read and thus offered the key to deciphering Egyptian hieroglyphs.

The Indus Valley civilization also quickly developed a system of writing. The idea of written language may have reached the Indus Valley from the Mesopotamians, because the two civilizations had contact through trade. The Indus script has been found on seals, pottery, and other objects—but so far remains indecipherable.

Because of its distance and isolation from Mesopotamia and India, writing in China was almost certainly an independent development. It is first documented circa 1500 BCE and was carved on bones used in Shang divination ceremonies that were used to seek messages from the gods. These early recorded characters demonstrate a well-developed writing system and suggest that writing had in fact already existed in China at least for some centuries—perhaps long before urbanization. The ancient Chinese characters—each of which usually represents a single word—are the direct ancestors of today's Chinese writing and provide the sole example of modern survival among the first ancient writing systems.

Later, in the first millennium BCE, writing would also develop independently in Mesoamerica—this area was completely separate from and unknown to the rest of the world (see era 9).

THE LATER BRONZE AGE IN WEST ASIA AND THE MEDITERRANEAN

Of the early civilizations, Egypt alone was remarkably stable throughout the Bronze Age. Egypt enjoyed long periods of firm government and strong regional power: the first, called the Old Kingdom, lasted from circa 2700 to 2200 BCE, the Middle Kingdom from circa 2000 to 1650 BCE, and the New Kingdom from circa 1600 to 1000 BCE. It was only between these long steady eras that Egypt fell into periods of collapse and disunity.

Egyptian culture did change over time. Pyramid building sharply declined after the Old Kingdom, the chariot transformed Egyptian warfare at the start of the New Kingdom, and political and religious power shifted between different urban centers. Yet for two thousand years, the Egyptian state generally remained politically, culturally, and artistically consistent. Fundamental challenges—such as efforts by the fourteenth century BCE "heretic" pharaoh Akhenaton to focus state religion on a single solar god—were quickly suppressed and buried.

In Mesopotamia, dominant regional powers began to emerge among the city-states in the late third millennium. Sargon, ruler of the Semitic peoples of Akkad (a city that has never been located), conquered the Sumerians around 2300 BCE and ruled a large part of West Asia—creating what is arguably the world's first empire. After Akkad fell, the already ancient city of Ur established a new Sumerian Empire around 2150 BCE. It fell to rival states and nomadic invaders around 2000 BCE. A century later, Babylon developed as the dominant power and reached its peak under Hammurabi. Babylon itself fell to eastern invaders, although it remained prominent under its new rulers alongside Assyria and other rising Mesopotamian states.

As urban civilization expanded, new West Asian powers emerged beyond the Fertile Crescent and a new group of people began to become prominent in West Asia and beyond, speaking a group of related languages known as Indo-European. Common word roots in modern and extinct Indo-European languages have enabled the original ancestral language, called Proto-Indo-European, or PIE, to be partly reconstructed. Indo-European languages would eventually include Sanskrit and many other tongues in the Indian region, Greek, Latin, and the Latin-derived Romance languages in Europe, along with Slavic, Baltic, Armenian, Germanic, Celtic, and other language families.

The PIE language is thought to have arisen by the fourth millennium BCE, and likely much earlier. Its reconstructed words and shared traditions inherited by later Indo-European-speaking regions suggest a culture that relied on farming, wheeled wagons, horse breeding, and livestock, with a pantheon of gods worshipped in sacrificial rites, probably by a caste of priests. Later Indo-European cultures seem to have inherited mythology and beliefs from these distant ancestors. Several, for instance, used related names for a chief celestial god: the Sanskrit name of the sky god, Dyaus Pita, is closely linked to the Greek Zeus Pater and the early Roman Diespiter (which later became Jupiter).

Many scholars believe the Indo-Europeans first appeared in the Central Asian Steppes, though others argue strongly that they originated in Anatolia. By the Bronze Age, Indo-European speakers were expanding into Europe, Persia, India, and the Near East. A people called the Hittites created the first major Indo-European-speaking power, forging an impressive empire in Asia Minor during the second millennium BCE. At their height, the Hittites challenged the dominance of the Mesopotamian powers.

The Minoan people thrived in Crete until the middle of the second millennium BCE: their origins and language are unclear, but they dominated the Aegean Sea with a powerful fleet and constructed large, artistically advanced palace cities. They were displaced by the Greek-speaking Mycenaeans, who emerged in mainland Greece in the early second millennium BCE. The Mycenaeans, heavily influenced by Minoan culture, built their own palatial city-states (the culture is named for Mycenae, probably the most powerful of these cities); they conquered Minoan Crete around 1450 BCE. The Minoan writing system, known as Linear A, has not been deciphered. The Mycenaeans adapted the Linear A symbols into their own writing system, called Linear B: their writing has been deciphered as an early form of Greek.

These cultures were all in contact with one another—particularly the most powerful states whose rulers were known to each other as Great Kings. Extensive diplomatic correspondence survives, particularly in Hittite and Egyptian documents. The various regional powers conducted extensive trade, exchanged diplomatic correspondence and diplomatic marriages, and frequently warred and raided each other for slaves, treasure, and territory. Conflicts between the Mycenaeans and the Anatolian city-state of Wilusa, on the edge of the Hittite sphere in western Asia Minor, seem to have inspired the legends of the Trojan War. These cultures were all literate and generally very bureaucratic: they kept voluminous official records on clay tablets, preserving detailed inventories of military equipment, slaves, commerce, taxes, and other items of government interest.

ERA 3: FROM IRON TO IDEAS: RELIGION AND FREEDOM TAKE SHAPE
(CA. 1700 BCE TO 400 BCE)

BRONZE AGE COLLAPSE AND THE NEW PEOPLES OF THE IRON AGE

The powerful states of the Bronze Age faltered over the course of the second millennium BCE. The Indus Valley civilization declined during the early part of the millennium, and its great cities were largely abandoned by about 1700 BCE. Reasons for the collapse remain unclear and much disputed. Speakers of the Central Asian Indo-European language family entered India from Persia some centuries after the Indus Valley cities died out. These Indo-Europeans laid the groundwork for later Indian culture, including its system of class castes and the roots of its later religions.

The powerful Shang state ruled central China for most of the second millennium BCE and maintained extensive trade ties and cultural influence throughout East Asia. Toward the end of the millennium, however, a rising rival state—the Zhou kingdom—overthrew the Shang and assumed power. The new kingdom's culture was similar to the Shang's and it would struggle to control an increasingly fractious China for most of the next thousand years.

In West Asia and the Aegean, the great Bronze Age powers plunged into sudden crisis late in the second millennium BCE. Over the span of a few decades, most of the great palace cities were sacked and pillaged, and many disappeared forever. The causes of this downfall remain unclear. Groups of marauding raiders, whom Egyptian texts call Peoples of the Sea, arrived from different places (including, most likely, the failing Mycenaean city-states). But it is difficult to determine whether the raiders actually caused the collapse or were merely a symptom of the crisis.

The Hittites and Mycenaeans reached the peak of their power in the thirteenth century BCE: it was only at this time that a Mycenaean ruler was ever hailed by the Hittites as a Great King and thus as one of the elite regional powers. Within a few decades, however, Mycenaean city-states and the Hittite Empire mysteriously met their demise; both had vanished by around 1200 BCE.

Even Egypt, the region's most stable power, suffered internal unrest and external crises at this time, including raids by the Peoples of the Sea. It never fully recovered.

Waves of migration coincided with this turmoil and were probably causes and effects of the chaos. Restless and rebellious peoples joined the looting waves that struck the old empires, and other groups were displaced in the changing political and cultural landscape.

As the great Bronze Age powers fell, once marginal peoples emerged from obscurity. The city-states of the seafaring Phoenicians appeared in what is now Lebanon. The Phoenicians would dramatically expand maritime trade in the Mediterranean, and their written alphabet would shape a new Greek writing system. This, in turn, would provide the building blocks for later European scripts (our word *alphabet* comes from the first letters of the Greek alphabet, *alpha* and *beta*).

The Kushites of Nubia had a rich, Egyptian-inspired culture. Although they had long been in Egypt's shadow, they conquered Egypt by the eighth century BCE. Persians migrated from Central Asia into what is now Iran. Five hundred years later, they would establish one of the world's first great empires and rule from the outskirts of Greece to the edges of India and China. In Greece, speakers of the Dorian dialect of Greek (whose origins are still the subject of much debate) gained influence and became a regional power after the Mycenaean collapse.

One of history's greatest technical innovations emerged during the turbulent aftermath of the Bronze Age. In the early centuries of the first millennium BCE, iron technology replaced bronze. Although iron was harder to work and took skill to extract from iron ore, it had enormous advantages. It was far stronger than bronze, particularly when alloyed with carbon to make steel. It was a great advance over bronze, just as bronze had been over copper and stone. Iron was also more abundant than copper and far more plentiful than the tin that is essential for making bronze. For the first time, metal tools and weapons became commonplace, widely available objects—no longer the exclusive province of the wealthy elite. The Iron Age had begun.

ANCIENT ISRAEL AND THE ROOTS OF EURA ANCIENT ISRAEL AND THE ROOTS OF EURASIAN MONOTHEISM

The Israelites were another people that emerged after the turmoil of the late Bronze Age. During the Bronze Age, the land that became the biblical Israel was known as Canaan—a territory that formed a crossroads between the powerful kingdoms of the Near East and Africa; the Egyptians, Hittites, and Assyrians struggled over it for centuries during the mid to late second millennium BCE. The Egyptian Merneptah stele of circa 1200 BCE describes an Egyptian military campaign against various cities and peoples of Canaan and mentions a rural or nomadic people called Israel among Egypt's enemies: this is the first known appearance of the Israelites in the historical record.

The biblical account maintains that Abraham, the founder of the Israelite peoples, came to Canaan from Mesopotamia; this may preserve memories of an ancient migration across the Fertile Crescent to the Mediterranean coast. Traces of Mesopotamian beliefs and practices survive in Israelite institutions such as the Sabbath day and in stories such as the biblical flood narrative. But scholars debate the origins of the Israelite tribes, and it is unlikely that they will find definitive answers. Like the neighboring Phoenicians, the Israelites were probably descended from the Canaanites. They may have been among the groups that emerged from uprisings against the rulers of the Canaanite city-states in the middle of the second millennium BCE. Scholars disagree whether second-millennium allusions to a people called Habiru might in some way refer to the ancient Hebrews.

The biblical narrative states that Israelites went to Egypt and were enslaved for centuries before they escaped through divine intervention, conquered the Canaanites, and seized the land of Canaan. External evidence for the biblical exodus is disputed, but Egyptian inscriptions record

Semitic slave names and laborers from Canaan; the Bible may also preserve genuine knowledge of life and locations in Egypt. Archaeologists disagree whether there are traces of an Israelite conquest in Canaan that might align with biblical memory. (Hazor and other sites show evidence of having been sacked and burned, although the chronology is uncertain. There is scant evidence of other biblical events, such as the siege of Jericho.)

By 1000 BCE, the Israelites pushed back the Philistines who had recently arrived in the region (most likely, they were among the Peoples of the Sea who marauded in the wake of the Bronze Age collapse). The Israelites established a kingdom based in Jerusalem; the Bible lists the first three kings as Saul, David, and Solomon. Recent archaeological discoveries, including a ninth-century-BCE text that refers to the "House of David," suggest that King David was an actual historical figure. After the death of Solomon, internal conflict split the realm into two separate kingdoms: Israel in the north and Judah in the south.

Uniquely in the ancient world, the Israelites officially worshipped only a single national god, called Yahweh—though it was forbidden to speak his name. Spiritual leaders, called prophets, held potent religious authority alongside the secular authority of the kings. At times, a prophet would force a king from his throne for failure to uphold the religious values of Israel. Archaeological finds, and recorded complaints by the biblical prophets, show that many still privately worshipped other gods—including Asherah, a female deity who some believed was Yahweh's wife. But the official national worship of a single god was nonetheless a marked break with other cultures.

The Assyrians soon established a new and dominant empire in the region, which demanded submission and tribute from Israel and Judah. When Israel rebelled in 725 BCE, Assyria conquered the Israelites. Many were taken into exile and never returned: these are known in legend as the Ten Lost Tribes of Israel. But then, a resurgent Babylon conquered Assyria and established another new empire. The Babylonians sacked Jerusalem in the sixth century BCE. After burning the Israelites' great temple, which is thought to have been built by David's son, Solomon, they forced many of the Israelites into captivity in Babylon.

The new and expanding Persian Empire, led by Cyrus the Great, defeated the Babylonians a generation later. The Israelite exiles were finally allowed to return and rebuild their temple. But the Israelites' suffering and salvation spurred a reexamination of their beliefs. They pulled ancient texts together into an early version of the Hebrew Bible. And for the first time, the Israelites denied the very *existence* of any god but their own. They proclaimed him the creator and ruler of the entire universe. This idea would ultimately have a profound historical impact.

THE REVIVAL OF GREEK CULTURE AND THE EXPANSION OF GREEK INFLUENCE

Greece entered a long "dark age" after the Mycenaean palace culture collapsed around 1200 BCE. This was a poorly documented period. The Dorian Greeks gained power and influence, but their origins are mysterious. The old notion of a violent Dorian invasion is no longer widely accepted. During this time of post–Bronze Age change, Greece entered the Iron Age.

The Mycenaeans' writing system, Linear B, disappeared with the Mycenaean city-states: few members of ancient societies were literate, and Greek writing vanished with the palace scribes who kept official records. Despite the lack of a writing system, oral traditions and bards' songs kept some Bronze Age memories alive. Echoes of palace culture and its warfare survive in Homer's epic poems of Troy, which probably preserved fragments of late Bronze Age tales recording a Greek war in northwest Anatolia. Scholars debate whether the Homeric poems were composed by one man or many and whether they were created at once or over time. It is likely, however, that the poems first appeared in the eighth or seventh century BCE as oral performances and were only later committed to writing.

By this time—which archaeologists called the Archaic period—Greeks were again on the move, and their culture was resurging. They had settled Cyprus, Crete, and the western coast of Asia Minor (where linguistic evidence places the origin of the Homeric poems). By the eighth and seventh centuries BCE, Greeks established trading posts in Syria and Egypt. In the eighth century BCE, Greek cities founded colonies in southern Italy and Sicily as well as in Thrace on the northern Aegean coast. Written Greek was reinvented, with a new alphabet derived from the Phoenicians. Unlike the Mycenaeans, who seem to have used their writing system almost exclusively for keeping records, the Greeks would soon begin to compose literary, mythological, religious, and philosophical texts that would profoundly influence world thought and history.

Greek religion continued to develop from its Mycenaean roots. The chief Greek gods, Zeus and Hera, are mentioned in Mycenaean texts. Greek myths, or complex and variable stories of the origins and deeds of the gods, were recorded in literary works. Sacred sites, such as the sanctuary at Delphi where an oracle was believed to speak for the god Apollo, emerged and were revered by all Greeks. Pan-Greek festivals, including the famous Olympic games at Olympia, fostered a strong sense of Pan-Hellenic (or all-Greek) identity.

Greek art, architecture, and poetry flourished during the Archaic period. Following the example of the wide-ranging Phoenician mariners, Greek settlers expanded their colonies on the shores of the Black Sea and in North Africa, southern Italy, and Sicily. Greek culture thus spread throughout the Mediterranean and to the frontiers of Asia and laid crucial groundwork for later cultures.

A new kind of Greek city-state also began to emerge during the Archaic period: the *polis* (plural *poleis*), a word that originally meant city but gradually came to mean a political state. Unlike the palace-centered Mycenaean city-states that focused on their kings' wealth and power, poleis would depend on the power and, ultimately, the participation of their citizens: a revolutionary concept. Beginning in the eighth century BCE, most poleis were led by aristocratic oligarchs—elite male citizens who had hereditary control of priesthoods, cults, and prominent local families. Kings still ruled some Archaic-period city-states, which often resulted in tension with the aristocratic councils.

In the seventh and sixth centuries BCE, political turmoil erupted in many city-states. It was fueled by tensions between old, established families and people who had gained new commercial wealth as well as dynamic new ideas introduced from the growing colonies and from contact with foreign peoples. Power frequently fell into the hands of dominating rulers, who the ancient Greeks called tyrants. And no matter who led them, the poleis were frequently at war, battling one another in a shifting landscape of regional powers, alliances, and conflicts. In turn, war fueled political change: the Homeric world of heroic single combat yielded to tightly disciplined units called the hoplite phalanx. The many citizens who worked in the hoplite ranks demanded and won greater civic status.

Major cities followed different paths. Corinth ultimately maintained its narrow oligarchy. Sparta's authoritarian, militaristic society had wide influence over other Greek city-states. But a number of Greek states would follow the lead of Athens—a minor city in Mycenaean times that rose to new prominence during the Archaic period—and move toward government based on popular sovereignty. Early in the sixth century BCE, the Athenian statesman Solon reformed the city's laws. Although the laws maintained many powers of elite citizens, they also granted a greater share of civic power to all citizens (defined as Athenian-born men).

In 510 BCE, the Athenians overthrew their last tyrant and unleashed another wave of reform under the statesman Cleisthenes. The city quickly established a democracy—or direct rule by its male citizens, who jointly governed through a citizen assembly. Although the institutions of

Athens would continue to evolve over the ensuing decades, its fundamental concept of democracy would prove profoundly influential in Europe, the Americas, and around the world. With the fall of its last tyrant and the rise of its democratic institutions, Athens ushered in Greece's classical era.

THE BRIEF GLORIES OF CLASSICAL ATHENS

By the first decade of the fifth century BCE, Greek cities on the coast of Asia Minor had fallen under the control of the vast, extremely powerful Persian Empire. Encouraged by Athens, which was increasingly focused on its democratic institutions and resented what it saw as Persian tyranny, these Greek cities rebelled against Persian control. After it finally crushed the rebels, Persia sent a punitive expedition against Greece. The Athenians and their allies surprisingly defeated Persia, which was by far the strongest regional power, at Marathon in 490 BCE. The vastly outnumbered Greek forces, drawn up in hoplite phalanx formation, advanced into the Persian lines: six thousand Persians died, and the Greeks lost only some two hundred hoplites.

The Persians waged a second attempt ten years later, sending a large fleet and army to crush the Greeks. Held back at the narrow pass of Thermopylae for several days by a small force under the Spartans' King Leonidas, the Persians finally broke through and sacked Athens. But the powerful Athenian navy, led by the gifted Themistocles, inflicted a heavy defeat on the Persians near the island of Salamis. Xerxes, the Persian emperor, withdrew much of his army back to Asia, and the remainder was defeated by the Greeks the following year at the battle of Plateia. The second defeat of the Persians established Athens as the preeminent Greek power.

After Athens led the Greeks to victory, a number of Greek poleis followed Athens's lead and established democratic governments. A defensive alliance of Greek city-states, called the Delian League, was formed with Athens as the clear leader. But as Athens gained power, it also grew more ambitious. It imposed its will on the other poleis, and the Delian League became an Athenian Empire in all but name. Other cities were forced to pay tribute to Athens, and their revolts against Athenian domination were sometimes brutally suppressed.

Wealthy and powerful, Athens flourished. Its democratic system continued to evolve, creating unprecedented political freedom for those it considered citizens: Athenian-born adult males. Led by Pericles, a general and statesman, the city was gloriously rebuilt after its destruction by the Persians in 480 BCE. Spectacular new monuments were created. Among the most impressive was the vast Parthenon, dedicated to the city's patron goddess Athena and built atop Athens's central acropolis. The Parthenon would help create a benchmark of classical architectural style still felt to this day. Athens became a center of art, literature, philosophy, mathematics, and science. The innovative tragic dramas of Aeschylus, Sophocles, and Euripides, along with the comedies of Aristophanes, formed an enduring cultural legacy. This period is still seen as Greece's Golden Age, and the Greek colonies helped carry these cultural achievements throughout the ancient Mediterranean world.

Yet although many non-Athenians were forced to help finance Athens's splendor, they reaped few of its benefits. Cities within the Delian League chafed against Athens's power. Other cities beyond Athenian control—most notably Sparta, with its fierce warrior culture—resented and feared Athens's dominance. In 431 BCE, the Peloponnesian War erupted among Athens, Sparta, and their respective allies. Twenty-seven years of fighting ensued: Athens was ultimately defeated and its empire was destroyed. But the war exhausted all of the Greek cities and drained them of their wealth and manpower. The war ended the Golden Age of classical Athens, and it weakened all of Greece.

ERA 4: THE CLASSICAL ERA: HELLENISTIC GREECE AND ROME FLOURISH *(400 BCE TO 476 CE)*

ALEXANDER'S EMPIRE AND THE HELLENISTIC LEGACY

The Peloponnesian War, which encompassed nearly thirty years of fighting between the Athenian and Spartan alliances, left Greece seriously battered. Sparta won the war in 404 BCE, but its victory resolved very little. The various Greek city-states were still constantly at each other's throats, and Persia again came to dominate the Greek city-states of Asia Minor. New bouts of fighting erupted in Greece over the ensuing decades, as shifting Greek alliances battled for supremacy—conflicts often encouraged and supported by Persia's emperors. After a brief Spartan-imposed tyranny, Athens restored its democratic system. But it was unable to reassert its power, and its internal dissension sometimes turned deadly. In 399 BCE, during the political turmoil following the overthrow of the tyrannical regime, Socrates—a great philosopher but also a constant critic of Athenian government and culture—died at the hands of Athens's citizen assembly.

Greek culture continued to produce influential ideas, art, and literature. In fourth-century Athens, Plato created an enormously influential body of writings on society, politics, and the nature of reality (his teacher Socrates, by contrast, had lectured without ever writing anything). Plato's own student, the Athenian philosopher Aristotle, would produce equally important contributions across a wide range of subjects including ethics, metaphysics, cosmology, and zoology. Yet politically, fighting between the city-states continued to pull Greece into chaos and weakness. Despite its many achievements, the Greek experiment in popular rule was unable to create broad unity among the Greek peoples.

By the mid-fourth century BCE, a new power was rising in Macedonia, on Greece's northern fringe. The fiercely militant Macedonians were a mixture of ethnic Greeks and other local peoples (southern Greeks considered them barbarians); they had maintained a culture that was distinct from their Greek neighbors to the south. Macedonia never developed the polis system of the Greek city-states and remained firmly loyal to its hereditary kings. King Philip II of Macedon, a strong ruler and a student of Greek arms and culture, dramatically increased Macedonia's regional power. The masterful soldier took advantage of the Greek cities' weakness and internal division and controlled most of Greece by the 340s BCE. Spurred by the brilliant Athenian orator Demosthenes, Athens and its allies challenged Philip at Charonea in 338 BCE—and lost.

Macedonia's victory allowed Philip to shift Greece's focus to its longtime enemy, the Persian Empire. After Philip was assassinated in still-mysterious circumstances, his son Alexander III used diplomacy and the sword to squelch any Greek resistance. Alexander's tutor Aristotle taught that civilized Greeks must conquer so-called barbarian kingdoms: Aristotle's message helped inspire Alexander to launch the invasion of Persia that Philip had envisioned. Alexander was a brilliant general and achieved stunning success against the massive Persian Empire. With an army composed mainly of Macedonians, he pushed across Anatolia, through Syria, down the coast into Egypt, and then up into the heart of Persia (present-day Iraq and Iran). As he went, he inflicted crushing defeats on Persia's army and its emperor, Darius. Alexander won a decisive victory at Gaugamela in 331 BCE against a Persian force far larger than his own.

As he advanced, Alexander padded his forces with peoples who had long been under Persia's rule. Many accepted Alexander as their legitimate ruler and even saw him as their liberator. Once he defeated Persia's emperor and took its capital, he could have dismantled the entire empire. Instead, he assumed control as its new master. He and his armies continued to press onward; they extinguished Persian resistance, solidified Alexander's hold on the empire and even expanded its borders. In the end, Alexander pushed into central Asia and, in the Persian province of Bactria, married a local princess named Roxana. He finally pressed to the borders of India—and discovered that the world was far larger than Aristotle had taught him. He defeated the elephant cavalry of an outlying Indian kingdom, but his own men—exhausted and thousands of miles from home—at last persuaded him to turn back.

After a difficult return—and after having conquered much of the known world—Alexander moved to establish himself as emperor at Babylon, near the heart of the Persian world. But he died shortly after he reached the city, when he was only thirty-two years old. His empire barely survived his death, as his generals fought over pieces of the fragmenting realm. Ptolemy took control of Egypt and Seleucus assumed power over Babylon and Persia, and the family of Antigonus took Macedonia and Greece. These so-called successor kingdoms gradually lost power. Weakened by internal rebellions and battles with one another over territory, they would ultimately fall to the expanding power of Rome.

Despite the almost immediate collapse of Alexander's empire, his rapid and unprecedented conquests brought lasting consequences. Alexander—who history would remember as Alexander the Great—had opened the lines of communication throughout western Asia, leaving Greek cities and settlers who left behind local pockets of Greek rule. New cities, such as Alexandria in Egypt and Antioch in Syria, became influential centers of Hellenistic culture and learning. Hybrid Greco-Asian cultures would persist for centuries, and their cultural effects would last much longer. Alexander had permanently drawn the Eurasian world, and its future cultures, more closely together.

ROME RISES

Ancient Italy was a patchwork of Italic peoples from diverse ethnic and linguistic groups. Originally, the Latin-speaking peoples were just one of many groups. They were neither the most powerful nor influential. For some time, those titles belonged to the culturally sophisticated Etruscans. The Etruscans, in turn, were heavily influenced by the Greeks, who established a strong presence in the region with colonies in Sicily and southern Italy. The Etruscans' literature is entirely lost, and their inscriptions are only partly decipherable. But their culture, art, government, and military prowess greatly influenced the early Romans.

Early Rome, the chief city of the Latin peoples, was governed by a series of kings: the position seems to have been elected rather than passed through heredity and were advised by a body of senators. In the late seventh century BCE, an Etruscan family assumed the Roman throne (although there is little evidence to suggest that the Etruscans actually conquered the city). At the end of the sixth century BCE, Rome overthrew the last of its kings and established a republic. Two consuls were elected annually by the citizens—who Rome defined as an elite class of Roman-born men— who governed in consultation with a Senate. The Senate was a body of three hundred elite Romans who were appointed by the consuls, though the system would change over time.

Although the Athenians pioneered the concept of democracy—or direct rule by the people— the Romans took an equally important step with their republic (a word derived from the Latin term *res publica*, "public matter": in short, a commonwealth owned by its citizens). Direct democracy, with all citizens able to act directly in the government, was impossible beyond a small and centralized population. The Roman model—in which elected officers served a fixed term and governed on the citizens' behalf in conjunction with a legislative body—was more practical and would deeply influence later political thought and practice throughout the world.

The Roman Republic was marked by often-violent struggles between the wealthy patricians (or hereditary aristocrats) and the plebeians, or commoners. Wealthy voters controlled the body empowered to elect the consuls and to enact many laws. However, ordinary citizens chose the body that elected the tribunes; the tribunes, in turn, could veto Senate resolutions and also enact laws. Despite their internal struggles, Romans remained deeply committed to the prosperity and expansion of their republic and were willing to sacrifice on its behalf. Rome's power quickly increased. By the third century BCE, it had defeated the Etruscans. In 275 BCE, after a bitter war with the Greek king Pyrrhus, Rome completed its conquest of the Greeks' Italian colonies; this was a major step toward full control of Italy.

The ambitious and expanding Republic then came into conflict with Carthage. Carthage was a North African state that was descended from Phoenician colonists; it boasted wide-ranging trade and a formidable navy. In the three Punic Wars against Carthage, which were fought between the mid-third and mid-second centuries BCE, Rome suffered serious setbacks. These included an invasion by the Carthaginian general Hannibal, who won fame by bringing his army, complete with war elephants, across the Alps into Italy (though few elephants survived the crossing). Rome's loss to Hannibal at the Battle of Cannae was the costliest defeat they had experienced. But Hannibal's invasion soon faltered and the Romans eventually prevailed, destroying and then colonizing Carthage. Now Rome was the dominant power in the Mediterranean, and it seized control of a vast empire that included Sicily, Spain, and North Africa.

In the wake of Alexander's death, Macedonian power was left weakened. The Greek cities had again fallen into petty warfare and internal conflict. Turning east, Rome soon absorbed the Greek mainland into its growing conquests. From its earliest days, Rome had been strongly influenced by the Etruscans—who were themselves strongly influenced by the Greeks—and by the Greek colonies that dominated southern Italy. Now the developing Roman sphere came to encompass Greece itself. All aspects of Greek culture were now part of the Roman world; now Greek artists, architects, authors, and philosophers worked and taught in Italy and across Rome's possessions. Greek culture became an even stronger element of Rome, which itself was poised to expand across much of the known world.

However, Rome's Republic became increasingly strained as its military dominance grew. Consuls and tribunes became more corrupt and autocratic, and military heroes increasingly dominated politics. Although service in the Roman army was a major privilege of citizenship, property qualifications barred many from its ranks. Small farmers were driven from their land, and non-Latin Italic allies, who served as Roman army auxiliaries, were repeatedly denied a route to citizenship. Periodic reform efforts generated controversy but resulted in little concrete change. In 133 BCE, the tribune Tiberius Gracchus proposed reforms to protect small farmers. His aristocratic enemies organized a mob that killed him. His brother, Gaius Gracchus, met a similar demise twelve years later.

As reform efforts failed, the republic tumbled into a series of civil wars between rival political and military factions in the first century BCE. Slave revolts, such as the rebellion in the early first century BCE led by the escaped gladiator Spartacus, added to the sense of chaos. An uprising by non-Latin Italian peoples (called the Social War) caused further disruption. Factional rule decayed toward outright dictatorship (*dictator* originally meant a supreme ruler appointed by the Senate to govern during an emergency), and Rome's response to the ongoing crises turned increasingly savage. Six thousand slaves, who were captured during the Spartacan revolt, were publicly crucified. In 82 BCE, Lucius Cornelius Sulla—whom the Senate had named as dictator—placed several thousand citizens on proscription lists. The dictator called these citizens enemies of the republic: anyone who found them could kill them and receive part of their property as a reward.

In 49 BCE, Julius Caesar led his army from Gaul across the Rubicon River into Italy. The move launched another wave of civil war that lasted until 45 BCE. The popular general was named dictator on his victory, but a conspiracy of assassins—including some of Caesar's former supporters—killed him in 44 BCE. Those who killed him feared that he intended to hold power permanently and hoped that his death would restore the republic (some of the conspirators, of course, mainly hoped to increase their personal power). The assassins, led by Marcus Brutus and others, held Rome only briefly. They were soon forced to battle Caesar's loyalists, led by Marc Antony and Caesar's adopted son Octavian. Octavian and Antony emerged victorious in 42 BCE and dealt the last blow to any meaningful restoration of the republic.

IMPERIAL ROME AND ITS BREAKING POINT

Octavian and Antony turned against one another almost immediately, and a new civil war erupted. Antony established a power base in Egypt, and famously allied with the Egyptian queen Cleopatra VII (a Greek ruler, descended from Alexander the Great's general, Ptolemy). Octavian's and Antony's forces met in the naval Battle of Actium, off the Greek coast, in 31 BCE. Antony and Cleopatra were crushingly defeated. Both committed suicide, and left Octavian in full control of the entire Roman sphere.

Despite his own increasingly monarchical powers, Octavian carefully avoided the appearance of monarchy. Indeed, the suggestion that Julius Caesar had wished to be king had helped bring about his assassination. Octavian shrewdly preserved the outward forms of the republic; he restored the pomp of the Senate and chose to be called *princeps*, or "first citizen." Yet he carefully ensured that all real power belonged to him alone. In 27 BCE, the Senate granted him the title Augustus ("majestic" or "venerable"): the term had religious connotations that evoked the mythical founding of Rome and also evoked the *auctoritas*—the recognized "authority" on which he based his claim to political power. The Roman Empire was truly born.

Under Augustus's rule, Rome dramatically expanded its territory—through diplomacy and through its powerful army legions. Augustus added Judea (formerly Israel and Judah), Asia Minor, Syria, the entire Mediterranean coast of North Africa, and much of Europe to the empire. Roman settlements, governors, and the legions that exerted Rome's power brought urbanization, trade, and Greco-Roman culture deep into Europe. Celtic and Germanic tribes were profoundly influenced. But the Celts and Germans also resisted fiercely and frequently, and the Germans did so with particular effect. In 9 CE, three Roman legions were wiped out in the Teutoburg Forest by an alliance of German tribes. Rome would hold its German frontier for centuries, but it would advance no further into German lands.

Augustus launched a great age of progress in Roman administration and engineering. His close advisor Maecenas befriended and supported leading authors; Rome's literary culture thrived with the classic works of Horace, Virgil, Livy, and Ovid. Roman art, which was heavily influenced by Greek traditions and often employed Greek artists and craftspeople, spread throughout Europe, North Africa, and western Asia. During the ensuing centuries, Roman roads and bridges connected the lands of the empire. Vast aqueducts brought new water supplies to growing urban centers, and Roman temples and civic buildings influenced architecture all over the empire.

In terms of political prowess, Augustus proved exceptional. Few of the emperors who followed him could match his extraordinary combination of ruthless ability and political savvy. The empire weakened under his immediate successors, especially during the disastrous reign of Nero. Chaos ensued; Vespasian, a successful general, took the imperial seat and ended the reign of the Julio-Claudians, the imperial line of Augustus.

Rome also became overextended. Its vast territories strained the empire's ability to manage and to pacify them. New territories often had to be abandoned shortly after they were won. Wars with German tribes became a constant problem, and other frontier peoples—such as the new empire of the Sassanian Persians—pressed in on Rome's more distant possessions. Inhabitants of the many provinces also pushed for full citizenship, which at first was restricted only to Italians. But even as citizenship became more widely available to Roman subjects beyond

Italy, the provinces became ever more independent and put further strains on central rule. In time, the army was left as the only real power in the Roman Empire.

By the late third century CE, the empire was near collapse. Amid constant rebellions of the soldiery and repeated assassinations, Rome saw more than twenty emperors—few of whom died a natural death—in less than fifty years. The emperor Diocletian worked at the end of the century to restore stability and order. He imposed a series of reforms to stabilize the currency and shore up the economy. He also tried to change the structure of Roman rule, seeking a system that could better manage the sprawling empire. Under his plan, the empire would be divided into eastern and western sections. Each would have its own emperor, or Augustus. A deputy ruler, or Caesar, would rule under each Augustus. Eventually, both Augusti would retire and pass power to their Caesars—who, in turn, would choose new Caesars.

Diocletian's reforms failed almost immediately. The Caesars pushed for greater authority, and generals plotted against them and the Augusti. As the fourth century CE opened, the empire was already tumbling back into civil war as rivals struggled bitterly to seize power. The man who would emerge as the victor, the emperor Constantine, would prove a pivotal figure in the history of the West.

CHRISTIANITY, CONSTANTINE, AND THE DECLINE OF THE WESTERN EMPIRE

During the early first-century reign of Augustus's successor, Tiberius, a Jewish preacher and moral teacher emerged in Roman-ruled Judea: Yeshua of Nazareth—or Jesus, in Greek. Most scholars view Jesus as a Jewish apocalyptic prophet, who taught that the worldly order would soon be overthrown and replaced by the just and peaceable kingdom of God. His message attracted a growing number of followers, but his apparent challenge to Roman authority in Judea led to his public crucifixion around 30 CE. Public execution was a favored Roman strategy, intended to terrify onlookers and instill obedience among Rome's subjects.

Jesus's followers believed that he had been raised from the dead after his crucifixion, and a growing number hailed him as the Jewish messiah (or Christ, in Greek): God's anointed, who was chosen to usher in the kingdom of God. His death transformed the meaning of what a messiah was: he was not, as had long been expected, a divinely anointed and triumphant leader. Instead, he was seen as the literal son of God, sent to suffer and to sacrifice himself to redeem others. The message of the early Jesus movement included forgiveness of sin and eternal life through belief in him. It quickly attracted followers in Judea and in the wider, mostly Greek-speaking Jewish Diaspora (Jewish communities beyond Judea). From there, the movement was influenced by early leaders such as Paul—a follower of Jesus and a Jew, who was determined to evangelize non-Jews and spread to the wider Greek and Roman worlds.

Most Jews rejected the idea that Jesus had been the messiah and continued to struggle for independence from Roman rule. A Jewish revolt in 66 to 70 CE led to the destruction of the Jerusalem Temple, which had been rebuilt a few decades earlier by the Roman-allied King Herod. The last rebels held the mountain fortress of Masada until a Roman siege led to their defeat and suicide in 73 CE. A second revolt, in 132 to 135 CE, centered on Simon Bar Kokhba—a man whose followers believed him to be the messiah and was destined to restore the Jewish nation. The rebellion was crushed and Judea was destroyed. The Romans renamed the province Palestine and expelled much of the Jewish population.

The earliest followers of Jesus anticipated his imminent return and the coming of the kingdom of God. But gradually, Christianity began to form a distinct religion and church. It emphasized the moral teachings of Jesus and taught salvation through belief in him as the Messiah. It ultimately split completely from Judaism. Roman law required that all citizens participate in sacrifices to civic patron gods. Like Jews, Christians refused. But although Romans respected Judaism for its antiquity and granted Jews an exemption, they argued that followers of the new faith were merely defying Roman law. Christians were not officially tolerated as Jews were and sometimes faced open persecution. During the third century CE, the emperors Valerian, Decius, and Diocletian launched particularly heavy crackdowns as they tried to suppress the growing Christian community.

Nonetheless, Christianity continued to gain followers. Late first-century accounts of Jesus's life and deeds—the gospels—were accepted as scripture, as were the letters of Paul and other books—though many other gospels, letters, and apocalyptic accounts also circulated before they were ultimately rejected. Despite the empire's official rejection of Christianity, it continued to gain in numbers, influence, wealth, and prominence. Romans had long accepted and absorbed foreign religions, and Christianity had wide appeal. In addition to its promise of eternal salvation, its commitment to charity and community made a strong impression in the turbulent and violent days of the faltering Roman Empire.

Just seven years after Diocletian's reign ended, Christians' situation in the empire reversed entirely. In the fighting that followed Diocletian's attempt to divide the empire, Constantine battled his way to supremacy. In 312 CE, as he fended rivals off in pursuit of the Western Empire, the general dramatically embraced Christianity. He later claimed that just before the battle for the Milvian Bridge outside Rome, he received a divine message: he would conquer if he became a Christian. His actual motivations are the subject of debate. Political calculation was probably at least one factor, because he knew that the Christian community was emerging as a potent force. Constantine soon secured the entire Western Empire and granted Christians official toleration.

Constantine was also soon at war with the eastern emperor: by 323 CE, he ruled the entire Roman world. Meanwhile, his open commitment to Christianity deepened. He built churches, officially supported the faith and its developing orthodox doctrines, and worked toward abolishing paganism. Rome and its bishop—who would soon be known as the pope—became the center of Christianity in the West; paganism was permanently banned by the emperor Theodosius in the 390s CE. But the empire itself soon shifted away. Constantine, who saw greater strength and wealth in the Eastern Empire, moved his capital to the eastern city of Byzantium (renamed Constantinople), which sat between Europe and Asia in what is now Turkey.

After Constantine's death, the empire began to fragment between eastern and western realms. Although the Eastern, or Byzantine, Empire, and its increasingly distinct church, grew under Constantine's successors, the Western Empire grew ever more unstable. Rome was forced to pull back its frontiers. By the early fifth century, the so-called Germanic barbarians (themselves displaced by Asiatic Huns who had pressed into Hungary and beyond) were pushing into Italy. Rome was sacked by the Germanic Goths and their leader, Alaric, in 410 CE. The last Western emperor fell in 476. But the linguistic, cultural, and religious legacies of Rome would continue to echo powerfully throughout the world.

ERA 5: RELIGION AND WAR: DRIVING CHANGE IN ASIAN EMPIRES
(1750 BCE TO CA. 1650 CE)

INDIA: FROM THE VEDAS TO THE GUPTAS—BUDDHISM, HINDUISM, AND THE WIDER WORLD

By 1750 BCE, northwest India's Bronze Age Indus Valley civilization had crumbled. Its great cities were abandoned and their inhabitants' fate is unknown. Speakers of an Indo-European language, who originated in Central Asia, migrated into India from present-day Iran during the centuries that followed. Although scholars used to call their entry an invasion, they now view the event as a more nuanced process, one in which the new culture fused with that of local peoples.

Between 1500 and 500 BCE, the Indo-European peoples of India began to create oral epics and sacred texts. The texts, the Vedas, are among history's first religious scriptures. They describe religious rituals, invocations, and hymns to a pantheon of gods, who shared links with Greek and Roman mythology through common Indo-European roots. The Vedas sky god is Dyaus Pita, which parallels the Greek Zeus Pater and the early Roman Diespiter (or Jupiter). The culture that created these texts is known as *Vedic*, and wrote them in the Indo-European Sanskrit language. Vedic religion and the Vedas formed the roots of the later Indian Hindu religion: a system based on belief in human reincarnation and a pantheon of gods with multiple manifestations and complex histories.

The Vedic culture gradually moved beyond the heartland of the Indus Valley civilization, south to the Ganges River, and then deeper into the Indian subcontinent. Society was divided into social levels, or castes, to which people were confined by birth. Vedic society believed in reincarnation, a process by which the soul gradually climbs to higher levels in successive lives. The priestly Brahmins occupied the highest level, followed by a warrior caste, a merchant caste, and a worker caste, each with numerous subdivisions. Below the castes were the so-called untouchables, who worked in trades that were considered ritualistically unclean, such as butchering animals or handling corpses.

By the fourth century BCE, the Vedic culture had produced enormous epic literary works. The vast *Mahabharata* tells the stories of Vedic princely families and contains the *Bhagavad Gita*, a major Hindu text that reveals the teachings of the god Krishna. The *Ramayana* epic, from roughly the same period, reflects on human obligations in relation to cosmic moral law.

Around 500 BCE, Siddhartha Gautama, prince of a small kingdom near the present border of India and Nepal, left behind his family, wealth, and position to pursue a spiritual search. Teaching that desire and attachment to the material world were the roots of all suffering, he would later become known as the Buddha (a Sanskrit word that means "awakened or enlightened one"). True enlightenment, he maintained, would allow seekers to reach nirvana, or the perfect state of mental freedom, and to escape from the cycle of earthly reincarnation. The Buddha quickly attracted followers, and the Buddhist movement was born. In the beginning, it was largely a personal quest for spiritual enlightenment. But it would gradually grow into a range of different religious movements with diverse interpretations of the teachings of the Buddha and his successors.

The vast Persian Empire subjugated parts of northwest India. In turn, Alexander the Great conquered the Persians at the end of the fourth century BCE and pushed to the edges of India. He learned of the great kingdoms still ahead along the Ganges—beyond what Greeks had believed to be the outer edge of the world—and wanted to add to his conquests. But his army refused to go any further. Greek contact with the outskirts of India, including long-term Greek settlements, would nonetheless leave a lasting influence on the cultures of the area that persisted for centuries and opened contact between India and the West.

In Alexander's wake, Indian rulers established the Mauryan Empire. It unified most of India for the first time and defeated Seleucus, one of Alexander's generals who ruled the eastern portions of his conquests after his leader's death. In the third century BCE, the Mauryan emperor Asoka renounced his own violent, militaristic past and converted to Buddhism. This was a significant moment for Buddhism: Asoka made his entire empire Buddhist and built great monuments to mark the places where the Buddha had preached and to preserve relics of his life.

The empire, however, fell soon after Asoka's death, leaving India vulnerable to a series of Persian and central Asian invasions. One group of invaders, the Kushans of central Asia, controlled northern India between the first and third centuries CE. The Kushan rulers adopted Buddhism and fused Indian culture with their own. Alexander's legacy was also felt, particularly in the Gandhara region (present-day Pakistan and Afghanistan): commercial ties to Rome greatly expanded and Greco-Roman aesthetics deeply influenced the Gandharan region, leading to a hybrid style of Buddhist art. The Kushans also opened trade routes into central Asia and China and thus allowed Buddhism to spread rapidly into Asia.

Southern India witnessed a political and cultural resurgence in the centuries that followed. From the fourth to the sixth centuries CE, the native Indian Gupta Empire gained control over most of India. India was now largely unified for the first time since Asoka's reign. The Gupta age was characterized by an artistic and cultural rebirth, and its artistic influence would spread along the trade routes as far as China. Most important, there was a revival of the ancient Vedic tradition, which gave rise to the modern Hindu religion that has dominated most of India through modern times. Meanwhile, Buddhism began to lose ground in its birthplace. Although it was well-established in East and Southeast Asia, it would virtually disappear from India by the early second millennium CE.

IMPERIAL CHINA EMERGES

The Bronze Age Shang kings were overthrown by the Zhou kingdom at the end of the second millennium BCE. The Zhou kings ruled central China for more than two centuries, but then regional states asserted their own power once more—and central control began to falter again. By the eighth century BCE, China had entered a long era of disunity called the Spring and Autumn period. The Zhou technically still ruled, but China's rival regional kingdoms fell to open conflict during the early fifth century BCE. China thus entered the Warring States period: China was divided and no single faction was able to control the nation.

These periods were marked by political disruption and discord and also by major advancements in Chinese thought, culture, and technology. During the Warring States period, bronze casting reached extraordinary levels of sophistication. Cast bronze coins, China's first metallic currency, appeared during the era. The revolutionary ability to cast iron emerged during the Spring and Autumn period. The classic treatise on military strategy, the *Art of War*—attributed to military strategist Sun Tzu (or Sunzi)—was most likely also composed during this time.

Around 500 BCE, the philosopher Confucius (or Kong Fuzi) created an immensely influential ethical system that emphasized familial ties, social obligations, and moral responsibilities for people at all social levels. During the fourth century BCE, the philosopher Mencius (or Meng Zi) offered a key interpretation of Confucius that highlighted the fundamental goodness of people, the duty of rulers to act justly, and the right of the ruled to overthrow villainous kings. The foundations of the religious and philosophical Daoist movement were also being laid at this time, which would seek the universe's guiding essence and the secret of human immortality.

By the third century BCE, the warlike and dictatorial state of Qin began to overwhelm its rivals. The Qin king finally defeated his last challengers and worked to exert his power throughout China. In 221 BCE, he declared himself Qin Shi Huangdi—the first Chinese emperor.

The Qin emperor imposed a harsh legal code, issuing deadly penalties for even minor offenses. He ruled by fear, suppressing dissent and burning books—including those of the Confucians—whose ideas might challenge his absolute authority. To that end, scholars were even buried alive. Seeking to thwart foreign invasion, he forced thousands of men to build a wall of stone and earth along China's northern frontier. This was the earliest version of China's famed Great Wall. Later dynasties would repair and extend the wall, although the now-famous stone structure would not appear for another fifteen hundred years.

According to ancient historians, Qin Shi Huangdi pursued immortality until it became his obsession. But he knew that his quest might fail, so he ordered the construction of a massive tomb beneath a colossal earth mound. In pits around the tomb, thousands of terra cotta soldiers were buried in order to serve him in the next world; there they lay until they were accidentally discovered in the 1970s.

After Qin Shi Huangdi died in 210 BCE, his empire began to crumble. His oldest son was murdered by rival courtiers, and his younger son assumed the throne. But he could not control his fractious and ambitious court—let alone his angry, restive subjects. Soon, the empire was wracked by a series of rebellions. The second emperor was defeated and forced to commit suicide in 207 BCE. The short-lived Qin Empire had brought unprecedented political unity to China, but the rigid and brutal system could not survive without the first emperor's unstoppable will.

However, the idea of a Chinese empire lived on. After Qin's fall, Liu Bang, ruler of the state of Han, emerged as the dominant figure and was proclaimed emperor in 206 BCE. The new Han dynasty was created, seeking to rule in accordance with Confucian principles. The Western Han dynasty ruled between 206 BCE and 9 CE, when disputes among court factions caused its downfall. But the Han emperors returned to power in a new capital in 25 CE. The Eastern Han dynasty lasted until 220 CE, when conflicts with outside peoples and internal agricultural failures led to political weakness, internal rebellions, and the final end of the Han dynasty.

The Han period is considered one of the greatest in China's history. The empire gained new territories and forever expanded China's cultural imprint. Trade routes into central Asia and beyond were opened; the famous Silk Road carried Chinese goods as far as the Middle East and enabled indirect contact with the Roman Empire. The Western Han capital, Chang'an, was one of the world's largest and most sophisticated cities. Art, poetry, history, philosophy, science, and technology all thrived, as did science and technology, including the pioneering development and use of paper. Even now, the Chinese call themselves the Han people in honor of the dynasty's defining achievements.

CHINA FROM TANG TO QING

After the fall of the Han, China entered another period of division called the Era of Disunity (or Six Dynasties period). Some of the era's transitory kingdoms were notable centers of art and culture, and it was at this time that Buddhism arrived in China along the central Asian trade routes. Buddhism became a major part of Chinese tradition, as Chinese thinkers and artists adapted Indian and central Asian precedents to their own needs. As Buddhism's influence declined in India, it gained an enormous following in China—alongside Daoism, Confucian philosophy, and other indigenous belief systems.

In the late sixth century CE, the harsh Sui dynasty reunited China. The Sui emperors adopted Buddhism to gain favor with the increasingly Buddhist population. Their reign produced notable accomplishments, including the completion of the eleven-hundred-mile Grand Canal. But they also imposed high taxes, forced labor, and fought an unsuccessful war in Korea. Their unpopular rule lasted fewer than forty years.

Then a new imperial line, the Tang dynasty, gained power. Its emperors presided over another of China's greatest periods: a golden age of art and culture known for its poetry, scholarship, painting, technology, and sculpture (Tang ceramic horses and camels are especially famous). The manufacture of porcelain expanded and improved under the dynasty and fueled a thriving export trade by land and sea as far away as Muslim Arabia. Most likely, gunpowder was also a Tang invention. The capital Chang'an, planned in a grid design, was the largest city in the world for some time. Its population peaked at a million people during the eighth century.

Progress and prosperity bypassed many Chinese, however. During this period, the wealthy began to break and bind the feet of their young daughters to create an appearance of the extraordinarily small and delicate feet that were considered a sign of beauty in Chinese culture. The practice also resulted in a crippling deformity that inhibited women's ability to walk, ensuring that these girls would grow into women who would never need to work or be mobile—a further sign of wealth and station.

During the Tang reign, China's territory grew. Extensive trade spread China's culture further and fostered a tremendous expansion of Buddhism throughout Asia. By the ninth century, however, the Tang's power was failing. Regional governors challenged the dynasty's authority, and a series of natural disasters raised popular fears that the rulers had lost the Mandate of Heaven—a powerful Chinese idea, which traced back to Confucius and Mencius, that divine authority supported just and legitimate rulers. Rebellions and internal schisms led to the Tang collapsing by 907, and a fragmented period of regional kingdoms opened.

In 960, the new Song dynasty reunited much of China (it failed to recover some of the outlying regions that the Tang had ruled). The Song ushered in new urbanization and oversaw one of the most glorious eras of Chinese art, particularly in painting and calligraphy. The Song also expanded the empire's talent-seeking system of civil service exams, which had started under the Han and which focused on the great Confucian texts. From the Song period onward, young men who could afford education could pass the exams, join the prestigious imperial bureaucracy, and thus gain the potential to rise to great power and fortune. (Predictably, these make-or-break exams also spawned an entire industry of cheating aids—men could, for instance, acquire silk handkerchiefs that displayed Confucian texts.) The exams required years of study that the truly poor could not afford: but some villages would join together to support a young scholar, hoping to benefit from his connections as he rose in the bureaucracy.

Song cultural achievements could not compensate for the dynasty's growing military weakness, and central Asian invaders pressed into China in the twelfth century. They drove the Song out of their northern territories and into a rump territory known as the Southern Song. During the next century, the powerful warriors of the Mongol Khanate began to overtake northern China. The great Genghis Khan, who had conquered much of central and western Asia, was their leader, terrorizing cities into submission. Under his grandson, Kublai Khan, the Mongols officially declared their own Yuan dynasty in 1271 and defeated the last southern Song resistance in 1279. The Mongols' Yuan dynasty would rule all of China for almost a century.

It was in the 1270s, during the Yuan conquest, that Venetian merchant Marco Polo arrived in China. His travel accounts circulated throughout Europe after 1300, and the narratives offered Europeans their first glimpse into the distant, mysterious lands of East Asia. Polo's narrative would inform European knowledge about China for centuries. Even when Christopher Columbus reached the Caribbean in 1492 (trying to reach China via the Atlantic Ocean), he sought everywhere for news of the "Great Khan" whom Polo had described.

As it happened, Columbus would not have found a Khan even if he had reached China. The Chinese revolted against Mongol control, overthrew the Yuan, and established the Ming dynasty in 1368. Under this lengthy dynasty, trade increased throughout Asia. In the early fifteenth century, large fleets under the famous admiral Zheng He reached as far as India, Arabia, and East Africa. But rival factions in the Ming court battled over these voyages. The winning faction argued that exploration and outreach were wasteful and unnecessary, and the Ming banned further expeditions. Limited trade with Europe, which was restricted to certain carefully guarded ports, such as Canton (Guangzhou), nonetheless began in the sixteenth century. European demand for porcelain and other Chinese exports soared, whereas foreign currency became an increasingly important part of China's economy.

The Ming capital moved to Beijing during the fifteenth century, and the walled Forbidden City—the imperial palace compound—was built. China's Great Wall attained its now-familiar stone walls, towers, and gates during this period: it was designed to deter central Asian invaders. Despite these massive efforts, Manchurians—a people from what is now northeastern China—launched a successful invasion during the seventeenth century. The Ming state was already struggling with agricultural failures, economic strife, and internal rebellion. The Manchus exploited these weaknesses, overthrew the Ming in 1644, and established their own Qing dynasty. It would last until 1911.

LANDS BEYOND CHINA: JAPAN, KOREA, AND SOUTHEAST ASIA

China strongly influenced the development of Japan and Korea. Japan's lengthy hunter-gatherer stone age, or Jomon period, lasted from circa 10,000 BCE through the late first millennium BCE and witnessed the first Japanese pottery. After 1000 BCE, Korea adopted rice cultivation and bronze technology from China. Japan developed rice cultivation in the centuries that followed, and metallurgy and the potter's wheel most likely reached the islands via Korea by 300 BCE. The roots of Japan's Shinto religious tradition also began to develop: people worshipped spirits, or *kami*, associated with ancestors and nature. At the same time, Korea began to enter the Iron Age.

Korea's earliest political states also developed by the end of the first millennium BCE and continued to absorb Chinese culture—especially during the Han dynasty, when China maintained military outposts there. But Korea's various states repeatedly resisted Chinese attempts to annex the Korean peninsula. After 300 CE, as three local kingdoms came to control the peninsula, Chinese cultural influences—including Confucianism, Buddhism, and Daoism—increased even further. After 600 CE, the Korean kingdom of Silla allied with China's Tang dynasty and unified Korea for the first time (relations with China remained often tense). In the tenth century, after a brief period of fragmentation, the peninsula was unified by the Goryeo (or Koryŏ, from which the name Korea comes) state, with a bureaucratic government system modeled on China's.

After 300 CE, Japan developed a system of clan leaders. The leaders of the dominant Yamato clan emerged as emperors. Japanese society moved deliberately closer to China's, because it adopted a writing system based on Chinese characters and taught Confucian precepts. The imperial system continued to develop during the seventh and eighth centuries. Buddhism became the official state religion, although Shinto beliefs remained influential. Japan was more physically isolated than Korea but also feared Chinese invasion. Japan's rulers admired China's cultural example but also wished to bolster their own power and protect their independence. In the ninth century, Japan severed all direct contact with China.

Japan entered an era of high cultural achievement in the Heian period, between the late eighth and late twelfth centuries. Powerful painting styles appeared as well as some of Japan's greatest literature, including the *Tale of Genji*—written by a female courtier and often considered the world's first novel. But even as its culture flourished, Japan's empire had evolved into a highly feudal system under powerful landholding warlords. Their strength increasingly threatened the standing of the emperors; by the beginning of the Kamakura period in the late twelfth century, the emperors were little more than figureheads. Real power belonged to the warrior rulers, or shogun. Also at this time, an elite class of Japanese warriors called samurai began to become prominent. Trained from childhood, samurai wore elaborate and fearsome armor and fought with exquisitely made steel swords, learning complex martial arts skills. Their culture was based on a code called *Bushido*—or the way of the warrior—which stressed bravery, stamina, honor, and loyalty.

Mongol invaders swept into Korea in the early thirteenth century, making it a vassal state and imposing a harsh occupation well into the fourteenth century. Once they took hold of China in the 1270s, the Mongols fixed their sights on Japan. Kublai Khan demanded that Japan submit to him and pay tribute, but Japan's military rulers refused. In 1274, the Khan launched an invasion against Japan.

A storm forced the Mongols to abandon their beachhead and decimated their fleet, so Kublai tried again in 1281 with a larger fleet that carried tens of thousands of soldiers. The well-prepared Japanese had fortified the coast and drove off the Mongol landing force. A massive typhoon soon struck, and the Mongol fleet–composed mostly of hastily gathered river craft utterly unfit for the open ocean–was virtually obliterated. The Japanese called it the kamikaze, or divine wind.

Over the next several centuries, power in Japan shifted between rival warlords. Although the imperial line continued unbroken, it held little power. Japan produced great art in this period, particularly painted screens and spontaneous ink painting inspired by the Zen sect of Buddhism (originally Chan Buddhism, in China). But the landscape was also dotted with massive castles, as military families struggled for dominance. In the 1500s, limited contact with Portuguese sailors and soldiers occurred; they introduced firearms to Japan. After 1603, the Tokugawa shoguns kept rein over the feudal lords and firmly closed Japan to outside contact. Few Western visitors were allowed, and they were confined to coastal enclaves. By 1600, Japan was manufacturing a massive number of firearms, but samurai warriors resented the threat to their traditional sword skills and ultimately forced the shoguns to eliminate guns from Japan.

In Korea, the Joseon, or Yi, dynasty took power at the end of the fourteenth century, after Mongol rule ended, adopting the Chinese Confucian tradition as the state ideology. The Joseon would last through many difficulties until Japan annexed the peninsula in 1910. Korean arts, especially painting and ceramics, flourished. But the peninsula remained a focus for outside ambitions. Japan launched a ferocious invasion during the late sixteenth century, in which soldiers and civilians alike were tortured. Although the Japanese were ultimately repelled, the war hit Korea hard. In the seventeenth century, the Manchus made Korea a vassal state: once the Manchus established the Qing dynasty in China, Korea would be technically independent but essentially under rule from China.

Since ancient times, Southeast Asia formed a crossroads for trade and ideas. Buddhism and Hinduism arrived from India, likely carried by merchants, and made inroads from Burma to Bali. China had frequent contact with Vietnam, repeatedly attempting invasion–sometimes successfully– and heavily influencing Vietnamese culture and language. Major Buddhist and Hindu kingdoms arose across the Southeast Asian mainland and even reached some of the region's large islands.

Perhaps the greatest of these kingdoms was the Khmer Empire, which was centered in the northeast of present-day Cambodia between the ninth and fifteenth centuries CE. Over several centuries, the Khmer built dozens of elaborate temple complexes dedicated to both Hindu and Buddhist beliefs; the most famous is the spectacular temple of Angkor Wat, whose walls carry over a mile of low-relief sculpture depicting religious mythology. Although kingdoms such as the Khmer incorporated Indian ideas and beliefs, they localized these practices, weaving them into indigenous systems of beliefs, values, and tastes.

ERA 6: THE RISE OF ISLAM: RELIGION TRAVELS ON A ROAD OF SILK (CA. 610 CE TO 1500S)

ISLAM'S ORIGINS AND RAPID CONQUESTS

We have few details about the religion of the Semitic peoples of Arabia before the seventh century CE. We know it was polytheistic, with multiple gods, demons, and *jinn* (spirits, or genies). But Judeo-Christian monotheism influenced the region heavily. A community of Jewish merchants had settled in Arabia, and some Arabs were practicing Jews. Christians—primarily members of offshoot sects that were distinct from the churches of Rome or Constantinople—probably also lived there.

Around 610 CE, a merchant named Muhammad was living in the Arabian city of Mecca and began to have divine visions. Muhammad, who was heavily influenced by the Jewish and Christian concepts of God, believed that he had been chosen to serve as God's final prophet. Over the next twenty years, his revelations on religious doctrine and law were recorded in the Qur'an, a holy book among his followers. Together with records of his teachings and actions, the Qur'an served as the basis of a new religion: Islam (or "submission to God's will," in Arabic). Adherents of Islam called themselves Muslims, or "those who submit."

At first, Muhammad's circle was small. His followers faced harassment from those who rejected Muhammad's claims, and they fled north to the Arabian city of Medina in 622. Soon, however, the Muslim community began to grow dramatically. By 630, Muhammad had raised an army and forced the surrender of Mecca. By his death, traditionally dated to 632, his followers were assembling a massive following, building a highly effective military force and rapidly taking control of Arabia. Through a combination of conquest and conversion, Islam would continue its rapid expansion in the wake of Muhammad's death.

The Eastern Roman, or Byzantine, Empire reached its peak under the emperor Justinian during the sixth century. But in the face of the seventh-century Muslim advance, it quickly fell back. Egypt, a Byzantine possession dominated for centuries by local Coptic Christians, was conquered and converted by 640, and Islam swept across the rest of North Africa. Since Constantine's fourth-century reign, Christian Byzantium had controlled Syria and the Christian Holy Land of Palestine. Both fell to Arab armies in the 630s, and the Byzantines were driven back into Asia Minor. By the 640s, Arab armies had also overrun the Sassanian Persian Empire. The last Sassanian emperor was killed in 651, and Persia was swiftly converted to Islam.

Within only twenty years of Muhammad's death, Islam controlled most of western Asia and North Africa. Muslims believed that they had a religious obligation to bring the world into the Islamic faith—or at least under Muslim political authority. The Qur'an uses the term *jihad* to denote "striving in the path of God," which may include war to advance the power and territory of Islam. Although jihad is restricted by rules of warfare—including protections for civilians—the struggle is considered a Muslim's duty. Those who die in its pursuit are considered martyrs who receive special rewards in the afterlife.

Although the new faith continued to grow, the pace began to slow and dissent over who could claim legitimate succession from Muhammad divided Muslims from within. Muhammad left no instructions on who should succeed him. Three *caliphs*—successors to Muhammad—followed him, fusing political and religious authority as he had. The first, Muhammad's companion and father-in-law, was chosen by Muhammad's close followers. His chosen successor, the second caliph, was assassinated in 644. Others, meanwhile, were loyal to Ali, Muhammad's cousin and son-in-law. They argued that he, as Muhammad's closest living relative, was the true Islamic leader, or *imam*, and should rule in place of the caliphs.

The third caliph was assassinated in 656, and Ali was acclaimed as his successor—before he too was murdered in 661. The schism proved permanent: Ali's followers, called *Shia* (or partisans), developed Shiite Islam with a separate set of doctrines and beliefs. The majority of Muslims rejected their claims and formed Sunni Islam. The Sunni majority rallied behind the Ummayad caliphs, who settled in Damascus after 660 and assumed control throughout the Islamic world. Conflict and open civil war would continue to flare between Sunnis and Shiites for centuries. More than 80 percent of modern-day Muslims belong to the Sunni sect.

Despite these serious internal rifts, the Sunni caliphate in Damascus had great achievements in a short period of time. The Ummayads established Arabic—the language of the sacred Qur'an—as the primary language of Islam. They standardized the currency throughout Islamic lands, which allowed direct trade across its vast territories. They also launched the first major campaign of Islamic architecture; they built Jerusalem's Dome of the Rock in 691, the new faith's first major monument, which marked the spot—once the site of the Jewish Temple of Solomon—from which Muhammad was said to have ascended to heaven in a mystical night journey. The Ummayads also expanded Muslim territory, pushing into Spain in the early eighth century and to the borders of China and India. Their attempts to push beyond Spain into France were stopped by the local Frankish rulers.

POLITICAL DIVISION AND CULTURAL ACHIEVEMENT

In 750, the Umayyad caliphs fell to the Abbasids, who were descendants of Muhammad's uncle Abbas. Their claim to power, which they based on their victory over the Ummayads, was not recognized by all Muslims. The new Abbasid caliphate moved its capital to Iraq and built the impressive, circular-plan city of Baghdad. As the new leaders turned from Syria toward Mesopotamia, they adopted aspects of Persian court culture and weakened Arab domination of Islam.

Muslim conquerors had not always systematically forced the people whom they conquered to convert, although many conversions took place as the new religion gained military and cultural supremacy over an expanding area. Under the Abbasids, pressure to convert grew. Islam had conquered extensive Byzantine territory with a large number of Christians and Jews—many of whom held to their own faiths and resisted conversion. Christians and Jews were tolerated as "peoples of the Book": fellow adherents to the God of Abraham and the biblical patriarchs. Nonetheless, they faced early expulsion from Arabia. Elsewhere, they faced political restrictions and heavy taxes, encouraging Jews and Christians to convert and escape these penalties.

The caliphate pressed for uniform Islamic practice within its borders, but Islamic culture also gathered ideas from other traditions. During the long era of turmoil that followed the fifth-century fall of the Western Roman Empire, monasteries preserved Christian texts—but most Greek science and philosophy works were lost. The Greek-speaking Byzantine Empire preserved far more, but it also faced serious decline as Islam rose. During the Abbasid caliphate, however, Muslims sought out, studied, and preserved Greek knowledge: it served as the foundation for much of medieval Islamic scholarship. Al-Farabi, the tenth-century scientist and philosopher, studied and circulated Aristotle's works. The physician and philosopher Avicenna, who lived during the tenth and eleventh centuries, was also greatly influenced by Aristotle and other Greek writers as he created works on medicine that would become hugely influential.

Muslims also established active trading ties with East Asia. They communicated directly with the Tang and Song Dynasties in China and also traded with Christians in the West. In doing so, Islam created the first major bridge between East and West. During the first millennium, China was more technologically advanced than the post-Roman West. Islam introduced Chinese innovations such as the magnetic compass, paper, and gunpowder to the West during the Middle Ages. Muslims also introduced the Indian game of chess and India's place-value number system to the West; Europeans still refer to the digits as "Arabic numerals."

Beyond carrying others' contributions to new places, Muslims influenced the East and West with their own contributions in science, mathematics, architecture, medicine, literature, and philosophy. The ninth-century Abbasid mathematician al-Khwarizmi helped develop algebra, the word for which derives from Arabic *al-jabr* (or the restoration of broken parts). Latin translations of his works introduced place-value numerals to Europe in the twelfth century, and the word *algorithm* derives from the Latinized form of his name.

The fourteenth-century Arab scholar Ibn Khaldun wrote influential works on the study of history, society, and economics. Omar Khayyam, a Persian scientist who lived during the eleventh and twelfth centuries, was a mathematician, philosopher, theologian, and poet. His four-line poems, or quatrains (called rubaiyat), explored love, time, and morality; they became famous in the West through a popular nineteenth-century English translation. Sufism, a mystical movement within Islam, began to develop by at least the ninth century. Beginning in the twelfth century, Iranian Sufists created new and exquisite forms of poetry.

There was a strong cultural flowering in Islamic Spain, where Muslims, Christians, and Jews enjoyed a generally peaceful coexistence. The twelfth-century Spanish Muslim philosopher Averroes followed the tradition of Al-Farabi and helped to reintroduce Aristotle to the West. Jewish scholars in Islamic Spain, such as the great twelfth-century thinker Moses Maimonides, also served as a cultural bridge. Maimonides created preeminent studies of Jewish texts but also philosophical works in Arabic. He was deeply influenced by Arab scholars and their study of Aristotle, and he worked as a physician for Islamic rulers. The cultural legacy of Muslim Spain would remain after the Christian reconquest of the Iberian Peninsula (where Spain and Portugal lie): the region's great Islamic architecture (often called Moorish, in reference to the Muslim rulers' North African origins) was frequently conquered and reused, rather than destroyed. Mosques were converted into churches, and Christian rulers moved into Muslim palaces.

Despite the dramatic cultural achievements of medieval Islam, the Abbasids' central political authority declined quickly. Its vast territories were difficult to govern, and local rulers, or sultans, began to gain power of their own across the Islamic world. Some regions were lost entirely: a survivor of the Ummayad Dynasty wrested Spain from the Abbasids in 756, and much of North Africa fell to local Muslim rulers. In the tenth century, the Shiite Fatimids seized Egypt and rejected Abbasid power. Shiites also conquered Iraq and reduced the Sunni Abbasid caliph to a captive figurehead.

During the eleventh century, the Seljuk Turks, a central Asian people who had converted to Sunni Islam, conquered most of the Middle East and seized much of Abbasid territory. They took most of Anatolia from the Byzantines and transformed the Greek and Christian region into a heavily Turkish and Muslim one. But the new Seljuk Empire itself declined almost immediately because it disintegrated into small rival states. European Christians, who had long resented the Muslim conquest of the formerly Christian Holy Land, took advantage of the Islamic infighting and launched the First Crusade. The crusaders took Jerusalem in 1099 and slaughtered a large part of its Muslim and Jewish population. They established several Christian kingdoms, called the Crusader States, in Palestine and Syria.

In the 1170s, a new Sunni sultanate (a government ruled by a Muslim sultan), led by the celebrated sultan Saladin, conquered Egypt and the Eastern Mediterranean coast. Saladin pushed the Crusaders from Jerusalem in 1187. Although he was ultimately defeated by the crusader Richard the Lionheart, the new crusade failed to retake Jerusalem. The Crusader States crumbled gradually during the following decades. Saladin's successors were themselves overthrown in 1250 by their Asian mercenaries, the Turkish Mamluks, who established their own Islamic sultanate.

AMID CHAOS, CONTINUED EXPANSION

The caliphate's central power diminished, but most areas that were once ruled by the Ummayads and Abbasids remained Muslim. After 1000, Christian kingdoms were established in northern Spain and began to slowly reconquer the Iberian Peninsula. By the mid-thirteenth century, only the southern tip of Spain was still in Muslim hands, and that would fall in 1492. Elsewhere, however, Islam continued to expand.

Since the Gupta Empire's fall in the sixth century, India had been ruled by a shifting landscape of Hindu states. By the tenth century, Muslim powers had moved into the far northern reaches of India (present-day Pakistan and Afghanistan). At the end of the twelfth century, Muslims from Afghanistan advanced farther into northern India. The Afghans' own Turkish soldiers seized control of these new conquests and created the Islamic Sultanate of Delhi. The sultanate would take most of the subcontinent over the next century before southern Hindu states drove it back into northern India.

Shortly thereafter, the Islamic world was soon overwhelmed by the massive westward invasion of the central Asian Mongol tribes. The feared Genghis Khan had united the Mongolian tribes at the beginning of the thirteenth century; he conquered lands from northern China to the Black Sea and struck terror with his savage brutality. In the mid-thirteenth century, his successors drove deep into western Asia—and the Muslim world was thrown into chaos. The Mamluks stopped the Mongols in the eastern Mediterranean, and the Delhi sultanate held northern India against them. But the Mongol hordes swept across Russia into Eastern Europe; in western Asia, they sacked Baghdad and captured Persia and Syria. But the Mongols themselves soon split into rival regional powers, and the Mongol rulers of Persia converted to Islam within a century.

Beginning in the twelfth century, merchants and missionaries carried Islam to East Africa. Strong trade relations, including an important slave trade, were established between East Africa and the Arab world. In the following centuries, Islam expanded to major West African powers such as Ghana and Mali. An extensive trade in African slaves, gold, salt, and other goods extended from these realms across the Sahara to the Middle East.

Islamic trade continued to expand and Muslim missionaries continued to follow the trade routes. By the thirteenth century, contact between Southeast Asia and Islamic merchants had increased. Islam had only limited penetration in the Buddhist and Hindu kingdoms of mainland Southeast Asia, but it began to make significant inroads in Southeast Asia's island states, including Indonesia, parts of the Philippines, and Malaysia.

LATER ISLAMIC EMPIRES

The Mongol invasion left most of the Muslim world disrupted and unstable. In what is now Turkey, the remaining Seljuk Turkish states narrowly staved off the Mongol hordes. Around 1300, a Seljuk ruler created the new Turkish Ottoman state in northern Anatolia. The militarist Ottomans quickly conquered most of Anatolia and pushed into southeastern Europe. The growing Ottoman Empire would ultimately become one of the most powerful and long-lasting in history.

As the Ottomans expanded, what little was left of Byzantium, or the Eastern Roman Empire, was forced to pull back even further. Even before the rise of the Ottomans, Byzantium had been in serious decline. It had gradually lost most of its once-extensive territories and had suffered a series of humiliating defeats. European soldiers engaged in the Fourth Crusade—an army that was intended to target the Holy Land—were hired by Venetian merchants en route to act as a mercenary force in Constantinople. In 1204, the opportunistic crusaders sacked the city and ruled it for several decades.

By 1300, the Byzantines had regained control of their capital, but the Ottomans were closing in on it. Byzantium managed to retain control until the late fourteenth century, when the Ottomans were dealt their own serious setback by the forces of Tamerlane: a Muslim Mongol conqueror who advanced out of central Asia. Between the 1360s and 1405, Tamerlane (or Timur Lenk, which means "Timur the Lame") conquered an enormous region from the edges of Anatolia deep into Asia. The Ottomans were left struggling to survive.

Tamerlane died attempting to invade China, and his empire crumbled. As it disintegrated, the Ottomans refocused their attention on Constantinople: the last remnant of Byzantium. Age-old tensions between the Catholic Church of Rome and the Orthodox Church of Constantinople—plus mutual ill will rooted in the crusader conquest of 1204—curtailed European aid to the Byzantines. After a long siege, Constantinople fell in 1453. The city was renamed Istanbul, and it became the Ottoman capital. Its grand, ancient churches were converted into mosques.

By the sixteenth century, the triumphant Ottomans had not only expanded into Iraq, the Levant, Egypt, and North Africa but also they had pressed into Europe as they took control of Greece, Bulgaria, and Hungary. The Ottomans would repeatedly try to dominate the Mediterranean and extend their conquests deeper into Europe. In 1571, the Holy League—an alliance of Spain, Venice, Genoa, and the Papal States—defeated a massive Turkish fleet off the Greek coast at Lepanto, thwarting Ottoman efforts to control the eastern Mediterranean. But Ottoman naval power was quickly reestablished, and it continued to threaten Europe for decades.

The Turks also made multiple attempts to seize Vienna. In 1529, Ottoman Sultan Suleiman I "the Magnificent" laid siege to the city for several months before he finally retreated. The last Ottoman siege of Vienna came in 1683; Polish monarch Jan Sobieski relieved the city, defeating the army of Sultan Mehmed IV after a desperate battle and making himself a European hero.

Tamerlane's successors ruled Persia until 1501, when the Safavid Empire restored Persian independence and converted the region to Shiite Islam. This laid a foundation for later Persian culture and ultimately for the modern Shiite state of Iran—although war soon erupted between the Sunni Ottomans and Shiite Safavids. Tamerlane's progeny achieved a more lasting victory in India. In the early sixteenth century, a Turkic-Mongol prince named Babur, one of Tamerlane's descendants, led his people from central Asia into northern India. Defeating the Delhi sultanate in 1526, he established the Mughal (or Mogul) empire. Mughal power soon advanced south and seized control of all but southernmost India.

The Islamic Mughals encouraged a culturally diverse society and advanced their own Muslim arts and beliefs even as they upheld tolerance toward India's Hindu majority. Mughal art, which combined elements of Persian, central Asian, and Indian styles, became greatly renowned. The seventeenth-century Mughal emperor Shah Jahan built the Taj Mahal as a funerary monument to his wife. It remains one of the most famous structures in the world. The Mughal Empire would rule most of India into the eighteenth century before gradually losing its grip as European powers increased their colonial presence during the eighteenth and nineteenth centuries.

ERA 7: EUROPE AFTER ROME FELL: THE MIDDLE AGES DESCEND (400S TO 1350)

EUROPE REBUILDS IN THE WAKE OF ROME'S FALL

Rome's Western Empire declined in the fourth and fifth centuries, and Germanic tribes increasingly dominated Europe. They, in turn, were driven westward when the nomadic Huns invaded Europe from the east. Rome was sacked in 410 by displaced Germanic Goths. The Vandals, a German tribe who had established a kingdom in North Africa, pillaged the city even more severely in 455. Under their fearsome leader Attila, the Huns ravaged much of southern Europe, including Italy, in the mid-fifth century. The Huns were ultimately defeated, but the Western Roman Empire was nearing its end.

The last Western emperor was overthrown in 476. The final collapse of Roman power in the West left the Germanic peoples' power virtually unchecked. Their advance across Europe continued, and they absorbed, displaced, or ruled the peoples they encountered along their way. A motley group of Celtic-speaking peoples, often at war with each other, had occupied Western Europe and had fallen under Roman control as the empire expanded. Now, the advancing Germans overwhelmed them: the Franks moved into the Roman province of Gaul (and renamed it Francia), and Anglo-Saxons reached Britain and pushed the Celts into coastal fringes that would become Wales, Scotland, and Ireland.

Although Rome's Western Empire disintegrated, its major legacy—the Roman Catholic Church—continued to gain authority and wealth. Rome lost its political might, but its bishops of Rome—who gradually became known as popes (from papa, or "father")—came to be seen as successors to St. Peter (the chief apostle of Jesus). By the time Rome fell, the popes had gained considerable religious power throughout much of the formerly Roman west. The popes maintained some of the stature and ceremonial trappings of the emperors. Even some of the language of Greco-Roman power survived in the Church: for example, *pontiff* comes from the Roman priestly title *pontifex*.

With Constantine's early fourth-century conversion and the adoption of Christianity as the empire's official religion, Rome's Catholic Church began to spread all across Europe. The incursion of the pagan Germanic peoples broke the Church's hold for a time. But papal missionaries—strengthened by dynastic marriages of Germanic rulers to foreign Christian royalty—succeeded in converting the new Germanic kingdoms of Western Europe in the fifth and sixth centuries. Beginning in the eighth century, the Church gradually succeeded in the more difficult task of converting the never-Romanized German peoples of central and Eastern Europe.

As the Western Empire toppled, the Eastern, or Byzantine, Empire continued to thrive from its capital in Constantinople. During part of the sixth century, Byzantium seemed poised to restore imperial rule to the now-fragmented Roman world. The Byzantine emperor Justinian set out to do just that, and he succeeded in retaking Italy and North Africa from their Vandal occupiers. Drawing on a long tradition of Roman judicial writing, Justinian created a legal code that aimed to restore uniform, systematic rule throughout his vast dominions. Justinian's code continues to influence modern European law.

But Justinian's European conquests and dream of a fully restored empire evaporated shortly after his death. During the seventh century, the new and rising forces of Islam invaded eastern Byzantine territories, draining imperial resources and helping to force the abandonment of Justinian's western gains.

Religion drove a divisive wedge between East and West. The churches of Rome and Constantinople diverged in doctrine and ritual, even as each waged its own internal battles over the nature of Christ and the use of religious images: followers of a given doctrine accused those who disagreed of heresy. The Nicaean Council met in 325 CE to try and settle these differences, as did six more Christian councils over the next two centuries. But persecution and violence, even over esoteric doctrinal divisions (for example, whether Christ had a single nature or separate human and divine aspects) continued.

The Byzantine Church was loyal to its own patriarchs and resisted the authority of the popes. The gap between the two churches—the Catholic Church in Rome and the Orthodox Church in Constantinople—continued to widen. And as Byzantine Christianity gained followers among Eastern Europe's Slavic peoples in the ninth century, its power and influence grew. Two centuries later, each church's leader excommunicated the other: the schism was complete.

The Germanic Franks gradually restored unity to much of Western and Central Europe. Frankish warrior kings, called the Merovingians, ruled in Paris from the fifth century and converted to Christianity in the sixth. From the next century onward, power passed to their palace stewards. One such "mayor of the palace," Charles Martel, staved off an invasion by Spanish-based Arabs at the battle of Tours in 732. His son, Pepin, finally overthrew the Merovingians and assumed the throne in 751. Pepin established the Carolingian line, so named in honor of his father. His own son, Charles the Great—or Charlemagne, would rise to become one of medieval European history's most important figures.

THE CAROLINGIAN EMPIRE AND ITS SUCCESSORS

From his capital at Aachen—on what is now the border of Germany and France—Charlemagne deliberately set out to re-create the lost glories of the Roman Empire. His conquests gave him control over much of Europe, including most of present-day France and Germany and parts of Spain and Italy. The papacy was also gaining power, yet neither it nor Charlemagne was secure enough to dominate the other. The popes had gradually taken direct political control of Italy's Papal States. In conquering and Christianizing the Germanic Lombards of northern Italy, Charlemagne gave additional territory to the pope. And on Christmas Day in 800, the pope crowned Charlemagne in Rome as the new emperor. Thus, each reinforced the other's power.

Charlemagne's revitalization of trade, scholarship, and religion changed Europe forever. He was a great patron of learning and attracted some of the finest scholars of the day to his court. From far-off England, Alcuin of York came to serve as one of his chief advisors on theology and education and introduced the classically inspired liberal arts (grammar, rhetoric, and logic) to Charlemagne's Palace School. A new script, called *Carolingian Miniscule*, was clear, fast, and employed to copy and preserve ancient texts that would have otherwise been lost forever. Some of Charlemagne's successors followed his example, and their collective efforts are known as the Carolingian Renaissance: the first major revitalization of literacy, literature, architecture, legal and religious thought, music, and the arts since the fall of Rome. Although the surge in creative energy was short-lived and largely confined to court and church elites, its influence was longer lasting.

Charlemagne's quarrelling successors soon dismantled his empire, and it split into rival kingdoms. In his wake, Europe was unstable and vulnerable to invasion. The Magyars invaded Hungary from the east in the ninth century and later attacked Germany (which was ruled by Charlemagne's heirs). North African Muslims also took Sicily during the ninth century and menaced the Carolingian territories. Most destructive of all, the Scandinavian Vikings (the Norse, or Northmen) began launching devastating piratical raids on towns and wealthy monasteries throughout Europe in the eighth century. The Vikings, however, were also traders, farmers, and seafarers. They established settlements in Britain, Normandy, Russia, Iceland, Greenland, and even North America—where they founded the short-lived Vinland colony (probably in Newfoundland) in the early eleventh century.

Central power was weak across much of Europe, so regional kings moved to secure local nobilities' support. They began to shift blocs of land to their nobles and to grant them strong local power on those lands. The nobles, in turn, began to organize the lower social tiers into dependent vassals—subordinates who held a grant of land, or fief, from the lord. Laboring serfs occupied the lowest tier: they were tied to the land and could never leave it. The nobles were laying the foundation of the feudal manorial system that would dominate medieval Europe and the lives of millions of people. Serfs were subject to their lords' manorial courts and could not marry without their lords' permission. Serfdom quickly became a hereditary status. Lords were legally required to provide for their serfs' needs, but the serfs' conditions were generally very poor. Although they could not be sold, serfs were nearly slaves.

In some places, centralized power began to recover. The new Ottonian imperial line rose over the remnants of Charlemagne's lands in Germany during the tenth century. Charlemagne had been crowned Holy Roman Emperor by the pope in 800. Following Otto I, founder of the Ottonian line, that title would transfer to the overall ruler of German lands. Otto was a powerful ruler who asserted the authority of the emperor to ratify papal elections and even to remove popes of whom he disapproved, and he successfully put down internal revolts in his own territories. But Germany remained a patchwork of semi-independent states, and the effective power of the emperors over the many German rulers would rise and fall over time.

A serious rivalry also developed between the Holy Roman Emperors and the Roman papacy, because both sides battled over the extent of secular versus religious authority. A dispute over who had power to appoint bishops (known as the investiture controversy) climaxed in the eleventh century, when Emperor Henry IV was excommunicated and forced to do penance before Pope Gregory VII in the snow at Canossa in northern Italy. But Gregory's triumph was fleeting—Henry pushed back and ignored a second excommunication. The empire gradually increased its power over northern Italy and even over the Papal States, sparking fresh conflicts over the papacy's political autonomy.

The popes and emperors built complex international alliances, and the balance of power continued to shift back and forth. Ultimately, the imperial crown lost most of its authority. After the fourteenth century, the rulers of the most powerful German principalities gained the right to elect the emperor. As these electors gained greater power, the emperor's title turned increasingly hollow. The empire lingered as an ever-more meaningless concept until the French emperor Napoleon abolished it in 1806.

Eastern Europe was also consolidating by the end of the first millennium CE, and it continued to adopt Byzantium's Orthodox Christian faith. Russia emerged in the ninth century: it was, at first, a Slavic state under the rule of the Rus Viking clan. Around the same time, Poland developed as an independent Slavic kingdom, the Magyars established a kingdom in Hungary, and Slavic Bulgars established Bulgaria. Byzantium maintained control of Greece and southern Italy. Along the Baltic Sea, different powers battled for influence. In the thirteenth century, the Mongols swept across Russia and into Eastern Europe. They launched a massive, devastating invasion that was only barely repelled.

THE FEUDAL STATES OF WESTERN EUROPE

Rome gradually withdrew from Britain, and abandoned it entirely in 410. Anglo-Saxon settlers gradually took over what would become England (or "Angle-land"), driving the Celtic Britons back into Wales, Cornwall, Scotland, and Ireland. According to legend, King Arthur led the ultimately futile British resistance in the fifth or sixth century. The small and shifting Anglo-Saxon kingdoms themselves later faced Viking invasion. Alfred, king of the Saxon state of Wessex, drove back the Vikings and began to create a unified England during the late ninth century. Over the following century, the Saxon monarchy became one of the strongest in Europe. Yet its power was rooted in a deep traditional belief that kings should govern only with the consent of their leading subjects.

During the eleventh century, England faced major troubles. The Danish King Cnut seized the throne in 1016. His early death, in 1035, sparked several years of strife before the Saxon Edward the Confessor claimed the crown. But Edward died without an heir. William, Duke of the Viking-descended Normans in France, invaded and killed the English claimant, Harold Godwinson, in 1066; he soon suppressed all resistance, installing his Norman barons in positions of feudal lord-ship across England. William's Norman successors would continue to build the strength of the English monarchy. Norman-French culture would influence England, and the Normans would adopt aspects of English culture—and would come to be influenced by the traditional limits the English had placed on their kings' power.

In contrast to England, France was far slower to unify. Frankish kings had ruled what is now France since the fifth century, and the land became part of Charlemagne's realm. But after his death and his empire's decay, the region became divided between powerful and often warring nobles—particularly the rulers of Burgundy, Brittany, and Normandy. The kings of France directly ruled only small parts of the country—their power sometimes barely extended beyond Paris. With the Norman conquest of England, the English crown also secured Norman possessions in France and sometimes ruled large areas. Not until the late twelfth and early thirteenth centuries, under King Philip Augustus, did the French monarchy begin to widen its authority. Philip Augustus fought off the claims of England's King John, but war with England would flare repeatedly over the following centuries.

During the Middle Ages, Italy emerged as a confused collection of city-states and small territories. Charlemagne had conquered northern Italy, and the Holy Roman Emperors battled to maintain control for centuries. The power and borders of the Papal States changed constantly in the face of local and imperial rivalries. This complex maze of states and factions sparked frequent wars and shifting alliances, which often involved the ever-contested power of the popes. The papacy based its claims to worldly power on the *Donation of Constantine*, a document—actually an early Medieval fabrication—in which the emperor Constantine had purportedly awarded secular control of the Roman Empire to the popes. Such claims would lead to frequent, heated political battles with monarchs all across Europe.

Southern Italy remained Byzantine long after Justinian's other European conquests had been lost. But Sicily fell to North African Arabs by the tenth century. A century later, Norman invaders took over both Sicily and southern Italy. They drove Arabs and Byzantines out, but lost their control of the territories during the following centuries. Some Italian city-states followed early Rome's example and established republics, which were led by wealthy and prominent citizens. As early as 700, Venice established an oligarchic republic (that is, rule by an elite group of citizens). Venice was a major port and became an important trading center. Its extensive trade with the Arabs created a bridge between European and Islamic cultures. The Tuscan city of Florence also became a republic in the twelfth century and would become a vital economic and cultural center—although its Republican system repeatedly decayed into near-monarchical rule by leading families, particularly the Medicis.

Scandinavia—the realm of the Vikings—began to Christianize during the ninth century (although the faith was slow to spread beyond the ruling elite). Denmark often dominated the Scandinavian region, though other local powers rose and fell. Christianity also advanced in Spain as Arab power declined. In northern Spain, Christian kingdoms such as Castile and Aragon became increasingly powerful by the eleventh century and began to push Muslims back. By the mid-thirteenth century, only Granada (on Spain's southern coast) was still in Arab hands.

Despite the deep and hostile divisions between the European powers, the Christian kingdoms united for the Crusades: these aimed to reconquer the Holy Land (which had been lost to Muslim conquerors in the seventh century) and purge heresies from Europe. In the 1090s—as the Seljuk Turks who had lately conquered the Levant interfered with Christian pilgrimage to Jerusalem—the pope and popular preachers called for a crusade. King, nobles, and commoners rallied to the call, repeatedly attacking Europe's Jewish communities as they went. They conquered Jerusalem in 1099, and slaughtered a large portion of its Muslim and Jewish populations.

There would be nine major crusades during the twelfth and thirteenth centuries and further attempts in the fourteenth century. Short-lived crusader kingdoms were established in Palestine and Syria. The Arab ruler Saladin retook Jerusalem in the 1170s, and the Third Crusade failed to reclaim it. The soldiers of the Fourth Crusade were hired as mercenaries by the Venetians and diverted to Constantinople. They sacked the city in 1204 and imposed Western rule until 1261—further weakening the fading Byzantine Empire. In 1212, waves of popular zeal swept tens of thousands of children and the wandering poor into the much-mythologized Children's Crusade. Although later accounts of the movement were widely exaggerated, thousands died from cold and hunger in their futile effort to reach the Holy Land.

The crusading spirit also turned against Europeans who were deemed heretics by the Church. In 1208, the pope launched the twenty-year Albigensian Crusade against the Cathars of Southern France: they were "dualists" who believed that a demonic force opposed to God had corrupted the material world. Inquisition and executions of Cathars continued for decades.

The Sixth Crusade briefly retook Jerusalem in the early thirteenth century, but the Crusader States were fading quickly in the face of Muslim resistance. The coastal fortress of Acre, the last Christian stronghold in the Holy Land, fell in 1291. Despite their ultimate failure, the Crusades helped shape European Christianity and medieval military culture. They promoted the ideals of knighthood and chivalry—even as they often succumbed to incompetence, corruption, and anti-Jewish violence—and deepened the divide between Islam and the West.

EUROPEAN COMMERCE AND CULTURE: THE MEDIEVAL REVIVAL

Despite early political fragmentation, abandonment of major cities, and frequent social turmoil, the European Middle Ages cannot simply be written off as a "dark age." Intellectual life continued as Rome crumbled, especially in the rising world of the Church. St. Augustine, a North African bishop who lived during the fourth and fifth centuries, would become one of the major intellectual figures in European history. He wrote extensively about the Church's role in the secular world and on the dependence of people on divine grace. Theodoric, an Ostrogothic German king, ruled Italy and was recognized by the Byzantine emperors at Constantinople during the sixth century. His scholarly Roman-born advisor Boethius was fluent in Greek and Latin and wrote important texts such as the famous *Consolation of Philosophy*.

In the centuries of confusion after the fall of Rome, monks kept Christian writings alive through ceaseless recopying and sometimes haphazardly preserved fragments of classical learning—although many important ancient works vanished and general levels of literacy declined. Parchment—animal hide used for books before paper became available—was scarce. Classical works were often scraped off old books and the parchment reused for Christian texts. Such sheets are called palimpsests; the traces of some of the original texts are still decipherable and have allowed the recovery of lost ancient works.

By the ninth century, Charlemagne's promotion of commerce, arts, and scholarship—through which he hoped to re-create the splendor of Rome—prompted a new burst of creative energy and interest in the classical past (see "The Carolingian Empire and Its Successors"). By 1000, large cities were beginning to redevelop around major religious centers and at important ports. Such ports built a growing trade across and beyond Europe, through the great hub of the Mediterranean.

Christian monastic orders continued to grow and diversify. They were often involved in local farming and craft, and they dominated scholarship—often excluding secular points of view. Millions of Europeans remained mired in the oppressive feudal system, because they were tied to the land as barely free serf laborers. But change was accelerating by the twelfth and thirteenth centuries. The foundations of modern banking were laid in Italy, particularly in Florence, where large-scale, long-distance trade required sophisticated financial transactions. Flourishing crops led to the development of more market towns and fairs, which spread opportunities for town-based trades that broke the stifling limits of the feudal manor system. Regional economies, which specialized in specific goods such as wool, food, crops, and textiles, gradually emerged.

Many communities sought to flaunt their growing wealth. Sponsored by the Church, state, and private donors, cathedrals in the new Gothic style literally brought architecture to new heights. During the early Middle Ages, Romanesque churches had dominated architecture. Although magnificent in their own right, these earlier churches' heavy walls had small windows that allowed little light. The Gothic style, pioneered near Paris in the early twelfth century, transferred much of the load-bearing structure to external buttresses—and thus made way for open walls and enormous stained-glass windows. At the same time, palaces, castles, and commercial structures also achieved new levels of grandeur.

Wealthy religious and secular patrons also funded a rebirth of painting and sculpture. Most surviving art of the period consists of religious devotional works, but secular arts also flourished. Led by pioneering artists like the Italians Giotto and Duccio during the late thirteenth and fourteenth centuries, painting attained a realism and depth that had not been seen since antiquity. The new Italian style, nourished in centers of commerce and culture such as Florence, would remake art across Europe and lay the groundwork for Renaissance artwork.

Scholarship and popular learning also surged. The monastic monopoly on texts began to decline as a commercial trade in manuscript books—which were mostly, but not entirely, religious—began to cater to wealthy buyers as well as socially middling readers like traders and small landowners. Even alchemy, the mystical effort to discover the deeper nature of matter (and in the process, transmute base metals into gold) helped lay important foundations for later chemistry.

Classical works also began to return to Europe's notice, partly from Arab regions such as Spain, where they had been preserved and studied. Knowledge of the ancient Greek scholar Aristotle was revived in part through the works of the Spanish Muslim philosopher Averroes. At first, Aristotle's works were challenged by the Church. But thirteenth-century religious scholars such as St. Thomas Aquinas reconciled his philosophy with Christianity: Aristotelian teachings about the nature of the world not only gained acceptance by the Church but also became unchallengeable Catholic doctrine.

Europe's burgeoning economic and cultural life was, however, dealt a severe blow in the fourteenth century. Severe famines descended on Europe in the early part of the century—and then the bubonic plague, or Black Death, arrived. This bacterial scourge, transmitted by fleas that in turn were carried by rats, reached the continent via trading ships, pilgrims, and other travelers in 1347. Within a year, it struck Western Europe. The epidemic shattered Europe and killed at least a third of the population by 1350. As agricultural land was left untilled and trade and economic life splintered, urban communities collapsed. The disease finally began to recede, although new epidemics would periodically flare. A full cultural, political, and economic recovery would take time.

ERA 8: THE RENAISSANCE: THOUGHT REBORN AND MADE BEAUTIFUL (CA. 1300 TO 1648)

THE CHANGING WORLD OF LATE MEDIEVAL EUROPE

The Black Death caused devastating catastrophe and loss throughout Europe. But it also dealt a major blow to feudalism, which had dominated Europe for centuries. Already, increased trade and economic opportunities had weakened the system as town dwellers broke free from manor lords' stifling grip. The plague shrunk the size of the workforce dramatically, so laborers gained bargaining power that helped them secure better working terms. Land, which had been controlled only by the feudal lords, was increasingly bought, sold, and inherited by nonaristocratic farmers and entrepreneurs. The lords made last-ditch legal attempts to preserve traditional social barriers; sumptuary laws—regulations designed to dictate how people spent their money—aimed to bar the rising middle classes from owning luxury items. To stop rising demand from driving up wages, mid-fourteenth-century laws tried to fix the price of labor. But the tides of change were unstoppable.

As feudalism declined and farmers took control of private land, the crushing institution of serfdom also began to unravel. Yet an escape from the virtual slavery of serfdom did not mean a dramatic improvement for lowliest members of society. It was larger-scale farmers who could now purchase land and town-dwelling merchants and artisans who were able to break away entirely from the manor system. Peasant laborers were now less likely to be bound to the land as serfs, but they still toiled in severe poverty. In many parts of Europe, peasants launched revolts seeking greater social rights—but the revolts achieved little.

Matters were even worse in Eastern Europe. Before the Black Death, feudalism there had been less advanced than it had been in the West. But pressure for food crops was now increasing, and serfdom in the East was becoming more entrenched—even as it declined in the West. Eastern Europe's system of serfdom expanded and defined large parts of the region until the nineteenth century. This would contribute to a deep developmental gap between commercially and techno- logically expanding Western Europe and the serf-based agricultural eastern region.

Following a centuries-old trend, monarchical states across Europe continued to solidify their hold. But frequent warfare often undermined many nations' gains. From the 1340s to the 1450s, continued English territorial claims in France—together with economic rivalries and French support for anti-English rulers in Scotland—led to the Hundred Years' War. After England's King Henry V defeated the French at Agincourt in 1415, the French king was forced to name Henry his heir—over his own son. But Henry's early death in 1422, the ascension to the throne of his infant son Henry VI, and feuds between the new king's advisors allowed the disinherited French prince (with help from Joan of Arc, the religiously inspired populist military leader) to strip the English of most of their conquests.

Europe's long and draining wars weakened the nations that fought them. Even as feudalism faltered, nobles were still able to take advantage of royal weakness in order to seize local power. In England, the inability of Henry VI and the loss of France inspired rival claimants to seek the throne (Henry's grandfather, Henry IV, usurped the throne from the autocratic yet ineffectual Richard II in 1399). The result was a long series of dynastic struggles called the Wars of the Roses: Henry's Lancastrian line and its Yorkist opponents would shift back and forth for decades until Henry VII's Tudor dynasty united both houses through strategic marriage in 1485. The wars drew in most of England's nobility; as one faction or the other fell from power, nobles on both sides lost their lives.

In many parts of Europe—away from the relatively strong monarchies of England, France, and Spain—small warring states still held sway. In Germany and Italy, complex leagues and alliances rose and fell. The papacy was a frequent player in these elaborate political contests, but the popes themselves were not immune to the effects. For much of the fourteenth century, political quarrels led the popes to avoid Rome and settle in the southern French city of Avignon. In 1376, the papacy itself fell into a forty-year schism, in which feuding nations and factions supported rival papal claimants.

Despite the turmoil, states had to collect taxes. This forced them to consolidate their admin- istrative systems, which strengthened their central authority. At the same time, the increasing burden of centrally imposed taxes led prominent subjects to demand a greater voice. Nascent representative bodies began to emerge through which elite subjects could grant money to their rulers by consent.

In England, an emphasis on representation and checks on monarchical power would become particularly important. Ancient Saxon tradition had expected kings to consult with their leading subjects, and the Norman kings had also become increasingly subject to legal checks. In 1215, England's barons had forced King John to sign the Magna Carta—the Great Charter—which defined subjects' rights and limited royal powers. (John immediately moved to toss out the char- ter, but his successors were forced to reissue it.) In the fourteenth century, such ideas became more entrenched as Parliament—a new representative body elected by a limited set of prominent men–placed fresh restraints on royal authority. In the following centuries, England's parliaments would gain in power and influence.

CLASSICAL REVIVAL, THE EXPANSION OF LEARNING, AND THE RISE OF THE RENAISSANCE

Intellectual inquiry, artistic innovation, and a renewed focus on classical texts had already begun in the late Middle Ages. Aristotle's works were reintroduced to Europe in the thirteenth century and they were ultimately accepted as definitive by the Catholic Church. By 1300, a new naturalism dominated painting and sculpture, beginning to displace the highly schematized styles that had dominated medieval art. Over the course of the fourteenth century, the pace of learning greatly accelerated, helping to inspire dramatic cultural change in the fifteenth and sixteenth centuries.

At first, the new intellectual ferment was centered in Italy. Interest in rediscovered classical remains–ruins, inscriptions, coins, and sculpture–surged. Ancient texts were sought in monasteries and recovered from the Arab and Byzantine worlds, where more had been preserved. This amalgam of late medieval trends, classical revival, and new innovations are known as the Renaissance (which means "rebirth"). Renaissance scholars were eager to emphasize the newness of their own achievements, and they therefore exaggerated the backwardness of the Middle Ages. They concealed their own indebtedness to medieval culture–and crafted an image of themselves as bearers of a new light after a long medieval darkness. But, even in clearer perspective, the Renaissance did mark a dramatic shift in thought and culture.

The vibrant republics of northern Italy, such as Venice and Florence, were hubs for new ideas as they began to recover from the Black Death's staggering blow. Republican principles were, in reality, far from consistent in these city-states. But even oligarchic control by prominent families–particularly Florence's prominent merchant and banking clan, the Medicis–enhanced the arts, literature, philosophy, and scholarship through patronage and support for active groups of like-minded intellectuals. Patronage for new arts and ideas was soon offered by wealthy nobles in many cities as well as by city governments, powerful families, and popes who were interested in the new artistic and scholarly exploration.

Renaissance artists gleaned inspiration from naturalistic classical sculpture and new scientific and philosophical ideas. They explored human anatomy intensely. They also began to investigate the complexities of space and developed theories of linear perspective–the illusion of depth in a two-dimensional work as all lines converge on a distant "vanishing point." The Middle Ages had viewed artists as craftspeople. But sixteenth-century artist Giorgio Vasari's *The Lives of the Painters, Sculptors, and Architects* shows Renaissance artists gaining self-confidence and growing more conscious of their status as creative individuals. In the second half of the sixteenth century, Italy was a remarkable cradle of artistic genius: it was home to Sandro Botticelli, Michelangelo, Leonardo da Vinci, Raphael, among many others.

A new classically influenced humanism influenced philosophy and learning as scholars' keen interest in human and individual perspectives looked past the rigid religious confines that had often defined medieval thought. Humanism, for example, challenged the authority of Church teachings and the historically undisputed power of princes. In the early fourteenth century, Marsilius of Padua rejected the secular power of the Church and argued that political power rested on the people's consent (in turn, the Church branded him a heretic). Florentine Niccolo Machiavelli (who lived during the fifteenth and sixteenth centuries) is best-known for *The Prince*, in which he offers cynical advice on the manipulation of power. But in other writings, he championed a Republican government.

Italian writers absorbed classical learning, and many of their poems and tales focused on the passions and relationships of individuals. Dante's early fourteenth-century *Divine Comedy* explored hell, purgatory, and heaven reflecting on God, contemporary Italian society, and the classical heritage (the Roman poet Virgil serves as Dante's personal guide in the first two poems). Dante, a Florentine, also rejected the Latin language of medieval literature in favor of his local Tuscan dialect of Italian. Petrarch, the fourteenth-century scholar and poet, is considered one of the first humanists. His lyrical sonnets profoundly influenced the development of the Italian language. His student, Giovanni Boccaccio, wrote the vibrant satirical tales of *The Decameron*, which lampooned contemporary culture and the Church's rampant corruption.

Classical study had powerful consequences. For centuries, the Church had based its claim to secular power on the *Donation of Constantine*, in which Constantine had supposedly entrusted the Church with his entire empire after an early pope healed him of a deadly illness. Secular rulers had long challenged the document. But in the mid-fifteenth century, Italian scholar Lorenzo Valla proved that it was no more than a medieval fabrication, after he compared the text to genuine ancient documents and exposed contradictions of newly uncovered ancient historical facts.

The Church supported great artists and often promoted the expansion of humanism and classical learning. But at other times, it harshly turned against ideas and practices that challenged its own doctrine. The Church was ready to use extreme measures to root out what it saw as dangerous heresy. After the 1540s, the Roman Inquisition (which also faced the rising challenge of Protestantism—see "The Reformation and Its Consequences") actively targeted those whose beliefs defied Church teachings; the Spanish and Portuguese Inquisitions used violence to enforce religious conformity (see "Exploration and the Roots of European Expansion").

The Renaissance spread beyond Italy to northern and central Europe by the early fifteenth century. Flemish artists pioneered the use of oil paints, which replaced egg yolk–based tempera. Oil paints created a new depth of color and enabled painters to show effects of atmosphere and light through subtle layering of paints. Oil-based paints quickly spread to Italy as regions continued to influence one another. Venice cultivated especially strong connections with the rest of Europe, serving as a bridge between Italy and the north (just as it had long connected Europe and Islam). Great artists such as Jan van Eyck, Rogier van der Weyden, Pieter Breugel, Hieronymus Bosch, Lucas Cranach, and Albrecht Dürer lived in Flanders, the Netherlands, and Germany. The northern Renaissance also led to innovations in commerce, urban life, literature, government, and religion.

Perhaps the most vital innovation of the era emerged in mid-fifteenth-century Germany. Johannes Gutenberg's invention of the moveable-type printing press enabled people to set and print any combination of letters multiple times—and thus did away with the need to hand copy texts. (The Chinese had experimented with moveable-type printing earlier, but there is no evidence that their process reached Europe or influenced Gutenberg.) The earlier, labor-intensive method of bookmaking had made books luxury items, even when commercial workshops were established in late medieval cities and university towns. The printing press transformed everything: it allowed mass production of texts at comparatively low costs. As printing spread across Europe in the later-fifteenth century, common people were able to enjoy and learn from books for the first time. Literacy and education rates increased and there was an unprecedented spread of new ideas.

EXPLORATION AND THE ROOTS OF EUROPEAN EXPANSION

Marco Polo's thirteenth-century narrative of his travels in China helped introduce the mysterious, almost mythical, lands of China and Japan to Europe. Indirect trade on the long dangerous Silk Road had made silk, spices, and other Asian goods highly prized commodities. But these goods had been scarce, and their supply further decreased after the Black Death. Trade along the

Silk Road (which was likely one of the plague's pathways in reaching Europe) fell sharply after the epidemic. In the mid-fifteenth century under the Ming dynasty, China ended its maritime outreach and thus blocked a new potential source of contact with the West.

China's isolationist maneuver did not stop Renaissance Europe from looking outward for broader knowledge, commercial opportunities, and even new Christian lands to aid in its struggle against Islam. As the Muslim Ottoman Empire continued to press into Eastern and Central Europe, rumors spread of a powerful Christian prince: at first, this mysterious king, the legendary Prester John, and his Christian people were said to live somewhere deep in Asia. As European knowledge of Asia improved and he failed to materialize, the stories migrated to East Africa—where there had been a Christian kingdom, Ethiopia, since the fourth century. The search for the mythical Prester John would persist well into the Era of Exploration, helping to drive expeditions into the African interior.

The small, seafaring nation of Portugal began to lead Europe's outward expansion during the early fifteenth century. First, the Portuguese explored the West African coast and gradually worked their way south. African peoples maintained firm control of their territories, so Portuguese attempts to seize strongholds along the coast were rarely successful. But Africa's powerful kingdoms and the Portuguese established trade ties, and the Portuguese imported African gold, ivory, spices, and slaves into Europe in exchange for European cloth, copper, foods, and other goods. This marked the beginning of Europe's African slave trade (an extensive African slave trade with the Middle East already existed at the time).

Portuguese mariners greatly expanded European cartographical knowledge—and they pressed on toward a sea route around the southern tip of Africa to the fabled riches of India and East Asia. Other European nations feared a Portuguese monopoly on Asian trade. At the time, Spain (which borders Portugal on the Iberian Peninsula) was becoming more powerful. King Ferdinand of Aragon and Queen Isabella of Castile united their kingdoms through marriage; thus Spain became a unified monarchy. They also completed the Christian *Reconquista* of Spain when they defeated southern Spain's last Muslim enclave, Granada, in 1492.

Ferdinand and Isabella were eager to top the Portuguese and funded the Genoese mariner Christopher Columbus. Europeans knew of no land mass other than Eurasia—although, contrary to legend, they knew the Earth was spherical instead of flat. Columbus thought that the Earth was much smaller than it is and argued that he could reach China by sailing directly west across the Atlantic. He was determined to establish direct Spanish ties with China and Japan, not only to secure the lucrative spice trade for Spain but also to harness the riches of the East for a final crusade against Islam.

The Spanish monarchs, and Spain's religious culture, shared his sense of climactic Christian mission. As the *Reconquista* advanced, Muslims were forced to convert or flee. In 1492—the same year that Columbus sailed and the final Arab stronghold fell—Ferdinand and Isabella ordered the expulsion of all Jews who refused conversion. Much of Spain's large Jewish population refused conversion, and they were driven from the country. But even among those who converted, many faced savage persecution. The Spanish Inquisition, which the Church created in 1478, and the Portuguese Inquisition, formed some sixty years later, aimed to root out deception and non-Christian practices among the *conversos*, or converted Jews and Muslims. Torture was routinely used to extract confessions, and accused heretics were often burned at the stake in the forced ritual of public penance called *auto-da-fe*, or "act of faith."

It was in this climate of Christian determination that Columbus planned what he formally called his "enterprise of the Indies." In 1492 and on subsequent voyages over the next decade, Columbus inadvertently discovered the Caribbean islands and the northern coast of South America. He remained convinced that he had reached the outskirts of China and asked everyone he encountered about the whereabouts of the Great Khan whom Marco Polo had described. (Even if Columbus had been right about his location, the Khans had been overthrown a century and a half earlier.)

Other explorers soon followed in Columbus's path and discovered that two unknown continents lay between Europe and Asia: from Europe's perspective, this was a New World. The discovery would unleash a long battle between the European powers for the wealth, territory, and resources of the newly discovered lands—with dramatic consequences for the Americas' indigenous peoples, for Europe's future, and, ultimately, for the direction of world history. The discovery closed the last great gap between human populations: peoples who had known nothing of each other's existence were now inextricably linked.

THE REFORMATION AND ITS CONSEQUENCES

In the churches of Rome's Eastern Empire, biblical scriptures had generally been translated into the local vernacular (or everyday language)—such as Greek, Armenian, or Coptic. But in the West, the Bible was available only in Latin. Latin stopped serving as a language of daily use and became a tongue used solely by the Church and for scholarship. By the Middle Ages, few besides priests could even read the Bible—and only through priests could most western Christians gain access to the scriptures and their promise of salvation. For most, the Church thus became a necessary intermediary between the individual and God. Not only was this view encouraged by the Church—it was put forth as formal doctrine.

Nonetheless, Europe's religious culture was changing by the late Middle Ages. Even before the printing press, educated elites had started to commission elaborate devotional manuscripts containing biblical texts for their own private worship. Schismatic groups were bolder, and they illegally translated the Bible into local languages. The humanistic inquiry that the Renaissance unleashed fueled critics of Church doctrines. Increasingly, they openly criticized those with power—including the Church, long known for its worldliness and widespread corruption. In medieval literary works such as Geoffrey Chaucer's fourteenth-century English *Canterbury Tales*, clerics' greed and dishonesty were openly mocked. Erasmus of Rotterdam, a leading humanist scholar in the early sixteenth century, loudly denounced monks' lack of virtue and other Church abuses.

One Church practice proved especially controversial. According to the medieval Church, most who escaped hell still needed to burn off their sins in purgatory before they could reach heaven. However, the Church could grant an indulgence: a promise that the penitent would escape part of the time in purgatory, in exchange for good works (such as giving alms to the poor, joining a crusade, or giving money to the Church). By the late fifteenth century the Church was selling indulgences outright and they became a major source of its revenue. The Church promised that when people bought indulgences, they could free themselves—and even their already-deceased relatives—from long stretches in purgatory.

The practice incensed Martin Luther, an early-sixteenth-century German monk. He had other concerns, fueled by Church critics such as Erasmus. During a visit to Rome, Luther was appalled by what he saw as rampant corruption and irreligion. He began to question whether the Church hierarchy—which grounded its legitimacy on apostolic succession, or the direct, unbroken line of Church leaders from St. Peter and the other apostles—had a legitimate biblical claim to authority. He wondered, indeed, if many Catholic practices had any biblical basis. Most radically, Luther questioned the need for priests as intermediaries between Christians and God. Luther demanded that the Church reform and return to what he argued were *true* biblical practices.

Rome branded Luther a heretic and ordered him to take back his accusations. He refused—and his German following grew. He encouraged people to read their Bibles privately, in their local languages; he himself translated the Bible into German. As the Church ramped up pressure, Luther's followers—including the rulers of several German states—became more determined and sheltered him from arrest. Ultimately, the attempts to suppress Luther drove him and his followers to total rupture with the Roman Catholic Church and the formation of their own Lutheran churches. The printing press, and the widespread literacy and learning it had helped create, enabled Luther's ideas to spread in ways that would have been impossible only a century earlier.

As Lutheran enthusiasm spread, the Protestant movement (those who protested against the Catholic Church) quickly extended beyond Luther's control. Other thinkers offered alternative visions for post-Catholic churches, and competing ideas dominated different regions. Some new leaders, such as John Calvin in Geneva, would prove extremely influential. Calvin ventured further than Luther, rejecting Catholic rituals that Luther still accepted and focusing on the gift of divine grace to a few "elect" individuals as the only path to salvation. Many also drew political insight from Luther's emphasis on individual thought and his attack on strict obedience to top-down authority. Luther himself feared unrest among members of the lower classes and rejected any extension of his ideas to government. Nevertheless, Lutheran-inspired peasant revolts erupted in Germany—where they were brutally suppressed. Through Calvin and others, the political implications of Protestantism would nonetheless continue to resonate.

At first, Catholic Church leaders were divided on how to respond to the Protestant Reformation. Should the Church offer concessions to reformers or seek to secure its authority at all costs? Supporters of the latter path won out at the Council of Trent, a series of deliberations that lasted from the 1540s to the 1560s. The result was the Counter-Reformation, in which the Church aimed to root out its own corruption and impiety while also holding firm to its doctrine and suppressing Lutheran heretics. Ignatius Loyola's newly formed Society of Jesus (or Jesuit Order) focused on curbing the spread of Protestantism. Meanwhile, Lutherans were a major target of the recently created Roman Inquisition.

The Counter-Reformation strengthened Catholicism among its adherents, but the schism with the Protestants only deepened. Europe began to fracture into rival camps. Italy remained firmly Catholic, although a Lutheran movement in Venice, fueled by its printing trade and connections with northern Europe, had to be silenced. Elsewhere, nations, cities, and peoples divided with often-violent consequences.

England became officially Protestant in the 1530s when King Henry VIII set aside his personal hostility to Lutheran doctrine, severed ties with Rome and took personal control of the Church in England. He did so mainly to secure a divorce from his first wife, who had not born him a male heir. Under Henry's son, Edward VI, England would become firmly Protestant. After Edward's brief rule, it would revert to Catholicism under Henry's daughter, Mary—who burned nearly three hundred Protestants—before its return to a more moderate Protestantism under Mary's half-sister, Elizabeth I. England would long remain divided; even as its Anglican Church gained strength, many stricter Protestants demanded a purer, less Catholic-style church without bishops or elaborate ritual. France was ravaged by religious wars from the 1560s to the 1590s, and other European powers took sides in the conflict. The wars finally ended in 1598, when the leader of the Protestant faction converted to Catholicism in order to take the throne as King Henry IV. He established religious tolerance with the Edict of Nantes.

Meanwhile, Spain faced Protestant rebels in its Dutch territories. The Dutch received English support under Elizabeth, which helped spark Spain's failed 1588 Armada against England. Germany's brutal Thirty Years' War (1618–1648) wrought the most devastating violence. Conflict erupted between Catholic and Protestant factions in the German states, and drew in Spain, France, Denmark, Sweden, and the Holy Roman Emperors. The 1648 Treaty of Westphalia settled some of Europe's territorial quarrels (for example, it granted the Dutch independence from Spain), established the sovereign power of the individual German states, and further weakened the Holy Roman Emperor. But the long war left Germany devastated—and still sorely divided, with its many states split into Catholic and Protestant factions.

ERA 9: AMERICAS NORTH AND SOUTH: THE "NEW" WORLD (CA. 20,000 BCE TO CA. 1500 CE)

EARLY HUMAN SETTLEMENT OF THE AMERICAS

The Americas were the last major continental regions to be settled. Despite extensive study, archaeologists disagree on when the first humans reached the American continents. Sea levels were lower during the last ice age, when much of the world's water was locked in glaciers. A land bridge, which geologists call Beringia, connected Siberia and Alaska across what is now the Bering Strait. This offered one of the first opportunities for a direct crossing from Asia (where humans had already lived for thousands of years).

In the past, scholars argued that as retreating glaciers opened an ice-free corridor, the first humans crossed from Siberia to Alaska (some twelve or thirteen thousand years ago). That population, it was thought, then spread across North America and formed the Clovis culture—which is known for its finely worked stone tools and sophisticated spear points.

However, more recent archaeological findings have overturned the long-dominant Clovis-first model. Human settlements were discovered in North and South America that predate the Clovis culture (the exact dating of the first settlements remains heavily disputed). During pre-Clovis times, the Bering land bridge was still blocked by glacial ice. Many scholars now argue that hunter-gatherer groups migrated along the ice-edge from Asia and down the Pacific coast, on land exposed by low sea levels. The land was later submerged when the glaciers melted; any remnants of their settlements and campsites would now be underwater, along the continental shelf.

Later, when retreating glaciers opened the Bering land bridge (twelve or thirteen thousand years ago), larger migrations from Siberia through the ice-free corridor probably began. These people were most likely the principal ancestors of the later Native American populations that settled most of North and South America. Slightly later migrants from Asia were the probable ancestors of the Arctic and subarctic Inuit populations. Many scholars argue that Kennewick Man—an ancient skeleton unearthed in Washington state in 1996 and dated to circa 7500 BCE—shows different Asian ethnic roots than most modern Native Americans. He may have descended from one of the early migrations from Asia, before the land bridge opened.

The first people in the Americas have long been known as Indians. But the term actually dates back to an error—one Columbus made during his 1492 voyage. He intended to reach China and Japan, which Europeans then considered part of "the Indies." When Columbus landed in the Caribbean, he believed that he had reached the outskirts of China. He never let go of the conviction and called the people he found Indians: a mistake that stuck.

A wide range of settlement and cultural patterns developed across the American continents. These patterns were significantly driven by resource availability and climate patterns (which ranged from ice choked to tropical in the Americas). Hunting and gathering opportunities also varied widely, as did the accessibility of raw materials for toolmaking, homebuilding, and other needs.

The last ice age ended about ten thousand years ago, and the climate proceeded to change rapidly. Sea levels rose, vegetation shifted to different regions, and ice age megafauna (mammoths, mastodons, and other very large mammals) met their demise; climate pressures and human hunting probably contributed to their extinction. As the climate and fauna changed, human communities were forced to adapt. Some groups moved to other regions, and others learned to use new resources. When this period of transformation ended, the natural environment stabilized—and more enduring cultures were finally able to develop as long-term, settled communities formed.

Geographical barriers often made interregional contact difficult. Useful inventions, domesticated crops, and livestock often spread very slowly between geographic areas—if they spread at all. For example, the writing system perfected by the Maya in Central America never reached the Inca in Peru or anyone in North America. The only indigenous pack animal in the Americas, the llama, never moved beyond its home in the Andes to Mexico or North America—neither of which had domesticated work animals before 1492, when Europeans introduced horses and oxen.

THE NATIVE PEOPLES OF NORTH AMERICA

Tribal hunter-gatherer cultures developed among many early North American communities. For many groups, some form of the lifestyle persisted until Europeans arrived. Native groups differed greatly from one another in terms of climate and terrain as well as language and culture. The different climate zones—for example, the Eastern Woodlands, Great Plains, Southwest, Northwest Coast, Arctic, and Subarctic—demanded that inhabitants use different animals, plants, and materials for building and toolmaking.

Over time, hunter-gatherer lifestyles became more complex. Many groups lived in settlements for some of the year, cultivating local plants and harvesting local resources; then they moved on to follow game animals or to reach other seasonal settlements. Deep rivalries existed between some peoples and led to frequent warfare. But groups also exchanged local resources through trade networks that sometimes extended over long distances. Tribal societies also frequently formed political and military alliances—one of the most powerful was the Iroquois League, which probably formed shortly before European contact.

From circa 1000 BCE to 500 CE, the Adena and then the Hopewell cultures built large ceremonial mounds as communal ritual centers along the Ohio and then the Mississippi River valleys. Many of these mounds, and those of the later Mississippian cultures, are still visible. The remains puzzled early European settlers, who could not believe that supposedly "primitive" Native American people could have built them. Later excavation and study established the actual date and origin of the earthworks.

Within the last two millennia, more heavily populated civilizations arose in North America. They developed permanent settlements and became dependent on organized agriculture. Crops such as maize (sweet corn), beans, and squash were introduced from Mesoamerica, where farming was already long established. Farming communities appeared in the Southwest, close to Mesoamerica, after 200 CE. These early southwestern farming communities developed complex irrigation systems and sophisticated home-building techniques. In time, however, deteriorating weather patterns and scarcity of water and other resources led to warfare. Increasingly, communities built their homes in more defensible locations—into the sides of cliffs.

Cultivated maize from Mesoamerica reached the Mississippi valley after 700 CE, and agricultural settlement enabled the Mississippian mound-building cultures to arise there. Large ceremonial centers of complex earthworks were surrounded by densely populated agricultural communities that dotted the region's fertile river floodplains. The city at the Cahokia mounds reached its peak around 1250 CE and its population was the continent's largest (there would not be a larger North American city until the late colonial period).

Many of these cultures were declining—or had already collapsed—by the time Europeans arrived in about 1500 CE. By that time, the Adena and Hopewell cultures were long-gone. The southwestern cultures were under siege, from Mexican peoples and from newly arrived Navaho and Apache bands, who had gradually migrated south from the region that is now Alaska and

Canada. The Mississippian cultures had become overcrowded, straining their resources and bringing disease to their densely settled communities; they were also in serious decline before European arrival.

THE NATIVE PEOPLES OF MESOAMERICA

Farming communities were well-established in Mesoamerica (or Central America) by 1500 BCE. In fact, agriculture was probably at least three thousand years older there. Wild plants were domesticated into cultivated maize, beans, chili peppers, and other crops. Animals such as turkeys, ducks, and dogs were domesticated and used for food—unlike in many other areas of the world, there were no large animals in Mesoamerica that people could domesticate as work animals.

As settlements expanded, some began to fuse together into denser communities with complex cultures and stratified social classes. Priests and kings began to rise over such communities and made some of the larger ones into unified political states. Civilization that centered on large, complex cities was emerging—just as it had in Mesopotamia, the Indus Valley, and China.

Sometime after 1200 BCE, the Olmec culture developed on the Gulf Coast of Mexico. This sophisticated civilization laid the foundations for much of later Mesoamerican culture. It developed elaborate temple architecture and religious beliefs, astronomical study and worship, colossal sculpture (some examples tower over ten feet and weigh many tons), an influential calendar system, and the rudiments of written language.

The Olmecs also introduced a religious focus on blood as a sacrifice that the gods demanded from their people. This emphasis would echo through later cultures in the region. Rulers made offerings of their own blood in ritual ceremonies, and human sacrifice—which generally involved prisoners—came to play an integral role in Mesoamerican spiritual practice.

The Olmecs probably also invented the Mesoamerican ball game. This complex sport was played with a rubber ball—the extraction of latex rubber from plants was another Olmec innovation—and became important throughout the region. Indeed, ball courts were a central feature in cities of many Mesoamerican cultures for millennia. The game had roots in ancient Mesoamerican religious myths and assumed great ritual importance. Evidence suggests that losing participants were sometimes sacrificed (that is, killed) after games.

After 500 BCE, the Olmecs were displaced by the militarist Zapotec culture. The Zapotecs, centered in the great city of Monte Alban, further refined written language as they recorded their conquests. They also refined the influential Mesoamerican calendar system. After 200 BCE, another major center emerged over the course of several centuries: the city-state of Teotihuacan. Its origins and its people's connections are unclear, but the city—which was one of the most architecturally magnificent in the ancient Americas—most likely controlled extensive trading networks. Teotihuacan reached its height during the fifth century CE. Although it began to fade, it was remembered throughout the region as a near-mythical source of culture and learning.

The Maya were one of the region's greatest civilizations. With sophisticated cities in present-day southern Mexico and Guatemala, they reached their pinnacle around 600 CE. The culture is known for its many impressive cities such as Tikal, Chichen Itza, Palenque, Copan, and Calakmul. The Maya developed a full written language, which they based on complex and highly artistic glyphs that represented linguistic syllables. Their script has been deciphered only in recent decades, and has entirely transformed the image of the Maya. They were once viewed as a society of peaceable astronomer priests, but scholars have discovered that theirs was a culture of priests and warriors, one that had much in common with other Mesoamerican societies.

Although they were linked by a shared language and culture (that included massive temple complexes with an emphasis on human sacrifice), Maya city-states were often at war with one another. In the late first millennium CE, the entire civilization began to decline. Warfare between the city-states increased and major cities were abandoned. There are various possible explanations for the decline, but worsening drought and battles over available resources are very likely reasons. The jungle reclaimed the great Maya cities long before the Spanish conquest.

The semi-legendary Toltecs—about whom little is known beyond the ruins of Tula, their major city—were regarded as powerful and cultured ancestors by later central Mexican civilizations, particularly the Aztecs, who built a powerful empire in the early fifteenth century. Their capital was Tenochtitlan (present-day Mexico City), an enormous planned metropolis built with great technical sophistication on a land-filled lake. At its peak, it was a city of more than two hundred thousand people—making it one of the world's largest at that time. The Aztecs were an artistically refined, militant warrior culture. They used a numeral system and a form of writing, although it was less developed and self-consistent than Maya writing. The Aztecs aggressively conquered many groups in their region and exploited them for labor, resources, and large-scale human sacrifices.

THE NATIVE PEOPLES OF SOUTH AMERICA

Early agriculture probably emerged in South America by circa 3000 BCE (and possibly some centuries earlier). It was concentrated between the Andes range, which runs down the western coast of the continent, and the Pacific Coast. By 1500 BCE, organized religious centers had appeared in the Andes. Patterns of worship developed that would strongly affect later Andean cultures. Similar to the roughly contemporary Olmecs of Mesoamerica, these practices included human sacrifice.

In the first millennium BCE, sophisticated cultures began to appear along the Andes range. Much of the coastal region was likely united in the worship of a deity revered at the mountain complex of Chavin de Huantar. Chavin cultural artifacts were found well beyond the immediate area, so the cult center's influence was likely widespread. The Nazca culture appeared in what is now southern Peru during the late first millennium BCE. It would persist until about 600 CE and is known especially for the Nazca lines: enormous symbols and images drawn into the landscape and visible only from the air (because they were created for the gods to see).

In the beginning of the first millennium CE, the Moche culture arose north of the Nazca. The Moche are known for their rich burials and lavish works of art, which included extraordinary gold funerary masks. The Moche were displaced around 650 CE by rival city-states. Power shifted over the succeeding centuries, when different cultures vied for territory that would enable them to exploit different climates and terrains between the mountains and the sea.

Beginning in the fourteenth century, a major new power—the Inca—developed in the central Andes region in present-day Peru. Similar to the Aztecs far to their north, the Inca emerged as conquerors and empire builders. By 1500, they controlled an enormous territory along the Andes Mountains. And similar to the Aztecs, they exercised tight control over the people whom they conquered—using them for labor, resources, and human sacrifices.

The Inca developed a highly advanced road system that linked the distant parts of their empire. They also created spectacular urban centers (including the famed mountaintop city of Machu Picchu) with stonework skills that have rarely been matched. Without a written language to organize their empire, the Inca kept records and sent messages with a complicated system of knotted strings called *quipus*.

In 1500, both the Aztec and Inca were young and vibrant empires at the peak of their power. Both would likely have ruled for centuries from their rich and grand cities. But visitors from strange and unknown lands were even then arriving: the Europeans, who would soon throw the powers of the Americas into chaos.

ERA 10: EUROPE'S GLOBAL EXPANSION
(1492 TO CA. 1700)

SPAIN TAKES ON THE NEW WORLD

As Portuguese explorers, Spain's Christopher Columbus, and others opened Europe's great maritime expansion in the late fifteenth century, Europeans went in search of "God, gold, and glory": the expansion of Christianity, wealth from trade and conquest, and national prominence and power. In 1493, soon after Columbus's first voyage, the Pope—who claimed broad authority in the quest to expand Christian control beyond Europe—decreed a new boundary line through the Atlantic Ocean: Spain, he proclaimed, would own all newly discovered lands west of the line, whereas Portugal would own all future discoveries east of the line. The 1494 Spanish-Portuguese Treaty of Tordesillas repositioned the line farther west: the Portuguese had almost achieved a sea route around Africa to India, and they wanted both regions firmly in Portugal's sphere.

Viking mariners from Greenland had found the northeastern tip of North America in the early tenth century and established the short-lived Vinland colony (which was most likely centered in Newfoundland, where archaeologists have discovered the remnants of a Viking settlement). But their voyages were long forgotten by Columbus's day, and he was unaware that any large land masses lay between Europe and Asia. Columbus, who completed four voyages to the Caribbean over the span of a decade, remained sure that he had reached the lands that Marco Polo had called Cathay and Cipangu (now known as China and Japan). People considered these lands "the Indies" and thus called Native Americans "Indians"—a name that stuck even after Columbus's error was exposed.

Later explorers realized that the Caribbean islands were not the fringes of Asia. Rather, Columbus had found the New World—a new one from the Europeans' perspective, at least. One of the early voyagers was the Florentine Amerigo Vespucci, who sailed on Portuguese-sponsored expeditions (and who has been widely accused of fabricating other voyages). Letters then attributed to him (many scholars now doubt their authenticity) claimed that *he* was the first to find the South American mainland (Columbus had actually landed there, although he believed it was part of Asia). Despite protests from Columbus's admirers, a mapmaker soon christened the new continent "America."

The Treaty of Tordesillas now came into play. Brazil, which was not discovered until after the treaty line was drawn, fell to the east of the line and therefore belonged to Portugal (a Portuguese expedition arrived there by 1500). But the rest of the Americas lay west of the line and by the terms of the treaty therefore belonged to Spain. By the beginning of the sixteenth century, Spain established a foothold in the Caribbean and instituted the *encomienda* system, in which Spanish settlers assumed control of native groups—supposedly to protect them and convert them to Christianity. In reality, encomienda rulers exploited the local Taínos peoples as slave laborers, forcing them to mine and farm as the Spanish extracted every drop of wealth from the islands. Although the Dominican priest Bartolemé de Las Casas and other Spaniards protested the cruel treatment of the native Indians, they were largely powerless to prevent the exploitation.

For the native peoples, disease proved even more devastating than the encomienda system. The Spanish unknowingly carried diseases to the New World. Although the illnesses were common in Europe, Asia, and Africa, the New World communities were physically and biologically isolated from the rest of the world and thus had never encountered them. A virgin soil epidemic results when a disease from the outside strikes a native population that lacks immunity to it—catastrophic epidemics erupted among the Taínos, and their population drastically dropped. Attempted rebellions against the Spanish, and against those local Indians who chose to ally with them, achieved very little—especially as the local population continued to plummet. In the 1530s, holy Roman emperor and king of Spain Charles V turned against the brutal encomienda system. But by 1550, overwork, exploitation, and disease had led to the virtual extinction of the Taínos. And the epidemics that helped spur their demise would spread only farther.

During his time in the Caribbean, Columbus had heard rumors of wealthy powers over the horizon, which he took as word of China and Japan: in fact he was hearing tales of the wealthy peoples of the Central American mainland. The Spanish colony in Cuba soon learned of the existence of Mexico and sent Hernán Cortés there in 1519. Local peoples subjugated by the Aztec Empire enthusiastically aided Cortés against their Aztec overlords. The native allies bolstered Cortés's five-hundred-member force, and allowed him to challenge the Aztec capital of Tenochtitlan—a city of two hundred thousand people, then larger than any city in Europe. The Aztec emperor Moctezuma (or Montezuma) met Cortés and invited him into the city as a guest (although legends that he believed Cortés to be a god are probably false).

The well-planned and constructed city greatly impressed the Spanish. However, they were appalled by the Aztecs' vast temples to pagan gods and their practice of human sacrifice. Cortés took Moctezuma hostage and tried to rule through him, but the effort failed and Moctezuma was killed. The Spanish fell back and rallied their local allies to besiege the city. The Aztec Empire fell to the Spanish in 1521; the Spanish granted their chief allies, the Tlaxcalans, special privileges—but also forced their conversion to Christianity. Most Mexican peoples were subjected to forced labor and conversion, and virgin soil epidemics spread through their communities.

After establishing their Mexican power base, Spanish adventurers then moved against the other great Native American empire: the Inca of the Andes. In 1531, the brothers Francisco and Gonzalo Pizarro led an invasion of Inca Peru. As Cortés had done in Mexico, they found allies among the local peoples who were dominated by the Inca lords. After defeating the emperor Atahualpa, the Spanish conquistadors held him for a massive ransom of gold and silver—and then offered him a deadly choice. If he converted to Christianity, he would be strangled. If he refused, he would be burned alive. After Atahualpa was baptized as a Catholic, the Spanish throttled him and installed his brother as a puppet ruler. Over the following decades, a period of repeated Inca revolts and constant Spanish infighting—including the murder of both Pizarro brothers by Spanish rivals—left the region in chaos. The Spanish crown only slowly managed to impose control.

OTHER EUROPEAN POWERS ENTER THE AMERICAS

The Portuguese took possession of Brazil, developing a system of sugar plantations and gradually expanding their settlements there. But Spain laid sole claim to the rest of the Americas. Its new American empire, called New Spain, tightened its grip on Central and South America—generating massive wealth in the process. It melted the native peoples' gold and silver treasures and forced them to dig for more of both. New Spain's precious metals filled the treasure fleets on which Spain's vast and growing global power soon came to depend. Together, the Spanish state and the Catholic Church worked to control the conquered peoples, imposing harsh government rule and squelching native religious practices that they saw as mere superstitions.

As gold and silver poured into Europe, the vast wealth of the New World caused economic chaos in the Old World. A massive discovery of Bolivian silver devalued Europe's silver currency, sparking a dramatic rise in prices and tremendous inflation. But the newfound wealth extended beyond gold and silver when valuable new crops and animals were taken from America to Europe—part of the large-scale transfer of plants, animals, peoples, cultures, and diseases among Europe, Asia, Africa, and the Americas that is known as the Columbian Exchange.

Europeans brought their livestock and crops to America. The horse, which was previously unknown there, would profoundly affect native life: in time, entire native cultures would be defined by mounted warfare and transport. At the same time, crops cultivated by Native Americans and animals they had domesticated or consumed were introduced to Europe, Asia, and Africa. Examples include maize, chocolate, turkeys, potatoes, tobacco, and chilies (the Spanish called these peppers, trying to compete with prized black pepper from Asia—a trade that Portugal dominated). The results of this exchange and diffusion would dramatically transform the economies, environment, and cultures of both hemispheres: new foods were adopted, new crops and new farming methods spread across the landscape, and new animals reshaped farming practices and transportation.

The Spanish expanded their control farther from their power base in Mexico: Ponce de Leon's 1513 expedition pushed into Florida, and Francisco Vázquez de Coronado entered the North American Southwest in 1540. But other countries were also drawn by the wealth that Spain and Portugal had found—and they did not accept the two nations' claims to sole ownership of the Americas. The English and French soon came probing. As early as 1497, Britain commissioned Italians John and Sebastian Cabot to find a route around the Americas to Asia. Instead, the Cabots found the North American mainland. Giovanni Verrazano sailed on behalf of France in the 1520s. He also sought a route to Asia but ultimately surveyed much of North America's eastern coast. French explorer Jacques Cartier followed him in the 1530s.

France's earliest efforts to settle North America were blocked by the Spanish. England's Sir Walter Raleigh tried to establish a colony at Roanoke (in present-day North Carolina) in the 1580s; a resupply mission, delayed by the Spanish Armada's 1588 attack on England, found the colony mysteriously abandoned. A larger British effort at Jamestown prevailed despite early crises, famine, and repeated wars with a powerful Native American confederacy. Founded in 1607, it formed the core of the new Virginia colony. The following year, French explorer Samuel de Champlain established Quebec, France's first permanent settlement in the Americas.

Although the Spanish vehemently protested such intrusion into what they argued was *their* land, their powers were limited beyond the Central American base. They managed to eject the French from Florida in the 1560s, but they were unable to block settlements farther north. Native peoples' ability to resist the growing European presence was also severely weakened. The virgin soil epidemics introduced in the Caribbean and Mexico soon spread north and probably peaked in the early decades of the seventeenth century. Even as the pace of European settlement accelerated, the native peoples' communities were collapsing. By the 1620s, as much as 90 percent of the indigenous population may have died.

Over the course of the seventeenth century, Britain, France, and Holland—a growing commercial power—made inroads in the Caribbean and established lucrative sugar plantations. In northern Canada, the British took control of Hudson's Bay, with its bounty of whales and seals. The French assumed control of eastern Canada, the lands around the Great Lakes, and down the Mississippi Valley to Louisiana. But their settlements were light: they focused mainly on expanding their fur trade with the Native Americans and establishing Jesuit missions to convert their Indian trading partners. France soon focused its efforts on the more profitable Caribbean sugar islands. The Dutch established the New Netherlands colony, which was centered on the trading port of New Amsterdam on Manhattan Island. The European empires constantly battled over control of these lands and frequently went to war.

The British soon controlled much of eastern North America. They initially hoped that their Jamestown venture would find mineral wealth as Spain had done in Central America. But when mining efforts mostly came up empty, they shifted toward permanent agricultural settlement. They grew cash crops such as tobacco, indigo, and rice and pushed the native peoples back in their relentless pursuit of farmable land. In New England, Puritan settlers aimed to create a godly world in the wilderness. Their self-supporting farming communities also demanded land, leading to increased tensions and sporadic wars with native communities. As the British consolidated their hold along the seaboard, they seized the New Netherlands from the Dutch and created the colony of New York. New Amsterdam was renamed New York City: a hub for trade with mainland Europe and with other colonies and an important center of economic opportunity for many who ventured to the colonies.

THE AFRICAN SLAVE TRADE INTENSIFIES

Even as Europe's power grew, sub-Saharan African kingdoms largely succeeded in repelling its incursions. The region had witnessed diverse local cultures and a succession of formidable regional empires. Powerful West African states such as Ghana, Songhay, and Mali converted to Islam during the Middle Ages. For centuries, they conducted an active trade in gold, slaves, ivory, and other goods across the Sahara to Islamic North Africa and the Middle East.

Coastal East Africa had also converted to Islam during the medieval period, and had conducted a heavy sea trade (including a large-scale slave trade) with Arabia. Trading ivory and mined minerals, the continent's southern and interior regions were also tied to the Islamic commercial network. The Shona Empire, which reigned in southern Africa during the fifteenth and sixteenth centuries, centered on the stone-built city of Great Zimbabwe. The Shona controlled hundreds of mines and exported gold and copper to the Arab world.

Europe had maintained strong ties with North Africa since ancient times and had sporadic contact with sub-Saharan Africa. In the early fifteenth century, Portuguese mariners began to explore the West African coast. Africa's coastal kingdoms were strong, and Portugal's efforts to seize territory largely failed (beginning in the sixteenth century, the Portuguese would have greater though still limited success in East Africa). Instead, Portugal established trade—including the purchase of African slaves—with the West African rulers.

By this time, slavery was already a way of life in Africa. The trans-Saharan slave trade with the Arab world had operated since the seventh century, and local slavery probably stretched far deeper into Africa's past. Africans could be enslaved by other Africans if they owed debts or if they were captured during war. Europeans would come to enslave Africans on the grounds of racial difference, an ideology that gained strength as slavery grew more entrenched. In Africa, however, there was little sense of racial distinction between peoples or regions. Instead, African peoples were most likely to enslave those with different ethnic or tribal identities. Slavery's scale and severity varied greatly by region and culture.

During the seventeenth century, Africa's slave trade with the West accelerated dramatically. By the time the Atlantic slave trade was finally suppressed in the mid-nineteenth century, more than twelve million Africans had been shipped to the Americas as slaves. The rise of commercial agriculture and the demand for labor drove the surge in the New World's slave trade. Because few Caribbean natives had survived the decades after European contact, the Americas' growing sugar plantations needed a new source of forced labor. Meanwhile, Brazil's Portuguese plantations also needed large labor forces. In the Southern colonies of British North America, cash crops such as tobacco had first been tended by European indentured servants, who paid for their passage to America by agreeing to fixed terms of service. But as Southern society became more settled and stratified, opportunities for rapid advancement dwindled: fewer Europeans were willing to indenture themselves with little hope of later striking it rich.

Planters in all these regions settled on the same solution: African slaves. Without much of a foothold on the African continent, European traders had to buy slaves from West Africa's kingdoms, many of which became immensely wealthy in the process. Rising demand sparked a sharp rise in internal wars, seizures for debt, and violent large-scale kidnappings as African traders aggressively sought captives to sell for Western goods—especially guns, which made Africa's wars and slaving raids still more effective and more deadly. Millions were marched to the coast by their African captors. Half of the captives died en route, and those who survived the treks were sold to Europeans at coastal enclaves that local African kings leased to European powers.

From the African slave ports, most slaves were shipped across the Atlantic in an inhumane months-long journey called the Middle Passage: slaves were packed into overcrowded ships and chained together so they could barely move. They were inadequately fed and exposed to constant filth and disease. Striving for efficiency, slave merchants stuffed as many as possible onto the ships—and simply assumed that some slaves would die during each voyage.

The vast majority of slave ships sailed to the sugar plantations of Brazil and the Caribbean islands. As severe as slavery became in British North America, the cruel sugar plantations were far more lethal: slave laborers often died in their unforgiving climate and brutal conditions, fueling a constant demand for fresh imports. A smaller number of slaves were shipped to the North American colonies. Survival rates in North America were much higher, and the local slave population grew naturally. The heaviest North American call for slaves came from large tobacco, indigo, and rice plantations in the South. Plantations in other areas such as upstate New York and Connecticut also demanded slaves. Elsewhere, they served as domestic workers and farm hands.

EUROPE EXPANDS INTO ASIA AND EASTERN COLONIALISM BEGINS

Portuguese navigators worked their way down the African coast over the course of the fifteenth century, pursuing a route around its southern tip to the riches of India and East Asia. By 1420, Portugal's Prince Henry—called "the Navigator," although he apparently never went to sea—sponsored voyages along the African coast that greatly enhanced the geographical and navigational knowledge of the day: these voyages also carried the first African slaves to Portugal. In late 1497, the Portuguese explorer Vasco da Gama successfully rounded the Cape of Good Hope, Africa's southernmost extremity. In 1498, he landed in India. He sailed to India again in 1502, forcing the raja (the prince or local ruler) of Calicut to accept peace terms and trading ties. Da Gama also landed settlers at Mozambique on Africa's southeastern coast, where Portugal would establish a territorial foothold.

Portugal's settlements and missionary activities grew rapidly. The Portuguese reached Japan and China by the 1550s, planting settlers and seizing trading ports wherever they went. They had found a sea route to the immensely valuable spices of the East and enjoyed nearly full control of the hugely profitable European spice trade—goals that had driven them for more than a century. But Portuguese dominance was short-lived.

In 1519, Ferdinand Magellan—a Portuguese explorer commissioned to sail for Spain—led a new attempt to find a route around the Americas to Asia. He succeeded, navigating around the southern tip of South America into the Pacific. In 1521, he touched down in the present-day Philippines and was killed there (the few survivors of the expedition—one ship from the original five—returned to Spain around India and Africa in 1522, completing the first circumnavigation of the globe).

Spanish sailors from Mexico soon pioneered routes across the Pacific to the Philippines (which they named for the heir to the Spanish throne, later King Philip II). In the 1560s and 1570s, Spanish settlers sailed from Mexico and took control of the islands, giving Spain a crucial foothold in the East—despite repeated revolts by the native inhabitants. Spanish colonists in the Philippines even urged King Philip to use the islands as a base for an invasion of China. (Philip declined: he was busy enough trying to protect his American conquests, fend off the Ottoman Empire in the Mediterranean, protect his Italian possessions, keep France in check, and put down Protestant rebels in the Netherlands.) In 1581, Philip also assumed the Portuguese throne and took full control of the Iberian Peninsula. For a six-decade span, Spain and Portugal fell under a common crown—with their holdings combined into a massive global empire.

Yet Philip's power was not unlimited. His repeated efforts to invade England and destroy its Protestant monarchy, which he had initiated with the great Armada of 1588, failed in the face of Britain's strong navy. Philip also struggled to contain a decades-long revolt by Protestant Dutch rebels—who soon cost the Iberians their dominance in the East as well. In 1602, the Dutch—still in revolt against Spain—created the Dutch East India Company to undermine Spanish and Portuguese interests in the Pacific. Skilled sailors and merchants, they established extensive trade with East Asia and took control of many Portuguese outposts. In Japan, the rising Tokugawa military governors, or shoguns, outlawed Christianity and expelled the Portuguese and their missionaries in 1639. But the shoguns allowed the Dutch to establish a limited trading outpost at Nagasaki—the only link between Japan and the West.

Dutch control also diminished in the face of more powerful European nations. The English, whom the Dutch had initially blocked from East Asia, shifted their focus to India—where powerful local Mughal rulers had prevented the Dutch from securing a foothold. By 1700, increasingly profitable trade in Indian spices and cloth, driven by the English East India Company, had led to a growing British presence in India.

Britain's growing grip on India provided a base for further expansion into the Pacific. A lucrative trade was established with China. Chinese porcelain, tea, and silk were exchanged for Indian goods—including the narcotic drug opium, which would bring dire consequences for China. By the mid-seventeenth century, the French had also begun to explore opportunities in India and the Pacific. Growing British, French, and Dutch colonial empires would build their power in India and Asia over the coming centuries.

ERA 11: THE REVOLUTIONARY ROOTS: THE MODERN WEST
(CA. 1600 TO 1800)

UNEVEN GROWTH AND ECONOMIC MODERNIZATION

During the seventeenth century, Western Europe urbanized dramatically as it focused on large-scale commerce. Rival trading powers Britain and Holland set the pace. Both developed banking systems that supported complex investments in powerful commercial bodies such as the Dutch and English East India Companies. Manufacturing and imports sharply increased as a more prosperous population demanded greater access to consumer goods, including Asian and American products such as tea, coffee, sugar, chocolate, and cotton.

Europe's population also grew exponentially as farming techniques improved and new crops such as maize and potatoes were introduced from the Americas. As the food supply stabilized, more members of society could venture beyond farming. Opportunities for advancement opened—even for rural people, who could enter into trade, move to cities, and sometimes even amass significant wealth. The new economy was based more on money and commerce rather than local barter. In many places, people were no longer shackled by their birth status; social mobility expanded as feudalism's rigid systems of landowning lords and land-bound peasants faded into memory.

As the power of nobles declined, centrally ruled nation-states took hold throughout Europe, uniting ethnic and linguistic groups into single polities. Spain, for example, had been divided between the crowns of Aragon and Castile. These realms now merged into a single nation, and linguistically separate Portugal, which had fallen under the Spanish crown, became a separate nation. France had been a patchwork of local aristocratic powers with only a central area around Paris under direct royal control. It now fell entirely under the monarch's authority.

As Europe continued to expand abroad, nations' overseas colonies emerged as important parts of a complex economic web. The colonies provided valuable raw materials for European manufacturers and consumption; they also provided growing markets for those manufacturers and enabled empires to provide their own suppliers and consumers without having to pay rival powers. States with strong central governments, such as England and France, increasingly barred colonies from manufacturing their own goods: per the mercantilist theory that dominated the era, colonies existed to enhance their mother countries' wealth, power, and status while diminishing the standing of rival states. This belief drove the frequent wars between colonial powers: each nation wanted to grow its empire at others' expense.

Nonetheless, the pace and extent of development varied greatly throughout Europe. Modern commercial states such as England and Holland offered economic advantage and opportunity to large and growing segments of their populations—but elsewhere people were less fortunate. Although France achieved wealth and power in Europe and overseas, the profits were enjoyed mainly by its large and disproportionately wealthy aristocracy. The vast French peasantry was still dominated by large landowners and only achieved slow, meager improvement in terms of status and rights.

The German states were devastated by the religious schism and brutal fighting of the catastrophic Thirty Years' War, which raged from 1618 until 1648. In the war's aftermath, innovation and advancement were slowed and Germans lacked the prosperity and prospects of the nations to their west. The war sharply reduced the population, and with it the labor supply: the German elite used harsh laws to keep the peasants under tight control—thus stalling economic development and commercial growth even further. At the same time, Eastern Europe was virtually moving backward. Even as serfdom withered in Western Europe after the fourteenth-century Black Death, the institution became entrenched in the East—and now it gained an even greater grip, keeping the economy heavily rural while depressing outside trade and commercial growth.

Warfare remained a common scourge in Europe as nations and royal dynasties battled over territory, resources, and imperial possessions. Nations that had achieved huge victories saw their dominance crumble within a generation. Spain had been Europe's dominant power during the sixteenth century, buoyed by the massive wealth it drew from the New World. But wars in Europe had drained its resources, lopped off its possessions, and undercut its royal line. By 1700, Spain's power was quickly fading; it would never again rank among the dominant European states. Under King Louis XIV, France emerged from the seventeenth century with much of the continental power that Spain had lost—though the French people faced a massive tax burden to pay for Louis's wars. England, which had a powerful central government to organize its economic expansion, began to displace Holland as Europe's dominant trading power and to dominate the seas.

By 1700, Eastern Europe risked being completely left behind. Russia's Tsar Peter I, or Peter the Great, launched ambitious reforms in order to draw isolated and stagnant Russia into the fast-modernizing European world. Early in his reign, he remodeled his military forces and bolstered Russia's power, expanding its grip toward the Baltic and challenging Sweden (which was then a strong regional power). He moved Russia's capital to St. Petersburg, physically closer to his European neighbors, and encouraged the importation of Western European culture and commerce. He also founded academies, modernized government administration, and even ordered Russian men to shave their traditional full beards or face a special tax. Although serfdom would long continue to dominate the rural interior, Peter pushed the nation onto the European stage with a forward-looking state and military.

FREEDOM VERSUS POWER: ENGLAND AND FRANCE IN THE SEVENTEENTH CENTURY

During the seventeenth century, power became even more centralized as European rulers took greater control of their nations. At the same time, wealthy nobles, landowners, and increasingly influential commercial middle classes pushed for greater rights of their own. Traditional legal privileges from the Middle Ages, the legacy of Renaissance humanism, and the Reformation's challenge to unfettered top-down authority all inspired such challenges to unlimited top-down authority.

In England, rejection of unlimited monarchical power stretched back to Saxon times; in 1215, the Magna Carta had enshrined specific limits. By Queen Elizabeth I's death in 1603, Parliament had secured still greater checks on royal authority. Crucially, Parliament now firmly controlled the nation's monetary supply. Taxation was defined as a gift from the people to the crown for the support of government. Parliament, which was defined as the people's representatives, thus assumed the exclusive power to raise taxes and fund the Crown. When they moved to America, the early colonists brought these concepts of taxation with them.

James Stuart, King James VI of Scotland, succeeded his childless cousin, Elizabeth I, as James I of England—joining England and Scotland under a single monarch for the first time. But James believed firmly in the divine right of kings and chafed at Parliament's efforts to limit his authority. Parliament, in turn, resented his imperious attempts to bypass their control of the monetary supply. England's religious tensions also ran high: the Catholic minority expected that James would be more sympathetic to their grievances than Elizabeth had been and hoped that he would grant them religious freedom. But James refused: like his predecessor, he eyed Catholics as a political threat to his Protestant throne. In November 1605, a group of English Catholic conspirators plotted to blow up the Parliament on the first day of the new session, planning to kill James and his ministers and to establish a Catholic monarchy. But the plotters' barrels of gunpowder were found in a cellar beneath Parliament and the Gunpowder Plot was thwarted. Guy Fawkes and the other conspirators were executed.

James was a shrewd politician and largely managed to keep the clashes with his rivals under control. His son, Charles I, was far less astute. Charles assumed the throne in 1625, and expected the English people to obey his divine authority. A clumsy would-be absolutist, he tried to bend Parliament to his will and to extract money from his subjects without Parliamentary consent. But Parliament pushed back, forcing him to endorse the Petition of Right, a 1628 document that explicitly defined the limits of his power. But despite his public agreement, Charles had no real intention of respecting the petition's terms.

Charles dissolved Parliament in 1629, and reigned without a legislature for eleven years (the "personal rule"). His highly ceremonial and ritualistic approach to religion, enforced by his unpopular archbishop William Laud, seemed almost Catholic to the many English Puritans; they demanded a return to stricter biblical traditions. Freed from Parliament's restraint, Charles worked to impose and increase taxes as he wished. "Ship money" was a traditional tax on port towns meant to fund the navy; Charles sparked heated opposition and court challenges when he extended the tax to the entire country. His attempt to force Anglican religious practices onto Scotland (a nation dominated by Puritan-friendly Presbyterians) led to war in 1640. His need to fund the war forced him to call a new Parliament. The "Short Parliament" immediately denounced the measures that he had taken during the personal rule, and it was promptly dissolved. But Charles still had to fund his war: he called another parliament later that year.

This "Long Parliament" forced major concessions from Charles. But as the demands of the Puritan-led Parliamentarians rose, the king's conservative supporters pushed back. In 1642, Charles's clumsy attempt to arrest five parliamentary leaders inflamed the crisis: England soon plunged into civil war. After heavy fighting, Charles continued to reject parliamentary peace terms, refusing to accept the limits they sought to place on his power. Forced to surrender to the Scots in 1646, he was turned over to Parliament but still refused to agree to terms. After escaping, he allied with the Scots in 1648 and made them an entirely false promise to impose Presbyterianism on England in return. The parliamentary army defeated the Scots and recaptured Charles. He was tried for treason and beheaded in 1649, and the monarchy was abolished.

Radical political ideas percolated during the English Revolution as stronger notions of popular sovereignty took hold. The Levellers, a particularly bold group within the Revolutionary movement, demanded broad legal and political reforms such as universal male suffrage, and they gained support from the lower social orders. But under the leadership of General Oliver Cromwell, the upper echelons of the parliamentary army gained power and formed a Republican commonwealth with strong central authority, limiting the vote to property owners. Cromwell put down the Levellers, violently subjugated Ireland, and waged territorial wars abroad. He ultimately suppressed the corrupt and difficult Parliament: although he refused to take the crown, his power approached that of a king. The Republican commonwealth disintegrated entirely after his death. In 1660, Parliament offered the throne to Charles's son. Charles II's restoration government pardoned most of the rebels. Most were relieved to end the commonwealth experiment: chaos and civil war had killed an estimated one-quarter of a million people in Britain, and Cromwell's crackdowns probably killed hundreds of thousands in Ireland. Monarchical power and the state-sponsored Anglican Church were quickly restored.

Similar to James I, Charles II balanced high-handedness with political savvy. Charles's brother and heir, James, was a convert to Catholicism. Tories—those who supported strong monarchical power—backed his right to the throne, whereas defenders of parliamentary power (the Whigs) tried to bar him. James II became king in 1685, but his autocratic ideas soon alienated almost everyone. In 1688, he fathered a male Catholic heir, which even his Tory supporters (who were staunch Anglicans) were unwilling to accept. Both Whig and Tory leaders invited Dutch Prince William of Orange and his wife, James's Protestant daughter Mary, to invade; James was deposed in the largely bloodless Glorious Revolution and allowed to flee the country. Parliament assumed greater control: it imposed limits on monarchical power, codified basic rights in the 1689 Bill of Rights, and proclaimed that the monarchical succession must henceforth be Protestant. The landholders and commercial elites that controlled Parliament had gained considerable new power.

While England moved toward a constitutionally limited monarchy and a powerful elected Parliament, England's traditional rival was moving in the opposite direction. As France emerged from its sixteenth-century religious wars, its monarchs struggled to impose firm control on the country. King Louis XIV came to the throne as a child in 1643; five years later, a popular revolt erupted (called the *Fronde*, or "sling" after the stone-throwing mobs) demanding greater local control of already excessive royal taxation. Power-hungry nobles exploited the unrest to launch years of plots against the crown and one another. Louis's ministers regained control by 1652, and Louis took personal control in 1661. The bold ruler quickly created a system of absolute royal authority that stood in utter contrast to the trend in England.

France had established institutions meant to defend the people: the States-General (a seldom-called assembly that represented clergy, nobility, and commoners) and the *parlements* (bodies in Paris and the provinces that could challenge royal laws). He also further weakened aristocratic power, forcing the many nobles to vie for his favor at his lavish court in Versailles. He increased the tax burden, expanding the treasury bureaucracy and the enforcement system. Louis was militarily aggressive, building up France's military and winning wide conquests. He also encouraged splendor in architecture, literature, and the arts, earning the description "the Sun King." Henry IV had ended the Wars of Religion in 1598 by issuing the Edict of Nantes, which granted full religious toleration to the Huguenots (the French Protestant minority). But Louis dismissed tolerance in favor of religious uniformity and complete popular obedience. He reinstated a policy of persecution and revoked the edict in 1685; two hundred thousand Huguenots fled for England, Holland, America, and elsewhere.

Louis XIV successfully created an absolutist royal state, but he left a troubled legacy. The Huguenot exodus deprived France of many skilled artisans and tradespeople, and the expansion of creative arts that he had encouraged early in his reign declined. His frequent wars were enormously costly and were financed by crushing taxes imposed on the French people by royal decree. After 1700, during the last years of Louis's reign, France's enemies rallied to inflict severe defeats on his forces. France was left weakened and impoverished. When Louis's great-grandson took the throne in 1710 as Louis XV, he inherited a stagnating economy, political weakness, religious disharmony, a bloated and unpopular aristocracy, and widespread discontent—all of which would haunt his son, Louis XVI.

NEW IDEAS EMERGE IN A RAPIDLY MODERNIZING EUROPE

In the sixteenth and seventeenth centuries, as Europe shifted away from the Renaissance into modernity, literary figures helped shape language and ideas. As they introduced new modes of expression and adapted foreign words, writers such as the actor-playwright William Shakespeare helped enrich and modernize the English language. The royally commissioned, team-translated King James Bible (1611)—surely the greatest work ever produced by a committee—further influenced English literary styles. Spain's Miguel Cervantes helped create the modern novel with *Don Quixote* (written from 1605 to 1615). Sixteenth-century French essayist Michel Montaigne questioned dogmatic intellectual certainty and called for open-minded inquiry, while early seventeenth-century English theorist Francis Bacon promoted rigorous scientific methods and other intellectual pursuits.

Many of the era's thinkers remained firmly Christian: René Descartes and Blaise Pascal—seventeenth-century French philosophers, mathematicians, and scientists—were both deeply religious, although they aimed to enhance knowledge by rigorously challenging long-standing assumptions. But by the late seventeenth century, skeptical inquiry in all disciplines—even religious thought—was gaining momentum. The ensuing age of philosophical, moral, and political skepticism—in which old ideas were challenged and sweeping reforms were demanded—is known as the Enlightenment (which, despite this commonly used term, was neither a unified nor coherent international movement).

John Locke, a Whig who opposed James II, was a founding figure in the English Enlightenment. His hugely influential *Second Treatise on Government* argued that rulers' powers were not divinely granted, as many divine right theorists (including James II himself) insisted. Instead, Locke said, power was delegated to the government by the people—who originally possessed all power in the "state of nature" before they formed a social compact and joined together to form a society. Society granted power to government in order to secure its own safety and protect individuals' natural rights of life, liberty, and property. Thus, if government acted against the people's interests, the people had the right to withdraw the power they had granted and to create a new government that would better serve their aims.

Such ideas had radical implications, allowing the public to demand an unprecedented degree of political authority. The overthrow of James II by the people's Parliament seemed to show Locke's ideas in action, and his words would echo through America's 1776 Declaration of Independence. But Locke's theories fell out of favor with the Whig parliaments of the eighteenth century, which took firm control and lost interest in bowing to the popular will. Writers who loudly opposed the often-corrupt parliaments had the greatest practical impacts in spurring resistance to abuses of power. And in America, the concepts of English liberty that were imported by the settlers and developed during decades of local self-government proved more potent than the works of outside theorists. Nevertheless, Locke's ideas offered strong backing for the British political opposition and, later, for America's increasingly disaffected colonists.

Locke's theories on education and knowledge were also influential. He argued that the human mind began as a tabula rasa, or blank slate, with no innate ideas or attitudes. His theory put enormous emphasis on the power of society and education to shape future generations and raised hopes that through such influences man could ultimately be perfected. A major eighteenth-century Scottish writer, David Hume, expanded on these ideas. Insisting that all aspects of the mind derived from experience, he rejected the notion that anything could ever be known with certainty. Encouraging skeptical inquiry into traditional ideas and opinions, Hume wrote important works on history, economics, aesthetics, and political theory.

Even in German states—as powerful monarchies rose in Prussia and Austria—influential theorists wrote on natural law, or the rules of fundamental justice that they believed God had built into the world. Despite its own authoritarian state, eighteenth-century France was home to a vibrant circle of probing intellectuals. In *Spirit of the Laws*, Baron de Montesquieu influenced European and American political theorists, arguing for the separation of legislative, executive, and judicial powers. Jean-Jacques Rousseau called for new educational models that would free people from society's corruption. His *Social Contract* rooted political power in the people. But unlike Locke—who emphasized society's obligation to respect individual rights—Rousseau envisioned a political order in which individuals were subordinate to the good of the whole society. Later, French revolutionaries would embrace this model.

The French philosopher known as Voltaire (the pen name of François-Marie Arouet) argued for rights to free speech and religion and denounced the power of the Catholic Church in the French state. Another religious skeptic, Denis Diderot, was the editor and a leading contributor to the great *Encyclopédie*: its twenty-eight volumes, with tens of thousands of articles and illustrations, were published between the 1750s and 1770s and investigated such issues as religious and political freedom, government, morality, education, economics, and artistic theory. Intellectual freedom did not come easily, however, and the French Enlightenment met fierce official resistance. Diderot was jailed for atheism in 1749, and the French government bent to pressure from the Catholic Church and banned his *Encyclopédie* in 1759 (although the project's powerful friends ensured that the ban was not enforced). Meanwhile, works by Voltaire and other *philosophes* (or philosophers) were publicly burned.

European science also advanced dramatically in the early modern era. In the mid-sixteenth century, Polish theorist Nicolaus Copernicus introduced an idea that would come to have profound consequences. Throughout history, most had assumed the Earth was the center of the universe. Europeans still relied on the geocentric model developed by Claudius Ptolemy, a Greek astronomer and geographer who lived in Roman-controlled Alexandria in the second century CE, to predict the motion of the heavenly bodies. Aristotle's similar concept of concentric, Earth-centered cosmic spheres became Church doctrine in the Middle Ages. But Copernicus sought a more accurate and efficient model and placed the sun at the center of the universe.

At first, his model was treated as a mathematical abstraction and aroused little controversy. But for the Church, his ideas had radical implications, challenging the Christian belief that the Earth was the center of God's creation, surrounded by the perfect and immovable heavens. Church officials began to push back—especially in Italy, near the center of its power. Italian philosopher Giordano Bruno argued that the sun was merely one star in an infinite universe and that other stars might support other worlds and other men—a direct challenge to the Church's view of man as God's chief creation. When Bruno refused to recant these claims, the Roman Inquisition burned him at the stake in 1600. However, Copernican ideas kept advancing. In the early seventeenth century, German astronomer Johannes Kepler made the new model far more practical and accurate by deducing the planets' true elliptical orbits.

A contemporary of Kepler and a fellow Copernican, the Italian scientist and mathematician Galileo Galilei used the newly invented telescope to discover the rough, cratered surface of Earth's moon and the distant moons orbiting Jupiter. His observations contradicted Aristotle's model of perfect, crystalline heavens in which all things moved around the Earth. Despite his indisputable astronomical observations, the Catholic Church ordered Galileo in 1616 not to promote the heliocentric (sun-centered) model except as a hypothetical abstraction. But his 1632 *Dialogue Concerning the Two Chief World Systems* was a barely disguised declaration of heliocentrism. He was charged with heresy and forced to recant his beliefs before the Roman Inquisition in 1633. Under house arrest for the rest of his life, he pursued and published innovative work on motion and momentum, laying key foundations for modern physics.

But as intellectual inquiry grew more fervent in the seventeenth and eighteenth centuries, science could not be contained. New telescopes and microscopes aided the exploration of nature. England's Isaac Newton investigated optics and motion and modeled the effects of gravity. Sweden's Carl Linnaeus developed an innovative system for classifying living organisms. America's Benjamin Franklin made breakthroughs in the study of electricity, ocean currents, and other areas of science and technology. Other scientists began to use comparative anatomy to reveal relationships between different animal species and to demonstrate that some fossil species were extinct—contrary to Christian teaching, which held that all created life was unchangeable. Still others used geological evidence to contradict a literal interpretation of the Bible's Book of Genesis and argue that the Earth was enormously old. But science was not untouched by the era's wider strains. For example, pioneering French chemist Antoine Lavoisier was also an aggressive royal tax collector, and revolutionaries executed him during the French Revolution.

AMERICA AND FRANCE ENTER THE AGE OF REVOLUTION

Evolving traditions of political freedom in Britain and America, together with the wider eighteenth-century spirit of defiance to ruling authority, triggered a profound crisis in the American colonies—which in turn helped inspire a shattering revolution in authoritarian France. British settlers had carried English notions of free and fair government to America since the seventeenth century. Americans themselves had further developed those ideas in their local colony governments, most of which featured powerful elected legislatures alongside governors whom the British king had appointed or approved.

By 1765, Britain's North American colonies were accustomed to substantial self-rule. British attempts to regulate American trade for the mother country's benefit sometimes caused friction, and smugglers routinely evaded or bribed British customs officials. But most Americans accepted the right of Britain and its Parliament to impose such rules—even if they often disobeyed them. As long as Britain did not interfere with the colonies' internal governments, colonial resentment remained limited and American loyalty to Britain and the empire remained strong.

Britain fought repeated wars with France and Spain over North American territory, and its American colonies were often involved. The last and largest of these wars, known as the French and Indian War (1754–1763) in America and the Seven Years War (1756–1763) in Europe, spread across much of the globe and led to the British conquest of French Canada. Britain's efforts in the war and its subsequent need to secure Canada were costly. The British government decided Americans should contribute to the costs: Parliament enacted the Stamp Act in 1765—the first direct British tax on the British-American colonies.

The colonists were outraged. Many already paid heavy local taxes to support their own governments, and several colonies had amassed large debts to aid the war effort. But the size of the monetary burden was never the major point of contention. In English tradition, taxes were a gift from the people to the king, made on their behalf by their representatives for the support of government. Yet Americans had no voice in Parliament and no control over its actions. Thus Americans had not consented to the new taxes, and Parliament's members were making a "free gift" of money that was not theirs to give. If Parliament could take Americans' money without their consent, what could it *not* do? For most colonists, subjection to such rule amounted to despotism and slavery, and deprived them of the rights Britons had struggled to win from the Magna Carta to the Glorious Revolution.

Britain's continued efforts to enforce parliamentary taxation and the colonists' rising discontent triggered resistance, trade boycotts, disaffection, and growing cries for self-rule—reinforced with appeals to theorists such as John Locke, with his model of power rooted in the people. The crisis finally culminated in war against British control. The American colonies declared independence as the United States of America in 1776. The colonists' long and difficult war was won with the aid of France—no friend to America's democratic aims but always ready to oppose its archrival Britain. The individual states and their larger union experimented with Republican constitutions, culminating in the 1787 Constitutional Convention and the inauguration of the new federal government in 1789. The new system was based on multiple, mutually balancing government branches; the first federal Congress added the Bill of Rights to protect individual liberties.

Meanwhile, France continued to struggle with the troubled legacy left by Louis XIV. The country was still dominated by a lavish and expensive court, where the enormous noble class hovered around the country's absolute monarch. Popular grievances continued to simmer dangerously under Louis XV and Louis XVI: heavy taxation, widespread poverty, gross inequality, and massive resentment toward the staggeringly wealthy elite. The people had no representation, no outlet for their discontent, and no means to enact change. But many French soldiers had served in America during the Revolutionary War, and they returned home much impressed by the new nation's democratic ideals.

In 1789, growing financial crisis forced Louis XVI to summon the States-General, a body—not summoned for 175 years—which represented the three "estates" of French society: the clergy, the nobility, and the commons (with popular representatives sent by the towns). The people were given a voice for the first time in memory, and popular anger erupted; the States-General quickly recast itself as a national assembly with direct political authority. Fears of royal resistance sparked popular violence: on July 14, 1789, crowds stormed the Bastille, a fortress used to house political prisoners, and the king was taken prisoner. The assembly passed the Declaration of the Rights of Man and the Citizen, and worked to create a new constitution, weakening the power of the Catholic Church and dividing power between the king and an elected legislature.

Louis XVI feigned cooperation, but attempted flight to friends abroad. Caught at Varennes, he was returned to Paris where he continued to plot secretly against the revolutionary government and the new constitutional monarchy. French conservative forces allied with the unnerved monarchies of Prussia and Austria (Louis's queen, Marie Antoinette, was Austrian royalty). In 1792, France preemptively declared war on Austria and Prussia invaded France. The newly elected French National Convention responded by abolishing the crown and creating a fully Republican constitution. The Convention tried the king for treason against the revolutionary government, and beheaded him with the newly invented guillotine in early 1793. Within days, France was at war against Spain, Portugal, Britain, and Holland.

The increasingly fanatical French Republicans turned to more radical theories of government and social order—they were determined to remake society in an utterly new and utopian image. Many embraced the view of Rousseau and other French Enlightenment thinkers that the good of the whole society took precedence over individual liberties. The result was a dangerous readiness to subordinate individuals' rights to what the leaders deemed the greater good of revolutionary society. As different revolutionary factions battled for power, the situation grew more precarious. In June 1793, the Jacobin faction (named for a revolutionary political club that met in a former Jacobin, or Dominican, monastery) pushed aside the more moderate Girondists and seized power under radical leader Maximilien de Robespierre.

Robespierre and the Jacobins purged moderates from the government, determined to create a thoroughly revolutionary society and to eliminate all suspected enemies of the revolution. After the king's execution, the Revolutionary Tribunal and the Committee of Public Safety had been created to defend France from foreign and internal enemies. Under Robespierre's ideological Jacobin dictatorship, the hunt for "enemies of the state" became a bloodbath. As many as forty thousand political prisoners, including aristocrats, priests, the Jacobins' political opponents, the deposed queen Marie Antoinette, and even some of Robespierre's most prominent former allies, were executed. In 1793 and 1794, the revolutionary government suppressed a monarchist revolt in the Vendee region on the Atlantic coast, slaughtering the local peasants and killing hundreds of thousands. In July 1794, Robespierre was deposed and guillotined, and the Reign of Terror finally ended. But Revolutionary France was still enmeshed in foreign wars and domestic chaos and continued to devolve into instability, confusion, and unrest.

The Age of Revolution affected England as well. America's revolution had many English admirers, who sought to increase popular power, expand the right to vote, hold more frequent parliamentary elections, and reduce the power of corrupt landowners in choosing parliamentary members. The French Revolution inspired an even bolder British reform movement, and political clubs and societies modeled on French groups rallied for bold political and social changes. But the French turn toward violence and extremism quickly created a strong conservative, pro-monarchical, and anti-French backlash in England; Edmund Burke's powerful *Reflections on the Revolution in France* warned of the chaos unleashed by upending the traditional social structure. The reformers were tarred as dangerous radicals, accused of plots to bring guillotines to London. The collapse of the movement delayed any meaningful political reform for decades.

ERA 12: THE INDUSTRIAL REVOLUTION: NATIONALISM UNITES
(1790S TO 1880S)

NAPOLEON'S EUROPE

The lofty aims of the French Revolution had quickly sunk into partisan feuds and ideological persecution. The bloody reign of Robespierre and the radical Jacobins ended with Robespierre's execution in summer 1794. But the year-long Reign of Terror left as many as forty thousand dead—quite aside from the mass slaughter used to suppress the royalist revolt in the coastal Vendee region. The chaos and carnage had permanently undermined the Revolution's ideals and left France dangerously unstable.

Moderates rallied in 1795 to form a stronger and more traditional government. The new regime rejected universal male suffrage and carefully curbed popular power: only property-owning voters would choose the two legislative houses. To avoid the risk of another dictator like Robespierre, executive power was split among a five-member directory, and the legislature, not the voters, chose the directors. Yet France remained bitterly divided, suffering financial crisis and popular discontent. The Jacobins were determined to regain power and conspired repeatedly against the Directory. In 1796, a cabal of disaffected lower class radicals launched an unsuccessful revolt aimed at redistributing property to the poor.

Growing more suspicious of radical agitation, some of the directors allied with the legislature's conservative royalist faction, which hoped to restore the monarchy. In September 1797, the royalists' rising power led to a coup within the Directory, which purged royalists and their allies from the government. After the coup, a new Second Directory reimposed harsh, dictatorial rule as it tried desperately to restore order and stability. The new government attacked the power of the Roman Catholic Church, largely shut the free press, and forced members of the old aristocracy to reapply for citizenship. Royalist exiles who returned to France were subject to military trial.

France's Revolutionary governments enjoyed greater success abroad than at home. By 1795, the nation had driven off many of its enemies: Prussia, Spain, and others made peace, freeing France from the threat of invasion. It was at this time that the militant patriotic song *La Marseillaise*—first sung by Revolutionary soldiers from Marseille in 1792—was adopted as the French national anthem. By then, a young and brilliant Corsican soldier was gaining tremendous prominence: Napoleon Bonaparte, a twenty-six-year-old artillery officer who had risen already to the rank of general. In 1796, France planned major campaigns into Germany, Austria, and northern Italy. The first two attempts failed, but Napoleon's invasion of Italy was a triumph: he broke Austrian power in northern Italy and established the French-controlled Cisalpine Republic in its place. In 1797, Napoleon pushed into Austria from Italy and the Austrians sued for peace.

Napoleon was now a French national hero and a rising political figure: he was heavily involved in the Directory's September 1797 anti-royalist crackdown. France now had only one real rival: England. In 1798, Napoleon launched an invasion of Egypt, which was then ruled by Mamluk pashas under the loose authority of the Ottoman Empire. Napoleon hoped to begin a French foreign empire that could challenge Britain's overseas domination and to cut off Britain's access to its growing power base in India.

Napoleon quickly defeated the Mamluks in the Battle of the Pyramids. But the French fleet was destroyed just days later in the Battle of the Nile by English admiral Horatio Nelson, cutting off the French army. Napoleon tried to push into Palestine but failed. In 1799, he abandoned his army and returned to France. The troops he left behind were worn down and finally ejected by British and Turkish troops in 1801. But Napoleon had also planned a massive cultural expedition. He brought nearly 150 of France's top scholars to conduct an enormous survey of ancient Egyptian monuments and inscriptions. They laid the foundations of modern Egyptology and sparked a European fascination with Egyptian culture. The findings of the French Egyptian survey, continued long after Napoleon departed, would fill twenty large volumes. French soldiers also discovered the multilingual Rosetta Stone—which the British soon seized and which proved the key to deciphering Egyptian hieroglyphs (see era 2).

Napoleon's Egyptian campaign was his first serious defeat. But it barely slowed his dramatic rise in French politics. Shortly after his return to France, Napoleon joined a coup against the unpopular Directory. The plotters created a new Consulate, with Napoleon as First Consul—in effect, the sole ruler of France. Though he claimed to uphold the Revolution's principles, Napoleon swept away all remnants of democracy and expanded the army to give the state unprecedented power. In 1804, he crowned himself Napoleon I—emperor of the French. Less than six months later, he was crowned King of Italy in the presence of Pope Pius VII—the end of a long saga in which Napoleon laid claim to the Papal States, faced excommunication, abducted the Pope, and finally reached a tense diplomatic settlement.

Over the following years, Napoleon created the Code Napoleon, a complete reworking of French civil law. Despite his own seizure of complete political power, the Code embodied key Revolutionary ideas—particularly in protecting individual liberties and in separating church from state. The Code proved enormously influential throughout Europe and left a mark abroad through Europe's colonial outposts. It still forms the basis of modern French law. Napoleon also ended restrictions on Catholic or Protestant minorities in countries he occupied, emancipated Jews from legal restrictions, and promoted public health and welfare through then-controversial smallpox vaccinations.

Napoleon defeated the Austrians in 1800, and made peace with Britain in 1801. But Britain remained suspicious of Napoleon's power on the continent and his threat to the Mediterranean: the 1801 peace accord dissolved by 1803. Russia, Austria, and Sweden joined Britain's new coalition against France. Completing a series of brilliant campaigns, Napoleon crushed Austrian and Russian forces at the Battle of Austerlitz in 1805. He also eyed an invasion of England, but Admiral Nelson demolished a combined French-Spanish fleet at Trafalgar that same year, asserting Britain's control of the seas and ending the invasion threat. Napoleon swiftly defeated the Prussians in 1806. Britain imposed a naval blockade on France; in retaliation, Napoleon forced much of Europe into the Continental System, a trade embargo against Britain. In 1806, he abolished the Holy Roman Empire. In 1807, he drew the defeated Russians into an alliance and occupied Spain with French troops. Napoleon had defeated the major powers and effectively controlled Germany, Italy, and Spain. He was left as the undisputed master of Europe.

In 1808, Napoleon moved to suppress a widely supported Spanish revolt and installed his brother Joseph as Spain's king. Britain sent an army under General Arthur Wellesley (the future Duke of Wellington) to support the Spanish rebels—whose irregular fighting methods introduced the Spanish word guerilla, or "little war," to the English language. The Peninsular War erupted in Spain—and for the first time Napoleon's hold on Europe began to falter. British victories in Spain failed to drive the French out, but they succeeded in tying down hundreds of thousands of Napoleon's troops. By 1811, Russia's Tsar Alexander I had again turned against Napoleon, and Napoleon launched an invasion in 1812. His vast army of over half a million men drove deep into Russia and took Moscow late that year. But the Russians kept pulling back, abandoning Moscow and destroying its food supplies. With the severe Russian winter setting in, Napoleon could only retreat. Facing bitter cold, growing starvation, and Russian guerilla attacks, Napoleon's army suffered horrific casualties. Few members of the massive invading force left Russia alive.

Napoleon finally abandoned his retreating men and raced back to Paris to save his tottering power. But it was too late: the French were turning on him and his enemies were closing in. After Napoleon was badly beaten at Leipzig by Austria, Prussia, Russia, and Sweden in late 1813, the German princes began to throw off Napoleon's control and withdraw their soldiers from his armies. In 1814, Napoleon was forced to abdicate (to renounce his throne). The victorious allies exiled him to the small Italian island of Elba, and mockingly named him its emperor. The old French monarchy was restored, and Louis XVI's surviving younger brother was installed as Louis XVIII. Napoleon escaped from Elba in 1815, returning to France and gathering an army. Many were still loyal: the French soldiers sent to stop him instead rallied to his banner, and the new king fled. But Napoleon's second reign lasted barely a hundred days. An allied army under the Duke of Wellington defeated him at Waterloo, in present-day Belgium. Napoleon was again forced to abdicate and exiled to St. Helena, a remote British-owned island in the South Atlantic. He died there in 1821.

In 1814, the allied powers assembled the Congress of Vienna to lay out a post-Napoleonic Europe. Masterminded by Austria's powerful foreign minister, Klemens von Metternich, the Congress stripped France of its conquests, and sought to restore the old monarchical order as far as was possible. But the Congress could not turn back the clock. At first, many Europeans had seen Napoleon as a liberator, expecting him to bring French Revolutionary freedoms to the rest of Europe. Such ideas died when Napoleon made himself emperor and moved to subjugate the continent. But revolutionary hopes still simmered across the continent after Napoleon's fall, and old regimes found it difficult to reclaim their power. Napoleon had permanently destabilized Europe's old order.

INDUSTRIALIZATION, TECHNOLOGY, SCIENCE—AND TURMOIL

Even as political revolution swept across Europe, an industrial revolution was also transforming daily life for millions. Britain's strong and innovative modern economy led the way in the second half of the eighteenth century. Trade and raw materials from colonial empires, together with huge profits from the Atlantic slave trade, had brought frenzied commercial activity and vast new wealth—along with periodic economic disasters caused when wild investment schemes collapsed. As rising wealth increased demand for consumer goods, new technologies developed to mechanize production and dramatically increase output. Since ancient times, skilled artisans had made manufactured goods by hand. Now, true factories began to emerge, with lower-skilled laborers operating machinery to produce goods en masse. The change began with textile factories in England. As iron-working technology improved, complex machines enabled still-larger factories. Many people left agricultural jobs and moved into the new industrial labor force.

At first, water power drove most factories. But the steam engine, invented in the early 1700s and perfected by Scottish engineer James Watt late in the century, had made huge strides by the early nineteenth century. Metalworking skills improved, and enabled new engines to handle high steam pressures without bursting. Water-powered mills relied on fast-moving rivers and streams, but steam-powered factories fueled their boilers with coal. Factories and worker villages began to appear in coal-rich areas of Britain. Steam's greater power enabled factories to grow even larger and more complex, further driving the advancing Industrial Revolution.

New canals carried goods from factories to towns and ports. In the 1830s, steam-powered railways began to carve new routes across the landscape, forever altering transport and facilitating travel at unprecedented speeds. Britain's landscape was quickly transformed, as factory villages grew together into vast manufacturing cities such as Manchester and Birmingham in the midlands and others in northern England, Scotland, and Wales. The development of interchangeable parts increased factory production even more, enabling individual components of manufactured goods to be made separately and then assembled in vast numbers.

British companies sold their technology to nations in continental Europe, and Britain's wealth and power soared. But the revolutionary new industrial system spread unevenly. Factories sprang up quickly in economically advanced areas with rich deposits of coal and iron. Northwestern Europe and parts of Germany industrialized most rapidly, along with the fast-growing United States. The United States attracted skilled immigrants and entrepreneurs from Britain, Germany, and elsewhere who saw and realized opportunities for enormous commercial success in the new nation. But in Russia, Peter the Great's early eighteenth century reforms had not spread modernization far beyond the main urban centers. The rest of the country remained heavily rural and clung to its traditional social order: Russia would not fully abolish serfdom until 1861 and was predictably slow to industrialize.

The Industrial Revolution improved the quality of life for many. Useful or desirable goods, which were once out of reach to all but the wealthy, were now being mass-produced and became available to a far larger part of society. Manufacturing created opportunities for investment and trade, which created a fast-growing commercial middle class—which in turn eagerly bought the newly available manufactured goods. But prosperity for some came at great cost to others. Skilled artisans had once been the backbone of the middle classes. In the late sixteenth century, for example, Shakespeare's father—a glove maker—had been one of the wealthiest and most powerful men of his town. But by the early nineteenth century, skilled craftspeople were being pushed aside as factories turned out goods in vastly higher quantities and at far lower cost. In the 1810s, England's Luddites sought to destroy the machines that were costing skilled workers their livelihoods: despite public sympathy, many of the vigilantes were hanged or deported.

As labor demand shifted to cities, farm workers increasingly left rural areas to find work in urban factories. But factories were grim places. Workers—including children—labored long hours for low pay, facing beatings if they showed fatigue. They constantly risked injury or death in the machinery and were often exposed to dangerous chemicals and pollutants. Factory workers found themselves trapped in urban poverty, living in overcrowded, dirty, and unhealthy conditions.

Demands for better conditions and a greater political voice helped spur radical political movements. Theorists proposed a wide range of socialist systems. Under socialism, the state would regulate or even own the industrial base—as opposed to pure capitalism, in which private wealth had sole control of commerce and industry. Socialist ideas were taken to their most radical extent by the influential German theorist Karl Marx. In the *Communist Manifesto* (1848) and *Das Kapital* (1867–1894), Marx and his collaborator Friedrich Engels depicted labor as a commodity, insisting that capitalist society unjustly deprived the laborer of the fruits of his labor. They argued that all societies evolved through fixed stages as the means of economic production changed: first slave labor, then feudalism, then commercial capitalism dominated by a bourgeois class of capitalist owners. Finally, Communism would arise from the inevitable collapse of capitalism. In a Communist society, all wealth would be owned in common by the workers who created it. Social classes would be nonexistent, and government would eventually become unnecessary.

Marx urged workers: "You have nothing to lose but your chains." His revolutionary exhortations gradually attracted greater attention, which helped fuel labor agitation and leftist political parties across Europe. Together with a fast-growing population and ceaseless competition for resources, such unrest sparked widespread political instability. And social pressures did not come solely from the poor. The growing commercial middle classes also demanded a greater share of the political power that was still mostly held by wealthy and hereditary elites. Yet even as the middle classes demanded more power for themselves, they resisted the demands of impoverished laborers.

Increasing numbers of Europeans, both laborers and members of the commercial classes, chose meanwhile to seek new opportunities in the rapidly expanding United States. Many went to seek farmland in the vast U.S. interior or to found commercial ventures of their own in the United States' prospering cities. After long journeys, many immigrants would in fact find themselves as low-skilled and low-paid laborers in those cities' factories—but they hoped still to win better opportunities for their children. Immigration spiked when European crises left few other options: a tragic example is the massive Irish exodus to the United States in the 1840s after a crop blight destroyed the food supply of Ireland's rural poor and created the Potato Famine.

Industrial development and commercial pressure also spurred profoundly important technological innovation and almost unthinkably rapid change. By 1800, New York's Robert Fulton and others were building steam-powered watercraft. By the 1840s, large steam ships were being built: for the first time, ocean transport was freed from the vagaries of the wind and dependent only on coal supply. The electrical telegraph was perfected in the 1830s and 1840s by U.S. engineer Samuel Morse. As cables were run over ever-increasing lengths—even, by the 1860s, across the Atlantic Ocean—instantaneous long-distance communication became possible for the first time in human history. Military technology also advanced rapidly, as nations vied to create iron-hulled warships and new, more destructive weaponry. Even as communication and transport tied nations more closely together, new armaments made potential conflicts more destructive than ever.

The climate of new ideas also helped foster breakthroughs in science and medicine. As scientists learned more about the Earth's ancient origins, the most basic assumptions of divine creation and life's origins came into question. Charles Darwin's *The Origin of Species* (1859) argued that animals change slowly over time and that natural selection—the survival and reproduction of those individuals better suited to their environment—caused the slow adaptive evolution of species. Darwin laid the groundwork for modern evolutionary theory, including the argument that humans descend from earlier primates—a direct challenge to traditional religious doctrines.

Another key scientific figure, the French researcher Louis Pasteur, demonstrated the transmission of disease by microorganisms, developed procedures to sterilize foods (called pasteurization), and greatly advanced the science of viral immunization.

NAPOLEON'S WAKE: RISING THREATS TO EUROPE'S OLD REGIMES

After Napoleon's defeat, Russia, Prussia, and Austria formed the Holy Alliance: its purpose was to restore and uphold the pre-Napoleonic monarchical order. All European monarchs (except the pope and the Ottoman sultan) were invited to join. Most agreed, including the new French king, Louis XVIII—who needed all possible help as he struggled to bury twenty-five years of revolution and rebuild monarchical power in France. Britain, ever wary of continental entanglements and more interested in maintaining its own dominance at sea, declined to join.

But unstoppable forces had been set in motion. Though Napoleon had never become the revolutionary liberator that many had hopefully envisioned, his example—and that of the American and French Revolutions—helped convince many that the old order was obsolete. And even as a conqueror, Napoleon had offered significant legal reform: his modern law code offered greater individual freedom from government oppression and greater freedom from religious authorities. With Europe unsettled and its traditional rulers weakened, long bottled-up national and ethnic divisions also rose increasingly to the surface—adding further instability to an already unsettled political landscape.

Joseph Bonaparte abandoned his claim to the Spanish throne in 1813 as his brother's empire faltered. Spain's absolutist monarch, who had been ousted in 1808, was restored to the throne. But the Spanish met the reinstated king with new defiance. In 1820, he was forced to accept a liberal constitution that restricted his authoritarian powers—but in 1823 the Holy Alliance sent troops to restore the king and the Catholic Church's Inquisition to full power. In the Italian states, similar risings were likewise crushed by the Holy Alliance—but liberal movements continued to grow. Spain's sitting queen was deposed in 1868, and a new king chosen by the revolutionary government. A short-lived republic governed Spain in the early 1870s—until the royal line deposed in 1868 returned to power.

In France, Louis XVIII at first maintained many of Napoleon's legal reforms. Bowing to the Revolution's legacy, he also governed in conjunction with an elected parliament. But as revolutionary fervor continued to stir, he turned to harsher, more repressive measures. His brother Charles X, who took the throne in 1824, was an open divine-right monarchist. He sought to rule by decree and ignored the will of the Parliament in appointing authoritarian cabinet ministers. As parliamentary elections turned more firmly against him, he tried to dissolve the unfriendly parliamentary majority, restrict the right to vote, and crack down on the press. The people rose against Charles in the July Revolution of the 1830s, and he was forced to abdicate. The provisional government chose the Duke of Orleans, Louis Philippe, as the new king. He vowed to rule as a constitutional monarch, the "citizen king."

England had faced internal pressures for reform since the eighteenth century—but the French Revolution's bloody excesses had helped discredit reformers as dangerous radicals and derail any serious change. By the 1830s, however, call for change were growing too loud to ignore. Only a tiny fraction of Englishmen could vote for members of Parliament (MPs), and the apportionment of parliamentary seats was archaic. Many of the new and growing manufacturing cities had no MPs. Many MPs, however, represented nearly abandoned old settlements, or "rotten boroughs": their parliamentary members were chosen by whoever owned the land. A handful of landholders thus controlled dozens, and millions of people in major cities were not represented at all.

Popular pressure forced Parliament to pass the Great Reform Act in 1832, which abolished the rotten boroughs and shifted representation to the growing industrial centers. The rising commercial middle classes gained a new degree of political power. But the Reform Act still left the great majority, including the many industrial laborers, without a vote—just as most U.S. states were moving toward universal white male suffrage. Demands for change inevitably continued. Another British reform act extended the vote to some urban laboring men in 1867. Universal male suffrage was not achieved in Great Britain until 1918, just ten years before the full enfranchisement of women.

Ethnic nationalism was also on the rise in Europe. Greece—with help from Western Europeans spurred by romantic visions of Greece's ancient glories—rebelled against the Ottoman Turks in 1821. Belgium, which was linguistically separate from the Dutch, split from the Netherlands in 1831. Poland unsuccessfully rebelled against Russian control in the 1830s and 1840s, and Norway sought independence from Sweden. In Ireland, the Potato Famine of the 1840s focused attention on British exploitation of the Irish: Ireland produced wheat and other food crops, but British law forced Ireland to export those crops to England—leaving the Irish to live on nutrient-poor potatoes. The famine not only fueled Irish emigration to the United States but also sparked fresh nationalist cries for Irish independence.

Decades of unrest climaxed across Europe in 1848. Crop failures magnified the social strains already caused by rising population growth and rapid industrialization. In France, Louis Philippe's government had quickly lost liberal support after 1830. Despite the promises of the "citizen king," corruption was rampant and the right to vote remained limited. The king's unpopular alliances with reactionary foreign powers only deepened popular discontent. In February 1848, revolutionary riots forced the king to abdicate. Louis Philippe fled to England, and the revolutionaries established the Second French Republic.

Agitation quickly spread. Austrians rioted against their emperor, demanding improvement in peasants' rights and successfully driving the arch-conservative Metternich from the government. Hungarian revolutionaries, led by Lajos Kossuth, declared independence from Austria. Popular uprisings in several German states demanded the election of a pan-German Parliament to draft a constitution for a unified German nation. Several Italian states also rose up to demand liberal reforms and a unified Italian republic. The Austrians—who had reclaimed much of northern and central Italy after Napoleon's overthrow—were forced to retreat. The pope, who still ruled the Papal States, was forced to flee Rome.

NATIONALISTS, CONSERVATIVES, AND THE UNIFICATION OF ITALY AND GERMANY

Conservative forces quickly rallied, and the revolutionary gains of 1848 proved short-lived. The German and Italian risings soon faltered as conservative elements regained control. The Austrians retook their possessions in Italy, and the pope, with military assistance from the new French republic, returned to Rome. Kossuth's independent Hungary eroded from within, as the majority Magyars rejected independence demands by Hungary's ethnic minorities. Aided by Russia, Austria was able to defeat Kossuth's republic in 1849, drive Kossuth into exile, and reabsorb Hungary.

The French Second Republic elected Napoleon's nephew, Louis Napoleon Bonaparte, as its first president. But this Bonaparte had his own ambitions. Since the death of Napoleon's only son in 1832, he had seen himself as Napoleon I's legitimate successor: he had repeatedly attempted to overthrow Louis Philippe, even facing exile and escaping imprisonment. In December 1851, after just three years as president, Bonaparte launched a coup against the Second Republic. In 1852, he established the Second Empire and had himself declared Emperor Napoleon III. The new emperor was careful to seek popular support: a national referendum officially confirmed his title, and a new legislative assembly was elected by all male citizens. But Napoleon's own power was supreme. He even dictated what legislation the assembly was permitted to consider.

Although the 1848 revolutions failed to achieve their aims, they did effect some change. The old regimes had been further shaken and new ideas gained greater traction. Radicals found a new voice in the anticapitalist theories of Karl Marx, whose *Communist Manifesto* first appeared early in 1848. And popular pressures continued to resonate. In France, for example, public unrest would persuade Napoleon III to increase the elected assembly's powers during the 1860s.

As nationalist fervor continued to grow, more conservative and traditionalist leaders also tried to harness its power. The Conte di Cavour was premier of Piedmont—a prominent state in northern Italy—and a strong supporter of Italian unification under a single monarchy. In the 1850s, he forged an alliance with Napoleon III's France and drove the Austrians from northern Italy, ceding border territories to France in exchange. Giuseppe Garibaldi, an ardent Italian nationalist, had also fought against the Austrians and continued to work aggressively for national unification. By the late 1850s, he had gathered a sizable but volatile nationalist movement composed of disparate forces with varying political goals.

Cavour and his king, Victor Emmanuel II, formed a sometimes uneasy alliance with Garibaldi's movement. (Garibaldi mistrusted Cavour and resented him for handing Nice, Garibaldi's own birthplace, to the French.) As Cavour consolidated Piedmontese control of the north, Garibaldi's forces took control of Sicily in 1860 and marched north toward Rome. Although Cavour stopped him from attacking Rome, fearing a new French intervention on behalf of the pope, Garibaldi had effective control of the south. Despite the tensions between Garibaldi and Cavour, Garibaldi supported Victor Emmanuel's claim to national rule. In 1861, Victor Emmanuel declared a Kingdom of Italy, with himself as its constitutional monarch and Cavour as his first prime minister. Cavour died soon after, worn down by effort and overwork. But Victor Emmanuel took control of Rome in 1870, completing Italy's Risorgimento, or rebirth.

In Germany, Napoleon had abolished the long-ineffective Holy Roman Empire in 1806. After his fall, the Congress of Vienna grouped the German states into the loose German Confederation, which Austria's emperors dominated. But the growing power of industrialized, militarist Prussia began to rival Austria's. Prussia's shrewd and brilliant chancellor, Otto von Bismarck, set out to shift the German states to Prussia's sphere. War erupted between Austria and Prussia in 1866. Prussia defeated Austria in mere weeks: Italy, allied with Prussia, took Venice from the Austrians, an important step in the Risorgimento. Bismarck formed a new North German Confederation under Prussian influence. Austria lost its power over the other German states and was forced to reach a new agreement with its Hungarian possessions to the east—which had been clamoring for independence since the 1848 revolution. Austria granted Hungary local self-rule, with its own parliament and constitution. Austria's emperor would also hold Hungary's crown in the dual monarchy of Austria-Hungary.

But Bismarck's ambitions were still not fulfilled. Even with Austrian influence broken, south Germany still lay beyond Prussia's control. South Germans feared French expansion: Bismarck deliberately sparked the Franco-Prussian War in 1870, rallying the southern German states against France and to Prussia's side. Prussia decisively defeated France. Bismarck's political success allowed him to merge the German states into a new federal union: Germany's Second Empire was proclaimed in Versailles's Hall of Mirrors in January 1871, with Prussia's King Wilhelm I as its emperor. Bismarck set about consolidating power, launching a divisive crackdown on the Catholic Church's power in Germany and negotiating an alliance with his former enemy, Austria, in 1879. Militarily, economically, and industrially potent, the new Prussian-led German nation would quickly become one of Europe's major powers.

In France, the Prussian war sparked revolution. Napoleon III was humiliatingly captured in 1870 during a major French defeat at Sedan, and his government quickly crumbled. A new National Assembly was elected to form a provisional government and make peace with Germany. But Paris rebelled, establishing its own government—the Paris Commune—in March 1871.

The Communards refused to end the war with Germany, called for a return to the revolutionary principles of 1789, and sought to establish socialist "social democracy." Paris demanded independence; government troops bloodily suppressed the revolt in a week of difficult street fighting, and the Communards murdered hostages. Waves of executions followed their defeat—though the failed revolt would inspire radical revolutionary theorists for decades. France, shaken and divided, was left to build its new Third Republic into a functional government.

The changing map of Europe, particularly the unification of Germany, dramatically altered the continent's balance of power. Britain and France had been enemies for centuries. But now, German ambitions—particularly its growing desire to challenge Britain's overseas colonial empire—seemed a far more direct threat to British interests. Britain itself was also growing more politically liberal as more men gained the vote and as Parliament became more representative of the people: Britain looked favorably on France's new republic and began to build a French alliance. The United States, fast becoming a global industrial power after its 1861–1865 Civil War, was also a traditional British foe—but again, a more liberal and anti-German Britain found democratic America an increasingly natural ally.

The era's climate of rapid and often unsettling change was also reflected in the European arts. In the late eighteenth and early nineteenth centuries, Romantic artists and authors turned inward to their own emotions and passions, musing on ruin and decay. By the mid-nineteenth century, Romanticism gave way to Realism, embracing the gritty and disturbing realities of contemporary life. French authors such as Victor Hugo and Émile Zola used their works to challenge social and political injustices, starkly depicting government oppression and the lives of downtrodden laborers. Russian novelist Fyodor Dostoevsky explored the darkness of criminality and corruption. His countryman Leo Tolstoy was born to nobility and wealth but turned eventually to Christian asceticism; his novels challenged society's norms, and he pursued humanitarian projects such as schools for the children of serfs.

By the mid-nineteenth century, Impressionist painters in France—who inspired imitators around the world—defied the traditionalist neo-classical art academies with a daring new spontaneity, using loose brush strokes to explore effects of light and create impressions rather than sharply delineated images. Many painters promoted a bold and authentic realism, rejecting the academies' grandiose historical and mythological scenes in favor of everyday urban, working-class subjects—trends also reflected in theater and opera. Musical composers also challenged traditional constraints on structure and tone: a musical impressionist movement moved away from established classical structures to experiment with the effects of sound.

ERA 13: MODERN IMPERIALISM: A RACE OF CONQUEST AND SUPREMACY (CA. 1790S TO 1900)

EUROPEAN EMPIRES FACE DECLINE IN THE AMERICAS

After it lost the American Revolutionary War to American and French forces, Great Britain was forced to acknowledge the independence of the United States in 1783. But the major European empires still held other colonies throughout the Americas. Britain owned Jamaica and other Caribbean islands and kept firm control of Canada. Disputes between the United States and Britain over Canada's boundaries helped spark the indecisive War of 1812. Britain, busy battling Napoleon, had little desire to fight its former subjects. But Britain continued to infuriate the Americans—it kept troops on the Canadian border, interfered with American ships bound for Napoleonic Europe, and pressed sailors from those ships into the Royal Navy. After years of sour relations, the United States finally declared war. American forces tried to invade Canada and wrest it away from Britain, but the effort was a miserable failure. After American naval victories, a British invasion of Maryland and Washington, DC, and an American victory at New Orleans (fought after the two sides had negotiated a peace treaty but before word of the treaty had arrived), the war ended in 1815 with little change to the prewar status quo.

By the 1760s, France had lost its largest American possessions. It ceded the Louisiana Territory to Spain in 1762 and lost Canada to Britain a year later. France held on to several Caribbean islands and their valuable sugar and coffee plantations, which were worked by large numbers of African slaves. The French Revolution, which championed the equality of all men, unleashed chaos in the Caribbean colonies. White plantation owners saw an opportunity to break away from France and take full control of the islands' trade. White royalists rejected France's Revolutionary government, and white Republicans supported it. At the same time, free black and mixed-race inhabitants demanded legal equality on revolutionary principles. Slaves, who made up the majority of the islands' populations, demanded freedom.

Royalists rebelled in Guadeloupe and declared independence; in 1793, the island's slave population revolted. In Sainte Domingue (modern-day Haiti) on the island of Hispaniola, Toussaint L'Ouverture led a slave uprising in 1791. Three years later, Robespierre's French Revolutionary government banned slavery throughout French territories. Toussaint became the governor general of Sainte Domingue in 1797. By 1801, he had driven out the Spanish (who had ruled the other half of Hispaniola) and made himself the nearly independent ruler of the island.

But Napoleon aimed to restore the enormously profitable plantations and bring slavery back to the islands. French troops descended on Hispaniola, captured Toussaint, and sent him to France, where he died in prison. Napoleon's troops also overran Guadeloupe and began to rebuild its slave system. The alarmed black population of Sainte Domingue rebelled, prompting a harsh French crackdown. But as the Napoleonic Wars resumed across Europe in 1803, the Americas became an unwanted drain on French resources. France reacquired the vast Louisiana territory from Spain in 1802, but quickly sold it to the United States. Most French troops withdrew from Sainte Domingue; the rebels gained independence in 1804 and founded the nation of Haiti—though the social and economic wounds inflicted by France have challenged the nation throughout its history. Their successful revolt alarmed slaveholders throughout America and the Caribbean. Yet France kept its other Caribbean islands, where slavery continued.

Slavery remained a divisive issue for many Western powers. In Britain, antislavery sentiment had increased during the eighteenth century. In 1772, the chief justice Lord Mansfield overturned slavery in England—but his ruling did not affect Britain's colonies, and the antislavery movement continued to gain strength. A push led by William Wilberforce secured a British ban on the African slave trade in 1807, despite vehement objections from Africa's slave-trading kingdoms—whose wealth and status rested on the lucrative trade. In his last major victory, Wilberforce pushed Britain to abolish slavery throughout its colonies in 1833—although heavy discrimination left freed Caribbean blacks scarcely better off. The United States banned the slave trade in 1808, the earliest date the U.S. Constitution permitted. France bowed to diplomatic pressure and finally abandoned the trade in 1830; it only abolished colonial slavery after its 1848 revolution.

Europe's direct hold on the Americas continued to weaken. By the early nineteenth century, sugar plantations and mineral deposits had made Portugal's Brazilian colony enormously prosperous—it began to surpass the wealth of Portugal itself. When Napoleon invaded Portugal during the Peninsular War, the Portuguese king and his son fled to Rio de Janeiro. The king ultimately returned to Lisbon, but his son stayed behind as Brazilian regent. In 1822, he successfully established himself as Pedro I, constitutional monarch of an independent Brazil.

In the early nineteenth century, Spain's grip on its vast Central and South American colonies was also slipping away. By this time, many colonists were of mixed Spanish and Native American ancestry. As the blended population grew, it sought greater rights and status. The American Revolution offered powerful inspiration: in the 1810s, with Spain consumed by the Napoleonic Wars and their aftermath, rebellions broke out and various regions declared independence. As Spain tried to rebuild in the 1820s, it also tried to reinstate its authority over its American colonies. In response, the colonists' rebellions only escalated.

Venezuelan patriot Simón Bolívar returned from exile in 1816 to lead South America's independence movement. By the mid-1820s, he and other regional revolutionaries had won independence for Colombia, Venezuela, Ecuador, Chile, and Peru. Mexico harbored its own independence movement, inspired by the American and French revolutions; Mexico achieved independence in the early 1820s. Although it fashioned its constitution after the United States', Mexico remained politically divided and fell repeatedly under military rule. The other Central American colonies also broke from Spain in the 1820s and formed a short-lived federal union. Spain retained Puerto Rico and Cuba and did not fully abolish slavery in those islands until the 1880s.

Despite the near collapse of Spain's American empire, Europe had not given up. The Holy Alliance, which was formed after Napoleon's defeat in order to rebuild Europe's old order, eyed a campaign to restore Spain's colonies. In response, an increasingly confident United States aimed to bar European powers from pursuing any new colonial ventures in the region. The Monroe Doctrine, proclaimed by U.S. president James Monroe in 1823, declared the Western Hemisphere a uniquely U.S. sphere of influence. The doctrine warned Europe not to attempt to reclaim its lost colonies or establish new ones: the United States would take any fresh European intervention in the hemisphere as an act of war.

In fact, the United States rarely needed to invoke the Monroe Doctrine—and arguably lacked the military strength to enforce it—until the late nineteenth century. But in the 1860s, Napoleon III's France made a significant bid for power. Mexico was weakened when American settlers in the Mexican territory of Texas rebelled and broke away, first forming an independent nation and then winning annexation as a U.S. state. Mexico then lost California and the American Southwest to the United States in the Mexican-American War (1846-1848). In 1861, Mexico could no longer make interest payments to its foreign creditors. With the United States consumed with its own civil war, Napoleon III swept into Mexico. He claimed to be upholding the rights of Mexico's creditors— but his true aim was to control Mexico's silver mines and dominate Central American trade.

In 1864, a rigged Mexican referendum—managed by the French—ousted the nation's president and installed the Austro-Hungarian emperor's brother as Emperor Maximilian of Mexico. But when the American Civil War ended in 1865, the United States shifted its focus to Mexico. French troops, threatened by the United States, were forced to withdraw. Mexico's deposed president, Benito Juárez, retook power in 1867, and Maximilian was executed. In 1876, General Porfirio Díaz established a long military dictatorship that lasted until a democratic revolution in 1911.

BRITAIN TAKES OVER INDIA AS EUROPE EDGES INTO AFRICA

After many years of regional dominance, India's Mughal Empire was in decline by the mid-eighteenth century. As Mughal control loosened, India's regional states battled one another and tried to reassert their authority. India's valuable exports and potential commercial markets attracted the English and French, and both moved to exploit the growing power vacuum left by the warring regional states. By 1700, the English East India Company (EIC)—a powerful privately owned British corporation that invested in foreign trade and managed a large trading fleet—had won access to vital Indian trading ports after violent conflict with the Dutch during the previous century. By the 1750s, the EIC had largely outmaneuvered its French rivals as well. Britain granted the EIC a monopoly on Indian trade—and the company built its own army, which began to subjugate and control uncooperative Indian rulers. Its bid to become the subcontinent's strongest power was well under way.

After 1800, the EIC tightened its control of southern and eastern India. By mid-century, it ruled most of the subcontinent. (Portugal still clung to small western enclaves such as Goa, which it refused to relinquish until the modern Indian state sent in troops in 1961.) Parliament gradually stripped the EIC of its commercial dominance in India, ending its trade monopolies in 1813. But although the British government asserted greater official control of India in 1813 and 1833, the EIC effectively continued to govern the subcontinent on behalf of the British Empire—and its imperious dominance created simmering Indian resentment.

Within the ranks of the company's Indian soldiers, or sepoys, resentment erupted into crisis. In 1857, rumors spread that their new rifle cartridges were greased with pig and cow fat. Hindus refuse to kill cows, and Muslims regard pigs as unclean—both groups thus considered the cartridges a deliberate religious insult. A mutiny erupted in the EIC army and quickly spread to parts of northern India. British garrisons were besieged and women and children in several British settlements were indiscriminately killed by enraged Indian rebels. At the EIC garrison in Cawnpore, the British were promised safe-conduct out of the area if they surrendered. Instead, they were massacred as they boarded boats to depart. Surviving women and children were held hostage and later murdered as British forces approached.

Outrage swept over England—the Indians had openly defied British authority and had randomly slaughtered civilians. British forces, including Indian sepoys who had remained loyal to the EIC, advanced on the mutineers' strongholds and killed thousands of Indians—including uninvolved Indian civilians. At Delhi, they looted and pillaged the city, killing thousands of civilians. The mutiny was suppressed, with the rebels cut down in battle or executed: the fighting and reprisals—on rebels and civilians—are thought to have killed at least one hundred thousand Indians and possibly far more. But the EIC's management of Indian affairs had been discredited. In 1858, the British crown took direct control of India, which became Britain's most important colonial possession. In 1876, Britain's Queen Victoria was named Empress of India.

Although British settlement in India was limited, Britain completely remodeled India's government and controlled its commerce. As the British built roads, canals, and railways across the nation, they argued that their subjects were fortunate: they now had access to education, Western ideas, and modern innovation—Indians' tax rates even fell. But Britain was in the subcontinent for its own gain. Indian soldiers were the backbone of Britain's forces throughout its vast empire. By the early twentieth century, British companies exported enormous quantities of manufactured products to India every year while importing the subcontinent's valuable raw materials. Despite inevitable local resentment, resistance stayed muted until a serious independence movement emerged in the early twentieth century.

Foreign inroads into Africa were more tentative. Since the fifteenth century, the Portuguese had maintained contact with Africa. By the early sixteenth century, they had established fortified settlements along the African coast; they also controlled strips of territory in present-day Angola (on the western coast) and Mozambique (on the eastern coast). In the 1650s, the Dutch established the Cape Colony at Africa's southern tip, a key point on the trade routes from Europe to India. But other European attempts to seize territory largely failed: many African kingdoms and alliances were significant powers in their own right and not easily susceptible to outside exploitation.

Although Europe and the Americas established a major slave trade with Africa, African rulers maintained control of the slave supply and most of the coastal trading points. European slave-trading forts and ports were generally rented from the local African kings, and the trade made many African states hugely wealthy—even as the African interior was devastated by slave-raiding wars and the sale of millions of people to the Europeans.

European interest in Africa increased in the nineteenth century. Explorers moved inland from coastal Africa to map the previously almost-unknown interior, paving the way for traders and missionaries. The British seized the Cape Colony from the Dutch in 1806 and gradually developed a larger South African colony of their own. Britain also established a growing presence in West Africa as it enforced the British-U.S. ban on the slave trade after 1807. The French invaded North Africa's Algerian coast in 1830 and also seized an outpost on the northwestern coast.

Territorial gains were still limited. But Europe expanded its impact through major Catholic and Protestant missionary activity. Islam still dominated northern and northeastern Africa, and indigenous religions were largely dominant elsewhere on the continent. Yet Christian converts began to establish growing enclaves in southern Africa and along the eastern and western coasts.

THE WEST'S HEAVY HAND IN THE PACIFIC

During the eighteenth century, Britain continued its aggressive push to become the world's dominant trading power. But to gain wider access to Asia's markets, and greater control over its tea and other exports, the British first had to displace Holland and its Dutch East India Company. The Dutch already held large parts of island Southeast Asia. But the British made major inroads as they pressed from India into Burma, took Singapore in 1819, and secured outposts in the Dutch-held islands. Some Southeast Asian kingdoms, such as Siam (present-day Thailand), maintained their independence and posed an ongoing challenge to the Europeans. But the colonial powers repeatedly managed to reassert and expand their control. The Dutch secured their hold on the island of Java in 1830, after a deadly five-year war against Javanese forces. But Britain dominated the surrounding seas.

Europeans discovered Australia in the seventeenth century. English explorer James Cook claimed possession of Australian territory in 1770, and a British penal colony was soon established there. British colonization grew during the early nineteenth century, and settlement expanded beyond convicts. Members of the Aboriginal population resisted, but the British violently drove them back, and virgin soil epidemics such as smallpox, influenza, cholera, and measles—European diseases to which the isolated Australians had no immunity—devastated the native population. The discovery of gold in the 1850s led to a fresh burst of immigration. Australia emerged as one of Britain's major possessions, a key anchor for its power in the Pacific.

But always, the fabled riches of China and Japan remained the West's true obsession. Japan maintained tight limits on trade and contact with the rest of the world, to the deep frustration of outsiders. Between 1853 and 1854, the United States sent a naval expedition under Commodore Matthew C. Perry to the island nation. Perry made a great show of the West's modern technology—particularly his powerful warships and their potent weapons. Under Perry's guns, Japan's shoguns signed a treaty opening key ports to U.S. trade.

Even before Perry's arrival, the shogunate faced internal economic crises and political unrest. The failure to resist Perry's pressure helped discredit the government entirely, and the people erupted into armed insurrection. In 1868, the Tokugawa shogunate was deposed after ruling for nearly three centuries. Under the shoguns, the emperors had been reduced to mere figureheads—but now the imperial line reclaimed power under the emperor Meiji Tenno. The Meiji Restoration ushered in an era of dramatic and rapid reform, and Japan used the coming decades to modernize along Western lines. The Meiji government swept away a millennium of feudalism and created a Western-style centralized and industrialized state. And, similar to its Western models, Japan began to nurture its own imperialist ambitions.

Japan quickly learned from its humiliation by the West: it would soon rival their industrial and military power. But China followed a very different path. China continued to exert influence in East and Southeast Asia—but similar to Japan, early nineteenth-century China severely limited contact with the West: it allowed Western trade only in heavily regulated port enclaves such as Canton (Guangzhou). The Qing emperors maintained a traditional, complacent confidence in China as the superior center of the world and were openly dismissive of Western overtures.

In the early nineteenth century, British traders tried to dodge China's official trade restrictions by smuggling large quantities of Indian opium (a narcotic derived from poppies) into China. Soon opium addiction raged across the nation. The Chinese government was also alarmed by the drug's economic consequences: by evading the regulated trade enclaves, the illicit opium trade was draining the nation's silver currency and avoiding government-imposed taxes. Chinese authorities cracked down in 1839, seizing thousands of crates of opium and banning further imports. British sent a naval force to China in 1840, launching the first Opium War. The stark reality of Western military power now confronted China head-on, and China was forced to yield in 1842. Britain forced an end to the opium ban, seized Hong Kong as a British colony, and imposed several treaty ports where foreign merchants were exempt from Chinese regulation.

Qing power in China was quickly eroding. In 1850, the devastating Taiping Rebellion erupted. The leader of the Taiping cult, Hong Xiuquan, believed that he was Jesus's younger brother and attracted a great following. Hong proclaimed a Heavenly Kingdom of equality and common property under his own religious rule, and his followers rose against the Qing government. The cult rebellion soon fused with more widespread grievances, including nationalist resentment toward the Manchurian Qing rulers. Civil war broke out. The rebels seized the important city of Nanjing; although they failed to capture the capital at Beijing, they took control of large parts of central China. The widespread warfare sparked disruption, famine, and disease, causing horrific casualties among soldiers and civilians alike.

As the Western powers watched China's crisis unfold, they saw opportunity. In 1856, Chinese customs inspectors impounded the *Arrow*, a Chinese-owned vessel out of Hong Kong. The British dubiously claimed that the vessel–based in their Hong Kong colony–was British and exploited the incident to launch the Second Opium War. After the British had suppressed the 1857 Indian Mutiny, they united with the French against China. In 1858, the two nations imposed a treaty that opened even more Chinese ports to Western trade and opened the nation's interior to European merchants and missionaries. When the Chinese emperor rejected the treaty, Western troops occupied Beijing and forced the emperor to acquiesce in 1860.

By now, China's government was in serious jeopardy. Although it finally suppressed the Taiping rebellion in 1864, the country was severely ravaged. The fourteen-year civil war and the chaos it unleashed had killed an estimated twenty million people. Meanwhile, the Russians were putting increasing pressure on Mongolia and Manchuria–the original homeland of the Manchu Qing rulers–and the West continued to tighten its grip throughout China.

LATE-CENTURY CLIMAX: THE DISINTEGRATION OF CHINA AND THE SCRAMBLE FOR AFRICA

France, Holland, Portugal, and Spain all retained colonial possessions in the late nineteenth century, but they were plainly in Britain's shadow. The British Empire, controlling India and other outposts throughout the world, was unquestionably the world's dominant colonial power. Adopting a phrase once applied to Spain's seventeenth-century dominions, Britain boasted of an empire "on which the sun never set" (British colonies spanned the globe: it was always daytime somewhere in the empire). But the newly unified German nation aimed to challenge Britain's supremacy–it demanded its own "place in the sun." Germany's ambition helped spur a sudden and dramatic burst of Western imperialism in the century's final decades.

China had been catastrophically weakened by the Taiping Rebellion and the Opium Wars, and its last-ditch efforts at internal reform achieved little. China was unable to resist escalating

Western demands: by the late nineteenth century, the nation had almost lost its sovereignty. Imposed foreign treaties divided it into separate spheres of influence—a single European power controlled trade within each sphere. Most of China remained technically independent: the European colonial powers agreed not to make the spheres into actual colonies. But there were exceptions: Portugal had controlled Macau, on China's southeastern coast, as a trading port since the sixteenth century. In 1887, it seized the city as a Portuguese colony.

China's regional influence inevitably crumbled. Vietnam, which China had long dominated, was seized by the French in the 1880s as French Indo-China. Japan, which was rising as a modern power even as China fell to pieces, also joined the quest to exploit China's collapse. After defeating China in the Sino-Japanese War (1894–1895), Japan pressed into Formosa (present-day Taiwan), Korea, and other formerly Chinese-controlled territories. Russia, alarmed by Japan's growing power and the threat to its own ambitions in China, persuaded France and Germany to join in the so-called Triple Intervention. The three European powers forced Japan to return the important Manchurian harbor of Port Arthur—on which Russia had its own designs—to China in exchange for financial compensation from the Chinese. Japan, which already resented its treatment by the West, was left with a simmering new grievance.

As China's government faltered and Western powers took ever-greater control, China's populist resentment rose. A mystic, antiforeign cult—the Society of Righteous and Harmonious Fists—emerged among the poor and economically exploited and even won the support of some Qing officials and courtiers. The cultists believed their ritual exercises, which included a form of boxing that gave the group its Western name (the "Boxers"), would make them immune to bullets. In 1900, cultist rebels besieged Beijing's foreign embassies. A multinational force was sent to suppress the rebels—who, contrary to their belief, were vulnerable to bullets after all. The foreign army sacked and looted Beijing and the surrounding area and forced China to pay reparations. The Chinese government was left weaker than ever.

Europe's late-century African moves—the so-called Scramble for Africa—were even more dramatic. In 1880, Europe controlled only limited coastal areas. But European industry demanded access to Africa's raw materials. Major colonial powers such as Britain and France had vowed to avoid dividing up the continent. But escalating imperial rivalries, including Germany's aggressive drive for its own empire, raised fears that some nations would ignore such agreements. Worried European powers began to make preemptive grabs for power and territory. Local incidents were magnified into convenient pretexts for incursions, and indigenous alliances were forged and exploited to stake out areas of control.

Beyond its obvious commercial potential—both as a supplier of materials and as a market for trade—Africa also had strategic importance. Vital maritime routes from Europe to Asia depended on ports and coaling stations along the African coast. A more direct route was created between 1859 and 1869: Egypt's Suez Canal, constructed by French engineers led by Ferdinand de Lesseps, connected the Mediterranean and the Red Sea. The canal immediately became Britain's chief route to India, and Egypt became key to the security of the British Empire. Britain took control of the strategically vital canal in 1875. In 1882, the British exploited an Egyptian revolt against Ottoman authority to take effective control of Egypt itself.

From the 1880s on, complex European moves and countermoves led to an astonishingly quick division of Africa among the major colonial powers. The French expanded their once-limited holdings to control much of western Africa and seized the island of Madagascar off Africa's east coast. The British moved south from Egypt into the Sudan and pushed on to Africa's east coast; they moved north from South Africa and took the Gold Coast and Nigeria in the west. In the 1880s and 1890s, Germany seized western Africa's Kamerun (modern-day Cameroon) along with territories that became German East Africa and German South-West Africa. Italy took lands around the Horn of Africa in 1889, and seized Libya in 1912. Belgium gained control of the central

African Congo. Portugal maintained holdings in Angola and Mozambique, and Spain carved out territory on the northwest coast.

Britain faced conflict and warfare with South Africa's Dutch settlers, or Boers—whose mineral-rich farmlands the British were determined to seize. Indigenous African peoples also resisted colonization and some rebelled against the colonial regimes. Under the fierce military leader Shaka (who ruled between 1816 and 1828), the Zulus of South Africa became a feared regional power. The British, determined to remove the Zulu threat, deliberately maneuvered the Zulu king Cetshwayo into war in the late 1870s. Despite stunning early Zulu victories—including the annihilation of an entire British force at Isandlwana—Britain crushed Zulu power in less than half a year's time. The British also eyed the mineral-rich territory of the Ndebele, or Matabele, people (who were close cousins of the Zulus) farther north. In the late 1880s, wealthy British mining magnate Cecil Rhodes tricked the Ndebele king Lobengula into allowing not only mining but also the outright colonization of Matabeleland. Rhodes's British South Africa Company army put down a Ndebele revolt and created the white-ruled colony of Rhodesia (today's Zimbabwe).

By 1914, virtually the entire continent was at least officially under European rule. In some cases, local African rulers invited the Europeans in: they sought allies and support against local and European adversaries and aimed to set up their own lucrative trading opportunities. In such places, European control was often more theoretical than actual—local rulers still maintained significant authority. Farther away from European-controlled cities, colonial power was generally weaker; local societies often continued to live with little outside interference. Overall, however, the expansion of colonial power was dramatic and widespread: Europe seized genuine control of vast areas, allowing Europeans to create their own settlements and exploit local peoples.

In some parts of Africa, colonial rule was oppressive and deadly. Tens of thousands of African workers died in British South Africa's hugely profitable but extremely dangerous gold and diamond mines. With the consent of other European powers, Belgium's King Leopold II arranged treaties with hundreds of local chiefs and took personal control of central Africa's Congo in 1885. To extract the region's rich iron and rubber supply, he blatantly enslaved the local population, letting European companies force obedience through starvation, mutilation, and murder. Leopold's savage rule cost an estimated ten million African lives. Brewing international outrage, driven by authors such as Mark Twain, Arthur Conan Doyle, and Joseph Conrad (whose 1899 novel *Heart of Darkness* described the horrors of racial exploitation in the Congo region), led the Belgian government to end Leopold's personal rule. The government assumed direct control of the Belgian Congo in 1908, but its rule remained harsh.

ERA 14: NATIONAL RIVALRIES: THE ERUPTION OF GLOBAL CONFLICT *(1880S TO 1918)*

EMPIRES IN COLLISION

As the twentieth century dawned, Europe was engaged in an extraordinary burst of colonial expansion in Asia and Africa—and political rivalries within Europe were growing dangerously tense. Newly unified Germany was a driving force. Germany pursued what it considered its rightful "place in the sun"—colonial power in Africa, China, and the Pacific islands, which would openly challenge the British Empire's global dominance. At the same time, Germany was determined to challenge France and Russia for domination of Europe itself.

The new German Empire, or Reich, became even more aggressive under its third emperor, Kaiser Wilhelm II, who took the throne in 1888. His mother was the daughter of England's Queen

Victoria and the brother of Victoria's son and heir, who became King Edward VII in 1901. Yet the new kaiser viewed his cousins as rivals. In 1890, he ousted his shrewdly practical chancellor Otto von Bismarck, the architect of German unification. Wilhelm II wanted a free hand to challenge the British Empire: he pushed for new German ships to undermine British naval dominance, pressed for expanded colonization efforts, and worked against Britain's colonial interests.

In 1806, Britain had seized South Africa's Cape Colony, which the Dutch had held since the mid-seventeenth century. The Boers remained throughout the region; in the 1850s, they established the independent Transavaal and Orange Free State north of British South Africa. The British annexed the Transvaal in 1877. The Boers rebelled three years later, sparking the First Boer War and soon reasserting the Transvaal's independence. But by the mid-1890s, the Boers were convinced that Britain was going to move against them again. The Transvaal and Orange Free State formed a military alliance—with Kaiser Wilhelm's open sympathy.

Fearing imminent British attack, the Boers launched preemptive strikes in 1899 and began the Second Boer War, a three-year struggle of savage guerilla warfare. The British placed Boer civilians in concentration camps, where many died of disease or starvation; Boer farms were systematically destroyed, and prisoners on both sides were often murdered. The British forced the Boer surrender in 1902. But Kaiser Wilhelm had continued to express sympathy for the Boer cause during the war and had hinted at the possibility of German intervention—further damaging relations with Britain.

The United States, another fast-rising global power, also sought power abroad. In 1895, Cuba—one of Spain's last colonial outposts in the Americas—rebelled against Spanish control. Americans already sympathized with the Cubans' fight for freedom—and then the U.S. battleship *Maine* blew up in Havana harbor in 1898. Although the explosion was likely accidental, the U.S. blamed the Spanish. The incident and resulting outrage offered a convenient pretext for a war the increasingly muscular United States already wanted. The U.S. navy quickly broke Spain's naval strength in Cuba and in the distant Philippines, and a U.S. invasion of Cuba routed Spanish forces (more Americans died from disease than in combat). Under the peace terms, Cuba gained independence—although the United States would have strong influence over it—and the United States gained Puerto Rico. The United States also bought the Philippines from Spain. Although America recommended eventual Philippine independence, it also firmly suppressed a Filipino insurrection against U.S. rule.

The United States also eyed China's enormous commercial markets. Although they technically refused to seize or colonize Chinese territory, the European powers and Japan had all carved out spheres of influence under their own commercial control. The United States had little desire to restore Chinese sovereignty: it joined the international force that put down China's antiforeign Boxer Rebellion in 1900. But the United States did wish to evade the other powers' spheres of influence. By 1900, the United States had pushed the other powers to accept an official "Open Door Policy" that granted all foreign powers full, equal access to China's trade. The other powers only reluctantly accepted the policy and tried frequently to ignore it. But even their limited acceptance reflected the United States' rapidly rising influence.

Modernizing Japan was also a fast-growing regional force. By the late nineteenth century, Japan was strong enough to renegotiate the treaties imposed by the Western powers in the 1850s after Commodore Perry forced Japan to open to the outside world. Japan's victory in the Sino-Japanese War (1894–1895) enhanced its international status and increased its power over China. The nation also gained significant territories in its victory. Japan's next major rival was Russia, which sought control of Manchuria and Korea—both areas over which Japan claimed control after it defeated China in 1895. Conflict centered on Port Arthur, a deep-water harbor on Manchuria's Liaodong Peninsula. Japan seized the peninsula from China in the Sino-Japanese War, but Russia,

France, and Germany forced Japan to return the territory to China. Russia, determined to win year-round, ice-free access to the Pacific, soon took control of the peninsula and the port.

Japan seethed bitterly over the loss of its Manchurian conquests. Tensions finally erupted in the Russo-Japanese War, which began in 1904. Japanese forces took Port Arthur in early 1905, after months of siege, and advanced up the Liaodong Peninsula. In May's Battle of Tsushima, the Japanese navy annihilated an exhausted Russian fleet that had labored all the way from Europe (the British denied Russia use of the Suez Canal, forcing the fleet to round Africa). The Treaty of Portsmouth, negotiated by U.S. president Theodore Roosevelt, ended the war and earned Roosevelt one of the first Nobel Peace Prizes. The war humiliated Russia and greatly bolstered Japan. Japan maintained control of Port Arthur, annexed nearby Korea in 1910, and continued to mount pressure on China.

Meanwhile, China tried to restore some semblance of its own authority—but the ineffective Qing imperial court had grown deeply unpopular. Liberal critics sought major government reforms or even a new Republican system. Trying to implement limited reforms, the Qing court increased regional governments' power. But the regional governments fell under reformist control, and armed revolt erupted in 1911. Large parts of China joined together to declare a republic, with reformist leader Sun Yat-sen as its provisional president. The last Qing emperor, six-year-old Puyi, was forced to abdicate in 1912. After more than two thousand years, imperial China was finished. But China remained badly divided: the new government soon collapsed and power fell to regional warlords until Chiang Kai-Shek brought most of China under his nationalist dictatorship through a bloody campaign in the late 1920s. Meanwhile, foreign powers continued to exploit China economically, and the United States still pressed the Open Door Policy.

EUROPE'S TINDERBOX

On the European continent, Germany posed the most immediate threat to France, which shared a large and disputed border with the Germans, and to Russia, which bordered Germany to the east. France and Russia had been at war with each other as recently as the 1850s, battling in the Crimean War (1853–1856) over Russia's ambitions in the Black Sea and a host of other issues. Franco-Russian tensions remained high. But after Germany's crushing defeat of France in the Franco-Prussian War, its 1871 unification and openly aggressive stance gave the Russians and French newfound common cause.

German unification humiliated Austria, which lost its dominance among the German states. But the Austrians recognized the reality of Germany's new power and accepted Bismarck's offer of a German-Austrian alliance in 1879. In 1882, Italy joined the pact to form the Triple Alliance. Bismarck tried to steer Russia away from direct conflict with Germany; but after Wilhelm II ousted Bismarck from power in 1890, the kaiser refused to offer Russia any further guarantees. In 1894, after long negotiations, Russia and France set aside their long-standing differences and signed their own military alliance: each vowed to fight for the other in the event of a Triple Alliance attack. Europe was dividing into heavily armed rival camps.

Britain had long focused on its overseas empire and naval dominance, carefully avoiding continental entanglements. But Germany's rapid naval construction and blatant imperial ambitions made Britain more willing to take part in continental affairs in order to contain Wilhelm II's Reich. By the late nineteenth-century, Britain and France began to set aside a millennium of mutual hostility as an increasingly liberal Britain found common cause with the French Third Republic against Germany. In 1904, as the Anglo-German naval race accelerated, Britain and France settled various colonial disputes through the new Entente Cordiale: among various resolutions, the French accepted British control of Egypt and the British accepted French control of Morocco. Although its terms were strictly colonial, the Entente's message of Franco-British cooperation was clear—and pointed directly at Germany.

Rather than balancing power and ensuring peace, the various rival alliances helped to escalate European tensions. In 1906, the British launched HMS *Dreadnought*, a boldly innovative new warship—the first "all big gun" battleship, with multiple large caliber guns arranged in rotating turrets along the ship's main axis. As soon as *Dreadnought* was built, every other warship on Earth was instantly obsolete—including the large fleet Germany had labored to build. But instead of ending the naval arms race, the new vessel further accelerated it. As Britain began construction of whole fleets of "dreadnoughts," the Germans followed suit. A new and even more deadly competition began.

Meanwhile, Russia faced serious internal trouble. Despite its enormous territory and manpower, the vast nation remained economically backward. Tsar Alexander II, Russia's emperor, moved to abolish serfdom only in 1861, and did little to better the serfs' harsh conditions. Modern industrial growth came slowly. Alexander II and his successors also maintained strong and often harsh autocratic power, resisting rising calls for political reform and an elected legislature. Heavy taxes and poverty burdened the country, and opposition finally reached crisis levels in 1905, when Russia's humiliating defeat in the Russo-Japanese War exposed the government's ineffectiveness. Tsar Nicholas II's troops fired on peaceful protesters in St. Petersburg; sailors on the battleship *Potemkin* mutinied, demanding radical reform; Communist groups seized the chance to create local soviets, or workers' councils, across Russia. As unrest spread, the tsar agreed to form a *duma*, or parliament. But he soon bypassed the new assembly and evaded meaningful reforms for the peasantry. Domestic tensions continued to mount.

Abroad, old tensions over the Balkans were mounting, which increased the risk of conflict between Russia and Austria-Hungary—and inevitably with Austria's dominant ally, Germany. The Balkans had fallen under the control of the Turkish Ottoman Empire by the fifteenth century. But by the late nineteenth century, the Ottomans were in serious decline—Turkey was widely branded "the sick man of Europe." As nearby Greece broke away from Ottoman control in the 1820s and 1830s, the Balkans' many Slavic peoples joined together in anti-Ottoman revolts. Austria, meanwhile, had eyed control of the Balkans since the eighteenth century—and when its power over the German states was broken by Prussia's new German Reich, the Austro-Hungarian Empire had shifted its expansionist aims even more explicitly to the Balkans.

The Balkans, like Russia, were Slavic and Orthodox Christian—and Russia saw the region as its natural sphere of influence. When Turkey drew European condemnation for its harsh suppression of a Bulgarian uprising in 1876, Russia seized the opportunity to launch the Russo-Turkish War (1877–1888). Russia defeated the faltering Turks and emerged with effective control over the Balkans. But at the 1878 Congress of Berlin, led by powerful German chancellor Otto von Bismarck, Germany and other European powers forced Russia to accept revised terms that greatly weakened its gains. Serbia and Romania were granted independence. Austria gained Bosnia, which had rebelled against Ottoman control in 1875. Hopes for a pan-Slavic Balkan state were thwarted, and Russia—deprived of what it saw as its rightful regional power—was left angry and resentful. Austria's 1879 alliance with Germany only hardened Russia's sense that both nations were threatening its interest in the Balkans.

Russia had already allied with France in 1894. With Austria continuing to tighten its grip on the Baltic and Germany growing more openly aggressive, Russia turned toward Britain as well. Britain and Russia were hardly friendly: they, too, had fought each other in the Crimea in the 1850s and had battled for decades over control of Afghanistan and other central Asian land routes to India. But the looming Austro-German threat trumped these concerns, and the 1907 Anglo-Russian Convention settled the central Asian disputes. Britain, France, and Russia now formed an alliance, called the Triple Entente—and it was clearly aimed at the Triple Alliance of Germany, Austria, and Italy.

Kaiser Wilhelm saw such alliances as plots to deny Germany its rightful position of power. He became still more aggressive—which in turn further alarmed the Entente powers. And critically, tensions continued to rise in the Balkans. In 1908, Austria enraged the Russians when it formally annexed Bosnia. Neighboring Serbia, independent of Ottoman control since 1878, considered Bosnia part of a larger Serbian nation: it also deeply resented the Austrian annexation. Threats from Germany, Austria's ally, forced Russia and Serbia to back down. But the two Balkan Wars (1912–1913) finally drove the Ottomans out of the region completely and ended with Serbia increasing its territory and influence—and thus posing a greater threat to Austrian Bosnia, where Serbian nationalists also launched terrorist attacks on Austrian interests. The Balkan Wars also pushed Russia into a close alliance with Serbia, which further increased Russo-Austrian tensions.

Europe's alliances eyed each other with heavy suspicion and hostility. Everything centered on Kaiser Wilhelm's Germany—nations were aligned either with him or against him, and his decisions were likely to decide the future peace of the continent.

EUROPE'S TENSIONS ERUPT INTO WORLD WAR

On June 28, 1914, during a visit to the Bosnian capital of Sarajevo, Archduke Franz Ferdinand (heir to the Austro-Hungarian throne) was assassinated by Gavrilo Princip, a member of a Serbian terrorist group called the Black Hand. In early July, Kaiser Wilhelm, convinced this was the time for Austria to end the Serbian threat, offered Austria-Hungary the so-called blank check: unconditional support, whatever its course of action. On July 23, the emboldened Austrians sent an ultimatum to the Serbs, demanding a massive crackdown on anti-Austrian groups, statements, and propaganda. Russia warned that it would not tolerate any Austrian seizure of Serbian territory, and France assured Russia of its support. Austria did not even wait for Serbia's noncommittal reply to the ultimatum and mobilized its army.

Britain proposed a conference to resolve the dispute, but Austria and Germany refused. On July 28, Austria declared war on Serbia. Germany, eyeing a possible continental war, tried to keep Britain neutral. Russia, despite German warnings and in the midst of much confusion in its own government, mobilized its armed forces, aiming chiefly at Austria. Germany issued an ultimatum to Russia, threatening war unless Russia immediately halted its mobilization. Germany pressured the French to stay neutral, but France refused to make promises. Britain, in turn, asked Germany to respect the neutrality of Belgium—a natural German invasion route into France—and the Kaiser refused.

France and Germany both mobilized on August 1. Wilhelm, more convinced than ever that enemies were plotting against him from all sides, viewed war as inevitable and was determined to bring it on at a time of his own choosing. That same day, he declared war on Russia, which had not answered the ultimatum. The next day, Germany demanded that Belgium allow German forces to cross its territory; Belgium refused. The Kaiser was convinced that the French would intervene for Russia. On August 3 he declared war on France and invaded neutral Belgium. The next day, the British responded to the violation of Belgian neutrality and declared war on Germany. Within weeks, there would be general war between the Central Powers (Germany and Austria-Hungary—Italy sidestepped its Triple Alliance obligations and stayed neutral) and the Allied Powers (Britain, France, Russia, Serbia, Japan, and others).

At first, the Germans made dramatic progress, trampling and savaging Belgium before cutting deep into France. But within weeks, the German advance had faltered short of Paris. The Western Front—the line along which the armies faced off, snaking hundreds of miles across northern France—would hardly move for the next three years. The fighting settled into a near-stalemate of bloody trench-to-trench warfare. Heavy artillery and new machine guns inflicted unprecedented casualties as armies poured in men and fought fiercely to gain mere yards at a time of battle-churned mud: more than two million men fought at the first Battle of the Marne in September 1914, one of the war's first major engagements—and nearly a quarter were killed or wounded. New armored and mechanized tanks seemed to offer the Allies an advantage in

1916—until the Germans matched them. Both sides used poison gas, which blinded and choked indiscriminately as it blew uncontrolled across the battlefields. Flashpoints along the front—places such as the Somme, Ypres, and Verdun—would become notorious fields of slaughter. Both sides had expected a quick and decisive war. Instead, they found themselves trapped for years in the hellish landscape of a nightmare.

In the east, Russia's lack of industrial modernization undercut its enormous advantage in manpower. With poor roads, inadequate equipment, patchy and badly functioning railroads, and inefficient communications, the Russian army proved disastrously ineffective. The first battles on the Eastern Front ended in serious Russian defeats. The Central Powers also persuaded Turkey to attack Russia, which further diluted Russia's fighting strength. But Austria's own military inadequacies, and the demand for German troops on the Western Front, turned the Eastern Front into another sapping stalemate. Italy ignored its past commitments to Germany and Austria and joined the Allies in 1915. It hoped to bite off Austrian territory—but most Italian campaigns were costly disasters, even against the stumbling Austrians.

Fighting spread gradually over much of the world. In Africa, British forces conquered Germany's colonies. In an attempt to take Turkish pressure off Russia, the British mounted a failed assault on the Dardanelles at Gallipoli that cost more than fifty thousand British and French lives—a catastrophic defeat for the young First Lord of the Admiralty, Winston Churchill. Seeking to control Middle Eastern oil fields and to further weaken the Ottomans, Britain invaded Ottoman-controlled Palestine. The British allied with an Arab revolt against Ottoman control (led in part by the British officer T. E. Lawrence, later known as Lawrence of Arabia). The British disingenuously suggested that the Arabs would gain independence after the war. But 1916's secret Sykes-Picot Agreement in fact split the Middle East between Britain and France: to embarrass the Western democracies, Vladimir Lenin's Russian Communist revolutionaries published the document in November 1917. The betrayal helped stoke Middle Eastern tensions and Arab anti-Western sentiments in later decades.

Around the world, naval combat flared, mainly in the form of small engagements against German commerce raiders, which preyed on Allied merchant ships. Both Britain and Germany had spent decades preparing for large-scale fleet battles—but only one major battle took place, off the Danish coast at Jutland. Its outcome was inconclusive, but the Germans were left fearful of risking their fleet and never deployed it again. Far more important was the Germans' innovative use of submarines, a relatively new invention, to attack Allied merchant shipping. Established rules of war held that merchant vessels must be stopped and warned before they were sunk. Tossing aside these rules, Germany declared unrestricted submarine warfare as its U-boats stealthily sank Allied shipping on sight.

The U-boat campaign posed a serious threat to Britain, which depended on foreign trade for food, fuel, and war supplies. It also risked conflict with the neutral United States, which—although determined to stay out of the war—sympathized with Britain. In May 1915, a U-boat torpedoed the British passenger liner *Lusitania* en route to England from New York; 1,198 passengers died, including 128 Americans. As the outraged United States seemed poised to join the war, Germany bowed to pressure and ended the unrestricted U-boat campaign. But by early 1917, Germany was desperate to break the European stalemate and resumed its unrestricted sinking. Shortly thereafter, the U.S. declared war on Germany. The Germans gambled that they could win the war before the United States could raise, equip, and transport an army large enough to make a difference in Europe.

Meanwhile, events elsewhere played into Germany's hands. Even as Germany resumed unrestricted submarine attacks, Russia—mauled by the war, its economy in shambles, its government unpopular and discredited—was near collapse. In March, a democratic revolution forced Tsar Nicholas II to abdicate. But the new provisional government under Alexander Kerensky was determined to respect Russia's obligations and stay in the war: popular resentment quickly rose afresh. Communist leader and Russian political exile Vladimir Lenin—who returned to Russia in 1917 with German help—took advantage of the chaos to launch a Communist revolution that November (or October, according to Russia's then-obsolete calendar); Kerensky was forced to flee Russia. The new Bolshevik government (named for the dominant Communist movement) left the war. Facing a civil war against the Tsarists at home, Lenin reluctantly accepted humiliating peace terms from the Germans and turned his attention to his domestic foes.

Germany was able to transfer large numbers of troops from the Eastern Front and launched a massive Western Front offensive in spring 1918. For the first time since 1914, the front began to move. For a time, it looked like Germany might sweep to victory—but it was, in fact, too late: U.S. forces were arriving, and they rapidly replenished the exhausted British and French lines. The German advance ground to a halt, and the Allies soon began to drive the Germans back. Germany was blockaded by the British navy and faced massive domestic pressure to end the war quickly. Now, Allied invasion seemed imminent. By early October, Germany's generals admitted that victory was impossible. Unwilling to endure the humiliation of surrender, the army told the civilian government to begin negotiations with the Allies.

Germany itself was unraveling. Kerensky's revolution in Russia had already inspired calls for change in Germany, sparking serious strikes among German home-front labor in 1917. The Russian Bolshevik Revolution that followed further radicalized Germany's laborers as well as soldiers. In late October 1918, as the German generals resisted the Allies' truce terms, the nation's top naval officers ordered their fleets into a final massive battle with the British. But rather than sail on this suicidal mission, sailors in two major ports mutinied. The mutiny quickly touched off a widespread revolt against the Kaiser's government. The revolutionaries ranged from Communists to Democrats, but they managed enough unity to proclaim a republic on November 9. Kaiser Wilhelm abdicated, and the new government accepted the Allies' cease-fire terms. Early on November 11, 1918, the Germans signed the armistice in a railroad car north of Paris to take effect at 11:00 AM Paris time.

The Allies now had to deal with their defeated enemies and create a post-war European order. The Germans faced the daunting challenge of building a new government in their divided, humiliated, and badly beaten nation.

A NEW WORLD OF SCIENCE, TECHNOLOGY, WAR, AND CULTURE

The First World War unleashed unprecedented slaughter. Machine guns, heavy artillery, and poison gas cut down waves of men. Faced with such gruesomely effective weaponry, nearly sixty thousand British soldiers were killed or wounded charging German lines on the first day of the July 1916 Battle of the Somme. Submarines preyed stealthily on merchant ships from beneath the surface. Mechanized transport and wireless communication enabled unprecedented coordination on the battlefield and beyond. These and other innovations resulted in almost incomprehensible carnage. All told, an estimated twenty million people died in the First World War. Nearly half were civilians caught in the destruction.

New means of transport, coordination, and communication also enabled something the world had never seen: targeted and systematic violence against an entire people. Massacres of hated minorities had always been common, but they had usually been confined to a single city or area: it had simply not been possible to coordinate mass slaughter across whole regions. The ancient nation of Armenia, on Turkey's eastern edge, had been ruled by the Ottomans since the sixteenth century and had straddled the Turkish-Russian border since the early nineteenth century. As Armenians agitated for independence, the Turks accused them of treacherous loyalty to Russia. In 1915, Turkey began to kill Armenian political and intellectual leaders. Soon much of the population of Turkish Armenia was rounded up and deported. Many died on forced marches, and others perished in concentration camps from famine and disease. All told, as many as 1.5 million Armenians (from a population of 2.5 million) were killed in this systematic campaign of eradication: a reflection of new, merciless, and modern methods of hate.

Such drastic developments—the carnage in the trenches of France, the ability to systematically exterminate an entire people—caught most combatants off guard. The brutal realities of modern technology had outpaced traditional ideas of war. Europeans rushed into war in 1914 expecting a quick and decisive conflict, but their tactics looked back to Napoleon, not ahead to the machine gun, airplane, and tank. Thus, the context for this unforeseen carnage was the tremendously rapid growth of science and technology in the decades before the war, which had changed the world more than most strategists and soldiers had realized.

Since the mid-nineteenth century, scientists—who were often closely tied to the technical needs of developing industries—had made great advances in understanding electromagnetic radiation. Electricity had been harnessed for practical use, enabling the rapid adoption of new electrical devices. Radio wave technology, advanced by Italy's Guglielmo Marconi and others, led to the rapid development of wireless telegraphy across ever-increasing distances—a vitally important advancement in times of peace and war. X-rays and nuclear radiation were discovered. Another revolution—the birth of modern theoretical physics through the work of scientists such as Albert Einstein and Niels Bohr—also began before the war; such discoveries, together with deeper knowledge of the atom and atomic radiation, would later dramatically affect the Second World War and its aftermath.

Improved methods of producing and using steel transformed many areas of technology. The use of steel frames brought buildings to new heights; older methods of building with wood or stone could never have supported such massive structures. New York's Flatiron Building, completed in 1902, rose nearly three hundred feet: such buildings ushered in the era of the skyscraper, which transformed urban landscapes and enabled vastly greater numbers to live and work in restricted urban areas such as Manhattan.

Daring uses of steel also enabled engineers to build ships on enormous scales. Such construction made it possible to construct naval vessels like the dreadnought battleships and gigantic commercial craft such as freighters and passenger liners—revolutionizing transport, trade, and naval warfare. However, the new technology of scale sometimes moved too rapidly for safety to keep pace. Many assumed that the enormous new passenger vessels could easily resist catastrophic damage—and old regulations were not updated, enabling vast new ships to sail with the lifeboats mandated decades earlier for ships less than a quarter their size. All of these factors combined in the April 1912 loss of the British liner *Titanic* (actually owned by a massive American commercial conglomerate), which collided with an iceberg on its maiden voyage to New York. The ship sank and fifteen hundred people died; although the ship had the capacity to carry thirty-five hundred people, it had lifeboat capacity for only twelve hundred. At first, overconfident passengers refused to board the lifeboats, and only 705 were saved. On the eve of the First World War, the tragedy served as a sobering reminder of the limits of technological progress.

The late nineteenth-century invention of the internal combustion engine led to pioneering work with automotive vehicles. The private automobile became a practical option beginning in the early years of the twentieth century. Horses and railroads remained the chief modes of transport, including during the war. But motor cars emerged as ambulances and as a transport option for officers. On the battlefield, they were developed into armored all-terrain tracked vehicles nicknamed tanks. These new motors' need for petroleum fuel—and the increasing conversion of warships to oil-fired steam boilers—would also drive post-war efforts to dominate the world's oil fields, with profound geopolitical consequences.

The internal combustion engine also helped fulfill an ancient dream of people: powered flight, which was pioneered by the American Wright brothers—who first flew successfully in 1903 and, together with other innovators, quickly turned the airplane into a practical technology. By the First World War, reconnaissance planes, fighters, and bombers of fast-increasing sophistication further transformed the nature of warfare. In a once-unimaginable mode of attack, German planes repeatedly bombed London. Fighter aces such as Germany's Manfred von Richthofen—the "Red Baron"—battled to dominate the air over the Western Front. Air technology, whose development was spurred by the war, would soon begin to transform peacetime contact and commerce within and between nations—and to further transform the nature of war.

The decades before the First World War were marked by economic modernization, international strain, and widespread social anxiety. But the era's stresses helped inspire radical new trends in culture and thought. Cultural movements looked toward bold reforms and social change, sometimes with profound effects. In France, courageous journalism by the reform-minded novelist Emile Zola defied the army and the Catholic Church by helping to expose the scapegoating of Alfred Dreyfus: a Jewish officer in the French army who was falsely accused and imprisoned for treason by conservative and anti-Semitic authorities. A young Austro-Hungarian newspaper correspondent named Theodore Herzl covered the Dreyfus trial. The experience helped inspire him to found the political Zionist movement, which sought a homeland for European Jews in the ancient land of Israel.

In Vienna, the pioneering work of Sigmund Freud explored the subconscious mind. His theories opened an important new field of study into individuals and human society: these developments profoundly influenced not only the new field of psychology but also art and literature. By the end of the century, many found the world disturbing, harsh, and alienating. The authors and artists of the international Decadent movement rejected the sentimentality of Romanticism and sought to describe the unconventional and shocking, defying social conventions in their works and in their private lives. By the last years of the nineteenth century—the *fin de siècle*—visual artists challenged social customs and launched bold experiments in ideas and forms. Sculptors such as Auguste Rodin and Edgar Degas broke with classical traditions and created works with roughly textured, powerfully expressive surfaces.

The literalism of photography, an increasingly common technology by the end of the nineteenth century, pushed artists to pursue bolder and more experimental directions. Turning away from literal representation of the visual world to explore psychological depths and the nature of human perception, French painter Paul Cézanne reduced the visual world to bold blocks of color and shapes. His work helped inspire Georges Braques and Pablo Picasso to create the geometric forms of Cubism. As the twentieth century dawned, artists increasingly tried to capture the disjointed and uneasy world around them as they moved into a new world of abstraction and grimly evocative expressionism.

ERA 15: DEPRESSION AFTER VERSAILLES: THE RISE OF TOTALITARIAN POWERS *(1919 TO 1930S)*

THE VERSAILLES SETTLEMENT AND ITS DISCONTENTS

The November 11, 1918, armistice ended the First World War's fighting, but it did nothing to determine the shape of post-war Europe. The defeated Central Powers—Germany and Austria-Hungary—were in disarray. The Austro-Hungarian Empire disintegrated as Hungary rebelled and broke away to form its own republic. Austria, now reduced to a much smaller, ethnically German core, also established a republic. Since November 1918, Germany had been administered by the provisional government that forced Kaiser Wilhelm II to relinquish power. Wilhelm went to Holland in exile, and in January 1919 a newly elected assembly met in the city of Weimar to adopt a Republican constitution. But Germany was still wracked by strikes and street riots. Communists declared an independent Soviet Republic of Bavaria, which the German government suppressed with military assault and hundreds of executions. Above all, nobody knew if the Great War had been, as many hoped, "the war to end all wars"—and if, as U.S. President Woodrow Wilson envisioned, it had truly made "the world safe for democracy."

The Allies' key question was how they should deal with Germany—whose aggression, in their eyes, had caused the war. In an early 1918 speech, President Wilson laid out his Fourteen Points, which offered an idealistic vision for post-war peace. Germany would not face crushing penalties, but it would lose territory: the disputed border regions of Alsace and Lorraine, which Germany had seized in 1871, would return to France; Russia would retake the lands that Germany had claimed in 1917; Poland—which had been divided among Russia, Prussia, and Austria since the 1770s—would regain independence. Other points focused on broader principles: the nationalist claims of peoples formerly subject to the Austro-Hungarian and Ottoman Empires were to be recognized, along with freedom of the seas and of trade. Wilson also aimed to establish an assembly of the world's nations to resolve international disputes.

Many Allied leaders resented Wilson's commanding tone—the United States had, after all, come late to the war and had been involved in comparatively little fighting. Although the Allies accepted his Fourteen Points as a basis for the 1919 Paris peace talks, they insisted on many harshly punitive provisions that Wilson had not envisioned. The Germans, who were barred from negotiating the terms that would decide their fate, were simply required to accept the final treaty. The June 1919 Treaty of Versailles forced Germany to accept full blame for the war and to pay heavy reparations to the Allies. Germany would be allowed only a token military, with no air force or submarines. Germany lost all of its colonies and lost disputed territories to Poland and France. As Wilson had hoped, the Allies created a global League of Nations. But Wilson—a Democrat—refused to make any concessions to U.S. Senate Republicans, who demanded safeguards for America's sovereignty. The Senate failed to ratify the treaty, and the United States did not join the league. With the United States quickly becoming a dominant world power, its absence crippled the league from the very beginning.

Separate treaties with Germany's allies—known collectively as the Versailles Settlement—further redrew the map of Europe. Agreements with Austria and Hungary created new nations from the former Austro-Hungarian possessions: Czechoslovakia, Romania, and, in the Balkans, a pan-Slavic state of Yugoslavia. A 1920 treaty with the Ottomans sought to create an independent Armenia—but Turkish nationalists, led by Mustafa Kemal, rejected such concessions and invaded Armenian territory. Soon, Armenia would be absorbed by Russia's new, expanding Soviet Union. In 1923, the Ottoman Empire fell. Turkey established a republic, dominated by Kemal's determined program of modernization and secularization: he won the title Ataturk, or "father of the Turks." Britain and France divided the Ottoman Middle East between themselves—and in so doing, betrayed their wartime Arab allies, who had expected post-war independence. Britain, which already dominated Iran, assumed control of Palestine, Jordan, and Iraq. Syria fell to France.

Germany was forced to sign the Treaty of Versailles—and was outraged by its severe terms. Regardless of their political views, most Germans argued that the treaty punitively and unfairly singled them out. They felt burdened with permanent humiliation and inferiority in addition to their already painful defeat. Even the Weimar government, which was still controlled by the moderate and Socialist parties that deposed Kaiser Wilhelm in 1918, strongly resented the treaty. Worse yet, the new government had little popular support—and thus little authority—in the angry, divided nation. The government faced opposition from all sides: old-guard monarchists, far-right militarists, and pro-Soviet Communists. In early 1920, enraged right-wingers launched a revolt called the Kapp Putsch, and drove the Weimar government from Berlin. Despite Weimar's low popularity, most of the country rejected the rebel government's authority and the coup collapsed.

But the militarist right wing was undaunted. Soon many were denying that they had even lost the war: they claimed that Germany had been poised for victory in 1918 before leftist revolutionary traitors at home—the "November criminals"—stabbed the unbeaten army in the back. Such claims ignored many inconvenient facts: by late 1918 the German army *had* been close to collapse and Germany *had* faced imminent Allied invasion. The army had told the civilian government that the war was hopelessly lost, and it had been the army commanders, who were determined to shift the humiliating burden, that made the civil government negotiate the surrender. But the facts made little difference to the growing *Dolchstoss* ("stab in the back") myth, which rapidly gained ground among angry veterans and right-wing agitators.

Dolchstoss paranoia fused easily with the German right's rampant anti-Semitism. Jewish leftists had been important in the November 1918 risings—but according to the anti-Jewish right wing, the "November criminals" had been a cabal of Jewish conspirators. Despite clear evidence, another widely accepted myth claimed that Jews had refused to fight for Germany. Many even insisted that international Jewish plotters had deliberately started the war in order to control war industries and reap the profits.

Adolf Hitler was a young Austrian-born corporal in the German army who was enraged by Germany's post-war degradation. He clung fiercely to the Dolchstoss myth and claims of massive Jewish treachery. As a failed artist in Vienna, Hitler had imbibed the city's pervasive anti-Jewish prejudices. He had come to see Jews as subhuman parasites on German civilization and blamed them for all his own failures and frustrations. He now refused to believe that the German military had truly been defeated, and argued that Jews had betrayed Germany. In 1919, Hitler took charge of a small right-wing nationalist party in Munich—the National Socialist, or Nazi, Party. His passionate, rage-filled denunciations of Jews, Communists, the Weimar state, and the Treaty of Versailles began to attract followers.

Even the Weimar government resisted Versailles when it could. The treaty allowed the Allies to arrest German officers for war crimes trials. But Germany's government refused to deliver any of the accused to foreign courts. The Allies reluctantly agreed to trials in German courts at Leipzig—but only twelve were tried, and all received acquittals or light sentences. The Allies protested bitterly. But even the Leipzig trials were too much for the German right, which seethed that the nation's military honor had been stained and that only Germans, among all the combatants, had been tried for war crimes.

The Weimar government also chafed against its loss of territory at Versailles. Per the Locarno Treaties of 1925, Germany formally accepted the redrawn French and Belgian borders in order to normalize relations with the Western powers. In exchange, Allied troops began to leave the occupied Rhineland along the French border, and Germany was invited to join the League of Nations. Yet, although it pledged that any future changes would be made peacefully, the German government refused to accept the new Czechoslovakian and Polish borders as final. Poland and Czechoslovakia felt betrayed by Britain and France, and continued to watch Germany warily. In violation of Versailles, Weimar Germany was secretly building an air force, submarine fleet, and other forbidden forces, employing foreign contractors and framing its projects as peaceful ventures to disguise its prohibited activities.

The dark, cynical arts of the early twentieth century flourished in the post-war period—and anxious, conflict-ridden Weimar Germany emerged as a prominent artistic center. The tortured emotions and twisted shapes of Expressionist painting, which emerged before World War I, flourished in its aftermath; new Expressionist cinema brooded on nightmarish effects and sinister scenes. Wartime had seen the emergence of Dadaism: it rejected tradition and even rationality as it delighted in the absurd—and gained many followers in the disillusioned post-war world. Surrealism followed, delving into the disturbing and bizarre worlds of the unconscious. Music also broke from its traditional emphasis on form and beauty, exploring harsh dissonance and abandoning the old structure of tonal notes and keys. Weimar art was among the most important of the twentieth century—but the culture that produced it was fractured, alienated, and dysfunctional. The period's arts spoke to the collapse of civic ties and institutions.

TOTALITARIANS RISING

Even though the United States never joined the League of Nations, Wilson's successors continued to press for new international peace efforts. The U.S.-led Washington Conference (1921–1922) resulted in international treaties to protect China's sovereignty (though with no real enforcement mechanism) and to sharply limit construction of new naval vessels. But obvious tensions remained, particularly over Japan's imperial ambitions in the Pacific. For every five large warships the United States and Britain were allowed, Japan was permitted only three. But with British and U.S. fleets spread over the Atlantic and Pacific oceans, the 5:3 ratio gave Japan enough ships to dominate the western Pacific. Japan's ambitions continued to rise in the wake of World War I. Expansionists took increasing hold of the government, determined to expel Europe's colonial empires from the Pacific and impose their nation's own imperial control in East Asia. Many Japanese strategists saw a war with the United States as an inevitable part of that process.

In Russia, Vladimir Lenin's Bolshevik Red Army waged civil war against the monarchist White Army until 1921. The Allies offered limited assistance to the White forces: a small force of British, French, Germans, and Americans held part of northern Russia from 1918 to 1920; Japan sent a larger army that occupied Siberia until 1922 (some Japanese leaders had hoped to seize the territory). But the Allied forces had little effect. Lenin prevailed over his divided and disorganized enemies and emerged as leader of the new Soviet Union. Outwardly, Leninism embraced the tenet of central rule until the people were ready for true Communist equality. But in reality, Lenin imposed a harsh authoritarian dictatorship until his death in 1924. Joseph Stalin, cruel and unpredictable even to those in his inner circle, triumphed in the power struggle that followed Lenin's death. By 1927, he had won complete power, purging rivals such as Leon Trotsky (who fled into exile only to be murdered on Stalin's orders in 1940). Stalin cracked down even further on dissent and free expression. He imposed Soviet control on neighboring territories and worked aggressively through foreign political organizations to export Communist revolution abroad.

In 1929, Stalin set out to forcibly "collectivize" Soviet agriculture: the properties of the landowning peasants, or *kulaks*, were to be seized, and the land reorganized into communal collective farms. When the kulaks resisted, Stalin ordered them massacred. The ensuing violent chaos severely undermined Soviet agriculture and led to a catastrophic famine, killing millions. Indeed, evidence suggests that Stalin engineered the famine to crush the peasantry that opposed him. He clung ruthlessly to power: in 1930, he established the dreaded gulag system of penal labor camps. Over the next two decades, his feared secret police would send millions to the brutal camps on the slightest pretext of dissident ideas or political opposition; the camps claimed an estimated three million lives. After the disastrous famine of the early 1930s, many leading Soviet Communists sought a more moderate leader. In 1934, Stalin killed his chief rival and rounded up that rival's supporters. In the Great Purge of 1936–1938, he killed much of the Communist Party leadership through staged show trials and forced confessions. Many members of the Red Army's officer corps were also murdered. Millions died in the purge, critically weakening the Soviet government and military on the eve of a new world war.

The Italians had joined the Allies during the war, and they gained territory in the peace settlement. But Italy had mostly been humiliated in battle, and its government was discredited in many eyes. In 1919, Benito Mussolini founded a new political movement that embraced fierce nationalism, total subordination of the individual to the state, and Mussolini's own absolute authority as party leader. He called the movement Fascism after the *fasces*: a tied bundle of sticks that signified authority in ancient Rome. The Fascists' violent, black-uniformed militias (called blackshirts) amassed power through intimidation, beatings, and murder. In 1922, Mussolini organized a massive Fascist march on Rome. With the capital in his grip, Mussolini was named prime minister. Officially, the Italian king retained his power, but Mussolini became the first Fascist dictator.

Meanwhile, Germany's Weimar Republic remained weak and unpopular. In 1923, as it struggled to pay the massive war reparations demanded by the Treaty of Versailles, the German currency collapsed. By November, it took billions of deutschmarks to buy a loaf of bread. Wages and savings became worthless, and the country was in danger of collapse. As Germany defaulted on its reparation payments, France and Belgium sent troops to occupy its industrial Ruhr valley. In 1924, the U.S. Dawes Plan tried to rescue the new German republic by restructuring Germany's reparation payments, helping to stabilize its banks, lending Germany money with its industrial assets as collateral, and arranging French withdrawal from the Ruhr. The currency was brought under control, and the Weimar government survived—for the moment. But the crisis had further weakened the delicate republic, and extremist sentiment had received a further boost.

In November 1923, as the economic crisis peaked, Adolf Hitler and his Nazi followers—including the general Erich Ludendorff, one of Germany's top wartime commanders—launched a revolt in Munich, capital of the German state of Bavaria. Hitler planned to seize control of the Bavarian government and imitate Mussolini's Fascist march on Rome with his own Nazi march on Berlin. Similar to Mussolini, he planned to oust the current government and force his own appointment to supreme power. The Beer-Hall Putsch (named for the hall where the Nazis gathered and launched the plot) failed completely. Although it was hostile to Weimar, the Bavarian government resisted Hitler's power grab. Local soldiers opened fire on the Nazi marchers, who were scattered, captured, or killed. Ludendorff abandoned the Nazis in disgust, but many members of Hitler's inner circle—including Rudolf Hess, Hermann Göring, and Heinrich Himmler—would remain fiercely loyal to the end.

The Weimar state tried Hitler for treason early in 1924, but the government again exposed its weakness through its hesitant treatment of the would-be conqueror. Hitler used the trial as a propaganda platform as the newspapers reported his speeches verbatim. His party was officially banned, but shortly after the trial ended, a thinly disguised Nazi front group won nearly 7 percent of the vote in a *Reichstag* (or German parliament) election. A few months later, as the furor over the failed revolt dissipated, the Nazis still drew 3 percent of the vote. Hitler was sentenced to five years in jail. He served only nine months, in easy conditions, and the ban on the Nazi Party was soon lifted.

Hitler spent his brief imprisonment composing a voluminous manifesto called *Mein Kampf* (*My Struggle*). The book, published in two volumes in 1925 and 1926, detailed Hitler's Nazi ideological program and his vision for Germany's future. *Mein Kampf* fused fury at Germany's Versailles humiliation, paranoid conviction that Germany had been betrayed and robbed of its victory by Jewish and Communist traitors, and Mussolini's Fascist model of nationalist state dictatorship. Hitler depicted Bolshevism as a force of evil corruption and painted German civilization as the sole savior of the Western world.

Hitler and his followers added obsessive racial theories to this angry right-wing mixture. In the late nineteenth century, racial theorists in France, Germany, and elsewhere in Europe had concocted influential, pseudo-scientific theories of racial hierarchy. The Germanic "Aryan" race— pure Nordic descendants of ancestral white Indo-Europeans—resided at the top of these hierarchies. Parasitical Jews and subhuman Slavs were at the bottom. Hitler embraced such theories with monomaniacal zeal, seeing Aryan German *Übermenschen* (supermen) as the natural masters of Europe. Although he insisted that Western Europe must accept German supremacy, he saw the East as fertile ground for German settlement: essential *lebensraum* (living space) for the master race, with the Slavs reduced to slavery. Other so-called inferiors must be removed from the Nazi sphere or eradicated altogether: gypsies, homosexuals, and especially Jews—whom the Nazis blamed for all evils, including the ills of *both* Communism and Capitalism.

Hitler's attacks on Versailles and endorsement of the Dolchstoss myth enjoyed widespread appeal, as did his vehement anti-Bolshevism. The Russian Revolution and Soviet-backed Communist parties in Germany raised widespread fears of workers' revolts. Many doubted that the Weimar government was strong enough to hold off Communist revolution. Many others, obsessed with the far left's role in the 1918 revolution, saw the Weimar Republic itself as little more than a Communist front. Nazi anti-Semitism was a natural fit, because the German right believed that Jews controlled international Communism. The Nazis, preaching state control of the economy, also promised to end the exploitation of workers by capitalist magnates—whom the Nazis also depicted as parasitic Jewish conspirators. Similar to the Italian Fascists, the growing Nazi movement relied on organized gangs of thugs—the SA or "brownshirts"—to terrorize those in their way. Gathering followers and silencing opponents, the Nazis began to build power bases across Germany. By 1928, the party had more than one hundred thousand members.

Both Stalin and Hitler exemplified a new and terrible twentieth-century phenomenon: totalitarianism. There had been many dictatorships and tyrannies before them, throughout the ages and all over the world. But totalitarian systems went further. They set out to destroy all social bonds and civic associations and to suppress all individual expression in an unyielding drive to impose their own mass culture. Government, police, education, and civic institutions all became tools for ideological indoctrination. The totalitarian state used widespread terror and enforced obedience to demolish popular belief in anything but its own relentless expansion.

THE GLOBAL DEPRESSION AND THE ENTRENCHMENT OF THE NAZIS

Despite their rapid growth, the Nazis' influence remained marginal in the 1920s. They were merely one of several small parties on the ideological fringe. In the 1928 elections, they won less than 3 percent of the vote and took just 12 Reichstag seats out of 491—down from 14 in December 1924, and from 32 in May 1924. It would take a profound upheaval to bring the Nazis to dominance.

That upheaval—dramatic and thoroughly unexpected—came in fall 1929. During the 1920s, the United States had experienced a vast, blindly optimistic investment boom that relied heavily on borrowed money. In late 1929, as doubts grew about the real value of soaring stocks and the safety of the money pouring into them, nervous lenders began to demand repayment of loans. The bubble burst, and Wall Street markets crashed. Within a few hours, billions of dollars in investments were wiped out. The U.S. Federal Reserve tried, too late, to rein in borrowing by raising interest rates; instead, it stifled business spending and made it impossible for debtors to raise funds. Meanwhile, a poorly planned U.S. tariff meant to protect American companies undercut foreign trade.

The massive expenses of the First World War had left European banks heavily dependent on U.S. bank loans. Now, faltering U.S. banks demanded repayment of those loans. European banks were unable to manage such sudden large-scale expenditures. With many banks in trouble, desperate depositors started runs on their banks to demand full payment of their savings. As too many people tried to withdraw their money at once, banks across the United States and Europe failed. The collapsing fiscal system took the entire economy with it. Businesses could not secure loans to pay their expenses, and consumers had no money to buy commercial goods or farm products: massive numbers of businesses and farms went under. Unemployment surged to catastrophic levels and drastic drops in tax revenue blunted governments' ability to provide aid.

Countries were tightly linked together by loans and trade, and the ravages of the Great Depression quickly spread throughout the developed world.

Germany, which relied on U.S. loans to finance its commercial growth, was hit particularly hard. Although a new U.S.-brokered plan had greatly reduced reparations payments earlier in 1929—another attempt to stabilize the Weimar state—Germany still owed billions of deutschmarks and needed U.S. loans to make the payments. By 1930, payments lapsed in the deepening crisis. German unemployment skyrocketed, and angry Germans blamed the usual suspects: the vengeful Allies and the reparations burden, the weak Weimar government—and the Jews, whom many blamed for all financial evils. Germans began to look for a savior—a strong, decisive leader who would purge the nation's enemies, save the economy, and restore the downtrodden nation to greatness.

The Depression spurred right- and left-wing extremists. Soviet-backed Communists made political strides in Europe, blaming global capitalist greed for the crisis and promising salvation through proletarian (or working class) rule. But far-right parties made even greater gains, exploiting both the crisis *and* widespread fear of Communist revolt. Suddenly, Hitler's violent rhetoric appealed to a far larger number of Germans. Sales of *Mein Kampf* jumped, and Nazi party enrollment soared. In the 1930 Reichstag elections, the Nazis emerged as Germany's second-largest party (behind the center-left Social Democrats, who had dominated Weimar politics). With more than 18 percent of the vote, the Nazis jumped from 12 seats in 1928 to 107 in 1930. The rival Communists secured 13 percent of the vote, finishing third.

Hitler was suddenly a serious political force, and his brownshirt thugs' violence and intimidation grew bolder. As a series of Weimar chancellors struggled to deal with the country's many crises, the Nazis continued to attract the desperate, disaffected, and enraged. Their rise was meteoric: in July 1932, the Nazis became the largest party in the Reichstag (they won 37 percent of the vote and 230 seats to the Social Democrats' 133; the Communists again placed third). The Nazis still fell short of a majority (which then required more than three hundred seats), and the centrist parties refused to join forces with them in a coalition government. Without a clear majority or any meaningful leadership, the Weimar government limped along.

New elections in November continued the stalemate. Although the Nazi vote share fell to 33 percent and 196 seats, it remained the largest party. Once again, there was no majority. Since 1929, Weimar leadership had increasingly fallen to monarchists, traditionalists, and military men who tried desperately to impose order. After the November 1932 election, the ruling politicians and the largely ceremonial Weimar president, Paul von Hindenburg—an aging hero of the First World War—cast about for an answer to the divided Reichstag. Their solution was to make Hitler Germany's chancellor—the most senior government position. Most of the other important cabinet posts would be kept in the hands of other parties. The political leaders viewed themselves as astute, well-bred, educated men who could easily control the low-class Austrian upstart and keep his thuggish Nazis in check.

Hitler became Germany's chancellor on January 30, 1933, and immediately outmaneuvered the politicians who had hoped to control him. Hitler used his powerful position to unleash his brownshirts in an unprecedented wave of terror. Nazi thugs attacked the homes and offices of Communists and labor leaders. Social Democrats and other parties were violently silenced and their newspapers were suppressed. Hitler had called new elections for March, and he was determined to ensure a Nazi majority. On February 27—only six days before the March 5 vote—the Reichstag building was set ablaze. Historians suspect the fire was arranged by Hitler's henchman Hermann Göring and his propaganda chief Joseph Göbbels, but the Nazis accused the Communists of causing the fire and planning a coup. The next day, Hindenburg accepted Hitler's decree declaring a state of emergency and suspending all civil liberties.

German industrial leaders hoped that a strong dictator would usher in a period of stability and growth. They supported the Nazis in the March 5 vote and worked to boost massive propaganda and voter intimidation efforts across the country. Even so, Hitler's party fell short of a majority, garnering 44 percent of the vote. But the results hardly mattered. On March 23, under heavy pressure—and with Nazi thugs gathered outside—the Reichstag passed the Enabling Act, which gave Hitler the power to rule by decree. The Nazi takeover was nearly complete. In 1934, President Hindenburg died: Hitler declared the president's office vacant, and assumed complete power as both chancellor and Führer (leader) of German—similar to the full-fledged Fascist dictator, Mussolini (called *Il Duce*, or leader), in Italy. The army was required to take an oath of loyalty not to Germany but to Hitler personally. The last remnants of the Weimar Republic had been swept away. The Third Reich (or German Empire) took its place.

Hitler was utterly ruthless, and he had no qualms about targeting even his longest-serving followers. When Hitler grew worried that the violent SA brownshirts could prove difficult to control and might even challenge his power, he launched a June 1934 purge of the SA leadership. The head of the SA, Hitler's old supporter Ernst Röhm, was killed along with dozens of others. Hitler also used the Röhm purge, or Night of the Long Knives, to kill off personal enemies and political opponents. The SA, which had been a major force in Germany, lost its power forever. From then on, the Nazi state imposed its tyrannical will through the feared secret police, the Gestapo, and Heinrich Himmler's elite party enforcers, the SS.

The Nazi state drove reemployment through massive economic regimentation. The success won Hitler solid support from business interests and boosted his popular standing in Germany. In 1933, he declared the end of reparation payments and withdrew from the League of Nations; the Allies, themselves wracked by the Depression, did nothing. To create a superior Aryan culture, Hitler worked to suppress all works of modern art, music, and literature that he deemed "degenerate." Political opponents and dissenters were sent to a growing network of concentration camps. As he implemented his plan of long-term conquest—detailed in *Mein Kampf*—he expanded the secret programs begun by the Weimar government to rebuild the armed forces. He envisioned German supremacy over all of Europe. Ethnic Germans in all nations would be united under the new Third Reich. The Slavic East would be seized and colonized, and the Slavs would serve as slaves. Jews were to be removed from Europe entirely. New laws and anti-Semitic propaganda blocked Jews from many professions. The Nuremberg Laws, passed in 1935, barred those with Jewish ancestry from German citizenship, and made German Jews the official targets of harassment and persecution.

Hitler's power was secure and he had begun his campaign to remake Germany—and then the world.

SCIENCE ADVANCES IN A WORLD OF GROWING DANGER

As political upheaval steered the world toward ideological collision—and ultimately toward a new and cataclysmic war—profound scientific revolutions were reshaping humanity's most basic understanding of the universe. The forces that these new sciences would unleash would, in turn, dramatically affect the coming war and make its aftermath perhaps the most dangerous time in human history.

Before the First World War, Einstein's theories of relativity had already begun to reveal a universe in which space and time were malleable, and in which both depended on the observer's frame of reference. The only absolute was the speed of light, a fixed point in a sea of relativity and a boundary no matter could break. In the 1920s, as study of atomic and subatomic particles advanced, the bizarre realm of the very small began to be revealed—the world of quantum physics, in which the act of observation alters reality and Isaac Newton's traditional laws of physics break down.

Study of atomic radiation had also progressed before the First World War. Now, quantum physics and related fields of study helped offer a new understanding of the atom and its structure. By the late 1930s, some scientists had begun to realize the world-changing potential of nuclear fission: if a neutron, one of the basic subatomic particles, struck the nucleus of a heavy metallic element like uranium, the nucleus would become unstable and split apart—freeing part of the enormous energies that bind the particles together. Neutrons released by the splitting nucleus would in turn split other nuclei, leading to a chain reaction. A controlled chain reaction could be used to create great heat, which could boil water to turn turbines and generate electricity. An uncontrolled chain reaction could create a bomb of unprecedented force.

The strangeness of relativity and the counterintuitive quantum realm sparked disbelief and even revulsion from many traditionalists. In the 1920s, even before the Nazis rose to power, a powerful scientific lobby dismissed such work as so-called Jewish physics, in contrast to the commonsense world of familiar Aryan physics. Albert Einstein, who was Jewish—and who actually resisted many of the bizarre findings of quantum mechanics—faced bigotry in Germany and beyond. He never received a Nobel Prize for his relativity theory, though he was repeatedly nominated. Despite clear experimental confirmation, the Nobel committee refused to accept his work as "proven"; in 1921, the committee declined to give a prize at all rather than recognize relativity. Einstein finally received the 1921 prize a year late—but for his work on electron emission (the photoelectric effect) rather than relativity. In 1922, Walther Rathenau, Germany's Jewish finance minister, was assassinated by anti-Semitic conspirators: Einstein faced similar threats.

The massive potential of nuclear research pushed the Nazi regime to protect some non-Jewish practitioners of modern physics as Nazi Germany pursued nuclear power and the atomic bomb. But many of Europe's leading scientists were Jewish or anti-Fascist and were driven to take refuge in Britain or the United States as the Nazi menace loomed over Europe.

Other scientific areas were also changing rapidly, including genetics and biology—fields the Nazis pounced on to bolster their theories of racial identity and advance their campaign to remove "inferior" racial stock. The Nazis were, however, far from alone in such thinking. Eugenics, the pursuit of so-called superior humans through selective breeding or gene manipulation, was supported by racially minded scientists and politicians in many countries, including the United States. Some hoped to breed out hereditary illnesses, deformities, or criminal tendencies. But for many, eugenics was a quest to cleanse the dominant white races of inferior Asiatic or African elements. Such ideas naturally fueled racial persecution. Some even planned to stop inferiors from breeding or to euthanize them outright—as the Nazis did with the mentally ill.

Technology was also moving swiftly in the 1920s and 1930s. Radio quickly advanced to transmit voices and music, enabling a new mass culture of news and entertainment to grow as home receivers became affordable. Study of radio waves also enabled the crucial invention of radar, which would have a dramatic impact in the next world war. Aircraft gained dramatically in range, speed, and power; fast delivery of mail became possible, and people could travel long distances at unprecedented speeds. But these new aircraft technologies also made intensive large-scale strategic bombings of cities possible, further blurring the line between combatants and civilians in wartime. This development would also have profound implications for the next war.

ERA 16: GLOBAL CALAMITY: APPEASEMENT FAILS AND GLOBAL CONFLICT RETURNS (MID-1930S TO 1945)

FASCIST AGGRESSION INTENSIFIES

Fascist Italy was solidly established in the 1920s, and Hitler's German Fascist regime emerged from the early 1930s in total national control. With the Great Depression still holding much of the world in its grip, dictatorial regimes had appeal for the desperate and disillusioned: they took rigid control of the economy, spurred reemployment, and instilled fanatical national pride. Powerful business interests continued to back the Fascist regimes as well, supporting their push for rearmament and regimented economic growth and strongly backed their militant anti-Communism. The Fascist police states, similar to their Soviet adversary, were also more than able to stifle any dissent. The secret police had eyes everywhere: people knew that any neighbor—or even a family member—might be a self-seeking or ideologically motivated informant. Even children, fed party doctrine in state-run schools and compelled to join party indoctrination groups like the Hitler Youth or Stalin's Komsomol, often could not be trusted even by their own families.

Germany's obsessive campaign of anti-Jewish laws, propaganda, and persecution made countries such as Britain and the United States uneasy. But prejudice was common. Many Britons and Americans agreed with Germany that Jews had too much power in society—and in any case, they considered German anti-Semitic policies to be Germany's own internal affair. But Germany and Italy were also casting a possessive eye on foreign territories. By the middle of the decade, Germany's aggressive intentions were becoming impossible for other countries to ignore—but Italy created international tensions as well: Mussolini was determined to make Italy a world power. The Italians had held colonial outposts in Africa since the late nineteenth century, and had controlled Libya since 1912. In 1935, Mussolini set out to expand his empire and invaded Ethiopia—which had successfully resisted Italian incursions in the 1890s and was now one of Africa's last independent states. The violent attack further alienated Mussolini's regime from the European democracies.

The Ethiopian crisis also exposed the powerlessness of the League of Nations, which had been founded after the First World War to prevent and contain international conflicts. The United States had declined to join the league because of internal disputes in the U.S. Senate, so the organization had lacked strength from its beginning. Fascist Germany and nationalist Japan—two of the most openly aggressive nations—left the league in 1933. In the wake of Italy's assault on Ethiopia, the league issued strong condemnations that Mussolini simply ignored. Italy would leave the organization in 1937.

Regardless of whether they supported the Nazis, most Germans opposed the punitive 1919 Treaty of Versailles. Even before Hitler came to power, Germany had violated essential terms of the treaty and had secretly worked to amass forbidden military technology. Under Hitler, Germany began to build its military more openly. In 1935, he renounced the Treaty of Versailles outright. But Britain and France, the major Western European powers, took no action in response. In fact, the British negotiated a new naval agreement that let Germany expand its navy significantly. The Anglo-German Naval Agreement replaced key terms of the Treaty of Versailles. By ratifying it, the British were effectively agreeing to discard Versailles.

Arms concealment was no longer necessary, and rearmament became Germany's top priority. The Nazis' state-controlled economy focused heavily on the military buildup: factories reached full production and unemployment fell sharply. Meanwhile, Hitler grew bolder. The Treaty of Versailles had ordered Germany to demilitarize the Rhineland—but in 1936, Hitler sent troops to reoccupy the territory along the French border. German rearmament was still in its early stages, and the formidable French military easily outclassed Germany's. Hitler's nervous generals were ready to beat a hasty retreat if French troops entered the Rhineland to oppose them, but the French did nothing. Hitler won another unopposed coup.

Hitler had described his long-term ambitions in his 1925 book, *Mein Kampf*. Although he never hid his aggressive posture, many countries simply failed to appreciate his ultimate aims. Few Westerners read *Mein Kampf*, and many who did dismissed it. Most assumed that Hitler would temper his ideology and pursue a more practical path once he gained power in Germany. In reality, Hitler and his followers remained completely committed to their ideological master plan. The Nazis' fanatical racial beliefs inspired their conviction that German survival depended on territorial expansion and the removal of the so-called inferior races that stood in their way. Nazis believed that racially superior Aryan Germans ultimately needed to dominate Europe.

They aimed to destroy Bolshevism, eliminate Jews from Europe, and reduce the Slavs to a slave race under German rule. Every move Hitler made was a step toward fulfilling his overall mission—and he took any attempt to stop him as an attack on Germany.

The success of Mussolini and Hitler inspired Fascist movements in many other countries, including Britain and the United States. Many Fascist parties remained small and thus had little chance of taking real power. But in Spain, civil war erupted in 1936 between right-wing nationalists—including Fascists—and an elected but Soviet-backed and anticlerical Republican government. General Francisco Franco emerged as the leader of the nationalist forces, combining Fascist ideas with more conventional military dictatorship, and forming a strong alliance with Spain's powerful Catholic Church.

Liberals in Europe and the United States offered their support to Spain's Republicans, whereas Italy and Germany supported the Fascist-leaning Franco. Germany unveiled its air force (which it had secretly developed), and it bombed Republican forces and devastated entire towns. The destruction of the Spanish town of Guernica—which Spanish artist Pablo Picasso immortalized in a starkly powerful painting—exposed the carnage and ruin that modern aerial bombing could cause. Franco triumphed by 1939 and made himself unquestioned dictator of Spain, and the Germans gained valuable experience with their new planes and fighting tactics.

Meanwhile, Japan pursued a policy of nationalist expansion inspired by its desire to control access to natural resources—and by its own conviction that the Japanese were a superior race, destined to rule in the East. Japan had looked toward imperial conquest since the late nineteenth century: it had built power over China, forced the Russians from Manchuria in 1905, and annexed Korea in 1910. Since the First World War, militarist expansionists had steadily increased their power in the Japanese government. When the Great Depression hit Japan in 1929, Japan avoided a severe economic collapse—partly because the government continued to stimulate growth by pouring money into the armaments industry. Though Japan had failed to seize Siberia during the Russian Revolution, they next targeted Manchuria, in northeastern China. The Japanese invaded in 1931 and created a puppet Manchurian state called Manchukuo. Japan installed China's former emperor, who had been deposed in 1912, as Manchukuo's nominal ruler—and then set to work stripping Manchuria of its natural resources for Japan's industrial and military use.

The Japanese military was indisputably the country's most powerful institution. During the 1930s, with Japan's emperor little more than a figurehead, the army came more and more to dominate the government, and Japan's military aggression sharply expanded. China was meanwhile weakened by internal division, particular Mao Zedong's Communist insurrection against China's nationalist government: in 1937, Japan launched an all-out invasion of China. The war began with a brutal six-week assault on Nanking and other cities, in which the Japanese killed two hundred thousand Chinese civilians. The global community denounced the onslaught, which would become known as the Rape of Nanking. Japan ignored foreign pressure and continued to widen the war.

Japan also eyed broader conquests, targeting other Asian nations and Europe's colonies throughout East Asia. It disingenuously called the project the Greater East Asian Co-Prosperity Sphere, which belied its true intent: Japanese conquest and total subordination of Asia's other peoples. Similar to Germany, Japan viewed any challenge to its expansion as a threat to its very survival—and had no intention of sharing the prosperity it won.

AS APPEASEMENT FAILS, EUROPE SLIDES TOWARD WAR

Even as the Fascists' aggressive aims became more blatant, the Western democracies' responses were weak and tentative. They were struggling to escape from the crippling international Depression, and many were desperate to avoid becoming entangled in a conflict that could bring back the horrors of World War I—or worse. Many strategists believed that the rise of new long-range high-capacity bombers had made war unthinkably terrible. Bombers, most believed, were unstoppable, and any European war would mean the obliteration of whole cities—a notion encouraged by the German destruction of Guernica. And, as the fury of 1919 faded, more Europeans had also come to see the Treaty of Versailles as unreasonably harsh: many considered Germany's grievances at least somewhat justifiable.

As the Depression dragged on and Fascism rose around the world, many in the West were also consumed by self-doubt. Some wondered if democracy was strong enough to stand up to the powerful new dictatorships. Fascists derided the democracies as decadent and faltering, and Westerners asked if Fascism's emphasis on national devotion, military strength, and state-controlled economies might ultimately overwhelm their own democratic systems.

Widespread fear of Communism also helped undermine a strong response to the Nazis. Hitler—with his aggressive military buildup, clear expansionist agenda, and obsessive racial ideology—represented the most immediate and urgent threat to Europe's peace and freedom. Though the equally despotic Soviet Union (U.S.S.R.) had worked steadily to seize and absorb small neighboring countries, Stalin was chiefly focused on crushing internal opposition and dissent: he had no near-term capacity for large-scale conquest. Nonetheless, Stalin's savagery was unquestionably alarming. Although the true scale of his atrocities would not be known until after his death, his brutality to his own people was staggering: millions had already died at his hands. And Stalinist Communism did represent a genuine danger to Western democracy. Ever since the 1917 Russian Revolution, the Soviets had worked actively to incite Bolshevik revolutions abroad by supporting and controlling Communist parties in Western nations. The Depression had reinvigorated U.S. and European Communists, who blamed capitalism itself for the economic collapse—and whose leaders, as their opponents correctly charged, were actively directed from Moscow.

Fascism and Communism threatened democracy and political freedom. But to some powerful people in the democracies, Communism's assault on private property and free enterprise was more alien to Western culture and posed the greater threat. Fascist states took state control of the economy but worked through private businesses and private wealth: the Nazis won early support from many German industrialists, who thought Hitler would restore Germany's prosperity. Prominent voices in the Western democracies—especially those who believed democracy was in decline and Fascism was unstoppable—admired Fascism's fierce anti-Communism and hostility to Stalin's U.S.S.R. Some influential politicians and industrialists, such as business magnate and U.S. ambassador to England Joseph P. Kennedy, argued that the Western powers should accept the inevitability of Fascist victory in Europe and ally with the rising Fascist states against the Communist menace.

All of these factors combined to encourage a policy of appeasement: tolerating Hitler's aggressive actions in order to preserve peace. Step by step, the democracies accepted Hitler's every expansionist move, hoping that each demand would be his last. But with every action that Germany's former enemies failed to block, Hitler only became bolder and escalated his demands. Some politicians, such as outspoken British statesman Winston Churchill, urgently warned about the dangers of appeasement. But he and others like him were widely dismissed as extremists, alarmists, or warmongers.

Nazi ideology demanded the union of all German peoples under a single Fascist government. Austria, Hitler's birthplace, was not yet part of the Nazis' German Reich, and Nazis in both countries considered the situation intolerable. Nazi agitation for an *Anschluss* (or "union") of Germany and Austria reached a climax early in 1938 as Hitler presented the Austrian government with an outright ultimatum. Austria's chancellor announced a national referendum to decide whether the country would remain independent. A strong pro-independence outcome was expected, so in March Hitler sent troops across the border to prevent the vote. Many Austrians welcomed Hitler's move, and those who did not were too terrified to fight back. Without resistance, the Anschluss was swiftly completed.

Again the democracies failed to respond—and Hitler moved on to his next demand. Czechoslovakia had been created in the aftermath of World War I. It contained parts of the former Holy Roman Empire, including German-speaking areas along its western borders known collectively as the Sudetenland. In his quest to unite all Germans under a single empire, Hitler now turned his eyes to these Czech territories, and demanded that Czechoslovakia surrender the German-speaking areas to the German Reich. Hitler falsely ranted that the Czechs were attacking and persecuting Sudeten Germans; war began to seem inevitable as his rhetoric grew louder. The formidable Czech army had heavily fortified the Czech-German border. Few German generals were eager to attack, and some even plotted to remove Hitler from power if he ordered an invasion.

Although the Czechs were prepared and willing to fight, the British and French were absolutely determined to prevent another European war—especially because they believed that the Sudeten Germans had a legitimate grievance against Czechoslovakia. British prime minister Neville Chamberlain and his French counterpart moved to intervene and defuse the crisis. That September, last-minute negotiations at Munich ended with the democracies' near-total acceptance of Hitler's demands. Britain and France agreed that Czechoslovakia should hand over the Sudetenland to Germany, and made it clear that the Czechs would not receive support if they chose to resist. Hitler solemnly promised that this was his last territorial demand in Europe, and Chamberlain proclaimed that the Munich agreement had achieved "peace for our time."

Hitler, by this time, was at the peak of his popularity in Germany: he had erased the shame of Versailles and again made Germany a dominant European power—all without war or obvious sacrifice. But as the Nazis gained still greater confidence, things grew rapidly worse for their targeted victims. In early November, just weeks after Munich, the Nazis unleashed a wave of anti-Jewish violence. Synagogues were looted and burned by Nazi thugs and thousands of Jewish businesses were destroyed. The smashed shop windows gave the event its name: *Kristallnacht*, or "night of broken glass."

At times—for instance, during the 1936 Berlin Olympic Games—the Nazis had tried to conceal the extent of their anti-Jewish persecution from outside observers. Now all pretense was dropped. Thousands of Jews were arrested and sent to prison camps. Germany's Jewish community was even ordered to pay one billion Reichmarks to cover the property damage caused by the Nazi mobs during Kristallnacht. The outside world looked on with distaste—but again, most argued that such events were Germany's own internal affair.

The violence did, however, help convince foreign powers that Hitler was still an active menace. Despite his announcement of peace after Munich, Chamberlain and others already had come to fear even during the Munich talks that Hitler could not be trusted. Hitler had insisted that annexation of the Sudetenland was his final territorial demand in Europe, and he had pledged to otherwise respect Czech sovereignty. But in March 1939, he suddenly sent troops to seize the rest of Czechoslovakia. Two facts were now obvious to the world: Hitler's ambitions were limitless and appeasement had failed. Britain and France realized that war was unavoidable. Now they only wished to avert conflict as long as possible while they ramped up their own rearmament programs.

Mussolini had long been unsure whether to regard Hitler as a natural ally or a threatening rival. But by 1938, Mussolini set aside his ambivalence and began to envision Germany and Italy as parts of a greater Fascist alliance. He also accepted reluctantly that the more powerful Germany would lead the alliance. Meanwhile, Hitler shifted his focus to the Slavic east: his next target was Poland.

HITLER SWEEPS ACROSS EUROPE

After World War I, part of East Prussia (a German territory along the Baltic coast) had been handed to Poland to allow the Poles access to the sea—the so-called Polish Corridor. The German city of Danzig had been taken by the League of Nations as an international port, and the remainder of East Prussia was left as an isolated German outpost surrounded by Polish territory. With the dismemberment of Czechoslovakia complete, Hitler now demanded the return of Danzig, free German access across the Polish Corridor, and special treatment for Germans who lived in Polish territory. Even the Weimar government had contemplated similar demands—but the British and French recognized that Hitler's true aim was the seizure of Poland itself, which would mark the beginning of his long-planned expansion into the Slavic east. They were no longer willing to buy Hitler off with fruitless concessions.

At the end of March 1939, Chamberlain and his French allies vowed to defend Polish independence. Hitler, who had always expected that his plans would lead ultimately to war, was undeterred. But to avoid a simultaneous war on both Eastern and Western fronts, Germany signed a cynical nonaggression pact with the Soviets in August. Stalin's Bolshevik Russia was Germany's ultimate ideological enemy and military target: Germany and Russia knew the treaty was merely a temporary ploy. But it was mutually beneficial: it allowed Hitler to seize Poland without Soviet interference, and Stalin gained time to prepare for eventual war. In addition, a secret provision of the treaty divided control of Poland between the Germans and the Soviets.

Two days after the Nazi-Soviet pact was signed, Britain signed a formal military treaty with Poland that guaranteed military assistance if Germany attacked. In early September, the Germans staged an incident on the Polish border: absurdly claiming that Polish troops had attacked Germany, they launched their invasion. Polish resistance was beaten down with tremendous speed. Complete German control of the air, massive bombing of Polish cities, and rapid movement of German tank divisions overwhelmed Polish forces. In mid-September, the Soviets moved into eastern Poland under the secret terms of the German-Soviet agreement. Fighting ended in just over a month.

Britain and France promptly declared war on Germany, but they made no move to aid the Poles during the brief and decisive German campaign. They still preferred to delay, using the time to increase their own military strength—which Hitler, of course, was also doing. The British and French leaders were now convinced that Hitler was dangerously irrational or even insane. Surely, they thought, the German military would realize the danger of an all-out European war and remove the Nazi madman from power. And so they waited.

In spring 1940, Britain tried to block Hitler from gaining access to neutral, British-friendly Norway, and even considered a preemptive invasion of its own. In April, Hitler used Britain's actions as a pretext for his own invasion of Norway. After a rapid victory, he installed a puppet government under Norwegian Fascist Vidkun Quisling. On May 10, after he secured control of Norway, Hitler launched a sudden invasion of Western Europe. Britain's prime minister, Neville Chamberlain, had already taken blame for failing to protect Norway. He was ousted the same day, and was replaced by the fiercely anti-Nazi Winston Churchill.

Germany's *blitzkrieg* ("lightning war") attack—a combination of aerial domination and fast-moving tank columns—quickly broke through the neutral Low Countries of Belgium, Luxembourg, and the Netherlands, and drove into France. Although France had a formidable military, it had relied too heavily on its outdated fortifications along the German border (the Maginot Line), which the Germans were able to outflank through Belgium and pummel from the air.

As the Germans pushed into France, the British expeditionary force was trapped against the English Channel. Aided by commercial ships, private yachts, and pleasure boats, the British managed to evacuate 330,000 soldiers from the French port of Dunkirk. But French resistance was crumbling. Many French leaders lacked confidence in the ability of their democratic institutions to fend off Fascism—and their doubts further undermined French efforts. France was defeated even more quickly than Germany had anticipated, and surrendered in June: Hitler made them sign their surrender in the same railroad car where the Germans had signed the November 1918 armistice. Northern France was occupied by the Germans. Southern France and the French overseas empire would be governed by a pro-German French regime based at Vichy. French partisans launched years of heroic resistance against Nazi domination but were unable to dislodge the Fascist enemy. In 1942, Germany would also occupy Vichy territory.

Once he had firm control of Western Europe, Hitler was determined to force Britain out of the war. For now, he was willing to leave Britain's overseas empire intact. In fact, he regarded the English as nearly the Germans' racial equals—and would have preferred to build an alliance with them. But he insisted that Britain leave Europe to Nazi control or face invasion. Germany launched waves of air attacks from France, which were intended to neutralize British air defenses and allow invasion forces to cross the English Channel. But Britain's well-coordinated Royal Air Force fought off the Germans' attacks in the furious Battle of Britain. Hitler postponed the invasion indefinitely and hoped instead to crush Britain's will to fight as he turned to heavy bombing of British cities. But this strategy also failed, because Churchill's Britain resisted fiercely.

In the United States, public opinion had grown more firmly hostile toward Nazi aggression, racism, and criminality. Although most Americans still wanted nothing to do with the war, President Franklin D. Roosevelt was convinced that Nazi control of Europe would endanger America and threaten the very survival of democracy. Despite a strongly isolationist Congress, FDR managed to press through increasingly open aid to Britain, including weapons, ships, and other supplies under the March 1941 Lend-Lease Act. The United States also began to protect British convoys from German submarines over large stretches of the Atlantic, claiming a right to protect American trade routes even in international waters.

Although British-Soviet relations were hardly warm, Hitler became convinced that hope of Soviet aid must be keeping the British from surrendering—and he was also impatient to implement his own aims for conquest in the east. In June 1941, he tossed aside his insincere treaty with Stalin and invaded Russia. Stalin had ignored clear signs that Germany was preparing to invade, still convinced that war against Germany was years away. Stalin had badly weakened the Red Army by killing many top commanders in the Great Purge of the 1930s. Now he was caught dangerously off guard by the Nazi attack, and the Germans made dramatic gains as they rapidly advanced toward Moscow. Despite strong Western hostility to Soviet Communism, the Nazi invasion forged an immediate common cause between the Soviets and the West: Churchill promptly formed an alliance with Stalin and Roosevelt extended Lend-Lease aid to the U.S.S.R.

GLOBAL CONFLICT AND THE DEVASTATION OF TOTAL WAR

In 1940, as Fascist forces trampled Holland and France, the Japanese invaded the Dutch and French Pacific colonies and the independent nation of Thailand in Southeast Asia. Seeking to improve its international position and ally with the powers that its leaders believed would win the European war, Japan also joined the Tripartite, or Axis, Pact with Germany and Italy that September. As Japan's expansionist aggression increased, the United States imposed escalating embargoes on the raw materials and oil that Japan so desperately needed. Japan became even more determined to achieve self-sufficiency through conquest and vowed to put an end to American interference with its plans. On December 7, 1941, Japan launched a surprise air attack on the U.S. naval base at Hawaii's Pearl Harbor.

Japan hoped that the Pearl Harbor attack would neutralize the U.S. Pacific fleet and stun America into a negotiated settlement. Instead, it shattered U.S. isolationism and drew a fiercely determined nation into the war. Hitler was already eager to attack the American ships that had been escorting British convoys: he thought war with the United States was inevitable and preferred to bring it on before the Americans grew any stronger. After the Japanese attack, he promptly declared war on the United States. FDR seized the opportunity he had long sought to combat Nazi Germany; even before the United States entered the war, he and Churchill had agreed that defeating Germany was their first priority.

The Allies fared poorly at first. Germany had pushed deep into Russia and was moving across North Africa toward British-held Egypt and the strategically important Suez Canal. In the Pacific, Japan conquered the British in Singapore and the Americans in the Philippines. But then the tide began to turn. As the Germans bogged down in the severe Russian winter, a Soviet counterattack stopped the Germans short of Moscow in December 1941; the Allies defeated the Germans in North Africa and had increasing success against German submarines in the Atlantic. Chiang Kai-Shek's nationalist government in China, aided by the Western allies and in an uneasy alliance with Mao Zedong's Chinese Communist insurgents, managed to bar the Japanese from making any more major advances. The Americans dealt a severe blow to Japanese naval forces in the June 1942 Battle of Midway, sinking four of Japan's carriers. And after months of brutal fighting in the jungles of Guadalcanal, they stopped the Japanese push toward Australia.

Industrial America produced weapons, ships, and aircraft at a rate no other nation could match. The full mobilization of national economies spurred economic development and social change around the world, as nations had to use all available labor. To boost their war industries, the Nazis forced conquered people from across Europe into slave labor. "Total war" blurred the line between soldiers and civilians as mass bombing of cities, initiated by the Germans over England, was soon inflicted on Germany. As U.S. forces advanced across the islands of the Pacific, they came within striking range of Japan and began to devastate Japanese cities with heavy fire-bomb raids.

The combatants raced to develop new weapons technologies. Chemical weapons had been used in the First World War and now biological weapons were available. But fears of retaliation kept both types of weapons from being used in major theaters (although Japan did employ both in China). In the 1930s, revolutionary scientific developments had opened the possibility of a massive bomb based on nuclear fission (the process of splitting atoms to release their internal energy). Now all of the major combatants tried to develop an atomic bomb. German efforts faltered: they were undermined by the flight of prominent Jewish and anti-Fascist scientists to the West. The Allies' Manhattan Project was bolstered by refugee scientists such as Niels Bohr, Enrico Fermi, and Edward Teller. The United States successfully tested a bomb in July 1945.

Germany and its widely feared secret police, the Gestapo, imposed oppressive rule throughout their conquered territories, and squelched freedoms as they killed gypsies, gays, political opponents, and others. But the Nazis' war on Jews, which Hitler had laid out in *Mein Kampf*, remained their fixation. Germany's Jews had already been systematically persecuted, degraded, and deprived of all rights. Determined to remove all Jews from Europe, German forces—particularly Heinrich Himmler's brutal SS—began mass killings of Jewish populations as they moved from Poland into Russia. By early 1942, the Nazis had settled on a program of outright extermination throughout Nazi-controlled territory: the "final solution to the Jewish problem." The young and fit served as slave laborers until they died, and others were murdered by mobile death squads or systematically annihilated in mechanized death camps like Auschwitz in Poland. By 1945, Germany had murdered some six million Jews, along with millions of other people whom they deemed "undesirables."

The Russians slowly began to push the Germans back; a decisive moment was the capture of the entire German Sixth Army in early 1943 after months of brutal house-to-house fighting in the Russian city of Stalingrad. Beginning in 1942, Stalin made urgent demands for an Allied invasion of Europe to open a second front and ease Russia's burden. The Allies invaded Sicily and then Italy in 1943; Italy soon deposed Mussolini and joined the Allies—but the Germans took control of Italian territory and continued to fight tenaciously. The Allies invaded France in the D-Day landings of June 1944. The Russians began to make major gains against the Germans, as they pushed the eastern front back toward Germany. The Allies liberated France and pressed on toward Germany. A last major German offensive in the West—the Battle of the Bulge—was defeated in December 1944, and German defenses began to collapse.

With his nation under siege from the Russians in the east and the Americans, British, and French in the west, Hitler committed suicide in his Berlin bunker in April 1945. German forces unconditionally surrendered within days of his death. Although it had been devastated by bombing, Japan refused to surrender. It appeared that a costly and destructive invasion of Japan would be necessary to secure an Allied victory, until the United States dropped the new atomic bomb on Hiroshima and Nagasaki in early August 1945. The Soviets had agreed to join the Pacific war once Germany fell, and declared war on Japan in the days between the two atomic bombings. Despite some Japanese officers' determination to continue fighting, the emperor decided to surrender days after the destruction of Nagasaki.

An estimated sixty to eighty million people—more than half of them civilians—died in World War II. After the war, the victorious Allies tried government and military officials in Nuremberg, Germany. The United States, which now occupied Japan, also tried accused Japanese leaders in Tokyo. Those found guilty were imprisoned or executed. The judicial tribunals went beyond the traditional categories of "war crimes" by pioneering the concept of "crimes against humanity": these were far larger crimes than battlefield abuses—atrocities committed against entire peoples.

ERA 17: POST-WAR WORLD: AN IRON CURTAIN DIVIDES THE GLOBE *(1945 TO 1960S)*

THE EMERGING COLD WAR*

The West's necessity-driven World War II alliance with the U.S.S.R was complex and difficult. After overthrowing Russia's democratic provisional government in 1917, Vladimir Lenin's Bolsheviks had quickly shown themselves to be autocratic, violent, and ruthlessly determined to exterminate their enemies. During the Russian civil war that followed, the World War I Allies had offered generally unsuccessful military assistance to anti-Communist forces (although a U.S. relief effort saved millions of lives after a catastrophic, two-year Soviet famine that began in 1921). Until 1933, the United States refused to even recognize the Soviet government—the last major power to do so.

Soviet dictator Joseph Stalin, who seized power after Lenin's death in the 1920s, was even more murderously savage toward his own people. His slaughter of land-owning peasants led to catastrophic famine, his purges of Communist Party and Red Army rivals unleashed bloodbaths, his Gulag system of labor camps killed millions as his feared secret police arrested those even suspected of dissent. Soviet Communists meanwhile worked to export ideological revolution abroad, seeking to undermine the West's democratic freedoms along with its commitments to private property and free enterprise. Stalin's coldly practical 1939 alliance with the fanatically anti-Bolshevik Nazis—which included a secret agreement to divide Poland between Germany and Russia—hardly improved the West's opinion of the Soviets. But when the Germans threw aside the two-faced treaty and invaded Russia in June 1941, the Soviets allied with Britain against Hitler and received aid from America. And when the United States entered the war, the U.S.S.R. became a major ally—by default.

*See U.S.16 and U.S.17 for additional information on the Cold War.

However, Western and Soviet long-term aims were incompatible. After the war ended, the differences could no longer be ignored. The paranoid, aggressive Soviets were determined to expand their territory and influence; they were driven by a mission to export Communism and were convinced they faced a constant threat of Western attack. The Soviets and the West managed only brief and limited post-war cooperation—forming the new United Nations (a more powerful organization than the defunct League of Nations) in June 1945, dividing Germany into Soviet and Western occupation zones, and jointly deciding the fate of the surviving Nazi leaders in the Nuremberg war crimes trials.

The rift between the two powers quickly widened. At the Yalta Conference with U.S. and British leaders in February 1945, Stalin had promised free elections in Eastern Europe—but he soon discarded his hollow pledge. The U.S.S.R. directly annexed many territories along its borders. Elsewhere in Eastern Europe, Stalin set about imposing puppet Communist regimes backed up by Soviet troops: all hopes of post-war democracy in the region were violently suppressed. Americans hoped the new atomic bomb would give them leverage over the Russians as the war ended, but the Soviets—armed with secrets provided by Communist spies in Western laboratories—were already at work on their own bomb. At a famous speech in Fulton, Missouri, in 1946, Winston Churchill—though no longer prime minister—warned that "an iron curtain" had descended across Europe, cutting off a repressive Soviet-controlled east from the rest of the world.

Bolstered by his new conquests, Stalin's ambitions grew bolder and more dangerous. Europe had thrown off Hitler's Fascist dominion—but now it faced the threat of brutal Soviet domination. In 1947, the United States' Marshall Plan committed billions of dollars to stabilize the war-ravaged democracies of Western Europe and head off Soviet-backed Communist insurrections. West Germany and U.S.-occupied Japan were swiftly rebuilt as anti-Communist bulwarks. Between 1948 and 1949, the Soviets demanded full control of Berlin and blockaded its Western-occupied sectors. An American-led airlift kept West Berlin supplied until Stalin backed down; the Western Allies meanwhile formed a mutual defense pact called the North Atlantic Treaty Organization (NATO). East and West Germany were soon divided between rival governments: the West was a democracy, and the East fell under a Soviet-controlled Communist regime. In August 1949, the Soviets detonated their own atomic bomb. The Cold War—a state of tense hostility that stopped just short of open conflict—had begun.

In China, Communists under leader Mao Zedong had sought power against the Nationalist Chinese government since the 1920s; in 1934–1935, Mao and his forces had broken out of Nationalist encirclement, enduring heavy losses on the difficult six-thousand-mile "Long March" to continue the fight from rural areas. Although Mao allied with the Western-backed Nationalists against Japan following the 1937 Japanese invasion, another civil war erupted between the Communists and Nationalists in 1946. The Nationalist Guomindang government of Chiang Kai-shek (or Jiang Jieshi) had long been corrupt, dictatorial, and unpopular. It enjoyed little support, and Mao's forces—aided and encouraged by Stalin's Soviet Union—drove the Nationalists into exile in Taiwan in 1949. The rise of so-called Red China, followed by its rapid expansion into Inner Mongolia and Tibet, fueled Western fears of a Communist wave in Asia.

Korea had been under Japanese control for decades and had been annexed by Japan in 1910. But the Soviets entered the war against Japan in its final days and won an occupation zone in North Korea, while the United States occupied the South. Korea soon emerged as a flash point. Under U.S. direction, UN forces repelled a Communist North Korean invasion of the U.S.-backed South Korea in 1950. When American forces threatened to overrun North Korea, Mao's China intervened on the North's behalf. The result was military stalemate, negotiation, and a permanent truce in 1953 that established a divided Korea. But the war had killed more than one million people, including many Korean civilians.

DETERRENCE AND THE UNEASY BALANCE OF THE SUPERPOWERS

The West had good reasons to fear Stalin's U.S.S.R. in the early years of the Cold War. He tightened his hold on Eastern Europe through violent crackdowns and bloody purges—tactics he had ruthlessly employed against his own people for decades. The aging dictator became ever more paranoid, aggressive, and dangerous. Tensions with the West rose steadily; many on both sides expected war. Within the U.S.S.R., Stalin launched new waves of oppressive violence through his feared secret police. Always anti-Semitic, Stalin now developed an obsessive fixation on Jews. Stalin's government accused a group of mostly Jewish Moscow doctors of plotting to assassinate him and other Communist leaders. By early 1953, the fabricated charges were being used to provide an excuse for a burst of anti-Jewish persecution, forcing Jews from their professions, arresting dozens, and sending many to the Gulags. Soviet propaganda spun stories of vast international "Zionist" plots, and a massive anti-Jewish purge looked likely. But then, in March 1953, Stalin suddenly died.

The inner Soviet power structure was left reeling in the wake of the dictator's death. They managed to put down an anti-Soviet rising in East Germany that June, but battled among themselves for permanent power. Lavrentii Beria, the powerful but much-hated head of Stalin's secret police, made a bid for control, but his rivals outmaneuvered and killed him. Nikita Khrushchev, a relatively low-level henchman of Stalin, gradually emerged on top. Despite his own violent past and his involvement in Stalin's 1930s purges, Khrushchev was no Stalin.

As premier, Khrushchev kept a tight hold on Eastern Europe, and vowed—lashing out with fiercely bombastic rhetoric—to destroy capitalism and "bury" the West. But behind the bluster, Khrushchev was a pragmatist. Though determined to maintain Soviet power, he was also determined to avoid a catastrophic global war. In 1956, he denounced Stalin's violent excesses at the Soviet Party Congress, boosting his reputation and helping him oust many of Stalin's former inner circle from power. By 1957, Khrushchev was in full control. He would hold power until rivals ousted him in 1964. But he had done much to move the Soviet Union away from Stalin's culture of casual murder: his enemies deposed him, but did not kill him.

In 1952, as the rivalry between the two nuclear powers escalated, the United States detonated the first hydrogen (or thermonuclear) bomb. Employing the nuclear fusion of hydrogen—the energy source of the sun—the H-bomb was vastly more powerful than the fission bombs that were dropped on Japan at the end of World War II. The Soviets detonated their own H-bomb in 1953. By that time, Stalin was dead and an armistice had been reached in Korea. Fears of immediate war eased. Yet the growing H-bomb arsenals meant that any war would probably annihilate both sides: a grim reality dubbed MAD (a fitting acronym for "mutually assured destruction"). World leaders hoped that fear of MAD would deter both sides from initiating such a conflict.

Deterrence required a constant buildup of forces and alliances to maintain a strategic balance. Both superpowers began to design intercontinental ballistic missiles (ICBMs)—difficult to destroy on the ground and impossible to stop once launched. With the Cold War now far more important than the memory of World War II, West Germany joined NATO in 1955. The Soviet Union created its own military alliance, the Warsaw Pact, with its Eastern European satellite states. Both sides also turned to espionage. Communist sympathizers in the West worked actively as Soviet spies, and an extensive espionage system operated out of Moscow. High-profile cases that exposed agents like Alger Hiss and Julius Rosenberg in the United States and the "Cambridge Five" in Britain raised anti-Soviet suspicions in the West.

The threat of thermonuclear war made the need for effective diplomacy more urgent. With Stalin dead and the more cautious Khrushchev in power, the superpowers began conducting summits in 1955 that aimed to limit the arms race and keep tensions under control. But relations often soured. Khrushchev was capable of behind-the-scenes pragmatism, but his public bluster and bombast deeply alarmed many in the West—and, indeed, he continued to press for Communist expansion and to keep an iron grip on Eastern Europe, brutally suppressing a 1956 anti-Communist rising in Hungary. Relations were further strained when an American U-2 spy plane was shot down over the U.S.S.R. in 1960 (the United States, assuming the pilot had been killed, denied the plane was intentionally committing espionage, but the captured pilot revealed the actual mission, to the great international embarrassment of the United States).

With Europe in an uneasy balance, attention shifted to Third World nations: developing countries that were aligned with neither Communist nor non-Communist blocs. Each super-power wanted to pull these nations into its own sphere of influence. To that end, the Americans and the Soviets provided nonaligned nations with aid and weapons and launched secret opera-tions to install friendly governments. This battle was for hearts and minds, and appearances on the global stage were essential as each side fought to prove its superiority. After their 1957 launch of the *Sputnik* satellite, the Soviets dominated the space race—the signature battle to show tech-nological dominance. But the United States, exploiting its superior resources in the longer term, decisively won the space race with its moon landing in 1969.

In 1959, tensions increased as the Soviet-backed Fidel Castro regime gained power in Cuba. The United States backed an invasion of Cuba (which was only ninety miles from Florida) by anti-Castro exiles in 1961, but the invasion ended in humiliating failure. The following year, the Soviet decision to secretly place nuclear missiles in Cuba sparked a massive diplomatic and military crisis. For several days, the world hung on the brink of nuclear war before a last-minute deal between Khrushchev and U.S. president John F. Kennedy defused the situation. Both super-powers had learned a sobering lesson and diplomacy improved. They turned away from direct confrontation and even more toward propaganda efforts and battles by proxy in the developing countries of the so-called Third World.

THE END OF THE COLONIAL EMPIRES AND THE RISE OF NEW NATIONS: SOUTH ASIA AND THE PACIFIC

As the two new nuclear superpowers stared each other down, European empires around the globe crumbled. The worldwide war against totalitarian conquest and occupation had helped discredit the idea of colonialism and boosted nationalist independence movements. The war also raised growing doubts among the European colonial powers about the wisdom and justice of imperial domination, which spurred rising protest at home against the continuation of empires.

Some of the most dramatic post-war developments came in India, where local opposition—led by Mohandas Gandhi, Jawaharlal Nehru, and others—had been actively seeking independence for decades through campaigns of nonviolent resistance. India had been the jewel of the British Empire since the mid-nineteenth century, and the British strongly resisted the independence movement. Although India's independence activists had set their campaign aside to aid the empire's fight against Germany in the First World War, many Indians were disinclined to support Britain in the Second World War. The empire offered eventual independence—at an unspecified future date—in exchange for Indian participation in the war, but that failed to silence Indian opposition. British-led Indian forces fought on many fronts—but thousands of Indians captured by the Japanese joined the pro-Japanese Indian National Army against the British.

After the war, Britain recognized that Indian self-rule was inevitable and began to plan for a rapid shift to Indian independence. But India's internal divisions complicated the process: the large Muslim minority, which had long been locked in mutual hostility with the Hindu majority, demanded a separate Muslim state in the Muslim-majority north. The final 1947 settlement resulted in a partition into India and Pakistan (which would later split into Pakistan and Bangladesh). Millions of refugees moved from one new state to the other amid heavy sectarian violence, which led to more than one million deaths. In the midst of the carnage, in January 1948, national icon Mohandas Gandhi—known by the honorary title *Mahatma*, or "great soul"—was assassinated by a radical Hindu nationalist. Gandhi was himself Hindu, but his calls for peaceful coexistence between Hindus and Muslims enraged Hindu extremists. India and Pakistan would repeatedly go to war in the following decades as they disputed border territories and harbored long-standing grievances.

In Southeast Asia and the Pacific, peoples who had fought to escape Japanese occupation now resisted a return to European colonial rule. The United States, which had proposed eventual Philippine independence—at an unspecified date—when it seized the islands early in the century, carried out its pledge in 1946. The British and Dutch gradually relinquished the majority of their Southeast Asian possessions by the 1960s; most Pacific island colonies gained independence by 1980, and Britain returned Hong Kong to China in 1997. Despite periodic economic crises, the newly independent nations quickly entered the growing global economy. They received heavy investment from outside corporations that were eager to develop new urban industrial bases.

The transition to independence led to power struggles between Soviet-backed Communists and Western-backed regimes (including democracies in some cases and, in many other cases, anti-Communist authoritarian regimes). After the battle over Korea, another major Cold War flash point emerged in French Indochina, a colonial territory that included the present-day nations of Vietnam, Cambodia, and Laos. A Communist insurrection drove out the French after defeating them in the 1954 battle of Dien Bien Phu. Just days later, the Geneva Conference divided Vietnam between a Communist government in the north and a Western-backed anti-Communist government in the south.

Communist North Vietnam soon launched insurgent attacks on South Vietnam. The United States feared a domino effect—would all of the nations throughout Asia fall to Communism if the North Vietnamese prevailed?—and actively supported South Vietnam's government despite its rampant corruption. As Vietnam's civil war deepened, America's involvement gradually increased. In 1963, the United States quietly supported a military coup, during which South Vietnam's unpopular ruler was killed. By 1965, South Vietnam's government was near collapse.

Despite an internal, Northern-backed Communist insurgency in the South, most South Vietnamese clearly opposed a Communist takeover. Yet the South lacked effective government, which meant that the fighting would fall mainly to the United States. President Lyndon Johnson remained convinced that U.S. defeat would weaken the nation's worldwide stature in the ongoing Cold War. He deepened U.S. involvement, stepping up combat operations, bombing Communist positions and steadily increasing the number of American ground troops. The costly and ultimately unsuccessful U.S. military effort would last a decade and sow dissent in the United States and abroad.

China remained the dominant Communist power in the East, supporting the North Korean government and Communist insurgencies throughout the region. But as Mao Zedong's revolutionary regime grew increasingly radical, even the Communist U.S.S.R. began to grow wary of Mao's unpredictability and of China's ambitions. At first, Mao's government was closely aligned with the Soviets. But the alliance eroded in the 1950s as Mao's increasingly ideological priorities pushed aside pragmatic policies and scorned international opinion. The Great Leap Forward, his failed attempt to force peasant communities into industrial production, undermined Chinese agriculture and created one of the most devastating famines in history. The crisis is estimated to have killed between twenty and forty million Chinese between 1958 and 1960.

By the 1960s, the Soviets had rejected Stalin's extreme, brutal practices. Relations with Mao, who had admired Stalin and his radical methods, further deteriorated. China detonated its first atomic bomb in 1964; three years later, it detonated its first successful H-bomb. This nuclear deterrent was aimed at the Soviets as well as the West, especially as Chinese-Soviet border disputes intensified. In the wake of the Great Leap Forward, Mao was threatened by more moderate Chinese officials who wished to move their nation toward a more restrained model—as the Soviets had recently done. Mao struck back in 1966 by launching the Cultural Revolution. The new Red Guard—a movement of students and young workers—worked to suppress moderate party officials, along with any other citizens—especially teachers and intellectuals—suspected of promoting Western or "counterrevolutionary" values. Against a backdrop of widespread violence, students closed their own schools and universities. Industry and the economy suffered, and China sank under a stifling wave of ideological oppression.

AFRICA AND THE MIDDLE EAST

Most of Africa, governed by powerful local states and empires, had resisted European imperial control for centuries. But in the late nineteenth- and early twentieth-century Scramble for Africa, the European colonial powers took advantage of their modern military forces—and internal African divisions—to rapidly seize most of the continent. During World War II, the European powers' demand for food and materials from African colonies led to increased industry, urbanization, and commercial agriculture. But this rapid modernization helped promote a demand for the same freedoms that Europe and the United States had fought for against the Fascists—a demand that India's successful 1947 bid for independence further encouraged.

At first, European powers resisted African demands. They continued to exploit African resources, even as such exploitation left the continent in deepening poverty. Africa's educated classes, trained to serve in the colonial administrations and in finding rising opportunities in the rapidly developing economies, built growing independence movements by the 1950s. By the middle of the decade, the large British and French African empires were crumbling. In some places, independence was achieved peacefully. In others, such as French-controlled Algeria, violent insurrections ultimately broke the European grip.

By the early 1960s, most of Africa was independent. In some cases, white minorities remained in control for decades before local nationalist movements finally achieved power. White settlers in Rhodesia achieved independence from Britain and established a white-controlled state. South Africa, which had been independent since the early twentieth century, remained under white-dominated Apartheid rule. New African states also fell prey to frequent government and military power struggles, along with internal ethnic schisms. The Cold War superpowers competed for influence in the newly independent states. Such competitions were a facet of the era's larger Third World proxy battles between the Western and Soviet blocs—but with the Americans and the Soviets arming and backing rival parties in several African nations, armed conflict between rival groups grew still more disruptive.

The Middle East emerged as one of the most contentious former colonial regions. During the First World War, Arab nationalists had allied with the Western powers against the Turkish Ottoman Empire, which then controlled most of the region. Post-Ottoman Turkey established a militarist republic, led by Kemal Ataturk, which held Turkey itself against European infiltration. But despite wartime promises to the Arabs, Britain and France took advantage of Ottoman collapse to seize much of the oil-rich Middle East in the early 1920s. Even Arab states that achieved independence often remained under heavy foreign influence: Egypt, for instance, remained under substantial British control until the military government of Gamal Nasser seized power in the early 1950s.

Since the nineteenth century, a Zionist movement—based mainly in Europe and the United States—had been pressing for the reestablishment of a Jewish state in the lands once held by ancient Israel. During World War I, the British government's 1917 Balfour Declaration endorsed the concept of a Jewish homeland located alongside the local Arab population. The local Arabs—who began to identify themselves as Palestinian in opposition to the Jewish claim—responded with anti-Jewish violence. In turn, Jews continued to settle in Palestine and strengthen their own communities, and Britain maintained uneasy control of the territory and tried to keep order.

During the Second World War, Germany tried to advance across North Africa to the Allied-held Middle East—and several Palestinian leaders actively worked with the Nazi forces, planning to eradicate the Jewish population in Palestine even as the Germans were working to do in Europe. Even after Hitler's defeat, the anti-Jewish Palestinian leaders continued to influence Arab nationalists across the region. In the aftermath of the Second World War, Arab states—including Syria, Jordan, and Lebanon—quickly achieved independence. The experience of the Holocaust, meanwhile, gave new impetus to Zionism. Jewish refugees flooded into Palestine, despite British efforts to restrict immigration to the territories. Jewish groups pressed for independence, and Jewish terrorist cells targeted the British authorities that still ruled Palestine. The horror of the Nazi atrocities helped convince many non-Jews to support Zionist claims: in 1947, the new United Nations proposed a complex partition of British-controlled Palestine into Jewish and Arab states, with Jerusalem falling under international control.

But the UN partition plan sparked fighting between Arab and Jewish communities. The Arab states of Egypt, Syria, and Iraq backed the Palestinian Arabs and joined the war against the Jewish nationalists, who in turn proclaimed an independent state of Israel in May 1948. Determined Israeli efforts defeated the Arab states by 1949 and took control of most of the disputed territory (although Jordan seized the Palestinian Arab territories of the West Bank and East Jerusalem, and Egypt took Gaza). Hundreds of thousands of Palestinian Arabs were displaced in the war and were forced into refugee camps in the West Bank, Gaza, and neighboring Arab countries.

Militarist nationalist regimes were still determined to eradicate the new Jewish state and soon gained power in Egypt, Syria, and Iraq. A succession of regional wars followed, including a 1956 conflict with Britain, France, and Israel sparked by Egypt's Gamal Nasser's decision to take direct control of the Suez canal—a conflict in which Nasser prevailed, when hostile world opinion and lack of U.S. support forced the British and French to accept Nasser's move. Cold War tensions also intruded: the United States and Europe supported Israel, and the U.S.S.R. provided aid to the Arab states. In 1967, after defeating another planned attack by the Arab powers, Israel would take control of the West Bank and Gaza—sparking new demands for a Palestinian Arab state in those areas. Despite occasional breakthroughs, including a 1978 peace treaty between Egypt and Israel, Israeli-Arab tensions would increase to become a major focus of world attention.

ERA 18: THE COLD WAR THAWS: UNEASY COOPERATION BETWEEN NATIONS (1960S TO PRESENT)

GLOBAL CONFLICT AND DIPLOMACY: DÉTENTE, CHINA, AND THE MIDDLE EAST

After the 1962 Cuban Missile Crisis and the close brush with nuclear war, direct communications between the superpowers improved. The following year, the United States and the U.S.S.R. negotiated the Limited Test Ban Treaty to end above-ground nuclear tests. The treaty was an effort to rein in the nuclear arms race and to curb dangerous nuclear fallout. But the rivalry between the superpowers continued through less-dangerous proxy conflicts, as the two sides battled for influence in the developing postcolonial nations of the so-called Third World. The longest, most divisive conflict was the United States' intervention in the extended war between North and South Vietnam.

Even as he struggled to resolve the war in Vietnam, U.S. president Richard Nixon moved to lessen the risk of conflict with the major Communist powers. Pursuing a policy of *détente* (or the easing of relations), Nixon hoped to slow the dangerous, expensive nuclear arms race through a diplomatic thaw with the Soviets. Greater cooperation resulted in the Strategic Arms Limitation Treaty (SALT), which directly limited the construction of weapons systems. This agreement between the superpowers marked a major shift in Cold War relations.

Even more dramatically, Nixon reached out to Communist China. The United States had refused since 1949 to recognize Mao Zedong's People's Republic, instead recognizing Taiwan's exiled nationalist government as the legitimate Chinese state. Communist China also resisted Western ties and supported North Korea against UN forces in the Korean War. Mao's extremism in the 1950s and 1960s soured his ties even with the Soviet Union and made improved relations with the West completely impossible. By the 1960s, the Soviets were openly repudiating the oppressive brutality of Joseph Stalin. Mao, instead, continued to grow more radical. Purging his own party of more moderate elements, he unleashed the savage chaos of the Cultural Revolution. Western influences were denounced as counterrevolutionary; those with Western learning were in danger of harassment, imprisonment, or death. China's acquisition of nuclear weapons further increased tension with the Soviets as well as with the West.

But the full fury of the Cultural Revolution could not be sustained. Damage to factories and labor forces undermined the economy, and the terrorization of teachers and closure of schools threatened the entire educational system. China's ruling Communists began anxiously pulling back from the full extremes of the Cultural Revolution in 1969. Although Mao continued to push for a rigidly ideological society until his death in 1976, even he began to retreat from the intense xenophobia that had gripped China. By 1971, he tentatively reached out to the wider world. Later that year, the United Nations granted China's seat, which Taiwan had held since 1949, to the People's Republic. The potent Security Council veto, which China had secured in 1945 as one of the five leading Allied powers (the United States, U.S.S.R., China, Britain, and France), was also transferred to the People's Republic. In 1972, Nixon paid a formal state visit to Beijing. His successor, President Jimmy Carter, established full diplomatic relations with China in 1979.

Other international problems remained. After escalating its involvement in Vietnam and failing to end the conflict, the United States and North Vietnam signed the Paris Peace Accords in 1973, which allowed withdrawal of U.S. forces. But beyond the American pullout, the peace agreement had little effect. North Vietnam continued to press its attack on the South. South Vietnam tried to continue the fight, but it was weakly governed and wracked by internal Communist insurrection. It was defeated in 1975, unleashing savage Communist crackdowns and mass flight by South Vietnamese refugees. Instability had already spread throughout the region. In 1975, neighboring Laos fell to a Communist insurrection—and the pro-U.S. Hmong minority was harshly suppressed. That same year, Communist Khmer Rouge rebels seized power in Cambodia. Dictator Pol Pot's regime murdered two million Cambodians in a fanatical effort to purge intellectuals, end Western influences, and force the nation back to an agrarian peasant society. In 1978, the nation was overrun by Vietnamese troops. In 1991, the United Nations finally reestablished the constitutional monarchy that Pol Pot had ousted.

Meanwhile, hostility between the Arab states and Israel continued. Under the leadership of Yasser Arafat's Palestine Liberation Organization (PLO), militant groups refused to recognize Israel's existence and demanded a Palestinian state in its place. In 1967, Israel launched a preemptive strike as Arab nations prepared to attack. In the swift Six Day War, Israel seized East Jerusalem and the West Bank from Jordan and the Gaza Strip and Sinai from Egypt. In 1973, Egypt and Syria attacked on Yom Kippur (a Jewish day of fasting and prayer). But after early setbacks and a difficult fight, Israel emerged victorious once more.

Western-Arab tensions had been high since Arab independence was denied after the First World War, and many in the Middle East resented Western backing for often despotic governments in strategically important oil-producing states. But the West's support of Israel exacerbated tensions with the Arabs and caused rifts with their governments. After the Yom Kippur War, the Arab states recognized the PLO as the sole legitimate government of all Israeli territory and imposed an oil embargo against Israel's Western supporters. A first major step toward stability in the region was the U.S.-brokered peace treaty between Israel and Egypt in 1978. Under the terms of the Camp David Accord, Israel ceded the Sinai peninsula—which it had taken from Egypt in 1967—and removed its settlements there. But PLO terrorism against Israel and Israeli crackdowns in the remaining occupied territories raged on. A 1982 Israeli invasion of Lebanon, a nation devastated by Christian-Muslim civil war since the mid-1970s, sought to deprive the PLO of a major base. However, the invasion mainly resulted in sparking further international dispute.

Increasingly influential followers of radical Islamic ideas aimed to purge Muslim nations of Western influence and create a strict, theocratic system of Islamic rule. In 1979, Iran's dictatorial, U.S.-supported shah was removed by Islamic revolutionaries. Iranian radicals demanded that the shah, who was in the United States for medical treatment, return to Iran for trial. They seized dozens of Americans in the U.S. embassy in the Iranian capital of Tehran, holding them hostage for months; their actions were part of a wider ideology of Islamic *jihad*, a doctrine of holy war for the defense and expansion of Islam that extremists claimed sanctioned acts of terror against Western civilians. Jihadists intended to force the West to withdraw support for Israel and to replace Western-backed Middle Eastern regimes with Islamist rule. But the West continued to support Israel, and tensions between the West and Islamic radicals continued to rise.

THE COLD WAR ENDS AND EUROPEAN COMMUNISM FALLS

By the 1980s, the Soviet Union was in serious economic trouble. After World War II, Stalin had promoted large, impractical schemes to transform the Soviet landscape—forcing crops into unsuitable climate zones and severely damaging agriculture in the process. By the 1960s, the state-controlled economy was focused on heavy industry: there was constant pressure to increase output, and attention to safety and quality standards decreased. The Soviets strained to maintain control of Eastern Europe and to preserve their massive military. In 1979, they invaded Afghanistan to defend a new Communist regime against Islamist rebels. The Soviets were opposed by U.S.-supported and -equipped Islamic Mujahidin guerrillas, who saw the war as holy jihad. The war soon turned into a quagmire that further drained the Soviets' overstretched resources.

Meanwhile, major Western powers were growing more conservative, and more militarily aggressive. Since World War II, many Western European nations had built complex state-supported social welfare systems. But over time, the expense of such policies grew, and taxation reached extremely high levels that many feared would stifle economic growth. In 1979, the Conservative Party's Margaret Thatcher became Britain's prime minister. Remaining in power until 1990, she worked aggressively to reduce the massive level of government spending and to rein in taxes. Opponents accused her of callousness as she cut taxes and reduced government-funded social services, but her supporters argued that the cuts were necessary to prevent government bankruptcy and economic collapse. She also firmly promoted a hard line against Soviet and Eastern European Communism.

U.S. president Ronald Reagan was elected in 1980 on a similar platform of shrinking the U.S. federal government and adopting a more aggressive foreign posture. He, too, focused intensely on eradicating Communism from the world—and he brought the dominant resources of the United States to bear on the issue. Reagan bolstered support for anti-Communist movements around the globe—including the Islamic rebels in Afghanistan. He also pushed for dramatic boosts in military spending to strengthen America's defenses. The Soviets were overburdened and their economy was struggling. American policymakers did not only intend to bolster the U.S. military. They hoped, by forcing the U.S.S.R. to match U.S. spending, to undermine the Soviet economy and bring down the Soviet Communist regime.

Although the United States' massive military spending created enormous budget deficits, the policymakers' predictions were correct: the Soviets' efforts to keep pace crippled them. Growing economic crisis boosted an internal Soviet reform movement. In 1985, Mikhail Gorbachev took power. The reformist premier quickly moved to modernize the economy, liberalize internal politics, expand free speech and personal rights, and retreat from aggressive foreign ventures. He called these policies *glasnost* (openness) and *perestroika* (rebuilding). In 1987, Gorbachev began preparing for withdrawal from the disastrous war in Afghanistan. Sensing an historic opportunity, Reagan pivoted to diplomacy. He startled many as he proposed a dramatic arms reduction treaty that the United States and the U.S.S.R. signed that year. In 1989, the U.S.S.R. withdrew completely from Afghanistan.

Eastern Europe had also been hard-hit by economic decline, particularly as the cash-strapped Soviets cut back on supports like subsidized oil. As Gorbachev liberalized the Soviet Union and the threat of Soviet crackdowns eased, pro-democracy movements gained strength in nations that had long been under the Soviet thumb. Poland's Solidarity movement, led by labor activist Lech Walesa and openly encouraged by Polish-born Catholic Pope John Paul II, began openly opposing Communism in the mid-1980s. Unrest rose elsewhere—and as relations with the West improved, Gorbachev loosened the Soviet hold on Eastern Europe and allowed states to shift away from Communism. In 1989, rebellious East Germans broke down the Berlin Wall. The Communist East German government soon collapsed.

Soon other pro-democracy movements spread across Eastern Europe. In Hungary and Poland, Communist governments negotiated settlements with opposition forces and transitioned to free elections. In Czechoslovakia, public demonstrations forced the republic's Communist regime to yield; in November 1989, dissident playwright Vaclav Havel became president of a free Czechoslovakian government. Bulgaria's Communist government fell to a coup and Romania's fell to an armed insurrection. The Soviet sphere quickly crumbled—and Soviet acceptance of these developments marked the effective end of the Cold War. Within months, the global political order changed profoundly.

The Soviet Union itself began to dissolve. The U.S.S.R. included the large Russian state and more than a dozen smaller, once-separate "republics." As Soviet policy liberalized and Communism crumbled in Eastern Europe, the republics began chafing for local control—and for the primacy of their own local languages, religions, and ethnic identities. Gorbachev tried to hold the U.S.S.R. together by force, but was gradually compelled to yield greater autonomy to the republics. In August 1991, hard-line Communists attempted a coup to reassert Soviet control. Boris Yeltsin, the recently elected president of the Russian Republic (which was the central component of the U.S.S.R.) led a popular street uprising that defeated the coup plotters. That December, the Soviet Union dissolved and was replaced by a loose Commonwealth of Independent States.

Since the 1919 Versailles settlement, Eastern Europe's many disparate ethnic and religious groups had been awkwardly joined together within often arbitrary national borders. Soviet control had kept these schisms forcibly submerged. But now the collapse of Communism allowed them to resurge. Czechoslovakia split into the Czech Republic and Slovakia in 1993. Yugoslavia, an awkward amalgam of Slavic peoples created in the ever-divided Balkans after the First World War, began to fragment by 1990; bitter fighting between ethnic groups soon followed. Long-buried splits also emerged in the Russian Republic. The Muslim province of Chechnya tried to break away, sparking a harsh Russian crackdown and a cycle of violence that is still unresolved. Germany was an exception: Cold War geopolitics had split a single people, who were reunited in a single German democracy in 1990.

Pressure against authoritarian Communism was not confined to Europe. China, which had opened to the West in 1970s, was increasingly affected by Western economic and political ideas. As Russia enacted liberal reforms under Gorbachev, popular pressure rose in China. Citizens, especially the educated young, wanted similar changes. Even China's ruling Communist Party was divided between those who resisted reform and others who favored concessions toward democratic change. The removal of a top reform-minded official sparked urban pro-democracy demonstrations in early 1989. In May, youth-led protesters captured the world's attention as they occupied Beijing's Tiananmen Square. In early June, the government sent the army to suppress the protests. Hundreds died in a crackdown that heralded a wave of arrests and executions. The pro-democracy movement was broken, but Chinese authorities were left with the difficult task of addressing widespread discontent without yielding their power.

THE CHANGING POST–COLD WAR WORLD

The post–Cold War world created a new mosaic of international challenges, and U.S. president George H. W. Bush helped form new relationships and alliances between nations. From 1990 to 1991, Iraqi dictator Saddam Hussein (whom the United States had supported during his long, bloody war against Iran in the 1980s) invaded Kuwait and menaced Saudi Arabia. The invasion threatened the United States' allies, global oil supplies, and the entire world economy. Bush skillfully assembled a broad international coalition against Hussein. He was also able to keep Israel—whose involvement would have alienated Arab states—from joining the war, even after Hussein launched unprovoked missile strikes against Israeli cities.

Western Europe continued a long-standing post–World War II push toward unity and economic integration. In 1993, the European Union (EU) was formed: it tightened political ties and harmonized foreign and economic policies—despite continuing conflicts over the extent of individual member nations' sovereignty. In 1999, a new single European currency called the Euro took effect (although Britain, always cautious about strong European ties, refused to use it).

Eastern Europe struggled in its transition to unfamiliar democratic institutions. Eastern European nations gradually moved toward EU membership in the early 2000s. Poland, Hungary, and the Czech Republic joined NATO in 1999. Other Eastern European nations followed suit, signaling a greater shift toward unified European policymaking. The single market and unified currency has created ongoing opportunities and ongoing challenges, because the European Union has tried to balance Europe's stronger and weaker national economies within a stable and coherent single system.

Despite the push for unity, nationalism and ethnic separatism persisted—particularly in the regions that had comprised the former Yugoslavia. In 1914, Serbian demands for control of Bosnia, with its large population of ethnic Serbs, had helped spark the First World War. In 1991, Serbians in Bosnia-Herzegovina launched a genocidal campaign of "ethnic cleansing" (or targeted extermination) against the Bosnian Muslim population. Their aim was to create ethnically "pure" areas, which Serbia could then annex. The resulting Bosnian civil war unleashed savage violence, war crimes, and civilian slaughter. In the southern part of Serbia itself, the province of Kosovo witnessed uprisings against Serbian rule later in the decade. In 1998, Serbia responded with a new campaign of ethnic cleansing in Kosovo, aimed at ethnic Albanians and Kosovar Muslims. In 1999, the United States led a NATO intervention: airstrikes and NATO troops drove the Serbians back, and Kosovo was placed under UN control. Kosovo declared independence in 2008, but its status remains disputed.

As the world struggled to achieve post–Cold War political balance, its economy was quickly shifting. Globalization–the trend toward an integrated worldwide economy, in which production and consumption are spread across the globe–had gradually been taking hold. For instance, factories had increasingly relocated to developing nations where labor costs were far lower and regulations far weaker. In the 1990s, the world was no longer divided into rival Cold War camps. Thus, globalization accelerated dramatically. Beyond the United States and Europe, new centers of economic growth were rapidly emerging.

India, the world's most populous democracy, focused heavily on economic development after achieving independence in 1947. The nation was a quickly expanding center for manufacturing and technology by the 1990s, even though its government struggled to deal with widespread poverty. Hindu India and Muslim Pakistan have remained hostile toward each other. Although the nations have not been at war since 1971, border incidents and diplomatic clashes have continued. India attained nuclear weapons in the mid-1970s, and Pakistan followed a decade later (although it did not openly test a bomb until the late 1990s). In spite of the tension, there have been periodic thaws and increases in cross-border trade.

Development has been difficult in Central and South America, which had long been under U.S. and European economic domination. In 1994, the North American Free Trade Agreement (NAFTA) cut restrictions on cross-border commerce. Since NAFTA, Mexico has produced more goods for the U.S. market and has developed close ties with the United States. But Mexico has also been severely hit by organized crime, drug trafficking, and lawlessness: there are large areas where the government barely has authority. Elsewhere in the region, post-war industrialization efforts often failed, and heavy borrowing led to debt crises in the 1980s.

Political instability led some nations into successive dictatorships. The United States sometimes supported these dictatorships, as long as they were anti-Communist. In 1973, the United States covertly helped Augusto Pinochet overthrow an elected Socialist government in Chile, which ushered in fifteen years of corrupt, brutal rule. Juan Perón, president of Argentina, flirted with Fascism after World War II. In 1976, Argentina fell to a military *junta* (a group of military officers in charge of a dictatorship), which murdered thousands of dissenters. The regime's unsuccessful 1982 attempt to wrest the disputed Falkland Islands from the British–aggressively fought off by Britain under Margaret Thatcher–finally led to its demise, and a new democratic government took power in 1983. South America's rich raw material resources–particularly oil and agriculture–serve as a springboard for future growth. However, the profits rarely reach large portions of the expanding populations, and serious ecological damage has been done. The destruction of vast areas of rainforest to create agricultural land has global environmental implications.

Development across Africa has been extremely uneven since post-war decolonization. For some countries, oil and other raw materials offered a path to rapid prosperity. As in South America, though, a drop in oil prices during the 1980s left many nations in debt. Some of them have successfully established democratic governments, but ethnic conflicts and political turmoil have continued to ravage the continent. During Nigeria's civil war in the late 1960s, nearly one million people died of starvation. Outbreaks of ethnic cleansing in Rwanda in the 1990s and in Darfur in the 2000s have drawn international attention but defied straightforward solutions. Poverty, HIV and AIDS, political crises, environmental decay, and continuing debt continue to impede new reform and economic development efforts.

International pressure and internal resistance helped bring down South Africa's white-dominated Apartheid regime. In 1990, South African president F. W. de Klerk began to repeal the country's Apartheid laws, freed Nelson Mandela–leader of the anti-Apartheid African National Congress–after twenty-seven years of imprisonment, and moved to enfranchise black South Africans. In 1993, de Klerk and Mandela shared the Nobel Peace Prize. The following year, Mandela was elected president of South Africa. His Truth and Reconciliation Commission sought to address the crimes of the old regime and avoid new divisions and further violence. South Africa, despite ongoing problems of poverty and ethnic tension, remains one of Africa's most successful democracies.

The Pacific Rim has experienced dramatic economic growth since World War II. During the post-war American occupation, Japan's growth was encouraged as a bastion against Communist expansion: industry and technology skyrocketed by the 1960s, as it became a major manufacturer of consumer goods and electronics. Within three decades, Japan was one of the world's dominant economic powers. Although a serious fiscal crisis blunted its growth in the 1990s, the nation's economy remains powerful. Other nations in East and Southeast Asia—including South Korea, Indonesia, and the increasingly reformist regime in Vietnam—have also become major players in manufacturing and agriculture and have received heavy Western and Japanese investment because of their lower labor costs. But there, too, destruction of rainforest and other natural landscapes for palm-tree plantations, other agricultural products, and urban expansion has done serious environmental harm.

RECENT TRENDS: GLOBAL TIES AND CONFLICTS

One of the most dramatic recent global developments has been China's emergence as a dominant economic power. By the 1980s, China was bending its Communist economic doctrines as it invited foreign investment through free-enterprise zones. In the wake of 1989's Tiananmen Square crackdown and growing popular unrest, the Chinese government recognized that it needed to improve the lot of its younger, more educated citizens. In the 1990s, the nation relaxed its rigid economic restrictions further: it allowed free markets to develop and privatized many state-run industries. When the British colony of Hong Kong was returned to China in 1997, China maintained its globally connected investment markets. The result was an economic boom for the educated classes—even though it depended on poor working conditions and meager pay for a large part of the Chinese population.

China's dramatic productivity and low labor costs have encouraged Western companies to outsource manufacturing to China, which in turn has become a major supplier of goods through-out the world. Although it has liberalized its economy, however, China has maintained its firmly authoritarian government. Other nations have criticized China for its autocracy and human rights violations. Tensions with the United States have repeatedly risen over regional power (including China's claim to Taiwan and territorial disputes with close American ally Japan), human rights abuses, and support for regimes such as dictatorial, militarist North Korea. But China and the West are now mutually dependent economically—which means that despite any ongoing disputes, at least some degree of cooperative coexistence is essential.

China's role in the world economy highlights the continuing importance of global economic interconnectivity. Modern telecommunications and the Internet strengthen these ties even more. Workers in developed countries with high labor costs have been squeezed out of employment as many low- or semi-skilled jobs move to less expensive overseas markets. Laborers in developing countries press in turn for opportunity and advancement, as pressure from foreign companies to keep wages low and productivity high often result in virtual slavery. Western popular culture—spread further by television and the Internet—has been embraced in many parts of the world, but it has also sparked backlash from cultural and religious traditionalists who feel threatened by what they consider decadent and immoral foreign ideas.

Cultural globalization has reinforced a sense of grievance in some Islamic communities, building on centuries of tension between the Middle East and the West. Opinions about pluralism and the wide circulation of diverse ideas have long differed: the first printing press did not appear in the Arab world until 1720, nearly three centuries after the first European press. Until the 1860s, independent newspapers were virtually unknown in the Arab world. But recently, Western technology, clothing, art, and music have been steadily embraced—and religious traditionalists have mounted significant resistance. The status of women, traditionally relegated to subordinate positions in Islamic culture, has prompted particularly serious clashes in some Muslim countries. Many women have pushed for greater social status, political rights, and equal employment, with widely varying success. The issue remains a difficult one, with women frequently facing social restrictions and even violent repression.

Conflict between Middle Eastern Muslims and the West mounted in the aftermath of the First World War, when the collapsing Ottoman Empire gave way to political and economic domination of the region by Europe and the United States. Even after direct colonial control of the region ended, Western powers continued to support dictatorial regimes to ensure their own access to vital oil supplies. Islamic militancy gained strength during the 1980s Afghan war against the Soviets, in which Islamic fighters or *mujahedeen* (who were aided and equipped by the United States) were central. Some militant groups that were active in Afghanistan emerged as terrorist bodies with far larger aims—particularly Saudi billionaire Osama bin Laden and his al Qaeda organization.

Although most Muslims around the world did not and do not endorse terrorism, the clash between Islamist militants and the West quickly emerged as one of the world's major post–Cold War fault lines. In the 1990s, terrorist groups turned their focus from Middle Eastern regimes to the West as they aimed to force the United States and Europe to withdraw entirely from the Middle East and end its support of Israel. In 1993, militants inspired by a radical Egyptian sheik detonated a truck bomb beneath New York's World Trade Center. In the mid-1990s, bin Laden's al Qaeda established bases in Africa and plotted anti-Western attacks on U.S. embassies in Africa. Later, as the radical Islamist Taliban took control of Afghanistan, al Qaeda relocated there. It launched attacks on New York City and Washington, DC, on September 11, 2001.

In the wake of the 9/11 attacks, the United States and several allies took military action to dislodge al Qaeda from its Afghan base. In the years following, enormous resources would go toward hunting down the organization's leaders and blocking further attacks. Meanwhile, hostilities widened. In 2003, the United States invaded Iraq after it claimed that Saddam Hussein was gathering weapons of mass destruction to use against the West. The claims against the Iraqi dictator proved inaccurate, and the war caused controversy across the United States and around the world. A resurgent Taliban continues to pose a threat in Afghanistan as U.S. forces begin with withdraw, and Pakistan—where many resent U.S. military presence in the region—has become increasingly radicalized.

Repeated efforts to restart Israeli-Palestinian peace talks, which had stalled, have resulted in little progress despite wide international support for a two-state peace arrangement. Palestinian groups continue to launch terrorist attacks and deny Israel's right to exist, and Israel has continued to expand settlement in the occupied territories that are seen by supporters of a two-state solution as belonging to a future independent Palestine. The Middle East was further roiled by the Arab Spring revolts of 2010 and 2011, as protesters across the Arab world—avoiding government censorship through the Internet—rose up against several dictatorial regimes. The outcome of those uprisings remains a great unknown, because pro-democracy activists struggle for influence against powerfully entrenched Islamist parties seeking to impose Islamic rule.

As the world moves into the new millennium, it faces challenges for the evolving global community: terrorism and peace, ethnic conflicts and border disputes, pollution and global climate change, resource management and population growth, the global status and rights of women and regional minorities, and democratization and its opponents.

Who Is Common Core

Common Core is a nonprofit 501(c)3 organization that creates curriculum tools and promotes programs, policies, and initiatives at the local, state, and federal levels, with the aim of providing students with challenging, rigorous instruction in the full range of liberal arts and sciences. Common Core was established in 2007 and is not affiliated with the Common Core State Standards (CCSS).

Common Core has been led by Lynne Munson, as president and executive director, since its founding. In six short years, Lynne has made Common Core an influential advocate for the liberal arts and sciences and a noted provider of CCSS-based curriculum tools. Lynne was deputy chairman of the National Endowment for the Humanities (NEH) from 2001 to 2005, overseeing all agency operations. NEH is an independent agency of the federal government that funds scholarly and public projects in the humanities. Lynne was the architect of Picturing America (http://picturingamerica.neh.gov/), the most successful public humanities project in NEH history. The project put more than seventy-five thousand sets of fine art images and teaching guides into libraries, K–12 classrooms, and Head Start centers. In 2005, Lynne led the first postconflict U.S. government delegation to Afghanistan to deal with issues of cultural reconstruction. In 2004, she represented the United States at UNESCO meetings in Australia and Japan, where she helped negotiate guidelines for cross-border higher education.

From 1993 to 2001, Lynne was a research fellow at the American Enterprise Institute, where she wrote *Exhibitionism: Art in an Era of Intolerance* (Ivan R. Dee, 2000), a book examining the evolution of art institutions and art education. Lynne served as a research assistant to NEH chairman Lynne Cheney from 1990 to 1993. She has written on issues of contemporary culture and education for numerous national publications, including the *New York Times*, the *Wall Street Journal*, *USA Today*, *Inside Higher Education*, and National Review Online's *The Corner*. She has appeared on CNN, Fox News, CNBC, C-SPAN, and NPR, and she speaks to scholarly and public audiences. She serves on the advisory board for the Pioneer Institute's Center for School Reform. Her degree in art history is from Northwestern University.

Learn more about Common Core at commoncore.org.

Trustees of Common Core

Erik Berg, National Board Certified second-grade teacher at the John D. Philbrick Elementary School in Boston, Massachusetts

Barbara Byrd-Bennett, Chief Executive Officer for Chicago Public Schools

Antonia Cortese, former Secretary-Treasurer of the American Federation of Teachers

Pascal Forgione Jr., Chairman of Common Core's Board of Trustees and Distinguished Presidential Scholar and Executive Director of the Center on K–12 Assessment and Performance Management at the Educational Testing Service

Lorraine Griffith, Title I Reading Specialist at West Buncombe Elementary School in Asheville, North Carolina

Jason Griffiths, Secretary of Common Core and Principal of Harlem Village Academy

Bill Honig, President of the Consortium on Reading Excellence and Executive Committee Chair of the California Instructional Quality Commission of the California State Board of Education

Carol Jago, Associate Director of the California Reading and Literature Project at the University of California, Los Angeles

Richard Kessler, Treasurer of Common Core and Dean of Mannes College The New School for Music

Lynne Munson, President and Executive Director of Common Core

Juan Rangel, Chief Executive Officer of the United Neighborhood Organization

Acknowledgments

On behalf of Common Core (CC), I would like to thank those whose time, knowledge, and passion created this invaluable resource for teachers. There are many who deserve heartfelt thanks; without their contribution, the Alexandria Plan would still be just an idea in our minds. My first thanks are to Kate Bradford and Lesley Iura at Jossey-Bass/Wiley, who advocated for publishing a new education series on history, despite the subject's having been marginalized for decades. They share our confidence that history is on its way back into classrooms.

Much of CC's Washington, DC, staff played—and continues to play—a significant role in shaping, shepherding, and promoting this work. Staff members include program manager Sarah Woodard, program assistant Lauren Shaw, and partnerships manager Alyson Burgess. Barbara Davidson, CC's Deputy Director, was fearless in her leadership of this effort.

Special thanks to the more than one hundred teachers who piloted the Plan in their respective classrooms. We are particularly grateful to Susan Hensley, elementary curriculum specialist for the Rogers Public Schools in Arkansas, for her lead role in the piloting effort. The piloters' enthusiastic and insightful feedback was an essential ingredient in our work. Also, recognition needs to go to CC's Alyssa Stinson for arranging the pilot project. Thanks also go to Russ Cohen of Schoolwide, Inc. Russ provided review copies of the more than eight hundred titles we considered for inclusion in the Alexandria Plan.

Many experts were involved in informing, shaping, and ensuring the accuracy of this work. Historian Harvey Klehr exhaustively reviewed our U.S. history era summaries to make sure we had our facts correct. CC trustee and past president of the National Council of Teachers of English Carol Jago reviewed and improved our text studies. Lewis Huffman, social studies education associate for the South Carolina Department of Education, provided keen, real-world guidance that was instrumental in making the Plan of service to teachers. Susan Pimentel and her team at Student Achievement Partners provided invaluable early advice that shaped the rigor of the Plan.

Research assistant Jennifer Foley's review of this work was incredibly beneficial. Our Plan was meticulously edited by Allison Lawruk to ensure that it was error-free and of maximum use to teachers. The materials were painstakingly copyedited by Shannon Last. Betsy Franz and Rebecca Hyman helped obtain the images that appear throughout the Plan. And Natanya Levioff drove our project deadlines to completion.

We are grateful to Ed Alton and his team at Alton Creative for their ingenious design of our website, commoncore.org. We are indebted to branding expert Christopher Clary, illustrator Amy DeVoogd, and copywriter Peter Chase for work that enhances both the website and this book.

There are three people who worked tirelessly for months on the Plan and who are most responsible for imbuing the Plan with heft, utility, and joy. Historian Jeremy Stern is not only our nation's foremost expert on state social studies standards but also a thoughtful, trenchant scholar who has the gift of writing the kind of history we all want to read. Jeremy brought extraordinary care and devotion to the crafting of each of the thirty-six era summaries that form the basis for the Plan and from which the topics for our text studies are derived.

Education policy consultant Sheila Byrd-Carmichael served as a writer and Common Core State Standards (CCSS) expert on this project. Sheila worked to ensure that the text-dependent questions and performance assessments for each suggested anchor text would allow students to meet, indeed surpass, the standards. She also brought forward essential academic vocabulary in each text study.

Lorraine Griffith is a teacher at West Buncombe Elementary in Asheville, North Carolina. She is also lead writer of all of CC's CCSS English language arts–based curriculum materials for grades K through 4. Lorraine identified the essential historical content in each of our anchor texts and made it the focus of the series of text-dependent questions that form the spine of our text studies, and of the Plan itself. Her uncanny ability to translate her passion for how great literature, history, and art can transform the learning experience for students is a gift to CC and to the teachers who use our curriculum materials.

Jeremy, Sheila, and Lorraine's depth of knowledge and passion for bringing quality resources to teachers inspired everyone involved in this project. We hope and expect that their enthusiasm will be evident to you as you begin to work with the material contained in this book.

It was a privilege for me to work alongside these inspired experts. I look forward to our next project together!

December, 2013

Lynne Munson
President and Executive Director
Common Core
Washington, DC

Index